Louisa C. (Louisa Caroline) Tuthill

Caroline Perthes

The Christian wife

Louisa C. (Louisa Caroline) Tuthill

Caroline Perthes
The Christian wife

ISBN/EAN: 9783742897640

Manufactured in Europe, USA, Canada, Australia, Japa

Cover: Foto ©Thomas Meinert / pixelio.de

Manufactured and distributed by brebook publishing software
(www.brebook.com)

Louisa C. (Louisa Caroline) Tuthill

Caroline Perthes

CAROLINE PERTHES

THE

CHRISTIAN WIFE.

CONDENSED FROM THE

LIFE OF FREDERICK CHRISTOPHER PERTHES,

BY

MRS. L. C. TUTHILL.

NEW YORK:

ROBERT CARTER & BROTHERS,

No. 530 BROADWAY,

1860.

PREFACE.

In the "Life of Frederick Christopher Perthes," it is evident, there was "a power behind the throne greater than the throne itself."

That "power" was the influence of a Christian wife;—a woman of remarkably good sense, of superior education, ardent affections, and earnest piety. She was the good angel, given by God, to reveal to Perthes "the beauty of holiness."

Her true womanliness, her devotedness to her family, over whom she exerted, whether present or absent, a felicitous influence, and her success in the education of her children, render Caroline Perthes a noble and a cheering example for all who would "do likewise."

It is fervently hoped, that many, who would never else have heard of Caroline Perthes, may now be benefited by her beautiful example.

Princeton, N. J.   L. C. T.

CONTENTS.

CHAP.   PAGE
I.—CAROLINE CLAUDIUS 7
II.—FREDERICK CHRISTOPHER PERTHES.............. 11
III.—STUDIES AND FRIENDS 25
IV.—FIRST IMPRESSIONS OF HAMBURGH.............. 36
V.—ESTABLISHMENT IN BUSINESS....................... 50
VI.—NEW ACQUAINTANCES 59
VII.—THE BETROTHAL AND WEDDING.................... 68
VIII.—THE BUSINESS AND THE FAMILY.................. 82
IX.—FAMILY FRIENDS 91
X.—PROGRESS IN RELIGION............................ 101
XI.—EVENTS OF THE YEARS 1805 AND 1806 119
XII.—LOSSES AND TRIALS 125
XIII.—THE FRENCH IN HAMBURGH........................ 135
XIV.—PATRIOTISM 150
XV.—CAROLINE'S ESCAPE FROM HAMBURGH.............. 163
XVI.—CAROLINE AND HER CHILDREN AT ASCHAU—1813.. 178
XVII.—THE WIFE'S TRIALS............................. 188
XVIII.—THE HAMBURGH SUFFERERS 193
XIX.—PERTHES AND CAROLINE AT BLANKENESE—1814... 206
XX.—THE RETURN 217
XXI.—MOMENTOUS EVENTS............................... 230
XXII.—DEATH OF CLAUDIUS............................. 240
XXIII.—JOURNEY TO FRANKFORT-ON-THE-MAIN............ 251
XXIV.—PERTHES' LETTERS TO CAROLINE 265
XXV.—CORRESPONDENCE CONTINUED 275
XXVI.—THE SUMMER OF 1819............................ 293
XXVII.—RELIGIOUS CONFLICTS OF THE PERIOD........... 300

(v)

XXVIII.—MARRIAGE OF THE ELDEST DAUGHTER............. 309

XXIX.—MARRIAGE OF THE SECOND DAUGHTER 325

XXX.—DEPARTURE OF THE ELDEST SON FOR THE UNI-
VERSITY.. 335

XXXI.—THE LAST DAYS OF CAROLINE........................ 852

XXXII.—PERTHES AND HIS MOTHERLESS CHILDREN........ 367

XXXIII.—GOTHA... 374

XXXIV.—PERTHES' VIEWS OF MEN AND THINGS............. 887

XXXV.—PERTHES' INNER LIFE—1822 TO 1825.............. 405

XXXVI.—CHANGES IN LIFE................................... 424

XXXVII.—CORRESPONDENCE ON THE RELATIONS OF LIFE... 438

XXXVIII.—CHRISTIAN ENTERPRISE............................ 456

XXXIX.—DEATH OF NIEBUHR................................. 466

XL.—DOMESTIC AND SOCIAL LIFE.......................... 471

XLI.—LAST YEARS... 487

XLII.—SICKNESS AND DEATH................................ 507

CAROLINE PERTHES

THE CHRISTIAN WIFE.

I.

Caroline Claudius.

N the high-road to the city of Lubeck, in Northern Germany, is the neat and pleasant town of Wandsbeck, in Holstein. Near the entrance to Wandsbeck, in the year 1796, was the residence of Matthias Claudius. Claudius was an excellent, popular author, and was familiarly called the "Wandsbeck Messenger," from a periodical which he edited, entitled the "Wandsbecker Bote." He was at once earnest and humorous in his writings, and cared less for the graces of diction, than for the inculcation of honest, noble, charitable and patriotic sentiments. The sickly complexion, the hair tightly drawn back and fastened with a comb, the ungainly figure, the homely dressing-gown, and the Low-Saxon dialect, would hardly have revealed the treasure that was hidden in this extraordinary man, had it not been for the heavenly fire which flashed from his fine blue eye.

Altogether opposed to the prevailing notions of the period, which had a tendency to subject religion and

politics, more or less, to the wavering opinions of man,
Claudius found in the revelation of Holy Writ the only
source of true religion. The belief that he was reconciled to God, being to him not a mere speculative
doctrine, but a state of mind acting upon his whole
inner being, all sad and disturbing, all gloomy and
anxious thoughts, were unknown to him and his household. " I found Claudius as harmless and as full of
German humor as ever," said Ewald, when he visited
him in 1796, in the expectation of finding a gloomy
fanatic ; " and," he adds, " whatever may be said of his
religious and political opinions, they have not changed
the man : he has no gloomy views, and is kindly towards all ; indeed, he laughs at many things which
would half kill with vexation many of our humanity
and tolerance and stoicism preachers."

The characteristics of the father's mind, which was
incapable of developing intellectual greatness and
depth otherwise than in a garb of unattractive comeli-
ness, or invested in forms that were all but ludicrous,
as well as the noble and womanly simplicity of the
mother, were reflected in the daily life of the family.
The great works of Palestrina, Leonardo Leo, Bach,
Handel, and Mozart, the language and literature of
England, and intellectual pursuits of all kinds, found
a home here, side by side with an extreme simplicity
of life. The daughters were brought up to discharge
the daily routine of domestic work. Claudius was
most careful to develop and strengthen the germ of
spiritual life in his children, but in every other respect
left them to themselves. It is true, that he had himself
to struggle with the enemy in the human heart, which
in his case led to the exhibition, in many circumstances,

of a seemingly inborn harshness of nature, and to his allowing a greater influence to the impressions of the moment than was reasonable ; this infirmity, however, in no way disturbed the free and unrestrained movements of the family life. Affected and pretentious alternations from the earthly to the heavenly were not known among them ; their life was simple and natural.

Caroline Claudius, the eldest daughter of the Wandsbeck Messenger, was born in 1774. Although there was nothing remarkable or dazzling in her general appearance, notwithstanding her fine regular features, her slender figure, and her delicate complexion, yet the treasures of fancy and feeling, the strength and repose of character, and the clearness of intellect which shone in her deep hazel eyes, gave her a quiet but irresistible charm. Throughout her whole life she inspired unbounded confidence in all who approached her. To her the glad brought their joys, secure of finding joyous sympathy, and to many of the afflicted both in body and in mind, she ministered consolation, taught resignation, and inspired them with fresh courage. Accustomed to the simple life of her parental home, contact with the bustle of the outward world appeared to her as fraught with danger to her childlike, simple walk with God. Household duties, study, and music, occupied her time. When more advanced in life, she retained a rich, clear voice, and a fine musical taste. She was acquainted with the modern languages, and had gone far enough in Latin to enable her subsequently to assist her sons.

While Caroline had remained at home, she had received but few impressions from without. She clung with reverential affection to the Princess Gallitzin,

1*

who was a frequent visitor at her father's house, and
who reciprocated the attachment with so much warmth,
that to the end of her life she preserved a motherly
friendship for her. By the Countess Julia Reventlow,
Caroline was equally beloved. She had been to Emkendorf on a visit of some months in the summer of
1795, and had become so great a favorite with the
family, that they would have taken her with them to
Italy, had they been able to obtain her father's consent.
The first great event in her life was the death of her
sister Christian, who was only a year or two younger
than herself. A letter that she wrote at this time to
the Countess Reventlow at Rome, has been preserved.

" I am," she says, " like a little child, who, when it is
in trouble, stretches out its arms to those it loves, and
finds pleasure in weeping on their bosom. How often
have I thus wished to be with you, dear Countess! but
though my arms cannot reach you, my letter may. We
have had a sad time! Our dear Christian was attacked
with nervous fever, and died on the 2d July. Gently
she fell asleep, after having suffered much ; and now
that the pains of death are over, I would not wish her
back. How dear has the death-bed become to me!—it
is at such times that we feel deeply, and in a manner
that we can never forget, how necessary it is to seek
for something that may support us in death, and accompany us beyond."

It was on the 27th of November, 1796, that Perthes
first saw Caroline in her father's house. " Her bright
eyes, and her open, clear look pleased me, and I loved
her," said Perthes.

And who was Perthes?

This short question demands a long answer.

II.

Frederick Christopher Perthes.

HE year 1772 was a very calamitous year for Germany. Dearth and famine were almost everywhere prevalent, while scarcely any district escaped the visitation of a malignant pestilence. It was in this, " the great hunger-year," as it was called, that Frederick Christopher Perthes was born at Rudolfstadt, on the 21st of April.

His father studied jurisprudence at the University of Jena, and on his return to Rudolfstadt entered into the service of the court. In the course of time he was promoted to the office of Secretary of the Exchequer, and exercised jurisdiction over the estates of many noble families. He was but seven-and-thirty years of age when his wife Margaretha Heubel stood by his death-bed.

The secretary left his family almost destitute. The widow found her pension of twenty-one florins entirely inadequate. She was soon received, however, as an inmate into a kinsman's family, which stood in need of her services as a nurse. Her mother, almost as destitute of means as herself, offered a home to the fatherless boy. But the grandmother died, when he was only seven years old, leaving him to the compassionate care of Frederick Heubel, his maternal uncle.

In 1779, when still a youth, Heubel had returned from the University to his native district, penniless like the rest of his brothers and sisters. An office in the Prince's service, though a help, was by no means a provision. He kept house in Rudolfstadt with an unmarried sister, Caroline Heubel. Though not possessed of beauty, Miss Caroline had great strength of character. Ever ready to help others, to accept help herself was even in extreme age intolerable to her : to independence in every form, even though associated with grinding poverty, she was almost passionately attached.

Such was the household into which the little Frederick Christopher was received and brought up, with tender and even parental affection. The impressions of his childhood were so deeply graven as to influence him throughout life. Born with a very excitable temperament, he always ascribed to his uncle and aunt the horror with which he regarded every kind of immorality ; and he also attributed to them that respect for the rights of others which is alien to extremely energetic characters such as his, in which there is too frequently a tendency to inconsiderateness.

The boy's first instructor was his uncle : he subsequently took part in the lessons of the tutors of some noble families ; and, finally, after frequenting for some time the classes of the court-pages, he entered the gymnasium of Rudolfstadt, when twelve years old, but not sufficiently advanced to profit by the instructions which he there received.

Heubel was promoted to the office of Master of the Horse, and Overseer of Forests, and resided in the castle of Schwartzburg. He took a deep interest in all the great movements of the time, and like his contemporaries hailed the French Revolution with delight. Yet, in the cause of his prince, he was ready, at any moment, to have sacrificed both fortune and life. The young Perthes was not fond of study, but his uncle, who was an ardent admirer of nature, succeeded in rousing into activity the same hitherto undeveloped "faculty."

Heubel would keep Perthes for months together in his apartments at Schwartzburg, and take him with him when he wandered over hill and valley in his official visitations of the forests, or when sojourning for a time in the huts of the fowlers. On these occasions he would exact from him great physical exertions. The remembrance of these excursions was never obliterated from the boy's mind. The dusky pines that clothe the mountain-slopes of that wondrously beautiful region, the roar of the Schwarza, as far below in the valley it winds round the base of the hill on which the castle is built, were indelibly impressed upon his memory.

When he had reached his fourteenth year, and had been confirmed, it was thought necessary to choose a calling for him. To allow him to continue his studies was impossible, and from the mercantile life, as known in Rudolfstadt, he shrank with aversion. His father's youngest brother, Justus Perthes, was a successful publisher and bookseller at Gotha, and it was natural for them to think of that business for the boy. Of its nature and details he was utterly ignorant, for there was

no bookseller in Rudolfstadt ; but that there must be
books for him to read seemed certain, and this was
decisive.

In the year 1786, Schirach the printer took the boy
with him to the fair at Leipzig, to seek a master. He
was then fourteen years of age. The first person to
whom he introduced him was Herr Ruprecht of Göttingen, an aged man, who spoke kindly to him, and
desired him to conjugate the verb *amo ;* but when he
found this too great a demand on his learning, he refused to engage him. He was then taken to Herr
Siegert at Liegnitz ; but the tall, gaunt figure of the
man in his long, flame-colored overcoat, reaching to
the heels, so frightened him that he could not say a
word ; " he was too shy for the book-trade," it was
said. At last, however, Adam Frederick Böhme, who
carried on business in Leipzig, and supplied the Rudolfstadt library with books, showed himself disposed
to take him, but " the boy must go home for a year ;
he is too delicate for the work yet." When a year had
elapsed, indentures were signed by the uncle and the
future master.

On Sunday, the 9th of September, 1787, the boy of
fifteen took his seat in the open mail, to begin the
great journey of life. " In the evening, at Saalfeld, I
felt very sad," he wrote to his uncle, " but I met with
many kind people." On a cold and rainy day he
passed through Neustadt, Gera, and Zeitz ; and on
Tuesday, the 11th of September, at three o'clock in
the afternoon, reached his master's house in Leipzig.

" Why, boy, you are no bigger than you were a year
ago, but we will make a trial of it, and see how we
get on together," exclaimed Böhme. His wife and her

six daughters and little son, as well as an apprentice who had been resident four years, all received him kindly.

" I like Leipzig very much," wrote Perthes, immediately on his arrival ; "and I hope all will go well, especially as my comrade is a very honest fellow. The young ladies also seem extraordinarily kind ; Frederika, my master's second daughter, came into my room in order, as she said, to drive away fancies and whims."

" Herewith," writes his master, " I have the honor to inform you that young Perthes has arrived safe and in good health. I hope we shall be pleased with each other. His pocket-money, which, according to this day's exchange, amounts to one dollar and twenty groschen, I have taken charge of, for we cannot tell into what company he might fall. One request I have to make, and that is, that when in future you favor me with your letters, you will have the goodness to omit the ' Well-born'* on the address, for it is not at all appropriate to me."

On the morning after his arrival, the first words young Perthes heard were these,—" Frederick, you must let your hair grow in front to a brush, and behind to a cue, and get a pair of wooden buckles—lay aside your sailor's round hat—a cocked one is ordered." This once universal custom had latterly disappeared, but Böhme tolerated no new fashions among his apprentices. "You are not to leave the house, either morning or evening, without my permission. On Sundays you must accompany me to church."

The two apprentices certainly were not spoiled by

---

* *Wohlgeboren*—Esquire.

over-indulgence. Their master's house was in Nicholas street, and there they had an inner chamber up four pair of stairs, so overcrowded with two beds and stools, the table and the two trunks, which constituted its whole furniture, as scarcely to admit of their turning in it. One little window opened on the roof; in the corner was a small stove, heated during the winter by three small logs of wood, doled out every evening as their allowance. Every morning at six o'clock they both received a cup of tea, and every Sunday, as a provision for the coming week, seven lumps of sugar, and seven halfpence to purchase bread.

"What I find hardest," said Perthes to his uncle at Schwartzburg, "is, that I have only a halfpenny roll in the morning—I find this to be scanty allowance. In the afternoon, from one till eight, we have not a morsel—that is what I call hunger; I think we ought to have something." Dinner and supper they took with the family, plentifully and well; but, alas! for them, when some fat roast, with gourd-sauce, was set upon the table, for it was a law that whatever was put upon the plate must be eaten. The "Er,"* with which Böhme was always addressed, not only by his children, but also by his servants and dependants, mortified Perthes, but he wrote cheerfully, "Not the slightest thing is required of me which could hurt my feelings; while other apprentices have to clean their master's buckles, to cover the table, and take the coffee to the warehouse, none of these things are required of us."

○ Used by children towards a parent only when a constrained respect is stronger than affection.

Böhme was not indeed a man of varied learning or great mental powers; but he had a good understanding, a character of the strictest integrity, and was not without reverence for knowledge and all noble things. He labored uninterruptedly every day, from seven in the morning till eight at night, with the intermission of one hour at noon. Sunday, after service, was devoted to the "Jena Literary Gazette," every word of which he faithfully perused, and then took a walk round the city. He never played, never entered a public-house, never received company at home, and drank nothing stronger than water. Occasionally in the summer he would go over to Entritzsch with his family, and drink a bottle of *gose*,* and once in the course of the year he was accustomed to make an excursion to the valley of Störm, about twelve miles from Leipzig, in company with his whole household—wife, children, and apprentices. He was exceedingly good-natured, but equally irritable, and apt when excited to give vent to a torrent of abuse. Great were the sufferings of Perthes from this irritability, during the two years of his inexperience in the business.

"That which troubles me most," writes the boy, "is my master's passionate temper. If we have made the slightest blunder, he breaks out upon us; this is very different from what I have been accustomed to, and I feel it very hard to bear, but I shall get used to it in time."

When the fit of passion was over, Böhme would good-naturedly endeavor to make peace with the boy by bringing him fruit, or sharing with him his after-

* A kind of light-colored beer.

noon coffee, and the accompanying lumps of sugar. This most temperate man, and stern disciplinarian, had a heavy domestic sorrow to bear. His wife was addicted to strong drinks, and the household economy accordingly, so far as it depended on her, fell into disorder. This melancholy failing frequently put the poor apprentices in the most painful position.

"I am often in perplexity," wrote Perthes, "out of which I cannot extricate myself, for Madame has things brought to her in secret, which she quickly disposes of. The master would fain know all that passes, and I would gladly, like an honest servant, tell all to one who though weak is so good at heart, were it not that I should thus only insure my own misery, for many occasions arise in which he cannot protect me, and which he is powerless to alter : from seven o'clock in the morning till eight at night, he is at business, and the children do as they please, the mother being quite unable to restrain them."

The time of the apprentice was wholly occupied by the work at the warehouse, which was situated in the old Neumarkt. "I have not much enjoyment of our little room," he writes, "for we begin work at seven o'clock, return to dinner at half-past twelve, and are at business again from one till eight ; then comes supper, and it is only after this that we have any time to ourselves. We dare on no account leave the house in the evening. On Sunday we must go early to church, and to none but St. Peter's. In the afternoon, after a sharp cross-examination, he lets us out for a couple of hours." The employment was, during the first year and a half, wholly mechanical. When books published by a Leipzig bookseller were ordered, if not among

Böhme's stock, they had to be obtained from other warehouses. This part of the business fell to the youngest apprentice, and gave him at first enough to do.

"There are so many little details in our business," he writes, "that it takes some time for a beginner to understand them, and the master booksellers use abbreviations for everything, such as the titles of books, and so forth. After a year or so one understands this, but a beginner is sure to make blunders, and if I ask a question, I get for answer nothing but 'Don't you understand German?'"

The work which fell to him as the youngest apprentice, kept him in the streets or in the warehouses of other publishers during the whole of the first winter. His vivacity, united with great modesty of demeanor, won for him the favor of all the trade; he was the only apprentice who was allowed the privilege of warming himself in the counting-houses while the books he came for were being fetched. His hard lot excited sympathy. When towards dusk he returned half frozen and with wet feet to the warehouse, he had to stand for hours upon the stone flags collating. Böhme, who had never been ill in his life, and was particularly hardy, never had the shop heated, but kept himself warm by dint of stamping his feet and rubbing his hands. He was not more considerate of others than careful of himself. The consequence was, that in the first winter of his residence at Leipzig, Perthes' feet were frost-bitten; Böhme saw his distress, but took no notice until he was unable to walk, when the nearest surgeon was at last sent for. Eckhold came, and at once declared that if another day had been allowed to

pass, it would have been necessary to amputate the
feet. Nine long weeks the boy lay in his bed in the
little attic chamber, but not neglected—for his master's
second daughter, Frederika, a lovely child of twelve
years, took him under her charge, and tended him with
care and affection. All day long she sat, knitting-
needles in hand, by the bedside of the invalid, talking
with him, consoling, and ministering.

Upon the floor, among other old books, lay a trans-
lation of Muratori's "History of Italy;" and the poor
girl, with never-failing kindness, read through several
of the ponderous quartos in the little dusky attic. A
devoted friendship between the children, the result of
these tender attentions, continued long after he had
need of her nursing.

But apart from the sufferings of these months, the
boy who, under the faithful and kind though strict
training of his relations, had grown up in the free and
unlimited enjoyment of wood and mountain, often felt
oppressed by the great city and its flat, treeless suburbs,
no less than by the unhappy relations subsisting in his
master's family, and that restraint and unbroken daily
routine of business-life, which permitted freedom neither
of thought nor of action. His heart turned with yearning to the years of early childhood, and especially to
the little incidents of the residence with his uncle at
Schwartzburg, where he had wandered at will over
hill and dale. All the letters written at this time, and
even those of a later date, bear witness to his tender
recollections of those happy hours which he was never
again to enjoy. "All is well with me," he writes on
one occasion, "but for a sort of melancholy of quite a
special kind; for when I am alone I fall to thinking

of my former happy life, now forever passed away. Now this well-known rock, now another, rises before me. Then the path to the fowling-floor, to Dettensdorf, and the spot where Spitz couched and Matzen yelped. Every bush is imprinted on my memory : often when I awake at night, or look out upon the early morning mist, I think now my uncle is saying to Matzen, ' To-day there will be good sport upon the fowling-ground.' Then I see you ranging the woods with your lanterns, and when you have caught anything, I fancy I hear you crying out, ' O that Fritz were here!' . . . Ah! how many sweet recollections of Schwartzburg, and of that bygone time, are in my heart." And he writes on another occasion, " Here, in a neighboring village, called Gohlis, there is a cowherd who blows his horn as skilfully as the Schwartzburg trumpeter of yore. I can hear him in my bed, and you can not imagine what a strange feeling comes over me, and the peculiar kind of sadness to which it gives rise."

Still the longing after his beloved Schwartzburg had not taken such absolute possession of the boy as to hinder his enjoyment of new books, and of such events as the varied life of Leipzig brought before him. Now it was a comment on some facetious scene out of Siegfried von Lindenberg, or the fine comedy of " Frederick with the Bitten Cheek," or a passage out of Villaume's " Logic," that filled his letters ; again Blanchard's ascent in an air-balloon, or some procession of the Leipzig students, delighted his boyish fancy ; six postilions in front, then the riding-master Herzberg, followed by eighty students on horseback, and sixteen curricles—a magnificent spectacle !

" To-day," he writes, " I have seen a military funeral ;

it was very grand, but I wish I had not seen it, for the officer lived in the suburbs, and I cannot go there now, the spectacle has made me so sad." But it was the annual Book-fair, the first he had seen in Leipzig, that excited him more than any thing else. It brought indeed days of severe toil ; " but I do not even feel the labor," he wrote, " when I think of the few minutes which I may spend with my uncle, who arrived from Gotha on Monday. He has been so kind to me during the whole time of his stay, that I often felt as if I had a father, and could confide all my thoughts and feelings to him."

During the first year and a half of his residence at Leipzig, Perthes had, indeed, gained but little knowledge and small insight into business from his own special labor, but he had acquired experience and considerable moral strength, for both of which he was chiefly indebted to the influence that his fellow-apprentice, Rabenhorst, exercised over him. The inward shrinking from all coarseness and impurity, implanted and cherished by the lessons of his aunt and uncle in his childish years, was to him an invaluable possession, of which he was deeply sensible.

" Dearest uncle," he writes, " if I am good now, and continue so, I have to thank you and my aunt for it ;— certainly not myself, for if I had fallen into bad hands, my levity of disposition might easily have led me into vice." His lively and excitable temperament could not dispense with some moral support even after he entered into Leipzig life, and this he found in Rabenhorst, then eighteen years of age, distinguished equally for his acquirements, for his business talents, and general character.

"I thank God," writes Perthes to his uncle, "that I came here, and that entirely on account of my comrade, whose conduct is so good an example for me ; if it had not been for this, the ways of the world would inevitably have led me quite astray. You thought that I should get into good society here, but this is impossible without money ; for those who have position or fortune are very exclusive, and the pride of the merchants' sons, who can afford to play a four-groschen game at billiards, and drink a bottle of wine out of their very pocket-money, presents an impassable barrier to my intercourse with them. The booksellers' apprentices are, with only two exceptions, dissipated youths, who spend the Sunday, their only holiday, at the taverns in all kinds of excess. Now you will confess, that had I been left to mix with these, I should have made shipwreck of all the good principles I derived from you. Men here must live like others, or make up their minds to be persecuted ; but Rabenhorst has been my support."

In other respects, the elder comrade was of great service to the inexperienced boy ; he taught him prudence in the troubled economy of their master's house, he made him attentive to such details of business as he could master without extraneous help, and was always urging him to exert himself in order to redeem lost time. But what he was chiefly, though unconsciously, the means of bestowing on his friend was, *ease* in his intercourse with others.

"You will think, dear uncle," he writes, "that I agree well with my companion, when I can praise him so highly ; but it is not so. Rabenhorst by no means possesses all the virtues that go to make a good companion; he is very proud, and most obstinate in maintaining his opinion; impetuous, and, withal, so susceptible and suspicious, that I often provoke him ten times in an hour without knowing why. Many a time I have to give up my own opinion, though fully persuaded that it is right; and when I have done so, and am thinking that our difference is made up, he will exclaim, 'How can you say yes to everything?—you fancy that I am deceived by your assent, but you are much mistaken.' I know, dear uncle, that you will regard this as very useful training, and you are right; for, from having been brought up alone, I used to be a most insufferable fellow in the society of young people, but I have now learned how to behave to others, and every one is surprised to find that I get on so well with Rabenhorst; he has, indeed, an unfortunate temperament, but he loves me, and that is enough."

In the summer of 1789, Rabenhorst left Leipzig to enter a bookseller's house at Berlin, and from henceforward Perthes stood quite alone.

III.

Studies and Friends.

N the first year after Rabenhorst's departure, Perthes had worked diligently, and acquired the confidence of his master to such an extent, as to be left by him in charge of the business during an absence of some weeks. He managed things so admirably, that, in acknowledgment of his services, he received a pair of silken garters. But Perthes now began to crave more leisure than business allowed, for the purposes of education. "My principal, indeed, teaches me all that is necessary for one who is to continue a servant, but very little suffices for that; a special knowledge of the trade I certainly do not learn from him, for he conducts his business in the most mechanical manner—he does everything in the way that first occurs to him, without being guided by any principle; if a question is asked, he replies, 'We will do it in this way,' but can never give a reason why it is done so, and not otherwise, for if the same thing occur again, he will do it in some other way. All the MSS. that he receives are submitted to the old antiquary, and then whether they treat of the three bread-earning studies—

2

reading, writing, and arithmetic—or of mathematics, philology, pædagogy, farriery, or polite literature, if the oracle declares 'it will do,' the thing is settled, and if it were by Geiker, junior, it would be taken; does he say, 'it will not do,' it is as certainly rejected. The antiquary is sagacious, no doubt, but it does not follow that he has travelled through all the realms of learning."

That satisfaction which he did not immediately find in his calling, Perthes sought in pursuits of his own. From 1790, when he attained his eighteenth year, he had been possessed by an evident desire for literary employment, but time and money were alike wanting. The entrance of a junior apprentice had, indeed, relieved him from the wear and tear of running the streets, and in winter he could now spare himself; still the only hours that he could call his own, were those before seven in the morning and after nine at night. He would, however, have taken lessons in languages at these seasons, had not his extreme poverty put it quite out of the question. The widow's pension of one-and-twenty florins, which his mother had with generous self-sacrifice given up to him, scarcely sufficed to provide him with shoes; his uncle contributed his half-worn clothes, but except in a case of extreme necessity, could do no more. His linen was taken by a carrier every fortnight to Rudolfstadt, where his aunt superintended the washing and mending. At Christmas his master always made him a present of two dollars, as pocket-money for the year. An extraordinary piece of good fortune would now and then come in the shape of a present, from his uncle at Gotha.

"If you could see me now, my dear uncle, you would

not know me," he writes in the summer of 1789, " for I am much taller, and through my uncle's kindness, very well dressed in a green coat with a short waist, and buttons behind, after the English fashion, trowsers of new English nankin, and a white waistcoat. What would you have more? But I must have a great-coat at Michaelmas, and then the old dollars must spin. Hurrah! I have the two still, but I shall look my last at them then."

Such a state of things made it impossible for him to remunerate a teacher, and though Perthes frequently tried, grammar in hand, to gain some knowledge of French or English, after nine o'clock at night, he could make nothing of it, and invariably fell asleep. His inclination and talents would have led him to the study of history and geography, but the prevailing fashion required of every young man who would enjoy any respect for his abilities, that he should be a *philosopher* as it was called, and Perthes could not resist the mandate.

" Dearest, best uncle," he wrote towards the end of the year 1791, " it is certainly true that he who strives after improvement, is thereby capable of exalted enjoyment ; and I have myself often had such bright hours when, by meditation on the perfections of God and his works, and by the consciousness of my own dignity as a human being, I enjoyed a foretaste of the destiny ultimately in store for me. At such seasons, all, all was joy, and I saw everything around me laboring onward to perfection—then all men were my brothers advancing with me to the same goal."

At other times the youth had to confess that he often deviated both to the right and to the left of the path which he saw to be the true one. "You say," he writes in a letter to his uncle at Schwartzburg, "that you are delighted with the principles expressed in my letters; and encourage me to cleave to them, and practise them in my life. I do indeed cleave to them, dear uncle, for they are not a mere result of reasoning: Oh no! they are so interwoven with my whole being that I have no power to think of myself without them, but allowing them to actuate my life is quite another matter. I should be a hypocrite if I were to tell you that they had been the never-failing guide of my conduct. Now passion triumphs, now habit, again a constitutional levity which is quite at variance with the results of my reflection; and then I have to pay for the errors which reason has made in deluding me by the exhibition of a perfection which seemed within my grasp, but which, I find, cannot be reached by a bound, but must be slowly and painfully worked out. The attempt to make such a leap always insures a heavy fall."

There were seasons when the youth had so absolutely lost courage, as to give up all hope of fulfilling what he conceived to be the destiny of man. "I must indeed struggle hard, if I am to expel from my heart all that disturbs my peace; for, alas! when I feel tranquil, it is but the sleep of evil inclinations which are gathering strength for a more violent outburst when opportunity offers. Ah! my want of firmness and my hot blood often destroy in one hour what it has been the labor of weeks to build up, and then I am the victim of a remorse which is not soon succeeded by the unreproaching self-possession of a heart at peace with itself. How often have I, with tears, deplored my perverse-

ness, when, after some stedfast resolution to cling to
the good, I have fallen, because too weak to overcome
some passion! At such times every one seems better
than myself, even those who have openly transgressed,
while I have erred only in thought; for I say to myself,—had others the same impulses to good as thou
·hast, they would assuredly have been better."

Then, again, came seasons in which the young man
was inclined to look complacently on these self-con-
demnations. "You see, dear uncle," he writes, "that
I have made a good beginning, for the being dissatisfied with myself is a sure proof of this."

The activity of Perthes both in his business and his
personal pursuits, as well as in the political and general movements of the age, by which he was profoundly
attracted, had developed his understanding, made him
acquainted with life in its varied relations, and given
him an intelligent interest in all the events of the period; but this very culture had at the same time made
him conscious of a void in his spiritual life, which caused
him many hours of sorrow.

Frank, open, and truthful, he keenly felt the want
of some one to whom he might pour out his whole
heart in the unreserved freedom of mutual intercourse,
and be met by a frankness and attachment equal to his
own. The natural devotedness of a child to father
and mother, had been denied him; for his interviews
with his mother had been too few and short to exercise any influence in the formation of his character.
To the uncle and aunt who had supplied to him the
place of parents, Perthes turned with ardent affection,
and never allowed an opportunity to pass of expressing the gratitude which he felt towards them. He

opened his heart to his uncle unreservedly ; to him he
imparted the struggles of youth, the grief which his
weakness occasioned, his honest joy at having been at
least enabled to prevent evil thoughts from running
into evil deeds,—all was communicated to this his fatherly friend. Still he yearned for the daily interchange of thoughts with some companion about his
own age, whose sympathies would be in unison with
his own.

"The most earnest wish of my heart," he writes, "is
for a friend to whom I might freely unbosom myself,
who would strengthen me when I am weak, and encourage me when I begin to despair; but, alas! I find
no such friend, and yet I feel an irresistible necessity
to unburden my heart; and so overpowering is this
longing, that I could press every man to my breast and
say, Thou, too, art God's image."   While thus deploring the want of a friend as one of the misfortunes of
his life, he had been powerfully attracted by the kindly,
though childish advances of his master's second daughter, who, by the force of a benevolent nature, had won
the affection of the friendless boy from the first day
of his residence under the same roof with her.

Frederika, then twelve years of age, was, as we have
seen, his faithful nurse during the illness of his first
winter, and continued to be his playfellow and comforter in subsequent years. She provided for all his
wants, giving him food, fuel, and light, and never failed to cheer him with her sprightliness. She had often
much to endure from the disorders of the house, and
when she or Perthes suffered from the unhappy relations which prevailed, they found comfort in each
other's sympathies.

"We were sensible children," writes Perthes subsequently; "we comforted each other, read together, and talked over all our troubles."

Together they grew out of childhood: the boy became silent and embarrassed, the girl shy and reserved. About this time a second apprentice, Nessig by name, came into the house; a smart, good-natured lad, with a wonderful gift for entertaining himself and others with light and lively talk. This was unbearable to Perthes when addressed to Frederika. He had been able to hold earnest discourse with her only touching the dignity of man and the perfectibility of the human race, of the love of God and of our neighbor, and such high topics, and when these were inappropriate, Perthes had nothing to say. "On this account," he writes to his uncle, "Nessig is more regarded than I am; people talk with him, while they leave me standing, and treat me almost contemptuously." Perthes felt irritated by the neglect, and soon became the victim of jealousy. He first became conscious of this by the ill-will that he felt towards the favored Nessig. This ill-will he determined to overcome; he opened his whole heart to the favorite, and promised to conceal nothing from him. A warm friendship between the youths, founded on their common feeling towards the beloved maiden, was the result; and this afterwards exposed Perthes to much ill-natured raillery, and eventually to many vexations.

His former playfellow had grown into a very handsome girl of sixteen, and the admirers of the elder sister, who had hitherto been regarded as the *belle* of Leipzig, were now dazzled and tempted from their allegiance by the sprightliness and superior intelligence of the dark-haired Frederika. Lovers without number soon gathered round her, and yet she could not do without the shy and anxious apprentice at the other side of the room, who numbered only nineteen years, and who never expressed his feelings to her except by the involuntary attention that he bestowed on everything she did and said.

"She is still," he writes, "most kind to me; she knows how, by a few words, to cheer me when I am troubled and depressed, and she speaks to me of her position in her father's house, as she does to no other. Ah! my dear good uncle, how sincerely I thank God that my former struggle with evil thoughts, which surely came without any intention on my part, is over! What the most serious reflections on the greatness and perfectibility of man could never accomplish, has been effected by the influence of a pure and innocent love. God will still protect me; may He also protect you and your wife and children, and what is my most earnest prayer, may He make Frederika happy.— Good-night."

The next letter from his uncle, as might have been expected, brought the inquiry, "What next?"

"Assuredly she is not in love with me," was the reply; "she has the choice of so many highly-educated men, that I, with my youthful twenty-year face, cut but a sorry figure among them, to say nothing of the advantages of dress and social position which they possess. It is true that the last-mentioned have no great value in Frederika's eyes; but a young man is at this very moment paying attentions to her, whose acquirements I respect so highly, that I should be the vainest of living men were I for an instant to put myself in competition with him. Yet one word, dear uncle: even if she loved me, and I were able to maintain her, I could never make her my wife ; for nothing on earth would induce me to commit myself irrevocably with Böhme's family, nor would I marry one who has first known me in the humble position which I occupy here. My heart is ready to break while I write thus, yet be not anxious on my account, dear uncle, I never felt so confident of my steady adherence to the right as I do now."

At this time Perthes would sit up half the night, seeking to allay the storm in his bosom, by the arduous study of treatises upon Kant's Philosophy and Cicero *De Officiis*. A better help than any which these wearisome studies could afford, and one of which he, up to that time, had had no experience, was at hand, in the society of young men of great mental activity and high moral character. Accident had given rise to an intimacy with seven young Swabians, considerably older than himself, who formed an affection for him, and drew him into their circle. The names of four principal members of this circle were Schröder, Duttenhover, Trefftz, and Meier. They were men of talent and good education, of pleasant humor, and considerable poetical enthusiasm. Perthes soon devoted all his leisure hours to them. Through them he became acquainted with Herder, Schiller, and Goethe ; and, moreover, had his first genuine experiences of the joyous life of youth.

"Never, since I came here," he writes, " have I enjoyed such pleasant heart-quickening hours as now, in the society of my beloved new friends. They are all Swabians, and closely united, and cultivate no society

2*

beyond their own limited circle ; but the moment I enter, I read my welcome in their eyes."

"I am one of the happiest of men," he tells his Schwartzburg uncle. "The friendship, and regard, and affection of good men accompany me at every step, and an annoyance of a particular kind that oppressed me, has now disappeared. The annoyance I refer to was this : when I saw other young men of my own age setting about everything with a sort of sprightliness that I could never command, I was grieved at heart, because I was convinced that nothing great or noble could be accomplished without ardor and vivacity. My weak spirits vexed me, and I even went so far as to blame all that was good in me, ascribing my good tendencies merely to the coldness of my temperament, which I consequently mortally hated. And now, dear uncle, all this is changed!— yes, I feel that there is enthusiasm in me ; but when this enthusiasm, which is now satisfied with lower objects, shall have religion, perfection, and virtue for its inspiration, then the last vestige of selfishness will disappear, and I shall love all,—all as my brethren."

The circumstances in which Perthes had grown up to youth, had, indeed, been narrow and limited, but his mind had been formed and strengthened by much valuable experience. "When I think of the years I have passed here," he writes in 1793, "when I carry myself back within the circle of ideas that I brought with me to this place, I am astonished at the transformation I have undergone. I shall ever look back upon Leipzig with affection and blessings ; for here my mind began to develop and to apprehend the greatness of humanity. I have had seasons of trial, but they have brought

forth much good. I came here a light-minded youth,
with many failings ; I have still many, but many too
are corrected. For all the good I have enjoyed I
thank God, who placed so many inducements to good
in my way, in order that my levity might not get the
upper hand." It was not without a feeling of pride
that, as the term of his apprenticeship drew near, he
contemplated his actual position. " It gives me pleasure," he writes, " to say to myself, Thou hadst no
father, no means, and yet thou hast been a burden to
no one, and in a few weeks wilt be independent of all
but thyself!" According to agreement the term ex-
pired at Michaelmas, 1793 ; but Böhme's friend, Hoffmann the Hamburgh bookseller, who had carefully observed Perthes and admired his business qualities,
requested his master to set him free before the close of
his term, as he wished to engage him as an assistant in
the Easter of the same year. Böhme consented ; at a
grand entertainment he came up to Perthes, told him
to rise, gave him a gentle slap on the face, presented
him with a sword, addressed him as "*Sie*," (they,*) and
the apprenticeship to the book-trade was at end, but
not the apprenticeship to life.

---

* The Germans use the third person plural instead of the second,
when addressing others—"they," instead of you. Children and servants are addressed by the second person singular—"thou."

IV.

First Impressions of Hamburgh.

O N the 13th of May, 1793, Perthes took leave of the city in which he had spent six years— "happy years of earnest striving," as he called them himself; he had now left behind behind him extreme poverty and abject dependence. He exchanged his cold little chamber in the roof for the comfortable travelling carriage of his new master, and the roughness of honest Böhme for the cultivated society of his travelling companion Hoffmann, a man of education, and one who also possessed considerable knowledge of the world. The country was in the first bloom of spring, and a bright moonlight night induced meditation on the past and the future. At Hochweisig, the first stage, the travellers fell in with Hoffmann's friend, Campe of Brunswick, his wife, daughter, and nephews. Campe was a member of the Council of Education, and enjoyed a wide-spread reputation as a man of talent and a distinguished author, and was on intimate terms with the most noted men of the period.

By Helmstädt and Uelzen, Hoffmann and he now journeyed to Hamburgh. "The next morning at five o'clock," he writes to his uncle, " we reached the Elbe, and had to be ferried over in a large boat to Zollens-picker, the first point in the Hamburgh territory ; this gave me great pleasure, as it was all new to me. From Zollenspicker to Hamburgh is eighteen miles, but the constant variety in the scenery made it seem hardly a league. The whole tract is one continuous village, a village cradled by the Elbe, surrounded by garden grounds, and houses such as one does not often see in cities — all kept with the greatest neatness, finely painted, and fitted up with Bohemian plate-glass windows. It is a fine sight! And just think, there are peasants who give to their daughters portions of ten and even twenty thousand dollars. It was at ten o'clock at night, on the 17th of May, the day before Whit-sunday, that we entered Hamburgh. I was astonished at the crowds of people, far greater than in Leipzig, even during the most thronged days of the Fair. Everything is grand and beautiful, surpassing all I have yet seen."

He was favorably impressed by the polite manners and kind-heartedness, the open candor and regular habits of the Hoffmann family. " Madame Hoffmann," he writes, " is a woman of superior intelligence. She is admirable as a wife and mother. But I find I must take heed to my manners, for you cannot think how particular she is, and what a way she has of managing us. The daughter is handsome, very handsome, and very good, too, but one is somehow compelled to keep at a distance from her."

Hoffmann was a good man of business, and, both as a man and a bookseller, thoroughly well-informed. He liked the luxurious, hospitable style of Hamburgh life.

The contrast between the dry tranquillity of his manner and the excitable vivacity of his wife, in nowise disturbed the harmony of the family. "Were you to see this respectable couple," writes Perthes, "you could not refrain from laughing ; for she is like quicksilver, and would know everything, while he, as you know, is rather phlegmatic. Though fond enough of talking, he has a great dislike to answering questions. She has consequently to keep up an incessant fire of interrogatories, as, ' I say ?—Do you hear ?—Hoffmann ?—Tell me ?—Don't you hear ?—Answer me ?'—and not unfrequently she pours out all these in rapid succession before she can extract a reply. At last he rejoins with, ' I have told you already,' and yet no one has heard a word. If she is too hard upon him, he growls a little ; it is of no use, he must do as she bids."

The business in which Perthes was now, under Hoffman's direction, to work, was one that called forth all his powers. Half a year after his entrance on it, he thus writes : "I was ignorant of many things, as is mostly the case with apprentices who have served their time ; but I have hit upon a situation particularly favorable for extending my information, for I have work to do here which is unusual even for an experienced hand. That this keeps my brain in excitement you may well believe ; happily, being left to myself, I can work as I like, and this is the only way in which I can get through much. Reflection has always been my best teacher, and just for this reason I find it very difficult to comprehend and to imitate any one who sets himself to show me the way to do anything."

Perthes did not find many leisure hours in his new employment: "We never close," he writes, "till nine o'clock at night, and once in the week we have to sit up half through the night. This is in ordinary seasons, but at the approach of a fair the work can scarcely be overtaken." Perthes had already learned in Leipzig to take advantage of the few hours which the uninterrupted routine of business life left at his disposal for mental cultivation and for recreation, and in Hamburgh, too, he found time to accomplish much.

He had been deeply interested with Herder's "Letters on Humanity," and Jacobi's "Waldemar." Schiller's "Essay on Grace and Dignity" had charmed and captivated him. "It is singular," he writes, "that works of this kind make the most profound impression on me, while special treatises on morality, and grave exhortations, however excellent, fail to interest, and even many leave me restless and unhappy. These suggest things which rouse all sorts of doubts and questionings in my mind, but a treatise, which, like that of Schiller's, is so convincing and exhaustive, and gives birth to so many new thoughts, has power to move me deeply.

On the holidays, the fine environs of Hamburgh afforded him recreation and numerous sources of pleasure. "He must be dead to the beauties of nature," he writes, "who could be unhappy here. You can imagine nothing finer or grander than the neighboring country. Every turn of the Elbe below Altona is unique of its kind, and reflects in its peculiar beauty the greatness and goodness of the Creator." Acquaintances he had readily found, and was no longer, as he had been in Leipzig even during leisure hours, dependent on the will of a master : he was quite disposed to avail himself of the many pleasures which were to be enjoyed in a great city.

But amid all the shifting scenes and impressions
that the change of life brought with it, Frederika's
image was still present with him. When Perthes left
Leipzig, they had promised that they would not forget
the days of childhood, and that they would correspond
occasionally. He was deeply affected at hearing that,
on the day he took his departure, she had sat for hours
at the window weeping. In his first letter to his
Leipzig friends, he says, "I still live wholly in the
past, and am now first aware how fondly I love Frederika; she is ever the centre round which all my
thoughts turn." True to the obligations he had taken
on himself, to keep back nothing bearing on his relations with Frederika from his friend Nessig, he sent
to him their whole correspondence. A strange intimacy thus grew up between the rivals, grounded solely
on their common affection for the girl. "You may
have secrets from me," writes Perthes, but "nothing,
nothing may you conceal of your feelings and thoughts
regarding me. Here the least reserve would be the
grave of friendship. Keep back neither doubt nor
reproach; write all, even though it should cost me
many a bitter tear."

Perthes was able to comment to his friend with
calmness, nay, even with some severity, on whatever
seemed wrong in Frederika, but he found excuses for
all in the trying circumstances of her home. "Men
may indeed blame her, but God condemns no one for
single and isolated failings. He has appointed a stern
discipline for the poor, dear, noble girl, and hereafter
she will reap the reward. If I knew any way to make
her happy," he writes again, "I would joyfully do so at
any cost. I have been long thinking how I can write

to her an affectionate letter of advice ; but though you may let a girl *feel* that you think her wrong, and although she is quite conscious of it, yet you must not venture to *say* it, or you will at once be made aware of the power which in such a case a woman always has over a man."

" Be her friend, her guide and counsellor," he writes to Nessig, " but guard against yourself, and do not harbor a feeling of security which is only imaginary. Your last letter betrayed the height of passion, and shows that you are given up to its intoxication. It were folly to strive to tear it from your heart, even if you could. No ; keep this love-sickness, be still an enthusiast, only forget not virtue and religion."

The calm judgment and self-forgetting anxiety which Perthes at one time exhibited, were at another over-powered by an outburst of passion : " You are still living," he writes, " under the eyes of my Frederika ! —*My* Frederika ? Yes, so I call her, for come what may, a part of her soul is mine, and will be mine for ever."

In another letter he says, " Frederika begins every-thing with me, Frederika is with me while I am occu-pied with it, Frederika ends it with me—in a word, Frederika is in my heart by night and by day. Ah ! my suffering is sometimes great, and it is truly terrible to have to will to subdue such a passion as mine, and yet I must and will subdue it."

Perthes had the firm conviction that the maiden loved his friend better than himself. " I would fain not confess it," he writes, " but I have long been aware of Frederika's preference for you—a preference ground-ed on your noble character, which is much stronger than mine. Believe me, brother, it often cost me a struggle, yes, a terrible struggle, not to be unjust to you, and not to make you smart for the preference you enjoyed. Once I was on the point of becoming your enemy, but I overcame, and now I am calm, though I must still weep. Write and tell me what is to be the issue of your love, and I will do all I can for you."

In such a mood Perthes would seek for solitude, where he might give himself up undisturbed to melancholy thoughts. "I have just returned," he writes, "from a solitary walk, which has done me much good; I was penetrated by the glory of Nature; certainly I was never better in soul than now. Dearest brother, be it what it may that now inspires me—God—Nature—Heart—do not grudge it me, but rather rejoice with me. In the twilight of memory, visions rise before me, and the misty figures of the distant loved ones hover around me."

"Imagination!" he says in another letter, "Imagination! no dependence is to be placed on thy votaries, says Campe; and yet, though thou hast caused me many sorrows, I would not be without thee. Imagination gave me blessedness—gave me love and melancholy. Oh, the melancholy which is the offspring of imagination, is the sweetest thing that I know! My brother, to lie in the stillness of nature, not knowing what one feels or thinks, and yet to know it so well! In such moments every blade of grass, every leaf is my friend—while as fancy prompts I can extract from each, food for my imagination, and would fain shed tears of sweetest sadness; there and then is it revealed to man that God is the soul of all."

Grateful as Perthes was for the happiness of his Hamburgh life, it was not long till he felt its insufficiency to satisfy him. " You cannot imagine, dear Campe," he writes, " what it is to be confined exclusively to the company of the young, and to be quite shut out from that of older men, and from all family gatherings, except on some rare festive occasions. Among the young men, however extended the circle of acquaint-. ance, an unbearable sameness prevails, and the whole conversation turns upon trifles. There can be nothing more perilous than constant intercourse with commonplace men ; even if the character do not sustain direct injury, a dry, dull, reserved condition of mind is induced, more or less inimical to freedom. When I first came here I was foolish enough to associate with a multitude of young persons, who at the outset appeared tolerable ; now that I have discovered how many precious hours they make me waste, I must take decided measures to get quit of them."

But though anxious to free himself from these connexions, Perthes by no means sought to avoid all society. His natural disposition, fostered by early habits, made it impossible for him to find entire satisfaction in what books alone could afford ; to become what he was capable of becoming, he needed both correspondence and personal intercourse with men capable of exercising influence over his mind, men of different positions, different degrees of culture, and of various tendencies. He became more and more conscious of this want. " My heart," he tells his uncle, " yearns for the society of many, and of cultivated men. Such society is a necessity for me, and I must compass it unless I am to sink entirely." Hamburgh, the most stirring city of Germany at that time, was exactly the

place where an ardent desire for the variety and excitement of improving society might best be satisfied.
As the first commercial city, and the first sea-port of
Germany, its world-wide trade had made it the centre
of the most varied interests, and consequently the
resort of strangers of all nations.

A comparatively small number of congenial families
formed the centre around which citizens and strangers
of distinction alike gathered. Büsch, whose writings
on political economy and commerce enjoyed a great
and wide-spread celebrity was already advanced in
years ; but the Commercial Academy, of which he was
President, was the means of bringing strangers from
all parts of Europe to his house, where all that was
most distinguished for wit, talent, or learning, was to
be met with.

When Perthes, then in his twenty-second year, first
came to live in Hamburgh, he was wholly unacquainted
with the opinions and objects that formed the centre-
point of this society ; but he saw that the life there led
was one of some significance, and longed to obtain admission into the circle. "How my heart beats," he
writes to his uncle, "when I think of such eminent
families, as those of Büsch, Reimarus and Sieveking,
and when I meet with young men who are privileged
to enjoy in their society the genuine pleasures of life.
I must and I will find an entrée speedily."

This was not, however, so easy a matter. The distinction between the business of the wholesale and
that of the retail dealer, a distinction grounded in the
nature of the occupations, was strongly marked at
Hamburgh, by the fact of its being recognized in the
very constitution of the city. The merchant might

become a member of the Senate, the tradesman only of what are called the burgher colleges.

Perthes, moreover, was poor, and had neither connexions nor introductions. It was a happy accident that first brought him in contact with the Sievekings; and his first appearance among them was an event of some importance to a youth brought up in the most limited circumstances—an entrance into an entirely new sphere of life. "My neighbor at the table," he tells his uncle, "was Büsch, a man of seventy, almost blind, and not a little deaf; he would insist on my helping him to everything; and as each dish was presented, he said, 'What's that?' Now I, you know, had neither seen, smelt, nor tasted any of the dishes before in my life, and as each dish was presented, I was obliged to proclaim my ignorance, in a loud voice, which was laughable enough both to me and to every one else!" The intimacy here quickly gained for him a welcome among the friends and relations of the family. Numerous invitations and much consequent mental excitement followed, but still the inward struggle and uncertainty were the same.

"I have," he writes to a friend, "tasted the intoxicating pleasures of a world in which all is collision and opposition; carried away by them, like many others, I am not: I have had my experiences, but I am not the better for them, and not to become better is to become worse."

In the society of the most distinguished families of Hamburgh, Perthes had hoped to meet with influences of an improving kind, which might give a new direction to his character; but the difference of years, of social position, and the fact that his spiritual wants were not experienced by his new friends, made this quite hopeless. Three men about his own age were now destined to exercise a powerful influence on his moral progress. " I have now," he writes in September, 1794, " become acquainted with three men, who, in spite of their very different characters, participate in each others' sentiments on almost every subject. One of them, Speckter, is a scholar, entirely devoted to the critical philosophy, and the intimate friend of the philosopher Reinhold. The second, Runge, is a merchant, the ablest mind with which I have yet come in contact; the other, Hulsenbeck, is inferior to neither."

Perthes was two-and-twenty years of age when he was introduced to these new friends. His small and slender, though firm and well-formed body, his curling hair and fine complexion, and a peculiarly delicate curve in the formation of the eye, gave to his appearance an almost girlish charm. Singularly susceptible, the slightest allusion to women brought the color to his cheeks. When he had determined on carrying out some settled purpose, the decision and resoluteness of his mind were manifest in the expressiveness of his slender form ; his strong sonorous voice, his bearing, and every gesture, indicated that he both could and would carry out his resolution. " Little Perthes has the most manly spirit of us all," said his friends ; and they had many stories to tell of the surprising power which his invincible will had exercised over the stubbornness and physical superiority of strong rough men. Perthes was conscious of his power, and in reliance on it, would often, both then and in more advanced life, advance boldly to encounter difficulties in circumstances under which men who possessed more physical strength would have quietly held on their way. He was not generally afraid of a coming evil, though he would tremble at the recollection of a danger past.

At the beginning of their acquaintance, Perthes exerted a gently constraining influence on the three friends, and on Herterich, who had recently been admitted to their circle. " Perthes is a man to whom I feel marvellously attracted by his tender susceptibility, and his earnest striving after all that is noble," writes Speckter at this time : " I thank you for having made me acquainted with such a man." Runge writing at a later period says, " I could not withdraw my eyes from him—the charm of his external appearance I could not but regard as the true expression of his inner nature." But the impression that Perthes on his side received was one of a far deeper kind : " I am now," he tells his uncle, " enjoying to the uttermost all that a quick and ardent sensibility *can* enjoy. I have found three friends full of talent and heart—of pure and upright minds—and distinguished by great and varied culture. When they saw my striving after the good, and my love for the beautiful,—when they perceived how I sought and endeavored, they gave me their friendship, and, oh! how happy I now am ! Through them I have attained what I stood most in need of. They know how to call into life and activity all that is best in me. I am like a fish thrown from the dry land into the water. Do not say that this is enthusiasm ; for a feeling is not to be regarded as enthusiastic because a man experiences it in its full power only in hours of peculiar elevation ; such hours are rather to be regarded as those in which a man is most truly himself." This friendship with men whose minds were more matured

than his own, gave him a deeper interest in the appearance of the great literary works of that period. " Have
you read Goethe's ' Lehrjahre," he writes ; how simple, and how grand ! and that there is anything finer
than ' Iphigenie ' I do not believe."

It was Speckter who first directed the inquiring youth
to Schiller's poem, " Die Künstler," (the Artists,) constantly urging upon him the lines, " It is only through
the morning gate of the beautiful that you can penetrate
into the realm of knowledge," and " that which we here
feel as beauty, we shall one day know as truth." Runge
then helped him to comprehend Schiller's æsthetic letters. It soon appeared to him as if a grand error,
embracing all time, had been overthrown by Schiller,
when he said, " It is not enough that all enlightenment
of the understanding is worthy of respect only in so
far as it reacts upon character ; this enlightenment
must also flow from the character, because the way to
the head is only through the heart. The cultivation of
our feelings is therefore the grand necessity." " I
entreat you to read the æsthetic letters," he wrote to
Campe ; " take pains to comprehend them, make them
your own, and you will reap your reward ; for the
views therein opened up of the beautiful, and of the
whole condition and capabilities of man, are the most
sublime and the truest that have ever penetrated my
soul." And again, " O brother ! let us become good,
genuine men, approaching more and more within the
sphere of the moral and the beautiful. When we have
ourselves attained a sure footing, we may then influence
others ; we may attain it, but only through the beautiful, for through it alone can goodness find entrance."

He was now penetrated with the liveliest gratitude

towards his friends for the new convictions which they had awakened within him. "I had despaired of myself," he writes, "while I was striving in vain to become virtuous by the sacrifice of all feeling, spiritual as well as sensuous. Constantly failing to fulfil my purpose, I lived in the constant dread of being an object of contempt to the men whom I loved. Where was I to find support? I had discarded as worthless all that was most peculiar to my character. You it was who taught me to recognize what I had thus discarded, and strengthened it in me by your love ; and your love will guarantee it to me as long as I am upon earth. You it was who led me to ' the morning gate of the beautiful ;' and now it stands open before me—and now I may, and will strive after that which is most wanting in me,—constancy and equipoise."

Perthes was soon to discover, that even within the portals of the beautiful there were paths of darkness and perplexity ; and it was well for him, that just as this experience was beginning to dawn upon his mind, he was forced to concentrate all his powers on the business of active life.

3

V.

Establishment in Business.

THE society in which Perthes now mixed made him feel keenly the defects of his own education, defects which he saw little likelihood of his now being able to supply. The daily calls of business occupied every hour. "In culture," he says, "I make no progress, and cannot hope to make any : this is a source of grief to me." He hoped, one day, to be able to retire, with a small sum, to some secluded spot, where he might devote himself to study, and give unity to his various but only partially digested knowledge. "Campe," he writes, "stigmatizes this desire for culture as vanity : 'A man must not live for himself,' he maintains, ' but to be useful to others.' But he is certainly wrong, and I do not agree with him." His future was pretty sure, as his uncle in Gotha had promised him the reversion of his business. "My plan of life is so simple," he said, " that I do not see how anything could occur to thwart it."

It was only a few weeks after he had thus expressed himself, that Reimarus and Sieveking proposed to him to enter into the publishing trade with a young friend of their own, promising to provide the necessary means: but, not feeling sufficient confidence in his knowledge of business, (he was then two-and-twenty,) or in the partner whom they destined for him, he gratefully declined the offer. But from that moment he formed the resolution to establish a business of his own in Hamburgh, as soon as he had acquired the requisite experience. He hoped to get his friend Nessig for a partner, and meanwhile succeeded in securing for him an engagement in Hoffmann's establishment.

At the outset indeed, Perthes regarded the book-trade as the means of acquiring property and achieving independence ; but a sense of the importance of his " beloved book-trade," as he was wont to call it, to the whole intellectual life of the German people, soon took such entire possession of his soul, that during the whole course of his long life, we are justified in saying, the mere question of gain had little weight with him. Where a large conception of the nature of the book-trade did not exist, it seemed to him that learning and art were endangered by its operations. " If there be no blower," he would say, " the greatest artiste would strike the organ to no purpose." In more than one district where literature lay dead, he had seen it revive and flourish by the settlement of an active bookseller in the locality.

Regarding the business from this point of view, he could not but complain that far too little attention had hitherto been devoted to this most interesting branch of industry. He had further observed, that where a bookseller possessed an educated taste, works of a high class were in demand ; and that where, on the other hand, the bookseller was a man of low taste and immoral character, a licentious and worthless literature had a wide circulation. Supported by these facts, Perthes ascribed to the book-trade in general, and to each individual bookseller, an important influence on the direction in which the public sought its mental food : and clearly perceiving the influence of literature upon thought and life, he was convinced both then and throughout his whole life, that the book-trade, and the manner in which it was conducted, had a most important part to play in giving direction to the course of events.

He was aware that the book-trade could be managed mechanically, and viewed merely as a means of livelihood, but he saw elsewhere also, among priests and professors, ministers and generals, some who, in giving their services, thought only of their daily bread.   A shudder came over him when he saw booksellers make common cause with a crew of scribblers who hired out their wits for stabling and provender.

" Where," writes he in 1794, " where will you find a body of men so deficient in the requisite information, and so negligent of the duties of their calling, as the booksellers?   Germany is deluged with wretched and abominable publications, and will be delivered from this plague only when the booksellers shall care more for honor than for gold."

His friend Campe had proposed to institute a tribunal of booksellers, and thus to render impossible the publication of injurious works.   But earnestly as Perthes desired the elevation of the calling to which with all the energy of his nature he had now devoted himself, he nevertheless regarded the execution of such a proposal to be not only impracticable but dangerous— introducing, in fact, a censorship of the press in another form.   It was only in the elevation of the whole body and of each individual member, that he hoped for progress. "Dear Campe," he writes, "in order to bring about all that is possible and desirable, let us first see that we ourselves are what we ought to be; let us also increase our knowledge, and strive as much as possible to win for our opinions friends and advocates among the young people of our own standing. There are now five of us, and what may not five accomplish if only they be in earnest? Let each strive to diffuse a high tone over his peculiar circle; let each seek out some choice spirits, and if we persevere, and God favor us, what may we not accomplish?—what good may we not be the means of bringing about? Write me your views on this subject, I entreat you, quickly, and at length."

Perthes desired to be independent, and to exercise a widespread influence by means of his calling. He had become so much attached to Hamburgh, that it seemed almost impossible to leave it; he was constantly revolving in his mind the practicability of founding a business there, and the change introduced shortly before into the manner of conducting the book-trade, appeared likely to facilitate the carrying of his wish into effect.

Perthes was of opinion that in the present position of the book-trade he might, without running any improper risk, found a business in Hamburgh, and by conducting it on liberal principles, stimulate the literary appetite to such an extent as to benefit rather than to damage the existing "Houses." He was only four-and-twenty, but "more at liberty on that account," he wrote to his uncle, "to enter on a great undertaking, as I may look forward to ten years of labor without thinking of marriage."

A thousand pounds of capital, however, was necessary, and Perthes had nothing. Nessig, however, was willing to become his partner, and to bring a capital of £300. A loan from one of his old Swabian friends, and the associating in the enterprise of a young Hamburgh merchant, gave him command of the necessary funds. The firm was to be under Perthes' name. In Easter, 1796, he left his situation and proceeded to Leipzig Fair, in order to open up communications with publishers. The circular which he issued was to the following effect :—

"I wish to signify to you my intention of establishing myself in Hamburgh as a bookseller, and to beg your confidence and support in this undertaking. In asking this, it becomes my duty to give some information concerning my past experience in the business I propose to conduct. Allow me to refer you to Herr Böhme of Leipzig, under whom I served six years, and to Herr Hoffmann of Hamburgh, whom I have served for the last three years. If you think it necessary to make any further inquiries, I shall endeavor to give you every possible satisfaction, either orally or in writing."

The old men were not without misgivings as to the prudence of giving credit to a young man of four-and-twenty, who so boldly established a business of his own. Perthes required larger sums of money than he had anticipated ; he fell into the most painful perplexity ; but the faithfulness of his three Hamburgh friends extricated him from his difficulties. "You will have heard," he writes to Campe, "how things fell out at the Fair, but happily, amid so many other childish pleasures, I had also that of procuring a few thousand dollars ; and that was pleasant,—very pleasant !"

In the midst of the throng and tumult of business, his old passion for Frederika returned. He had persuaded himself that his love was no longer a passion, nothing but pleasure in reflecting on the intelligence and gracefulness of the maiden, and had, indeed, engaged to renounce her in favor of his friend. But, in the presence of the beautiful girl, the fire that had warmed his earlier youth was rekindled. "There she stands before me," he writes, "in all her power and in the full consciousness of her freedom—earnest—free from all petty vanity—her eye full of thought, every feature beaming with life and expression; and, when her eye looks into mine, passion takes possession of me, and in the depths of my heart I feel that I am on the threshold of a great decision." The promise he had made to himself to win her for his friend, not for himself, he now regarded as an evil destiny. "Such overflowing happiness," he exclaimed, "I saw for myself in that beaming eye! and I find that in all—all, I have been the victim of self-delusion, and that I am poor and helpless. I ought to withdraw from her presence, and I cannot. Must I keep my purpose, even when it is I, not he, whom she loves? No; I cannot, for love to *me* gleams in her eye."

He saw but one way of escaping from this struggle between passion and duty. He at once wrote frankly to Nessig explaining all, and while awaiting his answer, he employed a friend to break the matter to Frederika. Perthes and Nessig each made an offer of his hand; the choice was to rest with her, and the rejected was to withdraw in peace, and, in all fidelity, to live and labor for the beloved pair.

"Frederika," wrote Perthes, "listened without changing color, remained silent for a short time, and then, with deep earnestness, replied,—' I love Perthes, I love Nessig ; but my hand I can give to neither.' And now," proceeds Perthes, " I feel sad and perplexed ; for is it not I who have called forth this decision of Nessig's destiny ?"

A letter from his friend relieved him from the load of self-reproach, but the future now appeared empty and desolate. " My whole life-plan is ruined—ruined by her! I have done with life. God give me comfort and strength !"

In another letter he thus expresses himself,—" You think the hard coldness with which I endure all this sorrow unnatural ; you would have me give way to tenderness and melancholy. Well, I will obey you, and in future learn to submit ; hitherto I have trusted too much in myself."

The necessity of working hard in order to give a fair start to the new business, was now a grievous burden to Perthes. " Would that I had never begun! but the thing is done. Already I am under heavy engagements to others, and these I must and I will fulfil, like an honorable man."

He returned to Hamburgh, and there had the delight of receiving his mother and sister, to whom he was now in a position to offer a home. He now devoted himself, with all the energy of his nature, to those preliminary labors on which the successful opening of the business depended. He was the first bookseller who displayed a selection of the best works, old and new, in all the various branches of literature, classified and arranged. His shop presented the appearance of a small but well-chosen library, and the addition of the periodicals of the day offered the means of gaining a general view of the actual state of literature, its movements and its tendencies. Perthes started business in a stirring quarter of the city.

" The house which I have rented," he writes, " for a thousand marks, is quite a wonder in Hamburgh, for, from top to bottom, all is literary. On the ground floor book-shelves ; up one stair the same ; up two stairs Dr. Ersch, as editor of the newspaper, recently set on foot ; on the third story, Dr. Ersch as littérateur and helper's helper to Meusel and his associates ; on the fourth, French booksellers in front, and at the back, the sleeping apartments of the young German booksellers ; up five stairs a loft, which may be used for a storeroom."

" My own domestic arrangements," he tells his aunt, " are on a small scale, but tolerably neat ; I think you would approve of them ; at least my love of order is becoming a terror to all the household."

The preparations being all made, Perthes announced the opening of his business by the following advertisement in the " Hamburgh Correspondent," of the 11th July, 1796 :—" I hereby make known that I have established a new bookseller's shop, which is now opened. In my shop the best books published in Germany, old and new, are to be found ; and I venture to promise, that I will procure any book which is to be had in other parts of Europe. A portion of my assortment is ready bound, in order to meet the wishes of the reading public more readily, to facilitate to the purchaser the knowledge of what he is buying, and to supply the wants of the passing traveller more adequately.

3*

" I am persuaded that by beginning in this manner, I have engaged in a useful enterprise. Whatever may be incomplete and defective in the manner of carrying out my arrangements, I shall endeavor to remedy as soon as I have acquired a better acquaintance with the wishes of the public. In order to make a visit to my shop agreeable, and, so far as I am able within my own sphere, to aid in diffusing a knowledge of recent literature, 1 shall take care that a copy of every German journal, every novelty of the day, and all writings of general interest, shall always lie in my shop for inspection. To attention, punctuality, and politeness to those who shall visit me, I pledge myself in all circumstances as a duty."

The business was now established with good hope of success. It was, as Perthes said later in life, a bold and adventurous youthful undertaking ; but it was founded on a correct insight into the important movements and necessities of the literary life of that period.

VI.

New Acquaintances.

N July, 1796, only a few weeks after Perthes had commenced business, a tall, slender man, with a finely-formed face, a darkish complexion, and glorious, thoughtful blue eyes, entered the shop. He appeared to be about fifty, but in all his movements there was the ease and power of youth. His dress, expression, and bearing, had the air of being studied and yet perfectly natural. His fine and noble bearing soon attracted the attention of Perthes; it was Friedrich Heinrich Jacobi, who having left Düsseldorf, was at that time residing in Holstein and Hamburgh. Superiority was stamped upon him, but it was neither cold nor repulsive. The attractiveness of his appearance inspired immediate confidence; and Perthes had scarcely given the necessary replies to his inquiries, when he expressed to the astonished author of Waldemar, the reverence and affection with which he had instantaneously been inspired. He, at the same time, gave the friendly listener a glimpse into his own earnest striving, and the uncertain ground on which he stood. Jacobi was pleased with his candor and animation, returned after a few days, and from that time became a frequenter of the shop, now turning over the leaves of the new French,

English, and German publications, and now conversing with their owner.

A few weeks later, in August, 1796, Perthes was invited to visit Jacobi at *Wandsbeck*, where he was then living. There he saw Jacobi's youngest son Max, who had just finished his medical studies in England, and the two sisters of his host, Charlotte and Helena. Clever, lively, and deeply interested in all the literary movements of the period, the sisters at the same time discharged all household duties with praiseworthy energy and self-denying care. From this time Perthes enjoyed the privilege of joining the circle at Jacobi's as often as he pleased, and that was not seldom. Helena became a real, motherly friend to him, and her brother a paternal counsellor, ever ready to enter into the feelings, to sympathize with the inward struggle, and to answer the doubts and questionings of his young friend, admonishing and instructing him, and thus doing much to further his mental development. " I love and honor the glorious man as I love and honor none beside," he writes to his uncle. " I met him with a full heart ; he recognized it, and thought it worth his while to occupy himself with my inner being."

Jacobi and Claudius were closely connected with the most cultivated society of Holstein.

A number of eminent men, most of whom were more or less intimate, were at this time living in Holstein, either on their estates, or in the smaller towns ; and these diffused life and activity throughout the whole duchy. The Greeks and Romans, nature and art, religious topics and politics,—all had their friends and partisans in this country. Niebuhr the father had been living at Meldorf in the Süderditmarsh since

1778, intimately associated with Boie, the editor of
"The German Museum," who held the office of Land-
vogt ; and, at the same time, like Niebuhr, had an extensive connexion with the men and affairs of foreign
countries.   Count Leopold Frederick Stolberg had,
on his return from Italy in December, 1792, fixed his
residence at Eutin, as president of the government of
the principality.   He was then, as during his whole
career, full of life, spirit, and love, and yet restless and
unsettled, because, as a Protestant, he could not find
for his religious convictions that firm external support
of which he felt the necessity.   Nicolovius, the late
director of the ministry of public worship in Prussia,
worked under Stolberg.   Voss had come to Eutin as
Rector of the Academy of Otterndorf, and had long
been known and esteemed among the Holstein circles.
Both the Stolbergs had been united with him in the
association of poets at Göttingen, and from 1775 to
1778 he declared that he had led the happiest life at
Wandsbeck, in the society of Claudius and his noble
friends.

At Emkendorf, between Kiel and Rendsburg, lived
Count Frederick Reventlow, who had retired to this
estate after his recall from London, where he had filled
the office of Danish ambassador.   As a zealous champion of the necessity of the closest adherence to the
Augsburg Confession, as Curator of the National University, and as a stanch maintainer of the rights of
the nobility, he incurred much odium ; but his talents
and integrity, joined to the refinement of his manners
and his knowledge of the world, excited general admiration.   His wife Julia, (born Countess Schimmel-
mann,) by her intellectual vivacity, her unassuming

piety, and her cheerful resignation under severe personal sufferings, as well as by her judicious kindness to her dependants, had won the friendship and respect even of those who did not share her opinions. This house was the frequent resort of Jacobi, Claudius, the Stolbergs, Cramer the father, and Hensler ; and the gravity and refinement by which it was distinguished were free from all formality, and interfered neither with the pleasures of literature, nor with the animation and cheerfulness of their social life.

The brother of Count Reventlow, the Count Caius, had his residence at Altenhof, near Eckernford, on the Baltic. In refinement of manner and general culture he was perhaps inferior to his brother ; but in energy, in business capacity, and activity of character, he surpassed him ; while in intelligence and extent of knowledge he was not his inferior. Closely connected with both was Count Christian Stolberg, at that time Warden of Tremsbüttel, a town situated about three miles from Hamburgh. It was not owing so much to the Count himself as to his wife Louisa, (born Countess of Reventlow,) that his house was peculiarly attractive to the friendly circle. By the acuteness of her understanding, and the thoroughness of her education, the Countess stood high in the estimation of her friends ; and she did not hesitate to assert, with spirit and independence, opinions, political and religious, that were diametrically opposed to those of the kindred and friendly families of Holstein.

Holstein was separated from Hamburgh by essential differences of character—differences which affected their mode of viewing all the events of the day and all relations of life. Notwithstanding this, Claudius,

Jacobi, and the two Stolbergs, were fond of Hamburgh, and, overlooking religious and political diversities, were often to be found there, enjoying its intellectual advantages. But the controversy regarding the Confession was connected rather with the influential circles of Münsterland, with the Princess Gallitzin as their centre, than with Hamburgh. For the elevated position which, since the year 1770, the archbishopric of Münster had occupied, it had been indebted solely to the Baron Frederick William Francis von Fürstenberg, who, as Minister of Max-Frederick von Königseck, Archbishop of Cologne and Bishop of Münster, had governed Münster since 1764. Fürstenberg was a statesman in the noblest sense of the word. But, apart from his merit as a statesman, Fürstenberg enjoyed a high literary reputation. He had at his command an amount of knowledge and experience seldom to be met with, and was quite at home in all the literary and philosophical movements of the period. Having been greatly addicted to the art of war in early life, and, in consequence, active in promoting the cultivation of mathematical studies and of a vigorous and manly style of education, he now, in his advanced years, devoted himself to the study of religion and philosophy.

To this man and to this country came the Russian Princess Gallitzin, on a visit, in the summer of 1779. She was the wife of the ambassador at the Hague. Her object in visiting Münster was to consult Fürstenberg about her son, with the intention of devoting herself to his education, in some country residence on the banks of the lake of Geneva. But so great was her admiration of the Minister, that she would not withdraw herself from his counsel and support, and,

consequently, became permanently established in Münster.

The princess, who was the daughter of the Prussian
Field-Marshal Count Schmettau, had received an education calculated only to fit her for entrance into the
fashionable world. In 1768, when in her twentieth
year, she had accompanied the Princess Ferdinand to
the baths of Spa, as her maid of honor, and there became acquainted with Prince Gallitzin, to whom, at
the end of a few weeks, she was married. In the
course of her travels she had acquired some experience
of court-life in Vienna, Paris, and London, and was
then called to play a distinguished part at the Hague,
as the consort of the Russian ambassador. Her ambition and vanity were flattered by the homage which
her talents no less than her position commanded, but
she was nevertheless far from being satisfied with her
condition. From her earliest youth she had experienced an earnest desire for the knowledge of the truth,
and the attainment of the ideal of moral perfection
which ever floated before her in a variety of forms.
The distractions of the great world had never quenched
this desire. From the unbroken circle of amusements
and visiting, of balls and theatrical representations, she
returned night after night with a craving after something better, that grew in intensity till it became a torture. She felt a wish to withdraw from society, and to
quiet the internal struggle by devoting herself entirely
to the acquisition of knowledge and the education of
her two children. It is somewhat remarkable that it
should have been Diderot who obtained the consent
of the Prince to her plan, although the philosopher
had been unable to comply with her request, that he

would introduce her into the realm of knowledge. At the age of twenty-four, the princess had retired to a small secluded house near the Hague—there with an energy bordering on passion, to follow out a course of scientific study.

In 1783, when she and her physicians alike despaired of her life, she had dismissed the priest whom Füstenberg had desired to attend her, because she was absolutely without faith in the efficacy or importance of the Sacraments.

During her long and tedious recovery, she for the first time, and much to her alarm, became alive to the fact that she was a slave to literary ambition and the pride of learning. "With this discovery," she said, "all pleasure in myself vanished." About this time her children were of an age to receive religious instruction, and she considered it to be her duty as a mother to impart it. In order at once to preserve her own integrity, and to keep from her children her doubts on the subject of Christianity, she resolved that the instruction should be purely historical. For this purpose she gave herself up to the earnest study of the Holy Scriptures, reading them by preference in the Latin version. What she had entered on for her children's sake, she soon continued for her own. The truth of Christianity, as set forth in the Scriptures, penetrated her heart; and once convinced, she ever after strove, with all the energies of her powerful mind, to bring her life and actions into the strictest conformity to the truths which she had imbibed. A small but distinguished circle gathered round this extraordinary woman. A woman who, like the Princess Gallitzin, surpassed, in breeding and culture, all her contemporaries of the same rank, and who now linked with her dazzling talents the faith of a little child, could not but make a deep impression on these powerful intellects. Goethe and Lavater, Herder and Hamann, felt themselves in a like degree, though in different ways, attracted and elevated by this remarkable character.

All the literary men of distinction lived in intimate union during the latter portion of the last century. Holstein and Münster also were brought into closer relations through Hamann. "Those times," said Perthes, fifty years later, "were very unlike these in which we now live. The Holstein families, as well as the Gallitzin-Droste circle, stood apart on account of their Christian tendencies. The prebendaries, and other dignitaries of Münster, with the single exception of the family of Kersenbrock, looked upon the Church with the eyes of mere men of the world ; while, among the burgher class, luxury and vice were universally prevalent. Earnest Christians, whether Catholics or Protestants, were closely united. There was no mutual suspicion or bitterness ; Claudius, Reventlow, Jacobi, and the Stolbergs, were often to be found in Münster, and the Princess paid frequent visits to Hamburgh and Holstein ; Claudius and his family especially attracted her. Their confessions of faith were indeed dissimilar ; Claudius was a decided Lutheran, the Princess a zealous Catholic. Her Catholicism was that of all times, so far as dogma and ceremonial were concerned ; but in so far as it was a life, and presented itself as such, it differed as widely from the new-poetic, and the historico-political Catholicism of the present, as it did from the frivolity of the French and the torpidity of the German Catholicism of last century. The great

fact of the Redemption, the common ground of Protestantism and Catholicism, exercised such a vital and
governing influence on the Princess, that, so far as the
Holstein circle was concerned, the diversity of confessions appeared comparatively unimportant ; while again
the names of Fürstenberg, Overberg, and the Princess,
were never mentioned in Holstein save with the greatest affection and respect."

No sooner had Perthes become a familiar guest in
the houses of Jacobi and Claudius, than his attention
was directed to these Holstein circles. They were
destined to exercise a powerful influence both on his
intellectual development and on his worldly position,
but for a while he knew them only by report.

An event of an important kind, one which was to be
the source of all his earthly happiness, was awaiting
him.

VII.

The Betrothal and Wedding.

A FEW weeks after Perthes had become acquainted with Caroline Claudius, he had been spending the morning, along with Jacobi, at the house of Caroline Rudolphi, the superintendent of the well-known Educational Institute, and had received an invitation from the former to spend the evening of the Christmas festivities with him.

Among the guests, Perthes found Claudius and his whole family. Before the entertainment commenced, accident threw him alone with Caroline in a side-room; he had not a word to say, but he experienced a calm and a happiness which he had never felt before. The Christmas games began, but Perthes had eyes for nothing but the expression of quiet pleasure which beamed in Caroline's face. In his opinion the best that the evening offered was hers by right, and yet her younger sister's gift seemed better than hers. On the topmost branch of the Christmas tree hung an apple, finer and more richly gilt than any; Perthes dexterously reached it, and, blushing deeply, presented it, to the no small surprise of the company, to the conscious Caroline. From that evening things went on between them as they usually do between those who are destined to share

(68)

the joys and sorrows of life together as husband and wife.

"Indeed," said Klopstock, as he was returning to Hamburgh with Perthes, after Claudius' silver wedding-day festival, on the 15th of March, 1797, "you young people are quite unconscious of the love that we have long seen in you both!" But Perthes was well aware of the affection that had taken possession of his heart, and which was daily growing deeper. He felt, however, that the distance between himself and Claudius was too great to justify his approaching him without friendly mediation. He at once told his secret to Jacobi and his sisters, and entreated them to ascertain for him whether there was any hope.

"Thank God! my dear Perthes," wrote Helena Jacobi on the 27th of April, "you are truly loved, and inasmuch as my courage is as great as yours is small, I see a prospect of great happiness for you. I could not hear anything yesterday from Caroline herself, for I did not find her one minute alone, but I ascertained from her mother enough to inspire me with great confidence, and Caroline looked so friendly that it was clear that she had something pleasant in her thoughts."

A few days later, on the 30th of April, Perthes applied to Caroline in person. "How can I ever forget that day of deep emotion in which I first revealed my love to you! Silent and motionless you stood before me; not a word had you to say to me, but as I was sorrowfully turning to leave you, you affectionately put your hand in mine." So in after days wrote Perthes.

Caroline's love was frankly confessed and pledged in the course of the evening, but to her father the decision not unnaturally appeared a hasty one. Perthes had only just entered his twenty-fifth year; he had boldly established a business which was attended with considerable risk, and he was too candid to conceal from the father the struggle of the conflicting moral principles that were fermenting in his mind. Moreover, Claudius was not altogether free from a species of jealousy. It was a pain to him to have to resign the protection of his daughter to another, and it was almost with grief that he discovered that she loved a young and inexperienced man better than her father. The saying, " Thou shalt leave father and mother," was to him a hard one. All he could do was to assure Perthes that he would not oppose the marriage, but his formal and full consent he could not yet be persuaded to give. Perthes was not uneasy on this account, and two days later, took his departure for Leipzig, with love and thankfulness in his heart.

" Know, my beloved Caroline," he wrote in his first letter, " that I would fain do, or leave undone, everything with sole regard to you. I am indeed happy, and have never loved the good God since my childhood so well as I love Him now. I have, indeed, felt love before, but it was torture and distraction ; now it is peace and joy, and I thank thee for it, my dearest Caroline." He long expected news from Wandsbeck in vain. At the end of a fortnight came a letter from Claudius himself, which ran thus :

"DEAR MR. PERTHES,—We are glad to hear that you arrived happily and safe, and that you are well and mindful of us. Caroline has received and read your letters from Brunswick and Leipzig, and thanks you kindly for them. She would answer them herself;

1*

but while the consent of her parents is not formally given, she is not at liberty to open her heart fully. It is better, therefore, that she should postpone her answer till your return."

A letter from Helena Jacobi explained matters. " Your Caroline said to her father, when he told her not to reply as if his consent were already given,—'If I may not write all that is in my heart, I cannot write at all ; you must write and say why I remain silent.' I pressed your dear Caroline more closely to my heart than ever," adds Helena, " on hearing this."

From Leipzig Perthes wrote to inform his three Hamburgh friends of the state of his heart. An alliance which drew him still nearer to Claudius and Jacobi, could not be regarded by them as a desirable one for their friend. " Why should the news of my engagement to Caroline have caused such bitterness in you ? Were you thinking of my former unhappy love ? It will live as long as I live! or, were you thinking on the fleeting and changing fancies that have often filled my heart ? It is possible that these too may move me again at some future time. If thoughts like these have suggested your letter, I cannot blame you. But listen to me. When I had succeeded in extinguishing my rejected love, I was horror-stricken to find that such love,—love with which the highest aspirations of my soul were associated, *could be extinguished*. A death-like coldness took the place of the burning flame. Shall love, then, whose source is in God, and in all goodness, be annihilated by external, adventitious circumstances ? There must at all events be something that is stable. If it be not love, it must be friendship. Friendship! I have nothing to say against friendship

—and yet shudder to think that this is all. Where, then, shall I find deliverance and help for my inner being? My soul craves something that shall not pass away ; my heart craves one who shall be all to me ; my spirit desires some abiding good ; my personality longs for union with some other being,—a union which shall endure even when the world is shivered to atoms ; and nothing but love is greater and more enduring than the world. *If I can in any way be preserved, it is only through Caroline ; in her I find peace and stability, devotion and truth.* The passion of love implanted by my former attachment is latent within me, but the love itself is no longer there. The passion which I then experienced can exist but once ; I can never love Caroline as I loved Frederika, but with her I can again lift my eyes to God, and this is the help from above which my soul requires."

On the return of Perthes from Hamburgh at the end of May, Claudius no longer withheld his formal consent. It was to the Princess Gallitzin that Caroline first communicated her happiness. " To you, my dear mother Amelie, I must myself tell the news of my being a bride, and a happy bride. This would at one time have seemed to me impossible, even if you had assured me of it, but my beloved Perthes has reconciled me to the step. I know and feel its importance for time and for eternity ; but I believe that I have taken it in accordance with the will of God, and now can only close my eyes and entreat God's blessing ; and you, too, must pray for me, dear Princess. I can say, in all truth, that my Perthes is a good man, who does not regard himself as formed, but who knows and feels that he is not yet perfect ; and I think, therefore, that he and I may make common cause, and, by God's help, make progress."

Perthes was now frequently to be found on the way to Wandsbeck, and letters were almost daily exchanged. Many of these have been preserved.

On the 15th of July, the betrothal, which in Holstein is a church-ceremony, was celebrated. The solemnity was graced by the presence of the Princess Gallitzin and her daughter, by Overberg, who was then on a visit to Claudius, and, much to Caroline's satisfaction, by the Count Frederick-Leopold Stolberg.

Shortly before the commencement of the ceremony, the bride was reminded by the pastor, that after it had taken place she was no longer free, and could be released from her vows only by the Consistory. "It is long since I took the step," she replied, "from which I could be released neither by you nor by the Consistory."

In the quiet of Caroline's maiden-life, the bride-like love grew deeper and stronger, and put even her tranquil nature in commotion. "Caroline would fain act the philosophic bride," writes the daughter of the Princess Gallitzin, "but in vain; her love perpetually betrays itself, and I believe that she dreams of nothing but the letter P, and if for a moment she devotes herself to me, you well know who it is that quickly comes and displaces me."

"Your brother Hans," writes Perthes to his bride, "brought the rose safely into the room, but then broke it. Thank you for this rose! Hans slanders you. He says that you can never find anything you are looking for. Even if you have this failing it matters not, since once, although not seeking, you yet found him who was

4

seeking the good angel of his life, and suffered yourself to be found by him."

The 2d of August was the day fixed for the wedding. On the previous day Perthes received the last
letter from Caroline as his betrothed bride. "I have
a great desire for a little black cross," she writes, "and
don't know how better to get it than through you, dear
Perthes, and why not? I have been to the pastor this
morning. The formula by which we are to be united
is neither cold nor warm, neither old nor new,—a
wretched neither one thing nor another. But it will
do us no harm, dear Perthes ; we will ask God to bless
us after the old fashion, and He will bless us after the
old fashion. Do it with me, dear Perthes, opening
your arms and clasping me to your heart. I am thine,
body and soul, and trust in God that I shall find it to
be for my happiness."

The marriage was solemnized on the following day,
the 2d of August, 1797.

In the first months and years of their married life, the
diversity of their minds and their habits was to be
brought into strong relief. Perthes had been fitted for
the sphere in which he now moved by natural character, by the circumstances of his early life, and by his
actual position in Hamburgh, by the variety of external
relations and impressions, by the efforts he had to make
in difficult and changing circumstances, but, above all,
by contact with men of the most opposite opinions.
On the contrary, Caroline had never come in contact
with the noisy outer world, but had lived a life entirely from within. To her the duty of man seemed to
consist in withdrawing as much as possible from worldly business and motives, and in abstaining from all

lively participation in the transitory. The first three books of Thomas-à-Kempis, taken as a whole, might be regarded as reflecting her views of life. Now that she had left her father's house, and experienced on all sides an infinite variety of new impressions, she could not fail to be disturbed and disquieted under their influence.

Her affection for her husband was, however, strong, and in the depths of her soul she felt that her new position was one of happiness and blessing. On one occasion, a few weeks after her marriage, when her father surprised her weeping in her room, he exclaimed, not without a measure of complacency,—"Did I not tell you that the first flush of happiness would not last if you left your father and mother?" "And if I am to pass the rest of my life in weeping," she instantly replied, " I should still rejoice that I am to spend it with my Perthes." But this confidence, which was an essential characteristic of her nature, could not overcome the uneasiness caused by the frequent disturbance and the many real or apparent hindrances to which the inner life was exposed from things without. In her sorrow and perplexity she thus writes to her husband : " A thousand times has my soul spoken out and told me, that I am no longer what I was. Formerly, God always held me by the hand and led me in all my ways, and I never forgot Him ; now I see Him afar off with an outstretched arm, that I am unable to grasp. This must not be always so, for the heart could not endure such a prospect. But I have made up my mind that so it will be upon earth ; and may God grant me the continuance of this inward longing, and suffer me rather to die of it, than to be content without it.

There are moments in which I take courage again, but they do not last, and it is no longer with me as it was once." In another letter she says, "When you are away, my beloved Perthes, I feel quite lonely and forsaken ; when you are not at my side to support me, I am a picture of grief. *Is* this to continue—ought it to be so ? It was otherwise once."

The letters written by Perthes, during short absences at Leipzig, Holstein, and Westphalia, show, that while he took pleasure in the exercise of his powers in public life, he knew how to appreciate the value of a life which looked within rather than without.

"Believe me," he wrote to his wife, in the summer of 1799, "believe me, my good angel, when I tell you, that you have much spiritual life ; do not then disquiet yourself. Our father acted wisely in keeping his children from active life and an artificial existence. Even if he had carried this too far, if he had rendered you unfit for the business of life, so that to you the whole world were foolishness, still you would have had the spirit of love, and the spirit of love is all in all."

The respect in which Perthes held the rights of individuality would have withheld him from any attempt to force his own mode of life upon Caroline, even if her character and her manner of looking upon life had not claimed respect from their own inherent merits. "To force upon one mind the opinions of another ; to graft the fruit of our own tree upon another stem, is sin," wrote Perthes to a friend. Besides, he clearly perceived that any such attempt upon Caroline's mind would be futile. "My Caroline," he wrote to his Schwartzburg uncle, "makes me unspeakably happy. She is a pious, faithful, true-hearted, and submissive creature ; but her inward course she shapes for her-self, and pursues it with a steady step."

As steadily did Perthes himself tread the path that seemed marked out as his. In 1798 he says to his wife, "I am more than ever persuaded that my destiny is an active, masculine career ; that I am a man born to turn my own wheel and that of others with energy." He was not diverted from his course by the difference between his wife and himself.

"Can you then, indeed, believe," he wrote in 1799, "that my restless labors, my activity and energy, can be detrimental to you? To you, Caroline! You should rather thank God that he has enabled me to take pleasure in things that might have been a weari-ness and a burden to me. How otherwise could I wish to exist? Dear Caroline, I am not always so good as you think me, but in this respect I am better than you think me."

Doubts, indeed, would occasionally arise as to the distracting and hurtful influence of his mode of life upon Caroline. "You have to fight against many failings in me," he writes. "I have asked myself what I would do, if it depended on me to remove you to a situation in every respect congenial to your tastes—whether to a convent or into the hands of a man who not only loved you as I love you, but whose disposition and habits entirely coincided with your own. No, dearest Caroline, I could not do it. You must live with me, or not live at all ; and, dearest wife, I know that in this you feel as I do."

That Caroline's dislike to all contact with the world, and her extreme susceptibility under the disturbing circumstances of her new position, were sanctioned by the claims of the inner life, Perthes did not for a moment believe. He was of opinion that a character like hers ought to show itself as an example in the world.

" Believe me," he writes, " I understand you and your present feelings thoroughly. While you lived in your father's house, you maintained, it is true, a constant walk with God. You had but one thought and but one path. But then your walk with God was the walk of a child, who knew sin and the world, and life, not at all, or only by name; still there was a unity in your existence. Now, simply because you are in the world, this condition must be disturbed. I have torn you from that childlike life, and brought you into the bustle of the world; you recognized in me an honest heart, full of love for you, but you have also seen in me, and through me, and in yourself, the sin of mankind. For a while, but it was not long, your love for me concealed all this. Now you can no longer walk so confidingly as formerly with the Unseen, and He no longer speaks to you as before. You are perplexed, and would gladly regain the purity and simplicity of the child, and are unable to bring order and unity into your thoughts. My dear Caroline, the want which you feel is entirely the offspring of your own imagination. You have, pious child, ardent faith in your heart, and in your mind entire subjection to the higher decrees of conscience : but where others would be contented and at peace, you are full of care and anxiety, because you would fain lead again the undisturbed and simple life of childhood, and cannot. Here, on earth, man has but a changing and unsettled existence ; he does not *all* live in any single moment, but only a part of himself.

The only things of value are love and truth, but would you, therefore, disregard all besides? Would you live apart from everything? But even if you were to withdraw to some retirement where no sorrow, no disquiet, could reach you, you would become cold because you love only the Highest and no other object, and coldness is always a horrible thing. No, we are not to drift away from the world; God demands not the sacrifice of natural ties, but the submission of our will to His. The sorrow and annoyances which may be our lot in the world where He has placed us, we should bear with inward tranquillity rather than seek to escape from them."

"Caroline does not find life easy," said Perthes to a friend; "in spite of her calm temper, and her rich and lively fancy, she feels it hard to have to do with the ever-changing and finite things of the world and of time. And yet, when I see her holding fast by her inward life, in spite of the annoyances which the tumult and distractions of her daily existence too often cause her, and also fulfilling the outward duties of her position in a manner so self-denying, kind and noble, she imparts strength to me, and becomes truly my guiding angel."

"Two creatures more different than Caroline and myself, in culture and tendency, it would have been hard to find," said Perthes later; and yet, in the first hour of our acquaintance, Caroline recognized what of worth there was in me, and loved me; and in spite of all that she subsequently discovered in my character, that was opposed to her own modes of thought and life, her confidence has remained unshaken and unalterable. I, on my part, soon perceived her love, and at once apprehended the true and noble nature, the lofty spirit, the life-heroism, the humility of heart, and the pure piety which now constitute the happiness and blessing of my life."

If Perthes and Caroline had not met till later in life, they would probably have repelled each other; but now the fusion of two characters so diverse was facilitated by the passionate ardor of youthful affection,—an ardor which long survived their marriage.

Many of the letters written by Perthes at this time have been preserved. They are often full of tender playfulness; frequently, too, we find in them the expression of fervid passion, and of deep reverence for that spiritual life of Caroline, still unattained by himself.

In a letter written in the third year of his marriage, during her absence for a few weeks, he says: "During my bachelor life, when one affection used to give place to another, when I loved Frederika, when I first knew you, my only aim was to conquer, to please; I sought only myself—was always *I*. But now in you I have lost myself—without you, I am nothing—I have nothing—am to myself nothing."

"You, yes you, my ever-youthful love, have given me a new life," he writes on the following day; "through you I am born again. While you are absent, all around me is cold and uninteresting: you alone give tone and coloring to everything. I did not know that my heart had retained such feelings; I had thought that the first love had passed away; but no! ever since you were mine, the first love is the first and the never-ending love. Where can it cease? Love, ever-strengthening love! every morning I rise to new love, and every evening I repose on thy heart. Ah! I can well understand now, how one may be cold and desolate, while yet, in the stillness, the heart is beating warmly."

"Dear child! dear Caroline!" he says in another letter, "I am exactly like our Bishop Kaspar; I would, without interruption, cry, Love, love, nothing but love! When I rise in the morning, I ask—Why should I? my Caroline is not here. When I am at work, I am thinking only of my return to you; and, alas! you are not here, and I have no home, no place of rest. If at evening I have done the day's work, and would assume a happy face—ah! for whom? my heart is not here. If you were to leave me, my angel, to leave me entirely, the good spirit would go with you. I believe, indeed, that I should love again, but how?"

Again he writes: "You fancy that I am jealous of our little daughter, because I would share your love as well as she; ah! I could wish you had twelve strong and healthy children, to be your joy; for you would have to thank me for all the twelve, my noble, excellent wife!" Caroline's return from a short excursion having been unexpectedly delayed for some days, Perthes wrote that the days passed as though a thousand pounds' weight were hung upon each :—

Just as the traveller's aching sight
  Explores in vain the morning sky,
Where, hidden in a flood of light,
  The soaring lark sings joyously:
So glance I anxious to and fro,
  Through wood and field, o'er hill and plain,
My songs one only burden know,
  O come, beloved, to me again!

4*

VIII.

The Business and the Family.

THE partnership into which Perthes had entered in 1796, was only provisional, and its continuance was contingent on the success which attended the undertaking. The returns during the first two years were so trifling as to cause a dissolution of the partnership in December, 1798. Perthes, when left alone, found himself in a position of considerable difficulty ; but, relying upon the attention which his mode of conducting business had already attracted among the literary circles of Hamburgh, Westphalia, Hanover, Holstein, and Mecklenburg, he did not lose hope of ultimate success.

Nothing, however, could be done without additional capital. The confidence which he inspired was such as soon to put 30,000 dollars at his disposal, and, so supported, he was enabled to weather the great commercial and monetary crisis of 1799.

From the nature of the business, Perthes had escaped the immediate influence of this wide-sweeping calamity, but indirectly he felt severely the general scarcity of money. By the help of his own energy and prudence, and the friendly assistance of his three Hamburgh friends, he not only stood firm at this great crisis, but was enabled to extend his business considerably, and amid the universal ruin, it acquired a name and received an impulse. He far overstepped, however, the means which he had in hand, and this prepared for him much anxiety and many painful perplexities.

"My engagements," wrote Perthes in 1799, "are now so manifold, that all my time and all my strength are required for the superintendence. What men commonly call good fortune, I may be said to possess, for success attends all my undertakings; but this good fortune has been anything but easily won, and when I weigh the hours of ease and tranquillity against the hours of labor and anxiety, the latter have an overwhelming preponderance. You know me well, and know what it has cost me hitherto to ask, to entreat, to put on a bold face; you know how difficult it has always been for me to seem harsh, stern, inflexible; and all this I have been obliged to be, or to appear. God, indeed, has come to my help, when most I required His aid. Good fortune, and that activity and energy which are called forth only by enterprise, never fail me."

Perthes had a lofty aim in the business which he had founded. Hamburgh, Holstein, and Mecklenburg were to be only the basis of his operations, from which it was to attain a position which would constitute it the medium of literary intercourse for all European nations, and would render accessible to each people the literature of every other. Hamburgh seemed to be the right place for a business so extensive in its relations: a branch was to be established in London as a support. But Perthes had not resources for carrying out so great a plan without assistance. He felt keenly the want of the necessary information, and more keenly still the inadequacy of his education—a want not then to be supplied. He looked around for help, and found it in John Henry Besser, who, from this period, may be regarded, both in joy and in sorrow, as his truest and most confidential friend, and who shortly became by marriage with his sister, a near and much-loved connexion.

Besser was one of those happy persons who are liked as soon as seen, whose society is sought by all, and with whom every one feels happy. His exterior was prepossessing, and as a young man he had been distinguished for his handsome figure ; his loving and love-desiring heart shone in his friendly eye, and gave expression to his delicate features. He had an instinctive perception of the wishes and wants of others, and without information or inquiry, he was ever ready to help to the utmost of his power. The favors of all kinds that he had conferred were innumerable. He attracted children as the magnet attracts iron, and could scarcely defend himself from their demonstrations of affection. Always, and in all circumstances, he acted with the purest integrity without the slightest effort, and without requiring to *will* to do so : that a man should speak contrary to his convictions seemed to him impossible. During the occupation of Hamburgh by the French, he would, with alarming *naïveté*, tell the plainest truths to the officers and functionaries, and yet, strange to say, he enjoyed their confidence. His many little peculiarities, his absence of mind, his habit of devolving on the morrow the business of to-day, often occasioned the most extraordinary incidents ; but these peculiarities were regarded by his friends as component parts of a character of such rare amiability, that they would not willingly have missed them.

Besser was born in 1775. His father was chief pastor at Quedlinburg, and had sent his son, well instructed in the modern languages, to Hamburgh, to learn the business of a bookseller. Here he so early won the confidence of his master Bohn, that. at the end of three years, he was sent to Kiel to take the sole charge of a branch-business in that town. Perthes, who had seen Besser in passing through Leipzig, was drawn into his society soon after he came to Hamburgh, and each recognized in the other a turn of mind which led to a strong mutual attachment. In 1797, Besser went to pursue his literary education in Göttingen. There he made good use of his opportunities, and attended lectures on the history of literature. On his return, in 1798, he entered into partnership with Perthes ; and although the business was still carried on in the sole name of the latter, the services of Besser became henceforward indispensable.

"It would be hard to find in any individual bookseller," said Perthes, at a later period, "so extensive a knowledge as Besser possesses, of the most celebrated books in all languages, their character and value ; and there is no one who knows, so well as he does, where to find, and how to procure them."

Besser, moreover, in spite of the gentleness of his disposition, maintained a calmness and presence of mind under harassing and complicated circumstances, which, united with the vigorous mind and active invincible spirit of Perthes, carried the business through great difficulties to a position of consideration and influence. The plan of making it the medium of the literary intercourse of the various European nations, was necessarily, in a great measure, abandoned, in consequence of the troubles and losses of the year 1806. Till then, it was steadily kept in view, and in the German book-trade, Perthes and Besser took an established and influential position. Even so early as 1802 Perthes could write from Leipzig,—"I do not think that any of our brethren in the trade have met with such distinguished kindness as I have; every one is ready to take trouble for me."

So great was the confidence inspired by Perthes, that numerous families in the north-west of Germany employed him to select periodically the works which he thought best suited to their respective characters and tastes—a duty which he performed with equal conscientiousness and success. It was impossible for Perthes, in his relations as a man with men, to be actuated by any mercenary considerations.

"I can forgive everything but selfishness," he once wrote; and in more advanced life nothing made him so indignant as petty narrow-mindedness in money matters. "Even the narrowest circumstances," he said, "admit of greatness with reference to mine and thine; and none but the very poorest need fill their daily life with thoughts of money, if they have but prudence enough to arrange their housekeeping within the limits of their income." In accordance with these opinions, Perthes, in time of pressure could accept freely from his literary friends the assistance they freely offered. Many of those who subsequently became his most intimate friends were originally only connected with him by the ties of business; while his extensive literary acquaintance was of considerable advantage to his interests.

But notwithstanding the flourishing aspect of affairs, he was very far indeed from being free from great and continual anxiety, and frequent anticipations of pecuniary embarrassment. The business meanwhile continued steadily to increase. "I am still," he writes in 1805, "in occasional straits for money, but yet in a sure way of becoming rich. I desire fortune only as a means of freedom and for the general good. God grant that I may one day be in a position to work with a more tranquil mind!"

It was with the warmest gratitude that Perthes acknowledged the blessings that had attended him in his calling. "A week ago," he writes, "I entered on the tenth anniversary of my establishment in business; how thankful should I be! For if the enterprise of 1796 had not succeeded, I should not now possess my dearest Caroline, nor my faithful partner Besser, nor my friends, nor my present wide and glorious sphere of action. I feel that I have found myself through my calling; for, owing to my previous negligence, this was the only way in which my powers were susceptible of development."

His family circle afforded a resting-place from the ceaseless turmoil and anxious cares of business, and maintained in him that cheerfulness and vigor necessary for the proper discharge of his daily duties. "You have penetrated into the profoundest recesses of my being," he writes to his wife; "there is no moment of my existence in which you are not with me, in me, and before me; and all I see, feel, and observe, I seem to see, feel, and observe only for your sake."

On the 28th of May, 1798, his daughter Agnes was born; on the 16th January, 1800, a son, Matthias;

on the 10th of January, 1802, a daughter, Louisa; and on the 25th of February, 1804, another daughter, Matilda. Joys and troubles, which are found in every family, become, wherever there are children, a means of education to the parents. One may indeed be induced by the love of God to withdraw from the external world, in order to give himself exclusively and without distraction to the cultivation of the spiritual nature; but the love of a mother for her children is, in its very nature, the closest of all links to outward and practical life, a direct and continual doing and caring, which leaves no time for a life of contemplation. Caroline's maternal love was the school in which she first learned wisely and vigorously to give to the hidden "man within the heart" an outward direction. Increasing household cares, the influence of her husband, and varied intercourse with men of the most opposite characters, further tended to bring out her capabilities, and to make her move freely in the world, so that amid the variety of external circumstances she was able to preserve an inward calm and self-control. She retained indeed to the end of her days a desire after a life of unruffled tranquillity,—a longing which would occasionally dispose her to melancholy.

" It is still the old story with me," she writes to the Countess Sophie Stolberg; " I desire much, and can do but very little;" and again to her husband, in the spring of 1804 on the day after his departure on a journey, " Agnes sends you word, she hopes you will cross the water safely, and is anxious—*my* daughter; Matthias only desires to know how his rocking-horse is, and is happy—*thy* son." Notwithstanding the continued longing for a life of outward repose, she had in the first ten years of her marriage attained to a measure of freedom, self-command, and tranquillity, which, when she was subsequently threatened with the loss of property, family, and all external happiness, she maintained with true womanly heroism.

She was now no longer disquieted, as she had often been at first, by the influence of her husband's position and mode of life. "I have just looked out into the night, and thought of thee," she once wrote to the absent Perthes. "It is a glorious night, and the stars are glittering above me, and if in thy carriage one appears to thee brighter than the rest, think that it showers down upon thee love and kindness from me, and no sadness ; for I am not now unhappy when you are absent. Yet am I certain that this does not proceed from any diminution of affection. If I could only show how I feel towards you, it would give you joy ; after all I may say or write, it is still unexpressed, and far short of the living love which I carry in my heart. If you could but apprehend me without words, you would understand me better."

" What you have now," wrote Caroline, in 1803, to a newly-married friend, " is only a foretaste, and will every day increase. At least, the merciful God has so ordered it for me these six years, and my eyes overflow as I think of it."

" My beloved Perthes," she writes a year later, on the anniversary of the day on which he had declared his attachment, " this is the 30th of April, and it is just nine o'clock. Do you remember this very moment this day seven years ? I thank God from the bottom of my heart for having made you think of me.

I have just come from looking at the children, who are already in bed, and while I gazed on them I had you in my heart ; thus, although you are so far away, we are still united. I bless the happy moment in which seven years ago you looked on me, and said ' I love you.' Yes, my ever-beloved Perthes, I thank God, and I thank you, for our happiness. May God continue to be with us and with our children, and preserve us to a peaceful and blessed end."

IX

𝔉𝔞𝔪𝔦𝔩𝔶 𝔉𝔯𝔦𝔢𝔫𝔡𝔰.

THE affection and ardor with which Perthes followed his calling, and the moral strength which he drew from his domestic life, enabled him to escape becoming the victim of vacillating indecision or of confused fancies—a danger to which his intercourse with men of such diverse and influential characters peculiarly exposed him. Next to his own, the house of his father-in-law was that which possessed the greatest attractions for him. "I have confidence in every one who esteems your father," wrote Perthes, in the summer of 1797, to his bride ; and in a letter dated in 1802, he says, "There is no one on earth that I think more highly of than our father. May God long preserve to us the noble, beloved man!" The uninterrupted and ever-increasing influence of Claudius was strengthened by many kindred impressions.

Perthes was a frequent and willing visitor at Klopstock's house, till his death in 1803. "The repose of death was greatly to be desired for Klopstock," wrote Perthes, shortly after his decease. "He said to me three weeks before he died, 'I prefer a state of pain to any other—all else is but torpor.' He died as he had lived, peacefully, simply, and with composure. No one, not even his brother, saw him during the last fortnight. Only his wife, Meta, and the physicians, were with him. His wife seems to have entertained mistaken ideas of upholding Klopstock's greatness, even in his last hours. I am sorry for this ; everybody knows that people do not die artistically. His funeral procession showed the respect in which the people of Altona and Hamburgh held their fellow-citizen. As the body was borne from the church to the grave, a chorus of young girls sang, ' To rise again, yes, to rise again !' It was a moment of general emotion ; but, even in death, Klopstock had to do penance for his toleration of the spirit of the times, and of his own insipid and shallow disciples, for N. delivered an oration over him."

In Hamburgh, Perthes still kept up his former intimacy with the Sieveking circle, and lived in free and familiar intercourse with his old friends, Runge, Speckter, Hülsenbeck, and Herterich ; but it was from Holstein that the deepest and most abiding impressions were now received.

The Countess Julia Reventlow of Emkendorf continued till her death to be the warm friend of Caroline ; and the unpretending sprightliness and gentleness of her disposition, which revealed itself even in her correspondence, made others more open to the influence of her opinions. Her husband's brother, Count Caius Reventlow of Altenhof, won the confidence of all who approached him by his genuine earnestness, and by his spirited and hearty manliness of character. Attracted by the goodness and candor of Perthes, the Count became his faithful friend in word and deed, notwithstanding the difference of age and position. "The Count was the last of the high-minded nobles of a bygone time," wrote Perthes to the widowed Countess Louisa, in 1804, shortly after her husband's death, "and a nobler than he our fatherland never possessed. He was a good friend and a benefactor to me at the period of my greatest need ; and there are many who will think of him with love and regret as I do now." At Altenhof, Caroline and Perthes had become intimately acquainted with the Countess Augusta, (born Stolberg,) who, as second wife of Count Andreas Petrus Bernstorff was the stepmother of the Countess Louisa. Many might have overlooked the gentle, pious woman without suspecting the treasure which lay concealed in her heart, but Goethe showed his wonderful power of discerning mental endowment in the well-known inscription to this unseen friend of his youth. To Perthes the Countess was wont frequently to refer, in letters full of intelligence and affection, and she always found in him a trustworthy friend. On his final departure from Hamburgh, she wrote, " Your life has taken such deep hold of mine, so intimately is it connected with many of the earlier and later associations of my heart, that your departure makes me very sorrowful. Forget me not."

Manifold were the impressions which Perthes was to receive from Holstein. His intimacy with the pious and venerable Kleuker introduced him to a more extensive acquaintance with theological questions, while the friendship of Reinhold exhibited to him the mental confusion engendered by the mutual repulsion of philosophical and theological views.

" Reinhold has received me in his old fashion, and with his accustomed kindness," wrote Perthes to his wife in 1799, " and has given up his own room to me.

He wins upon me as a man, the longer I know him ;
but his monotonous many-sidedness obstructs him in
his progress towards truth. He pushes back the curtain little by little, but he cannot draw it up. It will
be difficult to break down the partition-wall that sep-
arates him from Kleuker, because neither will allow
the two points on which the wall of partition rests,
and on which all depends, to be touched ; while, by
their mutual sarcasms, they continually provoke each
other."

Jacobi's influence with Perthes was also an abiding
one, and he was ever ready to converse with his young
friend on the works in which he was engaged. " Yesterday, Jacobi gave me his new MS. treatise to read,"
writes Perthes to Caroline, from Eutin, in 1801 ; "it
was hard work. I labored at it the whole of yesterday, and the 'tall papa' said admirable things apropos
of it ; to-day I have studied it again with him in right
earnest." In all his visits to Holstein, whether long
or short, Perthes felt himself improved and elevated
by the influence of the country and the people. He
says to Caroline, " I was at Sielbeck with Nicolovius ;
the day was glorious. Nicolovius is a charming man.
I felt so youthful, and so rich, and so thankful to God :
He has bestowed on me so many gifts ! such a long
and happy youth, and you, my love !"

With Catholic Münster, Perthes was no less closely
connected than with Protestant Holstein. It was in
the winter of 1798 that he had first become personally
acquainted with it, and on his journey thither he was
greatly impressed by the grand aspect of the lofty oak
forests and deep valleys of Westphalia, or more properly of Osnaburg. This short and hurried visit to

Münster was sufficient to give him an idea of the life with which, from other causes, he was afterwards to be so intimately associated.

The Princess Gallitzin, till her death, kept up her correspondence with Caroline ; and, notwithstanding the difference of creed, stood godmother to Perthes' eldest son, Klopstock and Claudius being godfathers. Caroline, on her part, preserved her affection and reverence for the Princess. In 1806, on hearing of her fatal illness, she wrote, " No one ever made so deep and so lasting an impression on me as she ; and from the first moment of our meeting, she has been, I may say, my guide to God."

Perthes had made the acquaintance of the Baron von Droste, a few weeks after his marriage to Caroline, when the three brothers, Kaspar, Clemins, and Francis had visited Hamburgh in company with Kellermann and Brockmann. He had been their cicerone, and they had gladly shared the frugal meals of the youthful couple. They were about the same age, and a friendship so intimate was then established, that neither differences of position nor of opinion had any power to shake their mutual affection and esteem. " I was particularly attracted by Kaspar," said Perthes, in his later years, " even then a suffragan-bishop, and one who, in depth of love, might have been compared with the beloved disciple."

In 1806, the Princess Gallitzin died. " The last few hours," writes Kasper to Perthes, " were hours of severe suffering, and yet rich in mercy. She met her end in perfect consciousness, and committing herself entirely to God, receiving her Lord and Saviour in the most holy sacrament about a quarter of an hour before her death ; and thus her beautiful, purified, sanctified soul departed in the most blessed and intimate union with Christ. A beautiful death, dear Perthes ; pray especially for her beloved daughter, that God may give her grace." "You believe as I do," he says in another letter, "in the necessity of illumination and grace from above, and that is everything." And somewhat later he writes, —"I am sure that you cannot rest on your present stand-point. The striving and hastening after the truth, which characterize you, and the need you feel of some firm footing, cannot continue ; for, dear Perthes, we are not now searching for the truth—we have it, we are not looking for the true faith, it is already ours. This only is our task and our duty, to show our faith by a real Christian walk, in all we do or leave undone. All our striving ought to have for its object progress in this path, and since we cannot advance without the grace of God, we pray to Him daily for this grace. Forget me not, dear Perthes."

Philip Otto Runge, the artist, a man animated by a deeply religious spirit, had for Perthes singular attractions. His morality was stern, his mind vigorous and racy, and full of humor. While to strangers he was, without intending it, a sealed book, he opened his whole heart without reserve to his friends, and displayed all the riches of his lively, witty, and original mind. A great religious idea would often unconsciously insinuate itself into the merest play of his pencil ; for everywhere in nature he saw traces of the mysteries of creation, redemption, and sanctification, and he regarded it as the great duty imposed upon him, to seek out those traces, and to represent them to others through his art. His apprehension of them was not always attainable by others, and thus many things in his compositions are unintelligible. When asked for an explanation, he used laughingly to say, "If I could have said it in words, I need not have painted it."

Runge could declare with the most solemn sincerity, that the artist who had gone so far as to make art a religion, should have a millstone hung about his neck, and be thrown into the deepest part of the sea.

"You have fully understood me," writes Runge in 1802, "and I think of myself just as you think of me, and not at all more highly." Even in his old age Perthes retained the impression he received on his visit to the Dresden Gallery with Runge in 1802. "Yesterday afternoon," he wrote to his wife at the time, "I saw Raphael's Holy Family, alone and unaccompanied, and I trust that this heaven will never pass away from my soul. To see creations such as these, from the hands of our fellow-creatures, is ennobling; pictures of this kind are the direct effluence and evidence of the Divine within us, and words are poor in comparison."

The friendships that Perthes had now formed were chiefly with men whose grand object, though pursued in diverse ways, was the cultivation of the inner life. His natural disposition, and the necessities of a calling that demanded the greatest activity, preserved the equipoise of his own mind in the midst of the various influences to which he was subjected. Two men of great eminence who shared his intimacy, Count Adam Moltke, and Schönborn, were perpetually exerting themselves to give intensity to Perthes' easily excited interest in the affairs of the world.

Count Moltke, a fine-looking man, with a noble fore-

5

head and a sparkling eye, had lived from the beginning
of the present century at Nutschau, a small estate in
Holland, which he had received as a trifling indemnity
for the lost family fiefs in Zealand.   His restless energy
and glowing imagination had been deeply stirred by
the French revolution, and he remained, for many
years, one of its most ardent, but, at the same time,
purest well-wishers.   After having travelled over a
great part of Europe, and experienced not a few of
life's bitterest sorrows, he returned to Nutschau, and
there, far from the cares of State, though deeply interested in political movements, he strove with a forced
resignation to live patiently through that iron time.
He required but little sleep, and sought to still the inward sorrow by the earnest and persevering study of
history ; particularly the history of the rise of the
Italian Republics of the middle ages, with which he
was minutely acquainted.   He had often undertaken
to present his own thoughts in poetry, or to give the
history of remarkable political events of former times,
but he was unable to express his ideas with that clearness and precision which were necessary to fit them for
appearing before the public.   He was thus excluded
from writing as well as from acting history ; but as, in
the days of his fervid youth, he had exercised a powerful influence on all with whom he came in contact, so
in his mature age he infused energy into every circle
that he frequented.   " He had attained the perfection
of his nature," said Niebuhr in 1806, of this the friend
of his youth ; " he had tamed the lion, the ever-restless
spirit within him, and he had used the fire of his youth
to animate Greek forms."

Perthes had met Moltke at Kiel in 1799.   " What a

man !" he wrote to his wife ; " what power ! and what
self-control ! I wish, Caroline, that you could see this
' mad Moltke,' as they call him. I esteem him as
highly as any of my acquaintances. His wife, too, is
a charming person." A few months later the two had
become intimate, and mutually attached. "Thank the
Countess for her delightful letter," wrote Perthes to
the Count, in the autumn of 1799. " Caroline and I
may well read with surprise what she wishes, and I
wish I had matters of corresponding weight and interest to write of to her." Moltke came frequently to Hamburgh at that time, as he did in later years ; and then,
all thought of rest for that night was at an end. Between nine and ten in the evening, when Perthes had
left business and had joined his family, he would find
Moltke waiting his arrival. Before many minutes
were over, they were involved in an earnest and im-
passioned conversation, and many a time the rising
sun reminded the disputants that it was time to break
off. When Moltke was in Florence in 1803, a report
reached him that Perthes was about to stop payment.
" Help my friend immediately with all that I have, if
I be yet in time," wrote Moltke to his man of business
in Hamburgh, at the same time sending the necessary
powers with the letter.

The Councillor of Legation, Schönborn, was in almost
every respect the direct opposite of Count Moltke.
Rist has preserved his name from oblivion in a characteristic sketch. From 1802 to 1806, he lived as a
guest in the house of Perthes. This extraordinary
man, whose unpleasing exterior was somewhat relieved
by the expression of resolution and depth in his countenance, would frequently remain in the house for

weeks together, rejoicing in the comfort of his dressing-gown and the disorder of his apartment, or buried in the literary treasures that the warehouse afforded. He was now nearly seventy years of age, and there was no person or thing in the circuit of the busy city that had any claim upon him; and thus in the enjoyment of a long-desired independence, he would submit to no restraints, except those which his own habits and his constitutional sluggishness imposed. About noon he was frequently to be seen standing in the door-way, dressed in a loose overcoat, with his stick under his arm, looking about in all directions, pondering with what friend or in what tavern to bestow himself for the hour, and then, after a while, reëntering the house to shut himself up again in his own room. In the house of Perthes he was regarded as a member of the family, and went and came just as he pleased, at one time enjoying the lively and ever-varying society, at other times passing hours in silent abstraction, or in a kind of dreamy, silent enjoyment with the children, or the visitors. "Silence," says Rist, "was no burden to him, even when fools were talking; but in later years, he would give vent to his displeasure in some one of those strong expressions which he had borrowed from the rude mode of speech not uncommon in Lower Saxony." When, however, Schönborn could be led to converse, and Perthes well understood how to bring him to the point, he became at once the centre of the circle, and the rare treasures of learning, and of general knowledge and experience of life, that lay hidden in his mind, were brought out in surprising turns, and in expressions emphatic and racy, the suggestions of the moment.

X.

Progress in Religion.

HE manifold relations in which Perthes stood to active life, and the distinguished men among whom he moved, could not fail to exercise a great influence upon him, and almost to fashion his mind anew. "I know," he says in a letter to his Schwartzburg uncle, "that you often think of your Fritz; but I am no longer the Fritz of whom you are thinking. You only know 'little Fritz;' you have to begin to learn to know me. Where shall I commence, and where leave off, in order to explain to you who and what I am? You knew me as a child who had something good in him, who was lovable and who was thankful to be loved, warmly returning the love that was given; as a child of quick perceptions and some cleverness, but also of most perilous vivacity, and of almost morbid susceptibility. Many years have since rolled away, and of all that the child cherished in his bosom, what is left?—what is added?—what has the child preserved of the childlike? If I were to endeavor to trace the path I have trodden, who shall certify me that I really and truly know it?"

From his earliest childhood, and amidst anxiety and poverty, Perthes had uniformly and earnestly striven

to bring his soul and his whole course of action into
harmony with the Eternal Will. As he grew in knowledge and in culture, he had always endeavored to attain his objects by spiritual means; and yet where
anxiety regarding his inward condition was stronger
than levity and self-confidence, he was forced to acknowledge that the will in his bosom was far from being the will of God, and that the tendency to oppose
his own will to the will of God, was still the master
tendency. Disturbed as he was by a consciousness of
this kind, the society of so many eminent persons, who
regarded the discovery of man's real position with regard to God, as the first and great business of life,
could not fail to give a religious direction to the further development of his mind. He had long ago given
up, as limited and perverse, his early stand-point, according to which man was to fashion himself to a ra-
tional existence by virtue of an intelligent will.

In 1799 he thus wrote to Caroline,—"N. was with
me yesterday; he thoroughly displeases me; his formal knowingness has dried up his brain and hollowed
out his heart. After all his much-boasted reflection,
he has merely satisfied a sort of tabular ethical system;
but in the (so-called) desire always to do right, he has
no share, he has lost spirit and vitality. He dare not
follow the promptings of his inner genius, for he must
needs reflect perpetually; and yet his reflection has
not been able to preserve him from a commonplace
style of mind, which was not natural to him."

Perthes had long regarded Feeling—the immediate
consciousness of the soul—as the only power that could
lead man through life with cheerful and courageous
views of God and the world. He had renounced the

hope kindled by Schiller, of seeing feeling purified and perfected by means of Art. "If," he writes to Count Moltke, " we could indeed so elevate and ennoble the Physical as to harmonize with the Spiritual, humanity would be perfected. But we are soon aroused from the delusive dream of such a hope, in a world where sorrow, want, and death, meet us at every turn."

Perthes had next, as we have seen, been brought under the influence of Jacobi, and listened to the voice of God speaking to and in Feeling; still there was disunion and discord in his mind. "Man is a twofold being," he writes to Jacobi, " the one mocks the other, and the latter in its turn despises the former. This is the state of every man who is not in harmony with himself." Latterly, in his intercourse with the circles of Holstein and Münster, Perthes had met with men who, in a manner that had not previously come under his observation, seemed to be in harmony with themselves. That it was the supremacy of Love that enabled them to preserve peace, joy, and inward harmony in the midst of the tumults of life, he was fully persuaded. "It is only one overpowering idea that can uphold a man, and make him forget sorrow and death, earth and heaven." He writes to Moltke, "All such forgetfulness is greatness ; but the greatness may be good and may be evil, according to the nature of the idea that has called it forth. We have seen men of angelic and of devilish minds, equally ready, firmly and fearlessly to confront the terrible. What is great is not always good, but what is good must always be great. Now, there is a something which is in God, and which He has kindled in us, that is always both good and great, and this is Love. Love can make even weakness great, and what

the highest greatness is without love we may see in the
devil.   Your stumbling-block, dear Moltke, is not the
want of Christian love in your heart, but the preponderance of Roman greatness in your head.   But why
should we think of greatness at all ?   It is but a poetic
dream for us now ; if we have made love our paramount idea, greatness will follow of itself."

" Only the man who is possessed by love," he writes
to Jacobi, "can solve the riddle of our being and of
our freedom.   Love is the visible form of freedom.
He who loves, and even he who does not love, can see
if he will that love is free as nothing in the world besides.   I am in bondage if I do not love, and I cannot
love if I am in bondage ; and he who loves knows, as
none else does know, that individual freedom and the
will of God are one and the same thing."

But in order to abide in love, as the permanent condition of the soul, Perthes felt the necessity of a human and personal medium; and no one stood nearer to
him than Caroline.   It was then through her, and her
alone, that he expected the essence of life, as he called
love, to be incorporated with his own being.   " That
I have something within me which lives and will live
eternally," he writes to his wife, " I feel with a degree
of certainty that is not to be expressed in words ; I
also feel that this eternal individuality can only find
its satisfaction in the love of God.   To him who
strives after this love, and who, in the midst of stumbling and falling, praying and thanksgiving, is in earnest, God will be gracious even if he worship a bit of
wood instead of the Crucified One.   For as the invisible is hidden behind the curtain of the outward world
of sense, every medium by which I venture to draw

near to the glory of God, is a sanctified means of escape from sin, and is not in itself idolatry. Evil rages within me and is powerful ; my prayers are but signals of distress, and do not help ; for I am not penetrated, as you are, by the holiness of the Supreme Being, by His light and glory ; but I am penetrated by the love of thee, my angel, and through the love of thee I shall rise higher, and draw nearer to Him, in whom I find I cannot participate without some medium." And in another letter, " Do not lose heart, my pious Caroline, and make me, by your instrumentality, as pious as you are yourself."

But Perthes now began to be conscious that the love of God is not a spontaneous development of that which he had spoken of as the love of man, but that it differs from this not only in degree, but in its object, and therefore in its essence. Although deeply conscious that his affection for Caroline was ever deepening and strengthening, he yet drew back timidly from God. He regarded his past life, and the present condition of his soul, as a partition-wall between himself and God, which even love had no power to throw down, and he could not but confess a desire to be without God, and a struggling against God as the predominant tendency of his heart. It seemed to him impossible that the alienation of man from God should be overcome by any human means.

" My internal anxiety," he writes to Caroline, " calls for some one who in my stead gives satisfaction ; and undefined feelings come across me, which seek after *a God who as man has felt the agony of man. I have leaned upon many a staff that has given way, and have seen many a star fall from heaven.* What is true, is

5*

given to us in science, but not The Truth. Human science can measure many things, but can take the *full* measure of none, and the great mysteries of life must for ever elude her grasp ;—have they, therefore, no existence, or are they, therefore, less certain or less vital ?"

He thus writes to Moltke, " That which is unusual, which does not repeat itself, but happens once only, we call unnatural, and if we have not ourselves been conscious of it, we call it untrue, and characterize the belief of it as superstitious ; and yet Nature itself, which is assuredly the most unnatural of all miracles, delights us, and we find *it* quite natural : and thus we, whose whole history forms but a moment of this great nature-miracle, pretend to decide upon the naturalness or unnaturalness of a particular event! No, the great mysteries of the world are not to be sought and found without us—the intuition of them is born in us ; our soul is intuitively christian, and that which exists in us as intuition, the mercy of God has revealed externally as actual, objective existence." Jacobi had maintained against Perthes, " I shall become a Christian, according to Claudius, if I can be certified of the perpetuity of the Pentecostal miracle ; but no historical belief can make up to me for the cessation of the Pentecostal miracle." To which Perthes had replied, " An individual man cannot be justified in disbelieving the perpetuity of the Pentecostal miracle simply because he has not himself experienced it." To Perthes the facts of Revelation were indubitable historical events ; " but," he says to Moltke, " the time when these facts are to become vital to me, and the measure of their vitality, depend on the grace of God."

An inward wrestling and striving now took place to realize in himself, as he expressed it, " the uncreated Son of the Father as in reality his God." The (to him) undeniable fact of the incarnation he desired for himself as the idea that should take entire possession of his being.

Holy Scripture now appeared to his soul in all its majesty, and Claudius was at his side, to aid, to animate, and to confirm, at one time in person, at another by his writings. Their personal intercourse had been continually growing more intimate and confidential, and Claudius' tract, " A Father's Simple Instructions about the Christian Religion," which appeared in 1803, in the seventh part of his collected works, had made a deep impression upon his son-in-law ; and he reached a certainty of conviction, and a repose of mind which he had never before known.

" You ask how it fares with me, dear Moltke ; I *know* what truth is, I *know* what man is, and what he shall be ; I *know* how to estimate the world ; I *know* that the richer a man becomes in himself, the poorer he is in the world. I thank God for this knowledge, and especially for the consciousness that I am a poor sinner, in myself helpless and comfortless. Those men are now a problem to me who seek satisfaction in themselves, and, if unsuccessful, try to find it in one fruit after another, in the hope of being satisfied at last, and are never awakened to the alarming consciousness that the sap is not there."

And in a letter to Caroline, " My youth," he says, " was healthy, and an unquenchable longing and an intense striving upwards possessed me, much more truly than now. But, on the other hand, I have now a clear insight into life ; I am conscious of power and vigor, of an assurance and actuality such as I never possessed before ; I know God, and this state of peaceful certainty is not indeed so pleasing, not so flattering I might say, as my former condition ; but perhaps, on this account, it is a surer evidence of the truth. If passions were less violent, and if we could escape from the troubles of the world, it might be better for us ; but it is presumption to require what God has not been pleased to ordain for us. An undisturbed internal assurance and perfect peace were possible to only one in this world, and that one was the God-man. Dear Caroline, when we have learned to be content, and to accommodate ourselves to times, circumstances, and outward relations, with tolerable calmness and composure, we thus advance more steadily than by all our striving and self-tormenting, towards the goal to which through the grace of God we are drawing nearer, but to which we can never attain on earth."

To Jacobi he says, " I thank you from my heart, my fatherly friend, for the kind tone of the letter in which you declare the difference between our inmost convictions ; I have only now to add, that by the words, ' Philosphical unbelief satisfies me as little as poetical superstition,' I certainly did not intend to indicate that which you, with an implication of censure, designate romantic. I believe that I take surer ground than others in my opposition to a wild, wanton, vain, and ever-wandering belief, because I take my stand on the revealed word of God, as the only word, the only law which is *above* us ; all besides is only *in* us, and whether it be a simple and compact, or a romantic and parti-colored philosophy, it wanders in a perpetual maze, till at last it finds that all is vanity."

"I am, like you, disturbed by Jean Paul's fluctuations whenever I read his works ; he indeed longs for truth and a settled faith, and yet he cannot abstain from representing the God-man as a mere creature of human imagination. But poems about the Messiah, whether written by Klopstock or by others, will never do." "It is far better," he says, after having read that amusing book, "Scenes from the World of Spirits," "to become a fool by philosophizing, than to graft our own imaginations upon the great truths of religion." "Winckelmann's letters are interesting, yet, like Winckelmann himself, they have afforded me but little pleasure," he says in another letter to Jacobi, "and Goethe honored him too much, when he called him a true-born Pagan, at the same time making him the representative of his own views of man and the world. But, on the other hand, I find in these letters the Goethean paganism more beautifully and forcibly developed than it is anywhere else, as the opposite pole of Christianity ; on this side, we have strength and unity through love, on that, self-renunciation. *Christianity is a free-gift-investiture—and in Christianity all is given by the grace of God*, and received by love ; while in heathenism all is nature, and every product is a self. The religious feelings of men appear as if begotten by nature alone ; every creature as if self-created is to stand only upon its own feet, man is to enjoy all things, and to resist or endure all unavoidable evil with a strength whose origin is in himself. Heathenism and Christianity exhaust everything ; and that which lies

between, call it by what name you please, is a mere
inconsistent fragment, mere patchwork and vanity,
resulting either in despondency or in pride.   That
Goethe should hate the pole that is opposed to him is
only natural ; and why should not the Christian also
choose rather the opposition of an avowed enemy, than
that of ten hobbling praters?   Let any man honestly
strive to become a Goethean Pagan, and truly to stand
on his own feet, it will give him work enough, and
will bring many proselytes to Christianity.   I must
confess to having received a good lecture from the
Countess Louisa for my praise of this Goethean work ;
but by appealing to Reinhold she herself proves that
I am right and that she is wrong."

Jacobi left Holstein in the spring of 1805, to settle
at Munich.   "God be with you," wrote Perthes.   "How
can I ever sufficiently thank you, who have been the
means of giving a fixed direction to my development?
It is through you that I have attained to the conviction, the religious certainty which I now enjoy, and
shall enjoy throughout eternity ; that conviction which,
though seeking, you had not, and I am compelled to
say, have not yourself yet found.   None but you persuaded me of the nothingness of self ; but that which
you have not been able to grasp, to seize, or retain
with your head or with your heart, was to be sought
in a direction different from that pursued by you.
Farewell ! God bless you and all your doings."

It was through anxiety and labor and after many
wanderings, that Perthes had won his way to the saving truths of Christianity, but he had won them as
part and parcel of his life.   It is true, indeed, that
neither at this nor at any later period did they reign

alone, nor did they hold habitual ascendancy in his
heart : the natural man too often asserted itself, in
sorrow and in joy, in the midst of the cares and activ-
ities of life ; but the truths he had gained were never
lost sight of ; and when, after many years, he lay on
his death-bed, they filled his whole soul, and had power
to take its sting from death.

XI.

Events of the Years 1805 and 1806.

HEN the imperial deputies met at Ratisbon in 1803, to parcel out the territories of the weaker powers, and divide them among the stronger, Hamburgh had had the good fortune to preserve its independence as an imperial city. Nevertheless, it was plain to all who looked at the power and violence of Napoleon on the one side, and the weakness of the empire on the other, that if there was any future for Hamburgh, it was to be found in its own political wisdom and strength ; and of political vitality, there was little then within the walls of the free imperial city. That indifference to all political affairs which pervaded the whole of Germany, had extended its benumbing influence to the council of the city, and to the once proud and sturdy burgesses. The citizens, careless and indifferent, had left the government of the city entirely to the council, formerly the object of so much jealousy and suspicion. The burgher colleges, whose duty it was to watch the proceedings of the senate, were deserted by all, save those whose duties compelled them to be there, for the citizens had ceased to avail themselves of this field of political activity. The civic government of the preceding century was, indeed, one

(112)

of great convenience, alike for governors and for the governed; but it was not of a kind to develop strength, confidence, or ability, either in the council or in the citizens, so as to enable them to act with independence in difficult and important circumstances; and the men whose eyes were open to European events, found it morally impossible to arouse to any lively political sympathies the torpid life which pervaded the imperial city.

The enthusiasm with which Perthes had, as a very young man, received the intelligence of the French Revolution, was converted to hostility when France declared war against the German empire. It was not in Prussia or in Austria, but in the smaller principalities, that the true national, imperial feeling was to be found, and Perthes, who had been born in one of the petty states, had grown up with a true Kaiser-loving heart. Hamburgh, it is true, relying on its foreign relations for its importance, did not afford the materials for a thoroughly German national enthusiasm, but the opposite feeling, at least, had no influence. The earlier leaning in that town towards the French Republic had been weakened by the growing connexion with England.

Although in the distinguished men with whom Perthes associated, the religious was the predominating element, he still took a lively interest in political events. He was not then committed to any definite political tendencies or doctrines; he remained entirely free, also, from a limited narrow-minded zeal for a particular part of the fatherland to the exclusion of all the rest. His political feelings, thoroughly German, were opposed to the cosmopolitanism which places

greater value on political doctrines than on national-
ities, as well as to that local or territorial patriotism
which cannot see the wood on account of the trees.

He saw Hamburgh only through Germany. He
had an ardent desire to gain insight into its great
political relations; and the circumstances of life in
which he was placed were of a kind to afford facilities
for the realization of this desire. Among his acquaintances were many men who had come into personal contact with European affairs. Schönborn had
opened his eyes to the internal condition of England
and its relation to the Continent, while the Danish
poet, Baggesen, who had moved for many years in the
most distinguished circles of Paris, and whose political
views were at once intelligent and profound, threw
much light on the confused politics of France.

Reinhard, the French consul in Hamburgh, was a
member of the circle in which Perthes moved, and by
frequent intercourse with him, Perthes imbibed enlarged views of political affairs.

Perthes longed for a political connection with men
who would not only give breadth to his political views,
but also share his political feelings, and by a community of hope and fear, waiting and striving, might impart warmth, clearness, and strength to his own convictions. It was easier to find political fellowship then
than in later times; for there were at that period but
two parties—a small one that saw political salvation
only in opposition to Napoleon—another and much
larger one which hoped to achieve it through his instrumentality. All who took up a hostile position towards France, and sought, at whatever cost, to preserve
the internal, and to retrieve the external independence

of the German nation, felt themselves politically one.
All the striving after this or that definite form of the
German political future, which subsequently gave rise
to numerous parties, was then merged in the general
desire to free Germany from the supremacy of Napoleon. Of all the men of German sentiment with whom
Perthes had intercourse, Johannes von Müller and Niebuhr exercised the most powerful influence over him.

Johannes von Müller had left Vienna for Berlin in
1804, as Prussian historiographer, and, in closest concert with Gentz, had put forth all his power to remove
the difficulties which opposed a simultaneous and united
rising of Austria and Prussia. Müller was at the same
time incessantly seeking to arouse the national feeling
of the Germans, and to excite their wrath against the
oppressor, by a series of spirited and powerful appeals.
It was one of these that led Perthes to write his first
letter to Müller, dated August, 1805. He turns to him
with warm and generous confidence, and concludes
with these words, "old and young, rich and poor,
strong and weak, all who love their fatherland, freedom,
law, and order, must now act together."—"Thanks, noble-minded man, for your letter," was Müller's reply ;
" it is refreshing to find such genuine feeling, and without having seen you, I have become your friend. The
time is come when all who are like-minded must em-
brace each other as brethren, and work together for
the national deliverance. This is now the only charm
that life has for me. There is an unspoken language,
an invisible brotherhood among the like-minded, by
which they recognize each other. This brotherhood
to which you, my friend, belong, is the salt of the earth,
and they who are united in it are brethren and friends,

far more really than many who have passed a lifetime together."

From this first exchange of letters sprung a correspondence, which, as a key to the opinions and tendencies of the years 1806, 1807, and 1808, is of great importance. A portion of it was afterwards printed. At Easter, 1806, Perthes went to see Müller at Berlin, and in the autumn of the same year, Müller came to Hamburgh to return the visit. Of this personal intercourse Perthes thus wrote to Müller :—"The esteem that is felt for a lofty spirit, for a great name, for a frank correspondent, is a very different thing from the personal attachment and affection felt towards the man ; and, now that I have seen you, believe that I entertain this personal feeling towards you. I for my part make no claim on you, except that you should recognize that a strong and warm heart beats in my bosom, and that I have some knowledge of the necessities of the times."

The friendship with Niebuhr, who had been long known in the circles frequented by Perthes, was of slower growth, but of greater depth. He had spent his sixteenth summer in Hamburgh with Büsch, in 1792, and had at that time made the acquaintance of Klopstock, Reimarus, and Sieveking ; and while studying at Kiel, from 1794 to 1796, had formed a close intimacy with the Stolbergs, Reinhold, Jacobi, and especially with Moltke. In the spring of 1798, he again passed some time at Hamburgh before his departure for England, and it was then that an acquaintance began with Perthes, who was about the same age with himself; this acquaintance soon ripened into a friendship that continued to increase in warmth, in depth, and in power, up to the period of

Niebuhr's death, in spite of one interruption that seemed to threaten its continuance.   While Perthes was
captivated by the noble character and the cultivated
intellect of the great man, whom he seldom named except as " My dear Niebuhr," Niebuhr, on his side, was
no less attracted by the "glorious power," as he was
wont to call it, and the manly aptitude for the business
of life that characterized his unlearned friend.   It was
to the uncultivated man of business that he sent his first
volume of his Roman History, in 1811, with these
words : " I am anxious to have your unreserved opinion
of my book.   I do not ask for a learned judgment ; but
if the great features of the work please you, I shall be
delighted.   On some points I fancy we are not agreed ;
but on others, I believe we are quite at one."

To Perthes' answer, Niebuhr replied some months
later.—" Your opinion of the first volume of my book
has been of inexpressible value to me.   Do not take it
as an overstrained compliment, when I say that Goethe's praise and your feeling about it suffice me, even
if hostile voices should be raised, as we may naturally
expect, at Göttingen."

Niebuhr's intellectual superiority, together with a
certain sharpness of manner, which not unfrequently
broke through the natural gentleness of his disposition,
caused even men who were themselves eminent in the
literary world, to feel a degree of restraint in his
society ; and this made the perfect freedom, and the
unconstrained ease of Perthes' intercourse with him, a
matter of surprise.   This perfect ease, which Perthes
never lost, even in his intercourse with the most distinguished men, was owing partly to his position, partly to his consciousness of desiring to pass for no more

than he was. His calling and his whole career precluded any expectation of learning or of statesmanship, and yet nevertheless he must have been conscious that he stood for something in society. In a letter to Müller he thus expresses himself on this subject: "I know who and what I am, and am always anxious to reveal rather than to conceal my ignorance, in order to prevent waste of time. Don't, however, give me too much credit for modesty, for though I am aware that I *know* nothing, I am also aware that I can *do* much."

The terrible years 1805 and 1806 were years of animated correspondence between Perthes and those last-named friends. The greater part of this has indeed been lost, and the letters written after the battle of Jena, show how heavily French espionage pressed upon epistolary intercourse; but enough remains to show the political principles and the hopes by which Perthes was animated. It was with bitter vexation and deep sorrow that he witnessed the stolid apathy which, since the peace of Luneville and the Diet of Ratisbon, had fallen upon men who were regarded as the pride of Germany, and from which neither the unutterable sufferings of their native land, nor the audacity of her tormentors, could arouse them. He was indignant at the appearance of Goethe's Eugenie at this season.

"Our hearts must and should be filled with shame, burning shame, at the dismemberment of our fatherland," he writes to Jacobi in 1804; "but what are our noblest about? Instead of keeping alive their shame, and striving to gather strength, and wrath, and courage to resist the oppressor, they take refuge from their feelings in works of art!"

A new hope of deliverance dawned, when, in the summer of 1805, the report of an alliance between England, Russia, and Austria, was propagated. But Perthes saw with dismay the political leaders of Germany array themselves on the side of Napoleon against England, and strive to work upon the minds of the people through the leading journals. "Our journalists," he writes, "take up the cause of the tyrant and the 'Grande Nation,' either from meanness, stupidity, fear, or for *gold.* I need name only Woltmann, Archenholz, Voss, and Buchholz;" and in a letter to Müller of the 25th of August, he gives vent to his stifled feelings. "Your letter distressed me, by the deep emotions that it stirred in my soul. If such men grow faint-hearted—what then? I am not so hopeless; my courage, indeed, has grown of late. True, I am young, and not well read in history. From the past you form conclusions as to the present, and so despond! But has not every people, till consolidated into unity, been ready to receive a leader, a deliverer, a saviour? This readiness is, I think, very observable among us. There is a universal panting, longing, grasping after some *point d'appui.* Much is already cleared away; I instance only this,— the end of the paper times. Twenty years more of such coquetting with literature, such playing at intellectual development, such hawking of literary luxury, and we, too, should have passed through a *siècle littéraire* still more insipid than that of our neighbors. Are not our youth now persuaded that the country does not exist to serve knowledge, but knowledge to serve the country? How many are now convinced that strength and virtue grow out of moral principles, and are the fruit of no other soil! Do not men regard

the love and care for their own houses as more important
than a widely-diffused love capable of no intensity ?
Are they not now disposed to honor a hearty and even
passionate love of country, rather than a cold cosmopolitanism ?   And even as regards religion, although
through the long-standing abuse of theological tenets,
infidelity and indifference have struck their roots deep
in our soil, still the want of religion is increasingly
felt.   I grant you that a miracle must be wrought before the country or the people can again have a faith,
but then many, many lament this, and would pray
without ceasing to revive the religion of the nation."
" Ought we not to feel ourselves great," he added,
" just because we are born in such evil times ? "

" I can give you but a very imperfect idea of the
impression made by your letter," wrote Müller in reply.
" You regard what we see around us as a preparation
for something better.   I wish it may be so ; but what
element of good has ever been found in a monstrous
empire full of the spirit of rapine, mockery, and vain-
glory ?   The cold hand of death is its sceptre, and
humanity and learning perish at its touch.   And yet
that is a sublime saying of yours,—' Must we not therefore feel ourselves great since we are born in such evil
times ?'   You are a man of a rare soul, and I love you."

It was but a few weeks after this letter was written,
that Austria, she scarcely knew how, found herself
allied with Russia and drawn into the war against
Napoleon ; and on the 20th of October, the Austrian
General surrendered his whole noble army to the
French.

After the disastrous day of Ulm, Perthes regarded
all lost if Prussia persevered in her indecision, and much

gained if Prussia, uniting her forces with those of Russia, should resist Napoleon. "What are we yet to pass through?" he writes to Müller; "what sufferings, what indignities, what degradation, are still in store for Germany, and for the world? And yet what opportunities Providence offers to men who have energy! Prussia can and must be the deliverer of Austria, even at her own peril. . . . Go to the King of Prussia and tell him what he, as a German, can do for the freedom of Germany. Prussia does not stand in this prominent position to no purpose. Let her raise the standard of Germany and all will flock to it, and will gladly give up their cherished local independence and look the danger in the face, as a united nation, rather than become the slaves of a people that has suffered itself to be made the instrument, by means of which one man may reduce the whole earth to the same degraded level. Should the historian have eyes only behind him? Never was a man so high in his position as you are. You can have no motive for holding back when duty says, Go forward. The anticipation of failure, and consequently, of doing something ridiculous, is nothing. Does one man know what is in another, and what there is to be aroused? It is not I who call you,—Germany calls you; if you knew our city it would inspire you, and be assured all Germany feels as we do. This hour is pregnant with greatness; but it is passing away and will never return." Soon after this he writes,—"I am not dispirited and will not be; free German hearts will never be wanting, and God will take care of the rest."

The battle of Austerlitz was fought on the 2d of December, 1806, and on the 26th of the same month the

6

luckless peace of Presburg was concluded. Bavaria
and Würtemburg had assumed the kingly title. It
soon became certain that Prussia, through its commis-
sioner Haugwitz, had pledged herself deeply to Napoleon. In January 1806, Russian troops invaded the
Hanoverian dominions, and closed the Elbe against
England.

In July was formed the Confederation of the Rhine,
and thus the very form of the Germanic Empire was
destroyed. " Events have now outgrown all political
calculation," writes Müller. " All customary expedients fail, and there is no appearance of help from any
quarter. God must remove one man, or raise up a
greater, or bring about something yet quite unforeseen.
I no longer feel either indignation or fear. The scene
is become too solemn. The Ancient of Days is sitting
in judgment ; the books are opened, and the nations
and their rulers are weighed in the balance. What
will be the end ? A new order of things is in preparation very different from what is imagined by those who
are the blind instruments of its establishment. That
which now is, is not abiding ; that which was, will
hardly be restored : and the difference will not consist
in the mere substitution of Corsican rule, for that of
some weakling of Italy, Germany, or Sclavonia."

By the annihilation of the empire, Hamburgh had
become, from a free imperial city, a sovereign state.
Perthes deslared that there were but few Germans
who would shed a tear over the downfall of the empire ;
the majority, and that composed of sensible men too,
rejoiced to be relieved of their disbursements to Vienna
and Ratisbon, and believed that Hamburgh would be
Hamburgh still.

Immediately after the battle of Jena, and while Murat, Bernadotte, and Soult were advancing upon Lubeck in pursuit of Blucher, Mortier had occupied Hanover, and on the 19th of November, 1806, marched into Hamburgh. " How you will have mourned over the fate of these districts," writes Perthes to Jacobi, "and over that of our city !   Why should I describe to you the awful fate of Lubeck ?"

Alarming accounts were now received from all parts. " Prussia will be annihilated," writes Niebuhr from Dantzig, "and that without leaving a single deed of heroism, daring, or patriotism on record."

" Our blunders are of such a kind," wrote Scharnhorst on the 11th of July, 1807, " that nothing short of a miracle can save us."

From Berlin, Müller wrote despairingly : " I call to mind the great seer of antiquity, who knew, by the signs of the times, that God was about to create a new thing upon earth.   Jeremiah had wept himself blind, but yet he saw that Asia, and also his own people, were given into the hand of the Babylonians, and he counselled submission as the only prudent course, although even when doing so he forgot neither his country nor the desire of his heart.   In like manner, in these days, in this wonderful year, are the nations taken as in the net of the fowler ; from Cadiz to Dantzig, from Ragusa to Hamburgh, and soon, everywhere, it will be *L'Empire Français*, whether for seventy years as in Babylon, or for seven hundred as it was in the case of Roman sway, who can tell ?

Immediately after the French occupation of Hamburgh, all intercourse with England was prohibited on pain of death ; all English property declared forfeited, and all goods purchased from English dealers, although paid for, were demanded from the owners, and trade was allowed to be carried on only under the restraint of a system of certificates. "All that was is annihilated," writes Perthes to Jacobi. "There is no longer any trade as it existed formerly." Owing to the general insolvency which followed the issue of the French regulations, Perthes's personal losses involved all that ten years of toil and anxiety had realized. In Mecklenburg alone, he reckoned his losses at 20,000 marks. Still his courage and hopefulness did not desert him.

XII.

Losses and Trials.

N those sad years of political oppression, the importance of the family life, in all its calm independence, revealed itself to many. It is true, indeed, that the family must always share largely in the joys and sorrows of the State; but as in seasons of the greatest national prosperity the family has still sorrows of its own, so in a season of national torpor and calamity it may yet be gathering strength and spirit, and generating courage and vigor for outward activity.

The darker the political horizon appeared, the more gratefully did Perthes acknowledge the value of the gift that had been bestowed on him in Caroline. His four children were strong and healthy, and on the 23d of January, 1806, another son, John, was added to the number, and on the 15th of September, 1807, a daughter, Dorothea. The domestic sorrows which grow only out of the family were now, for the first time, experienced by Perthes in the death of this infant, three months later.

"Dear mother," wrote Caroline immediately after, "God has taken my angel gently and calmly to Himself. I thank our heavenly Father that He has heard my prayer, and taken my darling child without pain. She looks so peaceful that we must be so too."

Perthes had, as we have seen, sustained heavy losses in 1806 ; but the excitement of the times, which left so many houses in anxious suspense, or led them to cautious limitations, afforded to his bold and active spirit, opportunities of extending his business. He could say with truth, "No one in Hamburgh has anything to do, but my business is more active than ever, and I look for a still further extension." His library was now regarded as the finest in North Germany. In 1807, Hüllmann had written from Frankfort on the Oder,—"You have the most extensive collection in Germany ;" and Niebuhr had sportively called him "the king of the booksellers from the Ems to the Baltic."

The spirit that animated him, and the domestic happiness which he enjoyed during those years of external and political suffering, are exhibited in a letter to Jacobi of October, 1807 : "My mind becomes every year stronger and more free, and thus I am able to meet all events with courage and cheerfulness. I am, indeed, an ever-erring mortal, but unhappy I am not ; I am, indeed, singularly happy, for one who has so restless a career allotted him. A multiplicity of interests for this world and the next ;—much love, much passion, many friends, many children, much labor, much business, much to please, much to displease me, much anxiety, and little gold ; moreover, a dozen Spaniards in the house, and for the last nine days three gens-d'armes to boot, who drive me almost to distraction."

"You ask how I am and how I get on," he says in

another letter of the same period; " I will tell you, as far as it is safe to write such things in these times. I am, then, rich in correspondence. Countess Louisa Stolberg writes to me diligently, and never without having something of importance to communicate. I receive regularly every fortnight a letter from Johannes Müller; and Niebuhr, frank as ever, has frequently something remarkable to communicate. Here we have Maréchal Brune for our governor, and find ourselves tolerably contented, as he on his part may well find himself. The *ci-devant* printer has already paid his compliments to the craft by visiting me. Old Zimmermann of Brunswick is still living at Altona; he is one of the most sensible men I ever knew, and deeply interesting to me. I love without trusting him. We occasionally see at our own house, or at Madame Sieveking's, Walmoden, and the young Countesses of Lippe-Bückeburg, two very interesting girls, and the youngest positively enchanting. Besides these, there are many eminent men coming and going, who keep life from stagnating, and put some spirit into us."

Bernadotte made a deep impression on Perthes; " He is in person, as in many peculiarities of manner and of habit," he writes, " very like Jacobi. He is uncommonly fond of philosophizing. Villers is often in Hamburgh, and likes it : he is very dear to me still ; but it is singular that while he will no longer recognize, and cannot understand the French, he looks the Frenchman all over."

To shut himself up within the happy and attractive circle of his family and his business was not, however, in Perthes's nature; his inclination and the influence of the times led him rather to take a lively interest in those events which commanded the attention of the whole civilized world. He now began, like many others, to consider Napoleon to be, and likely for some time to continue, an historical necessity.

"Napoleon, the ruler of the earth, is a unity, and is secure and firm in himself as no other is, because, more than any other, he seeks only himself: and like no other, he is a devil incarnate, because, like no other, he has made himself his god. 'He does not will, he is willed,' said Baggesen to me, with striking emphasis."

To this demon-like man Perthes believed the world given over by God—not to continue subject to his sway, but that through suffering, even of the most dreadful kind, the paralyzed energy of goodness might be resuscitated. All that was," he says, " is ruined; what new edifice will rise on the ruins I know not; but the most fearful result of all would be the restoration of the old enfeebled time with its shattered forms. By a practical path of suffering and distress, God is leading us to a new order of things ; the game cannot be played backwards, therefore onward must be the word. Let that which cannot stand, fall. Nothing can escape the crisis, and it is some consolation to see that events are greater than the circumstances that called them forth. He who would now turn the wheel backwards cares only for repose, comfort, and private happiness, and to these indeed the times are not favorable ; but to such things Providence cannot accommodate itself. We should rather consider ourselves to be the growth of the epoch ; and who could expect to compress the beginning and end of such a revolution into one lifetime ?"

Despairing of external help, and expecting nothing

from the existing governments of Germany, Perthes centred all his hopes for the German people in their unity.

"Whatever may be impending over Germany," he says in another letter written after the surrender of Ulm, "our first object must be, where special provincial interests still exist, to arouse the national German feeling and to keep it alive, bringing it more and more into the consciousness of the people."

The spirit to stake all in a worthy cause was inborn in Perthes ; once aroused to action, he knew no retreat. "And I thank God," he writes, "that I have a wife who shares my feelings, and who, if it come to the worst, will not shake my courage. He who has in him any element of intellect or power, of greatness or passion, cannot but turn his attention to what is now passing around him, in order, so far as he can, to influence the direction of events. He who has only an inward life in these times, has no life at all."

Perthes, however, was too practical and clear-sighted to involve himself enthusiastically in any undefined and ill-digested plans. He well knew that every deed of violence, and every individual act of resistance to the existing state of things, was mere madness, and was also criminal, notwithstanding the dissolution of political order. He knew, moreover, that it was impossible for any private individual to have any direct influence on the attitude of statesmen and governments, or on the political supremacy of armies and of gold. Still he regarded it as the right and the duty of every German to arouse and to strengthen, by every possible means, the hatred and the exasperation of the Germans against the oppressor. Yet even here it

6*

was impossible to his practical nature to stand, as it were, beating the air in his attempts to act upon others ; he must work from a centre, and that centre he found in his calling as a German book-seller. He regarded it as his first duty to provide for the printing and the general diffusion of the most weighty and stirring writings of men animated by true German feeling.

Sensible at the same time that isolated individuals could exert but little influence on the great mass of the people, Perthes regarded it as the duty of all who felt themselves capable in any way of arousing the spirit of the nation, to unite in some definite association.

Perthes had thought of Johannes Müller as the intellectual centre of a league of German patriots. Müller was thoroughly well informed as to the condition of Western Germany, and the secrets of Austrian and Prussian policy. He had the most extensive acquaintance with German statesmen, and with literary men of all shades of opinion : he was highly and universally respected ; and both as a man and as an author, he had shown that he was ready and resolved to act for Germany and against Napoleon when the time should come. There was no man who seemed so well suited as he to be the soul of the desired Germanic Union. But the results of the war of 1806 forced him into a different path. When Berlin was occupied by the French, Müller did not leave the city : Napoleon invited him to an interview, and he wrote in high spirits to Böttiger at Dresden, that he had talked for an hour and a half with the conqueror about all the great events of history, and all the great subjects of politics. Müller now delivered his celebrated oration on the glory of Frederick at the Academy of Sciences, went in the autumn of 1807 to Paris, and early in 1808 to Cassel as Secretary of State, and Minister to the King of Westphalia. "I shall no more forget Germany," he said, "than Daniel—who was never thought the worse of for having taken office at Babylon—forgot Jerusalem in that foreign court."

But this change placed Perthes in a very painful position. He had loved Müller, and a man whom he had onced loved, it was almost impossible for him to cease to reverence. "Give utterance to no harsh judgment against Müller," he says in a letter to Max Jacobi ; "you have never seen him, and one must have seen him to recognize his greatness, to know his goodness, and to have the key to all his weaknesses and failings." Perthes had regarded Müller as a man who meant truly and well to his fellow-countrymen, and he still believed that he had associated himself with the foreigner in order to work for Germany in the only way which was left open to him.

"As to the manner in which you will shape your future," he writes, "I have no fears. As surely as I know what right is, so surely am I persuaded that you will do nothing that can lead you to forget what you owe to yourself. I believe that you will take office *dans l'Empire Français;*" and he adds, sorrowfully, "where else could you take office?" Again he writes, "Your criticism of the Rhenish Confederation is fine, sensible, and spirited. It is the business of the scholar and spokesman of the country to take the nation under his protection in whatever form it is compelled to assume, and to give utterance to its rights and its nationality." When Müller's appointment to Cassel

was decided, Perthes writes thus :—" God give you
strength, and arm your heart and mind with firmness.
That is my special prayer for you. I would not be
the last to congratulate you on the important work
now before you. What we expect of you is, that you
stand forward as the peacemaker, the comforter, and
the arouser of your country. Such a destiny as yours
is rare. I know your piety too well not to be assured
that you recognize in all this the hand of the highest
wisdom." And when Müller had undertaken the
Ministry of Public Instruction in Westphalia, Perthes
writes—" Happen what may, you can and will be a
laborer in the Lord's vineyard. You are called to
preside over those establishments and institutions
which are the special organs of the German mind and
people. May God strengthen and preserve you for
the work ; I have never distrusted you, and I have
pledged myself for your fidelity and your truth."

But notwithstanding this personal confidence, Perthes could not mistake the nature of the impression
that the conduct of Müller had made on the people at
large. "To me," he says to Jacobi in 1807, " to me
he is what he ever was, but he is certainly wrong, and
is now lost to Germany." And shortly after the battle of Jena, he writes to Müller himself, "Your letter
was a great source of consolation to my friendship ; I
believe with you that God has delivered the earth
into the hands of Napoleon the Great, and that he is
therefore invincible. We must have patience with
the noble-minded of the nation. Your influence with
the people is no more. This should not have been."

Perthes himself was also greatly distressed, not by
any doubt as to the uprightness of Müller, but as to

the correctness of the principles on which he had acted.
Müller, dazzled by the unparalleled successes of Napoleon, had given up all for lost, and regarded him as
the instrument chosen by God for establishing a new
order of things in the world. He believed it impossible to form any idea of what lay hidden behind the
curtain of futurity, and he viewed it as mere folly to
oppose himself to this future. He felt that duty called
him to consider how the intellectual energy lavished
on the past might best be employed in the service of
the present. The earth was given to Napoleon ; that
was fate, the finger of God was there. " It is God
who sets up governments ; who, then, is at liberty to
set himself against them ? " he exclaimed. " Men must
rather accommodate themselves to them, and seek to
make the best of things as a whole ; not allowing
themselves to degenerate, but awaiting patiently the
further development of events over which they have
no control."

In March, 1807, Perthes had communicated to Müller in a letter, all the anxieties and torturing doubts
that agitated him on his account. " A whole friend or
no friend," he writes, " is my motto, and I therefore
feel compelled to tell you all that I see and hear about
you. These things have given me many a sad week,
and I have occasionally been quite overcome. They
declaim about hypocrisy, falsehood, treachery to the
cause of freedom and fatherland : and it is not only
the rabble yielding to the popular feeling of the day
who do so ; but men, who still love and honor you,
weep and lament over the grave of Johannes Müller."
" Believe me," he writes again, " amid all the troubles
of these uncertain and disturbed times, your present

relation to your country is to me one of the most pain-ful. The nation, believe me, is in perplexity and with-out leaders, and knows not if in future it is to hear your voice or not. I torture you—but I must have ceased to respect myself and to love you, before I could refrain from speaking. God be with you and with us all! The judgment of God will soon be given : I feel that I have still spirit and strength to be German, whatever turn things may take, and I trust that the road we are to follow will shortly be clear to us all."

XIII.

The French in Hamburgh.

ORTIER had taken possession of Hamburgh on the 19th of November, 1806, but it had remained a free sovereign city, although occupied by the troops of Napoleon. French, Italian, Dutch, Spanish, or German legions, under imperial generals, succeeded each other. Externally every vestige of independence was gone ; but the internal administration of the city, as in the towns of the Rhenish Confederation, remained in the hands of the former magistracy, subject, however, to the French code. The revenues of Hamburgh being derived wholly from its commerce, its territory being of no importance, were entirely annihilated by the continental system. More than three hundred Hamburgh vessels were now lying unrigged in the harbor, and the Assurance Companies sustained, in the course of the three years following the occupation, a loss of twenty millions of francs. While trade returns were thus incalculably diminished, the 130,000 persons who made up the population of the city and its territory, were given up to the unprecedented extortions of the French Government, and the shameless exactions of the French officials, among whom Bourrienne attained an infamous distinction.

Many wealthy men left Hamburgh, that they might not lose what they had, and those that remained went about in sullen sadness, tortured by anxiety and want.

Vague reports of great preparations in Austria, and of associations of resolute men in Prussia and Westphalia, reached Hamburgh, and kept Perthes in a state of continual excitement.

At Easter, 1809, he went as usual to Leipzig. "I rejoice that I have come here," he writes to his wife; "you would hardly imagine the general unanimity, Germany was never before so united."

On the 25th of April the news of the series of victories in which Napoleon, on the 18th, 19th, and 20th of that month, had defeated Austria, arrived at Leipzig. "Yesterday evening we got the tidings of the lost battles," he writes, "and with the greatest precipitation the people illuminated."

The battle of Wagram, fought on the 6th of July, and the peace of Vienna, signed on the 14th of October, 1809, confirmed the dominion of Napoleon.

There appeared but one means of developing German nationality, without running the risk of exposing it to the prying eye and crushing power of the enemy. Science, so long as it was only science, Napoleon neither feared nor regarded; and for centuries independent scientific life had been one of the essential characteristics of Germany as a nation. This consciousness of scientific independence and unity was not indeed sufficient of itself to uphold the national spirit, but it might help to do so; it might be the veil beneath which the national hatred of the tyrant might gather strength; it might be the undisputed medium of communication between patriotic men in all parts of Ger-

many, who, thus prepared, might, when the hour for
action came, be found armed with other weapons than
those of science.

In the months following the fresh conquest of Austria, Perthes had sought consolation for the present,
in the history of the past. It appeared to him that the
period of the Reformation, on account of the great
changes that it was the means of effecting—and that
of the Italian Republics, on account of the political
divisions of a spirited people—presented analogies
with the circumstances of Germany since the outbreak
of the Revolutionary war. "For the inner life of the
sixteenth century," he writes, " I committed myself to
Benvenuto Cellini, and then Robertson's ' Charles V '
was my guide. I have learned that a steadfast purpose
and will, that calm reflection and the attainment of
great objects, are possible even in times of the most
terrible outward disturbance and revolution. Sis-
mondi's ' Italian Republics' delights and cheers me at
present. For centuries Italy was without a centre of
influence and without political cohesion ; but in the
little circle of those republics there was power ; there
were men of understanding ; and Italy flourished anew
and produced men of deathless spirit, the memory of
whose glorious deeds is imperishable. And should we
despair ? No ! although our previous hopes have died
away, I am still full of confidence ; I love my fatherland—have often prayed, often trembled, and would
have fought for it, had there been hope of achieving
aught. ' I am,' to use Adam Müller's expression, ' afflicted with the disease of patriotic madness,' and,
therefore, not in despair ; but feel strongly convinced
that although the old form of the Germanic Empire is

fallen to pieces, the future history of Germany is nevertheless, not destined to be the history of its downfall,
if every one does what he can in his own station : I,
for my part, shall try what I can do in mine :" individuals can, and will do much.

It was only through his own calling that Perthes
hoped, individually, to be able to accomplish anything.
"The German newspapers," writes Perthes to Jacobi,
"are, with few exceptions, in bad hands. Some are
deliberately bad in their objects ; others, having been
established solely for gain, seek only to please the pal-
ates of their customers with the most recent novelty.
Such a state of things is at all times lamentable ; in
our own times, it is alarming. It is important, since
things will tell only when uttered at the proper moment, that Germans should know where they can at
once bring before the public anything which demands
and deserves publicity. A journal, appearing at short
intervals, which shall uphold the vital union of all
German-souled men, is a pressing want. I have this
object at heart, and my position is favorable ; the first
men of Germany are known to me either personally or
by connection, and I am sure of their coöperation,
while my shop offers facilities for the publication such
as are nowhere else to be met with. But perhaps you
will say, What avails your having it at heart ?—dare
you do it ? I answer with Jean Paul, ' The silence of
fear is not to be excused by the plea of coercion.'
There are many things that may be said, even under
the government of Napoleon, if only we learn *how* to
say them, and take care not to overlook the good we
have because of our hatred of the foreign medium
through which it comes to us. Indeed, there is much

to be learned from the French, and it is the native tendency of the German mind, to recognize and assimilate the good from whatever source it may come. The new journal shall be called the 'The National Museum.' It must not be prohibited, and must, therefore, be characterized, especially at the outset, by caution and circumspection; it must, at the same time, be read, and its object and tendency must, therefore, be evident to Germans. I shall go quietly forward in the firm conviction of reaching the goal, and, probably, without interruption."

Towards the end of November, 1809, Perthes began to send the prospectus of his "National Museum" to all parts of Germany, wherever men were to be found of whose patriotism and intelligence he had knowledge. In the private letters that accompanied it, many of which have been preserved, we find him presenting the enterprise to each in the point of view that seemed most likely to attract him. To one he urges the promotion of German science; to another the effect which such a periodical would exercise over the public mind; to a third the encouragement which the journal might afford to patriotic men who had been abandoned and oppressed by their respective governments, to reserve themselves for better times. To some he set himself to prove that a scientific association was the only possible bond of union in Germany, and that German Science should hold the first place in the 'National Museum;' while to a few, such as Jean Paul, he opened his whole heart.

He trusted that an alliance, unsuspected by their oppressors, might thus be formed among those who were called to be the intellectual leaders of Germany, every member of which, according to his ability and his position, might, without attracting observation, act as a centre of influence. When the right time came, the scientific alliance was to be transformed into a political one possessing the strength and union necessary for vigorous action. In order to extend this union as widely as possible among the people, the literature of Germany was to be presented in all its aspects. Rumohr was applied to for information relating to the works of ancient German art; Wilken for old national manners and customs, and for the truth or falsehood of the diversities of North and South Germany; Feuerbach was to write on German law and jurisprudence; Augustus William Schlegel on German, and Frederick Schlegel specially on Austrian literature; Sailer, at Landshut, on the religious life of German catholicism; Marheineke, of Heidelberg, on the importance of the German pulpit; Schleiermacher on the philosophical, and Plank on the historical theology of Germany. Schelling was reminded, by a reference to his oration on the Plastic Arts, how well he could adapt himself to the public mind, and Gentz was recommended not to keep silence, because he could not utter all he might wish. Innumerable answers poured in from the cities and from the most remote corners of Germany; and there were few that did not express enthusiasm for the undertaking, and gratitude to the man who had planned it.

Goethe, however, declined participation:—" I must, though reluctantly, decline to take part in so well-meant an institution," was his reply. " I have every reason for concentrating myself in order to meet, in any measure, my obligations; moreover, the character

of our times is such that I prefer to let it pass before
I speak either of it or to it. Forgive me, then, for de-
clining to share in the undertaking, and let me hear
frequently how it succeeds." Count F. L. Stolberg,
on the other hand, writes, " I rejoice to associate myself with you and yours, dear Perthes, and I need not
say how highly I love and honor the boldness of your
Address. Those parts of the announcement intended
for the public cannot but appear somewhat constrained,
but that is of no consequence : the unpractised reader
will not observe it, the practised will at once detect
the reason, and the patriotic will be deeply indebted
to you." The numerous replies which he received
from his widely scattered correspondents breathed
similar warmth and cordiality.

The " Museum" made its appearance in the spring of
1810. It contained contributions from Jean Paul,
Count F. L. Stolberg, Claudius, and Fouqué, with posthumous papers of Klopstock ; essays by Heeren, Sar-
torius, Hüllmann, and Frederick Schlegel, by Görres
and Arndt, Scheffner and Tischbein, and many other
eminent men.

Although Perthes was forced to confess that but little of what he would fain utter could be said in the
pages of the " Museum," its reception far exceeded his
expectations ; but the labor involved in editing it,
combined with the great political excitement to which
he was exposed, and the continual efforts for the extension of his business, almost exceeded the limits of
human strength.

Joys and sorrows in the family, too, added to his
anxiety. On the 2d of March, 1809, his son Clement
was born. " We rejoice in the birth of a boy," he

writes ; " through the youth now growing up we may
exert an influence on the future, which we cannot exercise upon the present." His daughter Eleonora came
into the world on the 4th of April, 1810 ; while his
second son, Johannes, a lively and promising boy, had
been removed by death on the 18th of December, 1809.
" His heart was overflowing with love and merriment,"
wrote Caroline, " so that he was our joy and delight.
We yearn after him, and cannot yet fully believe that
we must continue our prilgrimage without him ; we
have but a melancholy pleasure in the blessings that
God has left us."

After many years of labor, Perthes snatched a short
interval of leisure to revisit the beloved Schwartzburg
home. The two younger children were committed to
the care of their Wandsbeck grandparents, and in the
beginning of July, 1810, Perthes and Caroline set out
with the other four, by Brunswick and Naumburg to
Thuringia.

From Schwartzburg Caroline wrote to her mother,
—" Would that I could describe to you the grandeur,
the beauty, the loveliness of this country ; but words
can convey no idea of it. I thank God that we are
capable of feeling more than we can express : speech
is but a poor thing when we are in earnest. The hills
and valleys of Thuringia impress one just in the right
way. I love them, and shall remember them with
affection while I live. It is too much, I sometimes
think, and one has no power to repress the excitement
which this scenery stirs in the heart. In our flat
country, we cannot attain to such a height of joy in
the Lord of this glorious Nature, or to such intense
gratitude towards Him, as are possible in the midst of

scenes like these ; and I consider that it is a great gift
that the good God has permitted me to see all this, while
yet on earth. The valley of Schwartzburg surpasses
all the rest. There is an inconceivable wealth of mingled grandeur and beauty about it which rivets the
spectator to the spot, and compels him to stretch out
his arms in adoration of the Creator and Sustainer of
all this wondrous work. On the one side are vast
masses of rock, piled one upon another ; on the other,
hills of surpassing loveliness, adorned with meadows,
houses, men, and cattle ; in the midst of all, the
Schwarza runs clear and sparkling, rushing and roar-
ing bravely, far below in the hollow. Our reception
was very agreeable ; we had left the carriage, and
were walking towards Schwartzburg ; suddenly, from
behind the rock, the lieutenant-colonel made his appearance, and caught Perthes in his arms. My beloved
Perthes, thus disturbed in the tranquil current of his
thoughts, forgot nature like the rest of us in the pleasure of the reunion. This lieutenant-colonel is a fine,
vigorous, frank, and very dear old man, and I already
like him much. When we had walked a few paces
farther, we came to a broad, flat rock on which a
breakfast, brought in his own game-bag, was spread.
He was quite overjoyed, and never weary of recount-
ing the pleasure he had experienced long ago, in walking tours and fowling expeditions with Perthes. A
little further on we met the other uncle with his troop
of children ; we packed the little folk into the carriage, and walked slowly after it. The very depths
of my soul are stirred when I perceive the great and
general happiness which the return of my Perthes has
diffused ; my dear Perthes himself is like a child with

delight, and I thank God that He has let us live to see this time. They live the past over again, and are all twenty years younger."

After a stay of a few weeks, Perthes proceeded with his wife and children to Gotha, the home of Justus Perthes, his paternal uncle.

" Here, too," wrote Caroline, " we were received with inexpressible kindness, but our dear Thuringian hills are now only seen in the distance. The children long for the freedom of the woods, and to speak the truth, so do I ; and it is with difficulty that I can conceal my feelings. We had quite forgotten the French in our beloved woods ; but here we are daily reminded of them. For months cannon of enormous calibre had been passing through the town from Dantzig and Magdeburg on their way to Paris. Ah! here we have the world and artificial life with all their annoyances, continually suggested to us ; there is no place like hills and woods for forgetting ourselves and all our wants and infirmities."

They returned to Hamburgh by way of Cassel and Göttingen. "A journey such as we have enjoyed," writes Perthes to Schwartzburg, " is a real picture of life ; but that part of a journey which remains after the travelling, is, properly speaking, the journey. This still remains with us."

Ere long, rumors were afloat of new and violent changes contemplated by Napoleon in the German governments. The French Ambassador, Reinhard, had been in Hamburgh ever since the autumn of 1809, in order to settle the final destiny of the city. " He holds continual conferences," writes Perthes, " with deputies and others, as to the maintenance and perpetuation of

the Hanse-towns. The Emperor, after hearing the real
state of matters, is to determine the future of the cities."
More than a year after this letter was written, and
just before Christmas, 1810, the decision of the French
Senate was announced at Hamburgh. The Hanse-
towns with the whole north-west of Germany were
henceforward to be considered as forming part of the
French Empire. "Hamburgh, built by Charles the
Great," so ran the decree, "was no longer to be deprived of the happiness to which it had a hereditary
right, of acknowledging the supremacy of his greater
successor."

Hamburgh had now become a French city, and its
burghers subjects of Napoleon. At the same time,
Perthes, finding the impossibility of carrying out his
original object, in the form which it had up to this time
assumed, gave up the " National Museum."

" My sole aim in the establishment of this journal,"
he says, at the close of the last part, " was to unite the
well-disposed and wisest of our countrymen, and enable them to contribute, by teaching and counsel, in a
variety of forms, to the maintenance of that which is
of peculiar . worth in Germans, namely, energy, truth,
literature, and religion. Now that, as an inhabitant
of Hamburgh, I am, by the recent incorporation, made
a subject of the French Emperor, the obligations
thereby imposed are incompatible with this object, and
the ' German Museum ' can no longer be carried on by
me." " Your ' Museum ' is indeed silenced," wrote
Nicolovius, " but its spirit still lives, and will yet re-
dound to the glory of you and your endeavors."

He who now, after the lapse of years, gives a glance
at the contents of the " German Museum," cannot fail

7

to be impressed with a sense of German ability and honesty ; but only those who can recall the iron pressure of that period, resting on every form of life, will comprehend how the discontinuance of this Journal should, at a time of such unexampled tribulation, have been on all sides regarded as a national calamity.

The problem which Perthes, as a French subject and a man of business, had now to solve, was the maintenance of his business unimpaired under the new censorship. A widely organized system of espionage had been established, with its head-quarters at Paris, which imposed restrictions not only on the books which issued from the German press, but on their circulation through the empire. The bookselling trade suffered severely from the new laws. Perthes, however, perceiving the irregularities of their operation, arising from the ignorance of the officials, succeeded, by skilfully taking advantage of these, not only in preserving his varied and wide-spread trade connexions, but even in extending and giving increased efficiency to his business.

In the meanwhile, his intellectual life was kept alive by an active correspondence with eminent men of the most opposite tendencies and opinions ; such as Rumohr and Klinkowström, Stolberg and Droste, Steffens and Fouqué, Niebuhr and Nicolovius, Görres and Villers, Jacobi and Reinhold ; while the sittings of the jury, of which Perthes was a member, and a friendly intercourse with De Serre and Eichhorn, created other interests of a local kind.

" There will be no peace," wrote Görres, " till the whole generation contemporary with the revolution, is extinct to the very last man." But although Perthes could see no signs of better days, his firm conviction

that the present cloud would pass away, and that in
the meanwhile the best must be made of things as they
are, gave a tone of freshness and cheerfulness to his
conversation and to his letters, which attracted the
friendly sympathies of many persons of eminence far
and near who admired the spirit that he displayed.

"Your letter," wrote Fouqué,* "has baptized me
with fire and water—with the tear-water of the deepest
melancholy, but at the same time with the fire of a sure
and invincible faith and courage. If all the good men
of our times could regard the phenomena of the present with the same calmness, the same depth of feeling
and of penetration as yourself, then we should have
nothing to complain of as regards all that is highest
and most worthy of preservation among us."

"Niebuhr will tell you," wrote Nicolovius, "how
greatly we admire your manly spirit and your Christian serpent-and-dove demeanor. Do not doubt us,
but believe that, to the best of our ability, we keep up
our spirits, and will continue to be worthy of your
sympathy."

The great intellectual movements which were now
visible, and the opposing attitudes which political
parties now began to assume in Prussia, and especially
in Berlin, were not unobserved by patriotic Germans
of other countries. Perthes did not clearly see whether
this mutual clashing and fermenting of political opinion would be productive of good or evil, and in the
summer of 1811, was desirous to see and judge of the
state of Berlin from personal observation ; but he was
prevented from accomplishing his purpose. "I regret

* Author of Undine.

exceedingly that you are not able to come," wrote
Niebuhr ; " I had so ardently desired to see you ; you
could have passed a couple of days with us, and seen
none but your friends ; you are, perhaps, hardly aware
of the genuine goodness still to be found in those who
maintain either of the two principles which exist here
side by side—a goodness as pure and genuine as you
could wish.   I hate talkers and empty blusterers as
much as you can, but I would gladly have introduced
you to the salt of our wilderness, and I, as well as
Nicolovius, wish to talk heart to heart with you for a
couple of days.   Dear Perthes, if it is not quite decided, ask yourself again, whether you could not con-
trive to come to us.   I promise you that you shall not
repent it.   Your principles, indeed, are not exactly
those generally adopted here, but I have so long been
faithful to them that they have become a second nature
to me."

In July, 1812, Perthes accomplished his long proposed visit to Berlin, and passed some weeks there,
during the passage of the French armies on their way
to the East.   He made himself acquainted with the
views and objects of the ardent patriots who composed
the two parties ; and all that he saw tended to
strengthen him in his belief that the hour of deliverance for Germany was not far distant.

" The mental sprightliness of Perthes," wrote Niebuhr to the wife of the physician Hensler, " is very refreshing ; he left us on Friday ; we passed many cheerful hours together.   The facility with which he adapts
himself to every changing phase of the period, literary
and political, without ever compromising his independence, keeps, and will continue to keep him youthful, and

is greatly to be envied." And Nicolovius, in a letter of
the 12th of August, says, "Your visit has strengthened
me, my dear Perthes. You understand how to take
these evil times, so as not to be overwhelmed by them;
may God grant you strength for further struggles and
future victory."

Perthes had now seen with his own eyes, how heavily
and how fearfully the French yoke pressed upon Prussia. In Hamburgh it was no less galling. Trade and
shipping were annihilated. The once proud and flourishing city now presented the appearance of complete
decay. Harsh regulations were enforced with heart-
less brutality. Ground down by the exactions of greedy
officials of every rank, and harassed by arbitrary per-
secution, the inhabitants of Hamburgh had not even
the consolation of feeling themselves free from annoyance in their own houses; and when, towards the end
of the summer of 1812, the Gazette announced victory
after victory of the *Grand Armée* in Russia, all hope
of deliverance, or even of alleviation, seemed to be at
an end, and no man dared to attach any credit to the
faint rumors of misfortune and defeat which were subsequently whispered.

In gloomy and desperate dejection the citizens were
preparing to celebrate the Christmas festival, when, on
the 24th December, to the surprise of all, the publication
of the 29th bulletin confirmed beyond any possibility of
doubt, the tidings of the total annihilation of the French
host. A miracle had been wrought, and a star of hope
had appeared, which rekindled life and spirit in every
oppressed heart. Such a Christmas Eve was kept in
Hamburgh as had not been known for many a long
year.

XIV

Patriotism.

ERTHES had long been connected, in a variety of ways, with Ludwig von Hess, a remarkable and talented Swede, of noble birth, who had in early life filled the post of privy councillor in his own country. He had settled in Hamburgh in the year 1780, and his passionate attachment to his new home, his strict integrity, and the acuteness of his understanding, had secured for him universal respect. He was singularly fertile in expedients, and had a peculiar aptitude for stating complicated questions clearly and intelligibly.

Von Hess had always placed confidence in Perthes, and enjoyed his society; but it was Napoleon's Russian expedition that, by the excitement it gave rise to in both of these men, was the means of drawing them more closely together. They sought consolation and relief in the unreserved exchange of their opinions, hopes, and fears. Hess, a man of the past, and a foreigner by birth, had connected all his hopes and fears with Hamburgh, the home of his choice, but he possessed no German national feeling; Perthes, on the other hand, though attached to the city, and grateful for all that it had given him—education, friends, calling, wife and children, nevertheless did not hesitate to say—"If the freedom of Germany be not achieved, nothing in Hamburgh is of any consequence to me,—can interest me for a moment." But neither their political differences, nor their dissimilarity of view on more important points, opposed the slightest obstacle to their mutual and entire confidence. In speaking of this friendship in after years, Perthes used to say— "We were of different ages; our career in life, and our inward history, had been quite dissimilar; and our opinions were constitutionally opposed, and yet we became friends in the fullest and most genuine sense of the word."

The winter of 1812 drew nigh, and the burning of Moscow opened the prospect of a near and pregnant future. Perthes communicated his hopes to several men in whom he had confidence; first of all to Von Hess, and his old friend Hülsenbeck, then to Doctor Ferdinand Benecke, whose heart beat with the most self-sacrificing devotion to Germany, and to the Count Joseph Westphalen, who had been led at this time to Hamburgh, in the hope of finding there some field for his chivalrous spirit. The circle soon grew larger, and the opinions and plans of those who composed it more definite.

In January, 1813, the French garrison numbered scarcely more than 3,000 men. To oppose this handful of troops, there was the numerous and vigorous population of the great maritime and commercial city, accustomed to hard labor and perilous enterprise, aware of their physical superiority, and not wanting in daring. The words of the burghers waxed daily louder and bolder; even men who had belonged to the old magistracy of the city, gave their fellow-citizens to understand that when the hour came they might reckon on their support. All depended on giving form and cohesion to the powerful but undisciplined mass, and towards the end of January, Von Hess spoke to his friends about the establishment of a burgher force. The consent of the French authorities, tortured as they now were with anxiety, did not seem improbable, as they might regard the measure as being to some extent a security for themselves in the event of any wild outburst of popular fury. While Rist proposed the subject to the French generals, Perthes and his old friend Speckter formed a close intimacy with Mettlerkamp the plumber, a man of spirit and decision, and known and greatly beloved by the people. At their instigation, Mettlerkamp spoke to a number of the strongest and most determined among the people, chiefly of the laboring class, addressing each individually, and urging them to speak to others. Perthes, in like manner, availed himself of the extensive acquaintance that he had formed, partly through his vocation, and partly through his previous position as a member of the committee for billeting the troops. Lists were soon made out of men who engaged to be ready whenever the expulsion of the French was thought practicable.

While the excitement and the spirit of the burghers were at their height, General Lauriston appeared in Hamburgh, early in February, and withdrew the greater part of the garrison to Magdeburg, where a large body of troops was to be concentrated. The French generals who remained, Cara St. Cyr and Ivendorf, now fully recognized the dangers of their situation, and manifested their uneasiness by the vacillation and uncertainty of their movements.

Perthes had unbounded confidence in the strength and spirit of the burghers, and he was unwilling to owe the deliverance of the city to any third party ; still he could not overlook the fact that military discipline and experienced leaders were wanting, and that there was nothing to rely upon except the strong arms and the courage of the untrained citizens. He was, indeed, fully convinced, that an outbreak of popular fury which should annihilate the French garrison might, at any time, be counted on ; but then who was to conduct the defence of the city, and to lead the raw burghers against the French troops under French generals, who, in such a case, were certain to endeavor to regain the town ? Moreover, Perthes desired that the rising of Hamburgh should be regarded not as a local but as a German movement.

The solemn deliverance of the downtrodden city from its oppressors, seemed to him to possess importance as a signal for the rising of the whole north-west of Germany ; for, in the event of this, it seemed likely that the princes, who at that time were the victims alternately of hope and fear, would be driven to a decisive step. In order to give this character to the efforts of an isolated city, some man of high rank and of recognized position was wanted, to whom the command might be intrusted, and who would be able to provide the citizens with experienced leaders. The Duke of Oldenburg appeared to be the man, and Perthes thought himself at liberty to send him an urgent solicitation without delay.

"These eventful times," he says, "authorize the

7*

burghers to approach the prince with candor and
confidence, and the voice of the individual burgher is
also that of a band of united friends.   It is only through
herself that Germany can attain a real and permanent
independence.   And if, at this moment, even a small
body of troops, led by a brave German prince, having
under him men of irreproachable and recognized name,
both from the ranks of the nobles, and from the burgher
class, were to appear on our territory, the country
would everywhere rise to support him, and by God's
help Germany would, through her own unaided efforts,
be free to the Rhine.   The prince who now devotes
himself to the German cause may rely upon the nation.
The German has always loved his prince, and this affection still survives, and is now anxiously looking for
an object.   You are the universal object of hope and
desire, most serene Duke, for you have rendered your
own States singularly prosperous ; you have appreciated
German manners and German art, and you saved your
honor when with dignity you retreated before violence."

On the 21st of February Perthes, accompanied by
his eldest son Matthias, set out with this document to
the house of Count Adam Moltke at Nütschau. Moltke
took him, the next day, to Eutin, and there, through
the earnest eloquence of the Councillor Runde, the
President von Maltzan was persuaded to undertake its
presentation to the Duke. From Eutin Perthes went
to Lubeck, where he found the burghers animated with
the same spirit as the citizens of Hamburgh.

He returned home on the night of the 24th of
February, and found the whole aspect of affairs
changed.

On the 22d there had been great excitement in the city on account of a false rumor of the approach of the Russians.

"Yesterday morning," wrote Caroline to her father at Wandsbeck, "there were Cossacks at Perleberg, seventy-six miles from this,—ah! that I had a thousand voices to sing BENEDICTUS QUI VENIT! The city is all alive, and assuredly some great step is about to be taken."

On the 24th of February, the day before the return of Perthes, the citizens had risen simultaneously in different parts of the city. The Custom-house guard at the Altona gate was attacked, and the soldiers fired repeatedly on the people. The number of the killed was never ascertained; but the guard-house was taken and demolished, and a long row of palisades thrown down. At the harbor, where the prefectoral guard, which was composed of the sons of the burghers, was to have been embarked, the population of the neighborhood placed themselves in the road, and on the appearance of the Mayor, pelted him back with stones, and, proceeding tumultuously through the city, tore down the French eagles wherever they found them with shouts of triumph, and trod them under foot. The house of a particularly obnoxious French police-officer was levelled with the ground. There was no theft committed; the French only were sought for by the mob."

"There is no longer an eagle to be seen in the city," wrote Caroline to her father; "the tumult in the streets grows louder, God be praised; would that my Perthes were here!"

The French garrison suffered considerably, but kept

the people at bay. No leader stept forth from the
ranks of the madly-excited populace ; and the consequence was, that at nightfall, the mob dispersed,
leaving the French, though dispirited and full of
apprehension, still in possession of the city.

When Perthes, on the morning of the 25th of February, was made acquainted with the state of things,
he immediately sought out Von Hess, to urge upon
him the importance of overcoming a groundless but
passionate dislike of Benecke, and of acting in concert
with him and his friends Prell and Ewald. On Hess
declaring that he was willing to unite, Perthes added
Mettlerkamp to the number, and these six men held
their first meeting at the house of Perthes on the 26th
of February. When they learned from an announcement by the Mayor that the French authorities had
concurred in the propriety of arming five hundred of
the burghers, and had promised to supply them with
arms, the main difficulty was removed ; but the angry
warmth with which Hess in this first interview opposed
the ardent German nationality of Benecke, made him
fear that it was scarcely possible to induce these two
men to work together.

"It was then for the first time," said Perthes, "that
I saw the evil element of hatred show itself in Von
Hess, with a violence hitherto unknown to me ; I saw
that the business could only be carried on through my
mediation, and that a painful and laborious task was
thus imposed on me." Perthes persuaded the Committee to choose Hess as Commander of the burgher-
reserve. "I was certain," said Perthes, "that Benecke,
for the sake of the good cause, would gladly range
himself under him, and I hoped that Von Hess,

sensible of the honor conferred on him, would over-come his hatred."

On the 27th of February the invitation to the burgh-ers to enroll themselves in the reserve companies was issued. Men of respectability and spirit offered them-selves in sufficient numbers, and subjected themselves to the necessary military drill. The five Captains as-sembled at the house of Perthes, to master the manual exercise which they were afterwards to teach the men, in a timber-yard that had been cleared for the purpose. Some days of restless excitement followed.

"In the old town all is quiet now," wrote Caroline to her father, "but elsewhere all is confusion. In Lubeck the movement is in full progress, and there is no longer an eagle to be seen. Cossacks have crossed the Elbe into Hanover, but at present, it must be con-fessed, they serve the purpose only of alarm-drums; for we have letters from Berlin, and they have not yet been seen there; but all, old and young, are preparing; even Fouqué and Steffens are with them."

But the hopes that had been founded on the arming of the burgher-reserve soon disappeared. The rapidity with which this had been entered into, and the success of the movement, had excited the jealousy of the old burgher-guard, who felt themselves thrown into the background, and who busied themselves in disseminat-ing their suspicious and hostile views. At the same time the differences among the leading men of the re-serve force, were found to be past remedy. Hess opposed with frantic violence every national German sentiment, only because it was advanced by Benecke, and rejected with intemperate warmth every plan for the deliverance of Hamburgh that reckoned on the rising of the untrained and undisciplined masses, as an element of success; while Benecke and Perthes, on the contrary, perceived in the efforts of the people, irregular as they might be, a power which, in the present position of affairs, might be turned to good account.

"The rising of the 24th of February," said Perthes, "has shown that our people are ready for great events, and that they are neither bloodthirsty nor ill-natured."

"Above all things, the burgher-reserve must be popular," said Benecke, "and we must therefore avoid everything that would be likely to deprive them of the confidence of the people; their duty must then be confined to the protection of the persons and dwellings of their fellow-citizens, and they must on no account be called on to aid the French military or Custom-house authorities against the people. From this principle there must not be the slightest deviation."

Hess held quite contrary opinions. Perthes saw that the union of the citizens was endangered by these irreconcilable differences among the leaders of the Reserve, and was persuaded that the only means of averting this danger was its immediate dissolution. Supported by Mettlerkamp, he gained the consent of the Committee on the 2d of March, and on the 3d, the reserve companies were dissolved. On the very day that found him deploring the extinction of the hopes of deliverance which he had associated with this movement, his spirits were revived by glad tidings from Berlin."

"Here, in Berlin, all is life and activity," wrote Reimer, "and every one is engaged after his own fashion in raising the cry of Fatherland and King. The excitement and commotion has a charm for all, each lives a new life, and the individual disappears and is lost in his relation to the whole. Confidence has risen to the highest pitch by this visible manifestation of Divine providence, and the hope of a happy result has now become certainty. Such is the state of affairs with us, dear friend, and I hope that all Germany will participate in our joy, and do valiantly, so that a new day may dawn, and peace and happiness may once more take up their abode upon earth."

Now that there was no longer any possibility of openly training a large body of men in military exercises, Hess, Perthes, and Prell, assembled a small number of the most resolute and trustworthy members of the reserve, and went through the drill with them at the houses of different individuals. The object was to have ready for action a few leaders on whom, in case of need, reliance might be placed.

Without entering into farther details we may simply state that the French, aware of the growing spirit of discontent, and of the approach of the Russians, considered their position untenable, and much to the delight of the citizens of the town, evacuated Hamburgh on the 12th March. The city, however, was soon threatened with a siege.

When, on the 16th of March, General Moraud, with about three thousand five hundred men, entered Bergedorf, a village within a few hours' march of Hamburgh, and the excitement of the burghers had risen to the highest pitch, Perthes, Mettlerkamp, and some other friends, determined to make every effort to defend the city against the French, and to avail themselves of the popular fury, which was ready to burst forth on the slightest occasion. But the necessity of having recourse to this extreme measure vanished with the announcement that a detachment of Danish troops had taken up a position between Hamburgh and Bergedorf, and refused to allow Moraud a passage through the Danish territory. The latter found himself obliged, in consequence of this refusal, to transport his troops to the left bank of the Elbe. A body of some fifteen hundred Cossacks about the same time entered Bergedorf, having marched by way of Ludwigslust and Luneburg from Berlin ; and on the evening of the same day, a flying party of thirteen men, under the command of Captain (afterwards Councillor) Bärsch, rode for an hour through the streets of Hamburgh.

" As the detachment approached the city, and came in sight of the Steinthor Guard-house," wrote Benecke to Perthes, " the guard turned out, and our Captain with eight men, myself being one of them, advanced towards the Russians. At a signal from him, the Russian officer commanded a halt, and our Captain delivered the keys of the city to him with these words,—' Here are the keys of the free Hanse-town of Hamburgh—long live Russia and Germany, hurrah !' The shouts taken up by thousands after thousands, rendered the German reply of the Russian officer, who received the keys with dignified bearing and cordial friendliness, inaudible. The rejoicing passes description —' German, Russian, Cossack, Alexander !' were the only intelligible cries, and tears stood in many eyes. Dear Perthes, it was a moment to be had in everlasting remembrance."

During the nights of the 17th and 18th of March, the Russians occupied Bergedorf, over against Hamburgh, and on the morning of the 19th, entered the city. The streets were filled with crowds of happy citizens, anxious to behold with their own eyes those wild horsemen of another world who had hitherto been known to them only in nursery tales.

"My dear papa," wrote Caroline, a few hours before their arrival, "how can I give you any idea of the universal joy of old and young, rich and poor, bad and good? To have seen, and heard, and felt it, is, indeed, a thing to be thankful for. I will not inquire into the causes of the joy, but its expression was unspeakably grand, and it appears to spring from a good and pure source. An advanced guard of thirteen Cossacks entered the city yesterday evening, with long flowing mantles, and adorned with the spoils of the French,— at any rate adorned with parts of the French military dress. Every throat was strained to welcome them, and every heart thanked God in Heaven, and the Russians on earth. Never, dear papa, have I seen such a union of hearts, the feelings of thousands all centred in one point. Ah! could we but so centre ourselves in the best point of all, what a glorious Church we should form! The Cossacks advanced at a gallop, their lances lowered, and waving their caps, and looking wonderfully honest and friendly. The people crowded round them, bringing brandy, cakes, and bread. People who were yesterday quite desponding, are to-day full of hope and courage. If the depths of the soul were more frequently stirred, it could not but be attended with good results."

About noon, the Cossacks entered the city amid

wildest shouts of welcome, and all the sorrows of the
past and the dangers of the future, seemed merged in
the happiness of the present. And yet, scarcely a
German mile off, lay the enemy, who might, in the
course of a few hours, fill the city with blood and
desolation ; but no one thought of the enemy or of his
chagrin. To him who wandered through the streets
in the summer warmth of that spring evening, the city
presented a strange spectacle. The echoes of triumphant rejoicing had died away ; everywhere profound
stillness and the calm of security reigned ; there was
neither guard nor watch, not even a policeman was to
be seen. The moon shone brightly on the houses with
their sleeping inhabitants, and completed the picture
of peace and tranquillity. The joy-wearied city had
committed itself to the sole keeping of the Almighty.

XV

Caroline's Escape from Hamburgh.

HE Russian troops which Tettenborn led into Hamburgh were too few in number to enable the citizens to entertain the hope that the French would leave them undisturbed. Great exertions were now made to strengthen the government of the city, and to make preparations for a successful resistance in the event of the return of the French. Perthes worked with indefatigable energy, fixing the attention of all the leading men on himself as the citizen in whom most reliance could be placed in the hour of need ; and he was regarded by many as the centre of the efforts which were being made.

A few weeks after the evacuation by the French, Davoust, at the head of six thousand men, advanced to recapture the city. Without resistance he had made himself master of Harburg, which was separated from Hamburgh only by the Elbe, and the islands Wilhelmsburg, Ochsenwärder, and Feddel. On the 9th of May, at five in the morning, the drums sounded an alarm through the city ; the enemy had effected a landing on Wilhelmsburg, had driven back the Lauenburg and Hanse battalions by which it was occupied, and had taken possession of the island. Two companies of

Mecklenburg grenadiers and the first battalion of
Hanseatics advanced against the enemy as soon as
their leader, Von Canitz, had placed himself at their
head ; and, charging with spirit and in order, forced
the French to the extreme south corner of the island,
and even drove them back to Harburg. But to the
surprise and alarm of all, Tettenborn, on the 11th,
gave orders to evacuate the island which they had
so bravely regained, and on the 12th, after the two
Hanseatic battalions were to a man almost cut to
pieces, Feddel also was lost. The foe was now close
to Hamburgh, and on the night of the 19th of May,
the bombardment of the city began. "Dear Caroline," wrote Perthes to his wife, who had passed the
night at Wandsbeck, "I implore you from the depths
of my soul to be calm, and place yourself and me
in the hands of God ; trust me, and believe that
whatsoever I do, I shall be able to answer before
God. The bombardment seems more terrible than it
is, and even if it should be repeated, the damage will
not be so great as one would imagine ; there is often
far more danger hidden under common things."

During the night of the 22d, above five hundred
grenades were thrown into the city, but the spirit of
the burghers was still unbroken.

The Burgher-Guard, which at the most mustered
3400 available muskets, and was therefore, to a great
extent, armed only with pikes, had, since the 9th of
May, furnished daily from 800 to 1000 men to secure
Hamburgh Hill, the Stadtdeich, and the Elbdeich,
against the landing of the enemy. Every night a part
of them were obliged to bivouac.

Perthes now felt that his position in the Burgher-

Guard required him to exert all his moral and physical powers of endurance, all his elasticity of spirit, and all his influence over men's minds, in order to stimulate the courage, and to increase the steadfastness of his fellow-citizens, under circumstances which, trying enough in themselves, were rendered still more so by the conduct of the military authorities. Now, he afforded to Von Hess—who in restless excitement passed from the boldest confidence to the most abject despair, and from the most violent activity to a state of absolute torpor—the support of which he stood in need; now he might be seen quieting the citizens, when without any apparent cause, they had been summoned by the alarm bell, and were left to stand forgotten for hours together on the muster-ground; on other occasions, and generally by night, he sought out the burghers on the more distant posts, to many of whom his presence was a source of courage and of confidence.

"From the 9th of May," wrote Caroline, afterwards, " Perthes had not undressed for one-and-twenty nights, and during that period had never lain down in bed. I was in daily anxiety for his life. He was only occasionally, and that half an hour at a time, in the house. The three younger children were at Wandsbeck, with my mother; the four elder were with me, because they could not have been removed without force. I had no man on the premises—all were on guard. People were constantly coming in to eat and drink, for none of our acquaintances kept house in the city. I had laid sacks filled with straw in the large parlor, and there, night and day, lay burghers, who came in by turns to snatch a short repose. At the battle of

Wilhelmsburg we lost our Weber, and many of our friends. Day and night I was on the balcony to see if Perthes, or any of our relations, were carried by among the wounded. At the time when the cannon-ading was loudest, and the greatest terror and anxiety prevailed lest the French should land, Perthes sent to desire that I would instantly send him a certain small box, that lay on his writing-table. As I was running down the stairs with the box in my hand, I felt sure that it was filled with poison. I desired the messenger to wait, and went to my room to decide what I ought to do, for this great matter was thus committed to me; it was a dreadful moment. My horror, lest Perthes should fall alive into the hands of the French overcame me; and it appeared to me that God could not be angry with him for not willing this; and then the injustice of my deciding a matter between him and his God, seemed so great, that with trembling hands and knees, I, in God's name, gave the box to the messenger. Many hours elapsed before I heard anything further. It *was* poison, and poison prepared for the purpose I had feared, but not for Perthes, who assured me before God that he should not have thought it lawful, and was displeased with me for having so misunderstood him."

Tettenborn had entirely forfeited the confidence of the citizens, from the day on which he had given up the islands to the enemy. Many saw that he was not the man to whom the defence of the city, under such circumstances, should have been committed; and many feared that in the loss of Hamburgh he would see little more than the unlucky termination of a boldly planned and luckily commenced Cossack adventure. From the

city authorities no aid was to be expected ; the warlike
preparations which had been made, had been carried
into effect without their coöperation. The appearance
of the French on the Elbe had rendered the problem
that Herr von Hess was to solve, far too difficult for
him. All eyes were looking for foreign aid. As this
was neither to be expected from the great army of the
allies, nor from the corps under Walmoden, posted
between Boitzenburg and Magdeburg, hope was now
fixed upon the Danes. They had in Altona, at the
very gates of Hamburgh, an adequate force, and as
from the end of March they had entertained the hope
of being indemnified by the possession of the Hanse-
towns for the loss of Norway, they declared themselves
willing to undertake the defence ; but it was not till
the evening of the 11th of May, when the danger had
become imminent, that Tettenborn availed himself of
their offer of assistance.

Danish troops now marched in to the relief of the
besieged. But, unfortunately, at the same time Count
Joachim Bernstorff returned from London, whither he
had been sent to treat respecting the entrance of Denmark into the general alliance. He had been sharply
recalled ; for Denmark, having been led to believe that
she could escape heavy losses only by reliance on
Napoleon, felt herself compelled to espouse his cause ;
and thus, on the 19th of May, the Danish troops, in
obedience to orders, abandoned Hamburgh, and assumed
a more than equivocal attitude in Altona.

In this dilemma, Tettenborn placed his hopes upon
Sweden. The Crown-Prince of that country had not
yet indeed arrived at Stralsund, but a Swedish division lay in Mecklenburg, under the command of Gen-

eral Döbbeln, a man of dauntless courage and genuine integrity. On his own responsibility, and at his own risk, he marched into Hamburgh, on the evening of the 21st of May, with three battalions. No sooner, however, had the Crown-Prince arrived at Stralsund, than having learned that the Swedish troops were enclosed on one side by the French, on the other by the Danes, he ordered their immediate retreat, and thus Hamburgh was once more left to itself. General Döbbeln, for his independent and irregular conduct, was condemned to death.

Early in May, the conviction of the desperate posture of affairs had forced itself upon Perthes. "How should, how can this end?" he wrote. "The desire which we have to do our best is all that we have to rely upon. I will not speak of the people who act as though they wished to neutralize all our efforts; but what avails courage when there is not one citizen among us who knows anything of military movements, or even of the use of arms, and when no soldiers are sent to us with whom we might incorporate ourselves? Our neglect of our good old guard for so many years past is fearfully avenged now. If we had but three battalions of burghers, who could go through military drill, and were good marksmen; if we had but a hundred young fellows, who knew how to manage a cannon, we might still be saved; but now our preservation depends upon strangers."

Perthes knew but too well what was to be expected from such quarters. Of all the citizens, he was the only one who was acquainted with the political situation of Russia and Denmark, and only he and Von Hess possessed any information about that of Sweden.

In the meanwhile the turn that European affairs had taken, had cut off every chance of foreign aid; and, on the 26th of May, the day after the retreat of the Swedish force, Tettenborn's intention of leaving the city to its fate became known.

"The hours pass in uncertainty, dear Caroline," wrote Perthes, "and thus bring sorrow and difficulty. This evening will bring certainty, and two days hence you must leave the city."

With the departure of Tettenborn every hope of successful resistance vanished. In these circumstances, Perthes saw it to be his duty to make preparations for escape, in the hope of working for Germany in some other place, and through Germany for Hamburgh.

"I consider the thing as decided," he wrote to Benecke, "and can only place my trust in God. Farewell, beloved friend, I shall hardly be able to see you again. I am going into the wide world with a pregnant wife and seven children, without knowing where at the end of a week I may find bread for them; but God will help us."

Once more, on the 27th of May, a ray of hope shone out, when, at the urgent instance of Tettenborn, Walmoden despatched the brave Prussian battalion to Hamburgh, to take part in the defence of the city. "Our position is twice twenty-four hours older than it was the day before yesterday," wrote Perthes to Benecke,—"does that imply that it is better? I think not. Nevertheless, we must keep up from hour to hour; I am not yet disposed to give up all hope of deliverance."

On the evening of the 28th of May, Perthes sent

8

away his wife and children to Wandsbeck ; there, in
the Danish territory, they were safe from the perils of
war.

In a letter of some weeks' later date, to her friend
Emily Petersen in Sweden, Caroline thus writes concerning these sad days :—"You can form no conception of the anguish and dismay, the hopes and fears, of
our last three weeks in Hamburgh. My heart is full,
and I rejoice to be able to tell you how much more
kindness, truth and fortitude we all evinced, than we
had supposed ourselves capable of. We may speak of
it now, for it has been proved by exposure to want
and danger. How heartily do I thank God for this
experience ! I never knew how strong we are when
all concentrate their energies on one point. Dear
Emily, I never before felt such a universal ' willing' in
one direction. We were all elevated above small
troubles and difficulties, and desired only the one
thing needful, and desired that with all our heart,
each one in his own way, and without any doubt of
obtaining it. The 28th of May, the birth-day of my
Agnes, was the last I spent in Hamburgh ; then I bade
farewell to my dear sitting-room, with a sad, and yet a
thankful heart. I had sent the beds and linen to
Wandsbeck some days before, and the rest of the
things I had either hidden or given away ; the larger
pieces of furniture we were indeed obliged to leave
behind, because Perthes would not discourage the
burghers by making them aware of our preparations
for escape."

Caroline had left the city but a few hours, when, on
the night of the 28th of May the firing recommenced.
The enemy had passed over from Wilhelmsburg to the

isle of Ochsenwärder, and had attacked the Lauenburg battalion posted there with irresistible fury.

"The battle," wrote Perthes to his wife, "which began at two o'clock, still rages on Ochsenwärder, and, as far as we can observe, the smoke becomes more and more distant: we hope the best, for it has already lasted five hours." And again, a little later,—"We have no certain tidings yet; the fight continues. Trust me still, and believe that God is in my heart, and before my eyes. How, in my circumstances, could I act otherwise than I do?—how could I have appeared before you? That I repress, as far as possible, the outburst of sorrow and of feeling, is for your sake; for one hour of feeling does me more injury than ten nights of watching, and I desire to spare myself for you and for the children."

After an arduous struggle, the French remained masters of Ochsenwärder, the island immediately opposite the city, and there were now but few obstacles in the way of their triumphant reëntrance. The Danish commandant at Altona, at the same time signified on the 29th, that, in case of his being compelled to proceed to hostilities, it would not be in his power to give more than two hours' notice. The greatest excitement prevailed during the whole of that sad day. At one time it was announced that Tettenborn had commenced his retreat; then this, again, was contradicted. Perthes was on guard at the Steinthor with Von Hess; they were walking backwards and forwards in earnest conversation a little after ten o'clock at night, when Major von Pfuel drove through the gate and invited Von Hess to accompany him into the city, saying to Perthes that he would not detain him

long. About half an hour later, when Perthes was to
have met and concerted measures with Mettlerkamp,
(commanding the burgher-battalion posted at the Steinthor,) in case of a night attack, he was ordered by an
officer to repair immediately to Herr von Hess at the
Hühnerpost, distant about a mile and a half. On
reaching this station about midnight, he learned that
Tettenborn, with his whole force had retreated from
Hamburgh, and had conveyed his troops in safety to
Lauenburg, leaving the city to its fate. On the morning of the 30th of May, and only a few hours after the
retreat of Tettenborn, the Danes entered Hamburgh,
and saved the citizens from the vengeance of Davoust,
acting as a friendly and mediating power, and formally
putting him in possession of the city.

On hearing this sad news from Hess, Perthes had
set out for Wandsbeck; there, at two o'clock in the
morning, he told his wife that all was lost, and appointed Nütschau, the residence of his friend Moltke,
as her next place of refuge. The French troops were
now within a few hundred paces of Wandsbeck. To
escape a prison, and a rebel's death by the hangman's
hand, Perthes himself drove on through Rahlstadt
under cover of the night.

XVI

Caroline and her Children at Aschau, 1813.

I T was impossible for Caroline to remain long at Wandsbeck. In a letter written somewhat later to her sister Jacobi at Salzburg, she says,—" As soon as Perthes had taken leave of me in his flight, I began to pack, and then, exhausted as I was, set out with my seven children and the nurse, in a light open carriage. It was a very affecting parting ; my mother could not control her feelings, and my father was deeply moved ; the children wept aloud ; I myself felt as if turned to stone, and could only say continually,—' Now, for Heaven's sake !' My sister Augusta went with me, to comfort and to assist me ; truly willing to share my labors and anxieties. In the morning we arrived at Nütschau, where, finding only two beds for ten persons, I was obliged to divide our cloaks and bundles of linen, so that the children might at least have something under their heads."

Yet, on the evening of this day, Caroline contrived to write a few lines to her parents,—" I can only wish you good-night," she said, " for I am so weary in mind and body, that I can neither think nor write. If I had but met Perthes here this evening, safe and sound, as I had hoped, I believe I should have forgotten all my sorrow. I am still cold, and hard as a stone, and shrink from the thought of the thawing. I felt all day as if everybody were dead, and I was left alone on the earth. These have been weeks of life-and-death struggle ; God help every poor man who is in trouble of mind or body in these eventful times !"

On the first of June Perthes arrived. "And now," says Caroline, "we wished to pause and consider where we should go, and what we should do ; but my brother John came and told us that our friends advised us to lose no time, but to go farther away, as our house at Hamburgh had been searched, and Nütschau was too near to Lubeck. Perthes set out at once, and again I began to pack up, and, on the 3d, I left for Lütgenburg, to be *en route* for Augustenburg if need were."

Perthes, accompanied by his eldest son Matthias, had reached Altenhof, near Eckernförde, on the Baltic, the estate of Count Caius Reventlow. " I was so unaffectedly and kindly welcomed by the Count and Countess," he wrote to Caroline, " that it gave me genuine pleasure. The Count will give up Aschau to us ; it is, I am told, a dreary place ; but I think it will do very well."

On Monday, the 7th of June, the husband and wife met again at Eckernförde. " Here we wept freely together," wrote Caroline, " which, in all our trouble, we had never been able to do before."

Thence the whole family removed to Aschau, a summer villa on the Baltic, belonging to Count Reventlow, and made themselves as comfortable as they could. " And there," wrote Caroline, " I for a while

forgot all our troubles for joy that I had got my Perthes, and I can truly say that we were inexpressibly
happy in each other. I thought neither of the past
nor of the future, but thanked God incessantly, and
rejoiced that, out of all these perils, He had brought
my husband to me, safe and sound."

Perthes had lost everything. His shop in Hamburgh was sealed, his other property was sequestrated,
and his dwelling-house, after being plundered of every
movable, was assigned to a French general. Ready
money for the support of his wife and family he had
none.

"Do not suppose that I complain," he wrote to his
Schwartzburg uncle ; "he who has nothing to repent
of has also nothing to complain of. I have acted as in
the presence of God ; I have often risked my *life*, and
why should I be dispirited because I have lost my fortune? God's will be done! I do not yet see how I
am to provide bread for my wife and children in a foreign land. In the meantime, if I receive but two-
thirds of my outstanding claims, I shall be able to fulfil all my engagements ; but in our country no one is
in a position to pay, and I dare not press my demands
in the French dominions, and thus I may not be able
to avoid bringing others into difficulty ; this to me is
a great cause of grief."

Letters from creditors now came in from all parts,
and there is none in which such expressions as the
following may not be found, "Do not think of my
claims at present ; I know as well as you do, that
when you can pay, you will ; you acted as you were in
duty bound to act."

By the help of the business books, which had been

brought away, Perthes managed to get a tolerable insight into his position, he made such arrangements as were possible in the circumstances, and endeavored, at all events, to secure the creditors, through the debtors of the house. By exerting himself to the utmost he accomplished this.

"He works from morning to night," wrote Caroline, "with the exception of an hour after dinner, which we devote to thinking over our position, or rather to sleep ; for we rise at four o'clock, and require some repose during the day. Perthes is perfectly clear and calm, and, I may say, in some respects more cheerful than formerly, and so am I, while he is with me."

Perthes received strength and encouragement from the expressions of respect and consideration that were conveyed to him from all sides : "What I hear of you inspires me with the deepest respect," wrote the Duke of Augustenburg, "and your indomitable spirit fills me with admiration, and I esteem it as an honor and pleasure to have an opportunity of saying this to you. Your belief in a higher world is, indeed, a great matter ; it is this belief alone which is the source of your strength."

No sooner had Perthes set his affairs in order, so far as circumstances permitted, than he was informed by the Danish Government that it would be impossible for them to protect him, in the event of his being demanded by the French ; and that he must leave Aschau. It was true that the truce concluded on the 4th of June, between the Allies and Napoleon, kept the sword in the scabbard for the next few weeks even in North Germany ; but Perthes, who from his solitary retreat could see nothing of the state of external relations, desired to attain to such a knowledge of the position of affairs, as might aid him in forming some plan for himself, after the expiration of the truce. A number of influential men of all kinds were assembled in Mecklenburg, and thither he proposed to repair ; and, at the same time, he hoped to secure resources for the present support of his family, by collecting many outstanding debts due to him in that place.

In a letter of Caroline's, she says, " When we had spent a few weeks together at Aschau, Perthes said to me that matters were not yet settled, and that he must be off, in order to provide for our sustenance. Then it was that the scales fell from my eyes ; I knew, without asking, what Perthes intended to do—what, indeed, he was compelled to do, and once more I became exposed to all my former sorrows. Perhaps it would be weeks, perhaps months, perhaps we should be in the world above, before I saw him again. I feared for myself ; for I believe that with him I can bear all things, but without him I know not what will become of me. Ah ! and my soul is filled with sorrow, anxiety, and care, on his account. You know how earnestly I have desired more rest and leisure for him, and now that he has lost all that he had earned in seventeen toilsome years, he must take up the yoke again, and he will feel it to be heavier than ever. Pray for me that I may not grow faint-hearted."

On Thursday, the 8th of July, under the shade of the gloomy pine trees of Aschau, Perthes took leave of Caroline. " It was the most painful parting of my life," he wrote at the time ; and a journal which begins with this parting, and contains little else except short notices of facts, opens with these words, " I enter again

8*

into the world, into a new and unknown world, full of great possibilities, and also full of perils, but I have spirit and courage to meet them cheerfully. Resignation to the will of God, firm convictions and rich experience, a heart full of love and youthful feeling, truth and rectitude, such are the treasures which my forty years of life have given me;—Lord my God, I thank thee for them ; forgive a poor sinner, and lead me not into temptation."

The two elder children, Agnes and Matthias, accompanied Perthes to Kiel ; here he met Besser, and travelled with him by Lütgenburg to the little town of Heiligenhafen, situated on the shore of the Baltic. The feelings of his heart found expression in many letters written from that place. "About five miles beyond Lütgenburg, the aspect of the country changes entirely," he says in one letter : "all becomes wild and rugged, and the little inn of Bröckel is a very picture of desolation—not even a blade of grass does the barren wilderness produce. The host lay in his coffin ; strangers were listlessly conducting the business : even the poodle at the door was hardly to be called a dog, and though the color was evidently intended for black, it had got no farther than the dark grey of the surrounding scenery. But when we get over a few hills we come again into another world. There are, indeed, neither trees nor hedges, but the land is covered with the most glorious crops of green corn, and between the boundless green of earth, and the boundless light of the sky above, stretches a sea of the deepest blue, blending and harmonizing all. On the shore, looking inland, it becomes darker, till we reach the horizon, where it becomes brighter and more transparent, melting into the light of heaven. At my side stands in spirit my beloved, blessed Otto Runge, to point out to me all the mysteries and wonders that nature hides and reveals."

Perthes was soon left alone in Heiligenhafen, for Besser was obliged to return. "For many weeks past," he wrote to Poel, "one member after another of the old life has been removed from me; farewells follow hard upon each other: now Besser, too, is gone, and as the door closed after him, I felt as if the coffin-lid were shut down upon me, and I had passed from the old to a new world; but love and memory are fresher and more sacred in me than ever. I mean to go next to Rostock, in order to find out what there is for an honest and upright man to do in these momentous times. I have seriously put it to my conscience as in the sight of God, whether or not I should listen to the inward voice which impels me to rush again into the tumult of life, and I find that I must follow it. It is not ambition that urges me, for under any circumstances I shall fall back, if I am spared, upon the business I love. My still youthful heart is animated with an enthusiastic hatred of our oppressors, and to this my religion allows me to give full scope. Still, as I am not a military man, and have no scientific knowledge, and as there is no want of brave and strong men, I shall not enter the army; but if any leader were in want of a man who is accustomed to see his way through complicated relations, and who would unite the candor of a friend with the obedience of a subordinate and the duties and labors of an adjutant, I would shun no danger to fulfil the duties of such a post: Caroline would forgive me, and I should leave to my children a legacy of honor. If, on the other hand, on my arrival in Mecklenburg, I find things and persons in a state which seems to make it my duty to keep aloof from them, I shall then pay attention to my own concerns first ; go with my wife and children to Sweden for the winter, and in the spring to England, where I am sure, in a very short time, to achieve independence by following my calling."

Perthes was detained nearly a week in a small house at Heiligenhafen, the extreme point of Germany, by the prevalence of a strong east wind, which in spite of the bright, beautiful weather, prevented any craft from putting to sea. "A severe trial of patience," he said, " but since we suffer so much from men, why not from nature also ?" On the 17th of July the wind changed, and at five o'clock in the afternoon, Perthes, in company with some other Hamburghers, and Curtius, Recorder of Lübeck, sailed in a driving storm from Kiel across to Warnemünde, a seaport town near Rostock.

"So I am again on land," he wrote to Caroline " after a glorious passage! How I delight in those noble waves! My deepest feelings are called forth by them, and I become cheerful and courageous. I feel as if I were in my proper element. The waves were long and high, so that the open boat which just held us ten, was now poised on the edge of the billow, now deep in the trough of the sea. By the time it grew dark, all the passengers and one of the boatmen became sea-sick ; I remained well. At eleven o'clock that night, the strong gale had driven us to the point of Warnemünde, but the skipper was afraid to run in ; so we cruised about in the dark till morning. ' Nothing was to be seen but the monster billows which yawned for us in all varieties of horrid shapes. At dawn we found ourselves lying immediately opposite to Admiral Hope's ship, a colossus of seventy-four guns, surrounded by two-and-twenty other large vessels all bearing the flag of England. Far off across the sea the moon cast a strip of silver light, and the rayless sun a reflection of glowing red. I never received such impressions of the sublime as during that short voyage."

At this time tidings came from Hamburgh that a general pardon had been proclaimed. Ten men, however, were excepted, among whom was Perthes. " I thank you from my heart, my beloved Perthes," wrote Caroline, " that your name stands among the names of the ten enemies of the tyrant. This will bring us joy and honor as long as we live."

The general pardon failed to protect the city from the atrocities of Davoust. Bad as these appeared in July, they had not then reached their height. " It will do some good," said Perthes, " for if it had not been for this, the old-fashioned spiritless people would have relapsed into the indolent let-alone habits of their former life—still it is terrible, and it cuts one to the very soul when one hears of such horrors."

But still more grievous than the fate of particular cities was the miserable condition of Germany. The uncertainty as to the results of the truce filled all hearts with uneasiness. Would it end in a desperate renewal of the struggle, or in a disgraceful peace? Would Austria join the allies, or preserve her neutrality?

During the next month Perthes was actively engaged in reviving the Hanseatic Legion, and in taking measures for the defence of the Hanse-towns, and for their full recognition as an important political element in North Germany. He was well aware that no step of an important kind could be attempted without the support of Prussia, and it was therefore with considerable satisfaction that he discovered the opposition between the Government and the people, which now began to manifest itself. To the Privy Councillor Scharnweber, who possessed the entire confidence of the Prussian Chancellor, he sent a full statement of the position of North Germany, and concluded with these words :—" I build my hopes of deliverance for North Germany almost exclusively on the Prussian nation— on the earnestness, on the real German spirit, and the freedom which it is developing ; and whatever may be the particular tendencies and aims of the government of the day, they must, and will be overmastered by this spirit. Of your own personal desire and the influence you possess, I am well aware, most excellent sir, and I therefore commend our affairs to your protection. If you take up our cause, we have gained a *point d'appui* such as we need." It was amid this complication of cares, of labors, and of doubts, that on the 10th of August, the truce, which had for a time sheathed the sword in North Germany, came to an end.

XVII

The Wife's Trials.

N the 17th of August, hostilities recommenced between Walmoden and Davoust. Walmoden, whose division formed the extreme right wing of the northern army, under the command of the Crown-Prince of Sweden, was forced to retreat, and by the end of August, the enemy had taken Wismar, Gadebusch, and Schwerin. But early in September, Davoust himself was compelled to withdraw altogether from Mecklenburg, and to fix his head-quarters at Ratzeburg during the rest of the month ; while Walmoden sent strong reconnoitring parties to the left bank of the Elbe, and, on the 16th of September, cut to pieces a body of 7000 French on the Göhrde, occupied Lüneburg, and made incursions into the Hanoverian territory. Thus, when at the beginning of October, Davoust assembled the main body of his army on the Elbe between Lauenburg and Hamburgh, he found himself menaced by Walmoden's troops on the side of Hanover, as well as from Mecklenburg.

During these months of hope and fear, Perthes found full employment at his post in the Burgher-Guard, and in the Hanseatic Directory. The maintenance

(183)

of the Burgher-Guard he considered as a matter of the
first importance, both for the future external position
and inward development of the cities. It seemed to
afford the only means of diverting the burgher mind
from the one object of trade and commerce, and of
cherishing a vigorous self-reliant spirit, by means of
which the narrow city-life might expand into something
wider and more national. But to be in a position for
accomplishing this task, when it should return to the
citizen-life, the Burgher-Guard must, in the meanwhile,
have obtained general confidence and respect, and this
was only to be won by active coöperation in the struggle. General Vegesack's appointment of this force for
garrison-duty at Rostock, in the rear of the contending
armies, was consequently regarded by Perthes as an
unfortunate arrangement. He says to Mettlerkamp on
the 3d of September,—"We have sworn to risk our
lives for the liberty of the cities, and the hour is come.
Our brethren in the legion are ahead, we dare not
draw back. We burghers of the cities entreat to be
led out to war ; not because our little contingent can
add any weight to the army : it is for our own sake we
ask it." On the following morning he laid before the
officers and privates a petition addressed to General
Vegesack, requesting to be led into the field at once.
It was signed by the whole corps, but the General declared that he could not, without the most urgent necessity, consistently with the dictates of his own conscience or with his duty to the future authorities of the
Hanse-towns, oppose to the enemy a force composed
almost entirely of heads of families. The Burgher-
Guard accordingly remained in garrison during the
months of September and October, in Wismar, Gres-

sow, Calsow, and Grevismühlen, in the vicinity of the foe, but without participation in the strife.

Perthes had taken a considerable part of the labors of the Hanseatic Directory upon himself. These were continually increasing, on account of the growing necessity of procuring fresh supplies of money from England and Germany to provide for the support of the destitute exiles who were daily receiving additions to their numbers. The universal confidence in his integrity and his conscientiousness, was increased by the circumstance of his having thought it his duty distinctly to refuse every kind of support for himself.

The views of the Hanseatic Directory met with strong opposition on the part of the Conservatives of Hamburgh, who wished to see the old constitution restored. It seems to have been Sieveking who first saw the danger that might accrue to the future independence of the cities from this jealous opposition. In a letter written from Berlin on the 19th of September, he says, " We have laid before the Crown-Prince the Memorial relating to the measures which may be rendered necessary in the event of Hamburgh being placed under military authority. But I must confess, dear Perthes, that many an anxious foreboding has accompanied this step. The future independence of the Hanse-towns seems to me to be so absolutely contingent on their internal tranquillity, and on the result of the intervention of the Princes, that I would rather decline the avowal of our helplessness, and shrink from provoking the strife of burghers or admitting the interference of princes, even with the purest intentions. Let us keep our heads clear and our hands free, so that the fall of the Hanse-towns, which is perhaps a necessary result of the tendencies of the age, be not placed to our account. Let us not reckon too much on the indifference of our narrow-minded fellow-citizens ; there is fire enough under the ashes ; and you know as well as I, that Providence often makes use of the ideal in legislation to lead blinded men, by little and little, to political suicide. I am not sufficiently acquainted with Hamburgh to come to a conclusion as to the possibility or impossibility of restoring the old constitution ; but I am sure that it is only in the event of its impossibility, that we should be justified in hazarding much in the hope of gaining much ; and even then we must remember that we are are playing a game of chance. The reaction which is now fast manifesting itself, confirms my conviction of the necessity of avoiding every appearance of innovation."

The danger of attempting to carry out constitutional changes, by means of foreign assistance, was increased by a rumor that Von Hess had availed himself of his credit with the English Ministers, to induce them to take the Burgher-Guard into the pay of England ; thus throwing the power of framing the new constitution into his own hands. Rumor was also busy with reports of similar designs on the part of the Crown-Prince of Sweden.

At the sight of these opposing forces, the influence of which he could not avert, Perthes was greatly perplexed. "It is a momentous time," he wrote, "and I am able to comprehend it ; but the man often sinks into melancholy, and then all, all appears vain and miserable—all is falsehood, deceit, and illusion. Through such dark seasons a man must pass, they are part of human destiny ; and even he who was without sin was pleased to endure the like. I could not tell you in a thousand pages, my Caroline, all the thoughts and feelings that pass through my head in the course of the day; my days are often sad enough. How hard it is to present truth in its purity! it receives the coloring of each individual's mind, and of each individual's weaknesses and follies. How weak and corrupt are men, even the good! If man were not a poor sinner, he might regard himself as a god."

And in another letter, "May God enable me to do what is right, and keep me from self-exaltation. I will preserve my integrity; I will look upon my fatherland with a good conscience, and will return to our city with an open countenance and head erect."

The stirring events between the expiration of the truce and the middle of November, had demanded from Perthes mental and physical exertions and sacrifices of all kinds; but it had also been rich in experiences both of heart and life. Naturally disposed to self-confidence, he had learned that his powers were limited; "but," he said, "I have at the same time learned that the voice of an honest man is a mighty power, and has great influence."

There were seasons when the impressions made on him by the great agitation throughout Prussia, and the battles which were then being fought—remarkable both in themselves and in their consequences—rendered it difficult for him to preserve his sympathy and his energies for circumstances which, when compared with the momentous events of the times, were petty and circumscribed. Many of his friends desired a wider sphere of action for him.

"Would to God," wrote Niebuhr, "that you would

now step forth as a statesman in our fatherland! I call
to every one who has ears to tell me how you can in
future be brought into the administration of Germany."

Perthes, on the contrary, was convinced that he was,
by the previous course of his life, unfitted for working
for great things except in a small circle ; and since he
was excluded from any immediate participation in the
great affairs of Germany, he rejoiced the more in the
confidential relations in which he stood towards the
most eminent men of the North. He possessed the personal confidence of Generals Walmoden, Dornberg,
and Vegesack, as well as of the Hereditary Prince of
Schwerin, and Lieutenant-Colonel Witzleben who requested his intervention in numberless cases, when
fresh supplies were to be procured, intricate questions
to be determined, or young troops to be animated and
encouraged. The young men of the Legion were devoted to him heart and soul, and clung to him with
childlike affection and confidence. They delighted in
the sympathy of the slender, delicately-formed man,
who never shrank from the endurance of any hardship
with them, who took part in all their joys and perils,
and who never spared earnest and friendly remon-
strances in the hope of preserving them from the reckless license of a wild and irregular soldier-life. Perthes repaid their affection with the most cordial recognition. It was not without some mixture of personal
pride that he heard Witzleben and other experienced
officers praise the cheerful patience under hardships,
and the daring, even foolhardy rashness of the attack
of the newly-formed legion : he excused their occasional wildness as the exuberance of a poetical enthusiasm.
Tears stood in his eyes on receiving a letter from Wit-

zleben, in which the General wrote, "The infantry fought like lions, my dear Perthes, in yesterday's battle at Möllner Wood, and I am perfectly satisfied with their conduct; they have revived the glory of the old Hansa." Perthes writes on one occasion, "I see many fine youths here, who are developing noble qualities. The blessing of God will rest upon our youth, and through them He will make all right; such is my firm conviction, and it is my happiness that all our dear young people cling to me like children."

But the active and stirring life of three months was pervaded by a deep and heartfelt sorrow, arising from the position of his wife and children. He had been obliged, as we have seen, to leave them in the beginning of July at Aschau, a farm belonging to the Count Caius Reventlow. There, near the farm-house, and in the middle of the wood, close to the sea, stood the summer-house which had been the refuge of Caroline and her children, consisting of a sitting-room and a few small bed-rooms. The farmer was the only inhabitant within a circle of four miles.

In a letter written some time afterwards to her sister at Salzburg, Caroline says, "We could get nothing from the farmer, kind as he was, but milk and butter; bread, soap, salt, oil, and so forth, were not to be had within four miles, and my sister Augusta, with the two elder children, had to fetch them. For eighteen weeks we had neither meat nor white bread in the house. What was called the kitchen was about forty paces from the house; our cooking utensils consisted of four copper pots, a bowl, and a few plates. Fortunately, I had brought our spoons with me, and I purchased a few knives and forks; everything else we did without."

"And yet," she says, in another letter, "we are rich in
comparison with many others, for we have a hundred
thousand times more than nothing."

Caroline's confinement was expected in a few
months. The eldest of her children was a daughter
of fifteen, and the youngest, a boy, did not yet run
alone. The eldest son, Matthias, walked every morning at seven o'clock to Altenhof, a distance of three
miles, to receive instruction with the sons of Count
Reventlow. The education of the rest was in the
meantime interrupted. One old and faithful servant
had remained with them, and their means did not
allow them to engage a second. The damp garden-
house, with its twelve windows down to the ground,
and unprovided with shutters, brought ailments of all
sorts upon the children during the moist, rainy season,
and Caroline herself was often laid upon a sick-bed.
There was a friendly old farrier at Eckernförde, but
no physician nearer than Kiel, a distance of at least
twelve or fifteen miles.

The deserted wife, however, met with sympathy and
comfort. Her sister Augusta was ready for every
emergency by night or by day, "and the families of
Count C. Reventlow and Count C. Stolberg, vie with
each other," writes Caroline, "in their attention, and
in the readiness they manifest in lending us assistance
in our need. No words can describe the kindness of
our dear friends at Altenhof and Windebye." The
children, too, while adding to her anxieties, ministered
no less to her strength and happiness. "They refreshed me in my distress, each in his own way, and
out of the simple and genuine affection of their hearts,
—the little Bernard not excepted, who is often at a

loss to find expression for his love. I am indeed convinced from experience that God can give us no greater joy, or sorrow, than through a loving and beloved child. Nothing else so revives and sustains the heart, and shames us into energy. This I have experienced a thousand times ; and I scarcely think that I could have continued mistress of myself, if God had not given me my angel Bernard, and in him a living image of childish love and confidence. When I was in deep affliction and anxiety on account of Perthes, and in sorrow for my eight children entering upon life deprived of a father's counsel and affection, I was often on the brink of despair. And when at such times I folded my dear Bernard in my arms, and looked into his clear infant eyes, and saw that he was neither troubled nor afraid, but calm, sweet, and loving, I found faith again, and prayed to God that I might become even as my dear child."

The kindness of friends and the love of her children, might indeed uphold her against the heavy pressure of external circumstances, but when her anxiety for her absent husband was aroused, she could not be comforted. The communications with Mecklenburg being interrupted, letters from Perthes were seldom received, while the most contradictory and exaggerated reports were in circulation, as to the position he had assumed, and the dangers with which he was encompassed. Caroline's mind meanwhile was full of the saddest forebodings : in a future that did not seem far off, she pictured her children fatherless and motherless, helpless and forsaken. Her grief is revealed in letters evidently written under the deepest melancholy :—" I have need of hope," she writes to Perthes, "for the

present is mournful, and my condition and circumstances are more serious, and my sense of desolation is greater than you in the midst of so much activity
and hopeful labor can realize.   If I am to spend
my time here alone, if I am to remain here without tidings of you, while I know you to be exposed to
constant danger, I cannot survive.   I cannot sufficiently impress on you, my Perthes, the importance of making such arrangements as may prevent our being
separated during the coming winter.   I solemnly
assure you, that it is an act of injustice to leave
me here, without the most urgent necessity. . . . I am
surrounded by darkness and perplexity, and I see before me a sad and painful death-bed, to which I may at
any moment be called ; but I will not despair.   May
God protect and preserve you to us ; we will pray for
you by night and by day."

In a letter written somewhat later, she says, " If you
love me, take care that in the event of my death, my
children, especially my little children, be intrusted to
the care of those who will teach them to love God,
without knowing that they are learning it.   This is
the main point, and to little ones everything else is
comparatively unimportant : their hearts, in which so
much lies dormant, are first to be opened.   Ah,
my Perthes ! may God help us to awaken the love of
Himself in our children, whether we are to live together or apart in this world.   My hand trembles, and
I can write no more."

At other times her anxiety for the life of her husband overcame the thought of her own approaching
hour of danger :—" How can I persuade myself that
you, my dear Perthes, will be preserved to me ?" she

writes; "God takes away thousands of husbands as
much beloved by their wives and children as you are
by us. Perthes, my dear Perthes! to fulfil your slightest wish would be my only pleasure, were you to be
taken from me, and I were to have the misery of being
left in the world without you. Tell me, then, more of
your views regarding the children, and of what I can
do to please you."

The quiet energy and self-command with which
Caroline, even in her deepest affliction, presided over
her household, and the expressions of courage and
resignation which filled many of her letters written to
women who, like herself, were victims of the events of
the time, had impressed her friends with the conviction, that even if the worst should befall her, her
peace of mind would still remain unshaken. To her
husband, whom she had always found a sure refuge in
circumstances of trial, she, indeed, gave vent to her
oppressed heart in frequent complaints; but amid her
complainings she as often gave utterance, without
seeming to intend it, to the language of patience.

Thus she writes in one of her letters to Perthes,—
"I have the firm conviction that my trust in God will
never fail, but I cannot always rejoice in the will of
God, and I cannot make up my mind to resign you
without tears, and without the deepest anguish: you
are too entirely my all in this world; but believe me,
I do not murmur, I only weep, and I am yours for
eternity."

But it was only at long invervals that these letters
came into the hands of Perthes, and his answers sometimes lost, sometimes carried from place to place for
months together, afforded no help to Caroline in form-

9

ing her plans, and little or no support in her solitude.
To transport his wife and children to Mecklenburg
in the midst of the confusion of war, was impossible,
and to have visited them in Holstein, he was assured
by the Danish authorities, would have involved peril
to life or liberty. Perthes was, moreover, fully persuaded that he was in the path of duty. "I follow the
voice of God and duty," he says in one of his letters,
"and that voice is now clearer and more distinct than
ever;" but the privations and anxieties to which he
knew his family to be exposed did not on this account
affect him the less.

"Never, my Caroline," he writes, "permit yourself
to think that my love for you and for the children is
one whit less warm or deep than that of those who are
anxiously striving to preserve their lives for the sake
of their families. There are seasons in which the
whole weight of the anxieties which await us in the
future, and of the sorrow that is involved in the present, presses heavily upon me. Your task is, indeed, a
hard one, but mine is not light. Have patience, be calm
and self-possessed, my beloved Caroline, trust to my
sense and prudence, and leave the event to God. When
we took leave of each other, you wished to know what
was to become of the children in the event of my
death. It is not well to make minute arrangements
which are to have effect long after our death, for life
is always changing, and any disposition we can make,
may thus turn out unsuitable. I trust to your wisdom,
your energy, and your affection, and I pray to God to
give you what you want; and that is, tranquillity. If
I have a wish, it is that you and the children should
live near Nicolovius, and that Matthias should remain

under the tuition of Twesten for five or six years·
But man proposes, God disposes."

"Thank God," he says, in another letter, "that you,
my darlings, and my only earthly treasures, are well.
Dear Caroline, what a vast wilderness the world becomes when man has no home! That which I wanted
as a youth I want now, but in a different way. In my
youth you stood before me, the object of my love and
desire, like some fairy enchantment; I behold you
again in my thoughts, but it is in all the reality of
your truth and worth, and I cannot reach you. These
times are, indeed, wonderful and interesting, but it is
hard to be without a home, and the sad hours that I
spend apart from you, shifting for myself, are too many.
. . . . The sight of little children always brings
tears into my eyes."

"God will help me," he writes again; "I dare not
leave what I have undertaken. I am not so blinded
by vanity and folly as not to see that my own want of
ability and experience, as well as my age and my previous calling, unfit me for military life, especially considering that there is no lack of brave young men;
but it is my business to lift up my voice for truth and
justice, as opportunity offers, and to show that the will
of God is not altogether forgotten, in spite of the sinfulness and weakness that everywhere impede its clear
and perfect recognition. That in times such as these,
when the struggle betwixt good and evil, truth and
falsehood, is so fierce, a man cannot hope to achieve
anything without risking much; that, in order to do
homage to truth and right, a man must be ready to
give up heart, and life, and fortune, and estate—*that,*

my noble wife, you know as well as I. I have courage, and energy, and moderate desires, and I am at peace with God and with myself. I can pray as I never prayed before, and I pray much. My much-loved Caroline, take courage and be calm ; God will help you, and me also."

Again, he writes, " It seems as if God were blessing all my undertakings. Indeed much has been achieved, many things have received form, and in more than one instance harmony and stability have been secured by my efforts ; but it is not only in its results, as they affect the one great national object, that our separation has been useful : it has also enabled me to assist many individuals known and unknown. Large sums of money are placed at my disposal, and thus I am able to aid the distressed not only with sympathy and advice, but also with substantial assistance. Yes, dear Caroline, all the inducements that can move a man to sacrifice every earthly possession in order to work energetically and actively, combine to stimulate me now— honor, gratitude, affection, freedom, love of action. Comfort yourself, as I do, by thinking on what has been done."

On the 17th of September Caroline and her children had left Aschau for Kiel, where Count Moltke had given up to them the apartments which he usually occupied when he was staying in that city. There Caroline found indeed medical help, friends and relations ; but she had still to endure the most severe privations from the want of money. Her own illness and that of her children added to her sorrows. Her anxiety for the fate of her family, in the event of her not sur-

viving her confinement, was also increased by her total ignorance of her husband's circumstances, and
even of his place of residence.

From the 7th of August to the 2d of October she
was without tidings of him, and knew not whether he
were alive or dead. Towards the end of October she
wrote, " I struggle ever more and more to keep thought
and fancy, heart and yearning, under control, but oh,
my beloved, I suffer inexpressibly !"—and then after
details concerning the children, she adds, " I tell you
everything, for you should know how things actually
stand, that you may be able to do what is right in the
circumstances ; but I do not write thus to induce you
to draw back. I take God to witness, who is more to
me than even you are, that I do not wish you to do
anything but your duty."

These last words were conveyed to Perthes with unusual rapidity, and within a few days he was transported to a sphere of action which enabled him to assure his wife that she had now nothing to fear for his
life, for that he was employed on a peaceful mission.

XVIII.

The Hamburgh Sufferers.

CIRCUMSTANCES arose which rendered it desirable that Perthes should remove to Bremen, to prosecute there his labors on behalf of the Hanse-towns. With all the zeal, the untiring energy, and the self-sacrifice which we have already seen him display, he continued to labor until he was deputed to represent the Hanse-towns at the Diet of Frankfort, where the affairs of Germany were to be deliberated upon. On the 3d of December, in company with Sieveking, his fellow-deputy, he left Bremen, and on the 8th reached Frankfort.

On the following day Perthes had the satisfaction of obtaining from Baron von Stein, in a long and very candid conversation, the most positive assurances of the Independence of the three towns. "The Germanic Empire," said Stein, "will be restored ; but till peace is concluded, it is not advisable to proceed to any definite arrangements, lest we should thereby give rise to misunderstandings. But the feeling of the great allied powers is entirely favorable to the Free Cities ; they will not be subjected to any prince, but will preserve their independent place in the empire. They have nothing to fear from the Crown-Prince of Swe-

(198)

den; he and his intrigues are well known." He highly approved of the proceedings of the Hanseatic Directory, and considered it as a matter of justice that a Provincial Committee should be appointed for Hamburgh, in order to carry out the requisite changes in the Constitution." Stein entirely agreed with Perthes in his opinions respecting the Elsfleth duty. "Duties," he said, "imply no restriction on trade; even England admits them; only a duty should not be levied for the benefit of a single district. A regular scale of duties should be fixed for the whole empire, from Holland to Russia." "Stein spoke so freely and openly," said Perthes, "that I poured out my whole heart to him, and told him all my feelings with reference to our German Fatherland and our Hanse-towns, and I soon perceived that he listened to me with pleasure."

From Stein Perthes and Sieveking went at once to Herr von Pilat, private Secretary to Prince Metternich. On the 10th of December the deputies were introduced by Pilat to Prince Metternich. "The Prince received us very kindly," wrote Perthes, "assured us of the independence of the Free Cities, and spoke with confidence of the restoration of the Germanic Empire. On my observing that the cities would not be disposed to return to a simple neutrality as before, but would desire to be included in the Empire;" he replied, "I see that you, like the rest of us, have given up many of the chimeras of former days."

On the same day the deputation was admitted to an audience of the Emperor Francis. "You have suffered much," he said, "but matters are improving, for now we are all Germans, and I will soon help you." Then turning to Perthes and Sieveking, he added, "Yes, it goes hard with Hamburgh, and that wild fellow Davoust avenges himself cruelly, but what I can make good, I will."

While the kind assurances of the Emperor had increased the previous affectionate attachment of the deputies to his person, the abrupt harshness of the King of Prussia, by whom they were received on the following day, was in no way calculated to lessen the dislike which was then felt in North Germany towards the Prussian supremacy. By the Chancellor Hardenberg, by Wilhelm von Humboldt,[*] and by the Privy-Councillor Hippel, the freedom of the Hanse-towns was spoken of as a political necessity, but a secret misgiving as to the designs of the Court of Berlin still remained.

Many were the political impressions that Perthes received during his short stay in Frankfort. At the table of the Chancellor he met the most distinguished personages of Prussia ; Count Nesselrode spoke kindly to him of the importance of the Hanse-towns to the trade of Europe, while the Hanoverian Count Hardenberg hastened to assure him of his friendly feelings.

"This day," writes Perthes, on the 16th of December, "terminates our journey of discovery, and we have found that the *terra firma* which we sought is not yet in sight ; but our hearts are filled with gratitude and praise to God, for showing us how much kindly feeling exists among the great European powers towards our Fatherland and the Hanse-towns." While Smidt remained at head-quarters, Perthes and

---

[*] Wilhelm von Humboldt, the younger brother of Alexander, distinguished as an orientalist and philologist — and in other respects as one of the most eminent men of the period.

Sieveking returned to Bremen, and arrived there on
the 20th of December. The Emperors Francis and
Alexander, and King Frederick William had in writing recognized the Independence of the Free Cities,
and the deputies were thus able to render a joyful account of their journey in the Council-hall at Bremen,
where the senators assembled to meet them.

Perthes had been disappointed in his hope of finding
letters from Caroline at Bremen : he was the more
anxious, because Holstein had become the seat of war.
Finding no letters at Bremen, he hastened to Lubeck,
carrying with him the guarantees of the Independence
of the cities. Here he heard that Caroline had been
safely delivered of a son, Andreas, on the 10th of December. On Christmas night he travelled to Kiel,
now no longer threatened by a hostile army, and arrived there the next day at five o'clock in the afternoon. "Unexpected, and in the twilight, he entered
my room, after a separation of nearly six months,"
wrote Caroline : "Matthias saw him first. I had the
happiness of restoring all the children to him safe and
well, with the addition of a darling, healthy infant.
What this was none can know but one who has experienced it."

Shortly after his return, Perthes was requested by
the staff-general of the Crown-Prince of Sweden, to
associate himself with two other gentlemen of Lubeck
and Bremen, who were also named, to administer the
large sum of money which the Prince had granted for
the relief of the exiled Hamburghers. For this purpose, Perthes again left his family on the 1st of January, 1814 ; and in order to be as near as possible to
the scene of suffering, he took up his quarters at Flott-

beck, a small town on the Elbe, about nine miles above Hamburgh. Here the situation of the city revealed itself to his eyes in all its horror.

While the greater part of Germany had long been delivered from the French, Davoust had maintained himself in Hamburgh, although confined within the limits of the city by the besieging army of General Benningsen, who had succeeded to General Woronzow, towards the end of December. What Davoust did may perhaps find its excuse in his position as a beleagured general, but the manner in which he did it could only have been devised by the rage of a disappointed villain. He began his cruelties with the robbery of the Bank, and most cruel treatment of the burghers. On the week following the Christmas festival, the suburbs, all the surrounding villages, and the fine country houses on the Alster, were set on fire after only eighteen hours' notice, and twenty thousand people were driven out of the city destitute and homeless; first the young and strong as dangerous, and then the old and weak as superfluous. The children were next brought out of the orphan-house, the infirm poor from the almshouses, the criminals from the prisons, and all were driven outside the gates, and there left to their fate. At mid-day, on the 30th December, Davoust gave orders that the hospital in which were eight hundred sick and idiots, should be vacated, and set on fire, and by the same hour on the following day it was in flames, but not till, through the incredible exertions of the burghers, the helpless inmates had all been removed, while bands of drunken soldiers were struggling with the sick for their clothes and their bedding, and scenes of reckless plundering were being enacted on every side.

The troops, at the same time, set fire to the adjoining houses, and gave themselves up to deeds of unmitigated atrocity. The intense excitement, and the bitter cold of a January night, cost six hundred of the sick their lives.

The tidings of these horrors filled with sorrow and indignation the minds of Perthes and his friends at Flottbeck, while the misery which came under their own personal observation was equally heart-rending. For miles round, the snow-covered country presented the appearance of a vast waste of ruins, above which, here and there, a wall, or a half-consumed tree, might be seen, while women and children wandered about amid the desolation, seeking their property. Every night the sky was illumined by the glow of freshly-kindled fires. In the streets of Altona, and in the neighboring villages, half-frozen figures were seen wandering about and crying for food and clothing, and for shelter from the frost and cold, while long lines of the sick and the aged, of women and children, might be seen on the roads to Lubeck and Bremen, under the escort of a troop of Cossacks, on their way to seek in the sister cities the assistance they so sorely needed.

"You will have heard of the misery of this district," writes Perthes to Caroline, "but no words can give any idea of it. It must be seen: all the trouble that I have witnessed and shared for the last nine months, is as nothing in comparison. How will it end! May God graciously shorten it, and bring us safely through it."

Much was done to alleviate the wretchedness; the most strenuous efforts were made in Altona, Bremen, and Lubeck ; contributions poured in from far and near ; a committee of Hamburgh burghers made great exertions at Altona, and those appointed to administer the Swedish contribution did what they could : " but all we can do," wrote Perthes, " is to relieve cases of individual suffering, we cannot meet all the necessities of the present ; may God save the future! We must in the meantime summon all our energies to prevent the burghers and the city from sinking into depths out of which there will be no possibility of raising them."

It seemed as though the destiny of Hamburgh for years to come had been sealed, by what had been already done. Everything depended on Davoust's abandonment of Hamburgh being insisted on, as the preliminary condition of the next truce or treaty between the allies and Napoleon. Perthes turned to Smidt with the most urgent entreaties that he would continue to press on Metternich, Hardenberg, and Nesselrode, the importance of making the evacuation of Hamburgh a preliminary condition of any treaty with Napoleon. With the same object Perthes availed himself of his personal influence with the Duke of Oldenburg, to request his mediation with the Emperor Alexander. "The Princess, lately won for Germany, appears at the present crisis as a heaven-sent deliverer among us," wrote Perthes to the Duke : "one word of hers to her imperial brother may rescue thousands from wretchedness and suffering." "The Duke will write to you himself," replied Zehender, " but for the present I must tell you that in all probability a courier will shortly be dispatched to the Emperor, who will carry with him a good word for the unhappy Hamburghers.

Perthes sought to minister to the pressing wants of the Burgher-Guard, by applying to Benningsen and to his friends in London, but without success. He then had recourse to a loan, by means of which food and clothing were to a certain extent provided. He next drew up for Smidt an estimate of the losses that Hamburgh had suffered through the French occupation, and he was incessantly busied in bringing to Benningsen's head-quarters, men who could give information required by the General.

The letters belonging to this period which have been preserved, give evidence in general of an almost incredible number of references made to Perthes during his residence in Flottbeck, touching matters great and small, far and near. From the Russian and Swedish head-quarters, from the leading men of Bremen and Lubeck, from men of all parties, and from the unfortunate, he received applications for information, counsel, money, or for assistance in carrying out their plans. Perthes held no office, he had neither rank nor title, and yet he appears at this time to have occupied the centre around which all business revolved that had any bearing on the destiny of Hamburgh.

XIX

Perthes and Caroline at Blankenese.

1818.

ERTHES had passed the last days in Flott-beck in sorrow and depression, working amid many anxieties. On the 17th of January he wrote to Caroline, "No letter, no word from you, my beloved Caroline—how is this? I am very unhappy, and long to be with you and the children ; but I dare not leave, for an important decision may depend on my presence. Never since our departure from Hamburgh have I been so un-happy as I now feel myself, and yet I have no tidings from you. Surely some great calamity has overtaken you. Is my darling Bernard still alive?—he was un-well when I left."

This child, a boy of uncommon beauty and vivacity, was indeed still alive when Perthes wrote these lines, but he was even then struggling with death, and within two days the Lord took him to himself. "My dear Perthes," wrote Caroline, immediately after the death of the child, "what I feared has happened ; our dear Bernard is very ill, and although the physicians assured me yesterday evening that he was not in danger, I am full of care and anxiety, and fear the worst. I wish

above all things, both for your sake and for my own,
that you were here. . . . May God be our help! Why
should I conceal it longer from you?—our angel is
with God—he died this morning at half-past nine. He
looks wonderfully beautiful, and I implore you to come
as soon as possible, that you may see his dear remains
before any change takes place."

Owing to the irregularity of the posts, Perthes had
neither received this letter nor a former one acquaint-
ing him with the illness of the child; and on the 21st
of January he stepped cheerfully into Caroline's room
with the question, "Are all well?"   "I had to lead my
poor Perthes to the corpse of our beloved child," wrote
Caroline to her sister: "his grief was excessive, and
my anxiety for *him* carried me through this painful
day."

Perthes had been only a few hours in Kiel when he
received an invitation to repair to the Russian head-
quarters at Pinneberg, in order to consult in the name
of the Crown-Prince, as to what further measures ought
to be taken for alleviating the sufferings of the outcast
Hamburghers, and for obtaining the voluntary cession
of the city. "Called at such a time and under such
circumstances, you must go," said Caroline.   But
Perthes was physically unable.   "Caroline's heroic
spirit was greater than my bodily strength," he wrote.
He was unable to leave the house till the 27th January.

"Thank God, nothing has suffered by my absence,"
he wrote from Pinneberg. "Be strong, my beloved!
May God spare us further trials. We are quiet just
now. I have no more to say to you at present; but we
understand each other for eternity without words.

May the Lord protect you and my dear children, and keep for us those who are now at rest."

The misery that Perthes met on every side left him no time for the indulgence of his own grief. He exerted himself to the utmost to give unity to the efforts which were being made to relieve the sufferings of the Hamburghers, and was the means of bringing into operation a Central Relief Board, under the able presidency of Senator Abendroth ; and in this way much was effected for the relief of the more urgent necessities of the fugitives. In order to be as near as possible to the seat of suffering, Perthes had fixed his quarters at Van Smissen's Mill, near the Devil's Bridge at Flottbeck. On the 9th of February the Russians converted the mill into a temporary hospital for their soldiers, and he had to carry on his work amid the groans of the wounded and the dying.

"My letter of the 7th of February, your fortieth birth-day, my still young and ever youthful bride, you will have received before this," wrote Perthes ; "and gladly would I have hastened to your arms and pressed you to my heart. Be comforted, my dear Caroline! True love is immortal, and by some bonds of love I feel sure that our departed little ones are still united to us. Here, since three o'clock to-day, things look very, very serious. The French are attacked on every side, at Wilhelmsburg, at Neuhof, and in Harburg, and many of our people have already been brought in wounded. One fine, brave young fellow, Volkman, fell to-day. He went out yesterday full of spirits. His father, a stout artisan, was obliged to flee from Hamburgh on his account, and is in deep distress, but is supported by the thought of the honor his son has won by his self-

sacrifice. Close to me lies a Russian captain, a man
upwards of fifty ; as the surgeon was cutting out the
ball, he said that he felt the house shaking. And here
I sit amid blood and moaning, groans and death, but
I trust in God that the end is approaching. Here
come three wagons full of wounded, and there is not
a spare corner in the house. Nine corpses are now
lying in a row in the snow before my door. It is
strange to look upon these once wild men, now so still
and tame." The misery of the exiles, and the sufferings
of the wounded, now that he was brought into such
close proximity with them, filled the heart of Perthes,
already saddened by the loss of his child, with a horror
such as he had never before experienced.

He was compelled to be almost perpetually in motion,
passing and repassing over ground covered with snow,
while suffering severely from a contusion on his foot,
which he had received by a fall from a carriage. A
dangerous fever at the same time prevailed in the reg-
iment stationed at the mill, and Perthes carried the
germ of this with him, when on the 16th of February,
he left Flottbeck for head-quarters, and for Lubeck,
with a view to complete arrangements for the relief of
the destitute.

He arrived in Kiel on the 19th of February, and
then it was found on examination that a bone of his
foot was broken. "I hope my future biographer will
record," he wrote playfully to Sieveking, " that I have
walked about for nearly a fortnight, and driven twenty
miles in a requisition wagon, with a broken bone."

For nine long weeks he was now confined to bed,
and for the first part of the time was in great danger
from a severe attack of nervous fever ; but a good

constitution carried him through all, and he had soon
only to endure the pain of lying still. "Here," he
wrote to Besser, "after many journeyings up and down,
I have been obliged to cast anchor at last. Such a fate
is hard to bear at the present moment. If a ball had
done it, one might have been better pleased." His
spirits, however, never flagged ; and his wife could
write,—"My dear Perthes is always the same, whether
lying and enduring, or travelling and acting ; and
during the whole period of his confinement, he has
never been cross or impatient. I rejoice that he was
with us when he fell ill, and that I had the happiness
of nursing him. The children were all well, fortunately, and we made the best of it."

Intellectual excitement was not wanting meanwhile.
As soon as the state of his health permitted, he was
visited by his numerous friends, who passed many cheerful hours by his bedside. He took advantage also of
his being laid aside from public duties to consult with
Besser, whose faithful friendship afforded him comfort
and support in this, as well as in many other seasons
of trial, as to the ways and means of resuming their
business ; and he gave himself up with fresh delight to
the pleasure of reading, of which he had been so long
deprived. Nicolovius directed his attention to Neander's "Life of St. Bernard." "Read Neander's 'Life
of St. Bernard,'" he wrote ; "you will be astonished
at Neander's wealth of inward experience, and his exalted view. Fr. Leopold Stolberg wrote to me about
it with the most enthusiastic admiration, inquiring
whether the author were old, or whether he might be
expected to write more. His popularity in the university here is great, and his influence must be good. It

is touching to see the simplicity with which he brings forward the most sublime opinions, and the results of the most laborious study." But all other objects of interest were soon cast into the shade by the events of the time. By an active and extensive correspondence, Perthes endeavored to bring order, harmony, and regularity into the plans for the assistance of the exiles, and even from his sick-bed his efforts were attended with success.

The conferences at Chatillon, the fresh victories of Napoleon, the onward march of the Allies, their arrival before Paris, were known to him before he had left his room, and many a word of hope for the future found its way to distant Kiel. "We are living in a time of miracles," wrote Nicolovius, in a letter that the Countess Louisa Stolberg transmitted to Perthes; "what we, with sad hearts, *desired* for our children, but never dared to expect, we ourselves have lived to see. And what a glorious day this beautiful dawn promises! A generation that has raised itself so high will never sink again."

On the 9th of April, Perthes at length received permission to leave his bed. On this occasion he wrote to Max Jacobi,—"I have borne this trial of patience with tolerable composure and cheerfulness. I have been strengthened by the victory of truth which is once more bringing back freedom, order, and love to mankind. God is with us, and all now feel that they have been doing more than they thought."

On the 19th of April, Perthes left Kiel with his whole family, and on the 20th arrived at Blankenese, a fishing village a few miles below Hamburgh, where he purposed remaining till the French evacuated that place. Although the day of Hamburgh's deliverance seemed uncertain, it was evident that it must come in the course of a few months, and in this certainty all those hopes and fears for the political constitution of the city that had been thrown into the background by the pressure of the moment, now started once more into life.

The thoughts of all now naturally turned to the question of the future constitution of the Hanse-towns. As to Hamburgh, Perthes was decidedly of opinion that some innovations should be introduced. He was desirous above all to see a perfect civil equality among the three confessions, and to infuse fresh blood into the hereditary *Bürgerschaft*, by the admission of deputies from the hundreds, the educated classes, and the Jews. It was in the executive, however, that he thought reform most indispensable. But apart from any reference to his own peculiar views, Perthes had begun to doubt whether any open party strife was not likely, in present circumstances, to be more perilous to the interests of the city than the restitution of the old and defunct constitution. From the head-quarters of the Allies came an emphatic warning against all internal division. "It is all over with the Hanse-towns," wrote Smidt, "unless they see the necessity of avoiding all that may lead to foreign interference. The Allies can look upon each city only as one body politic, not as divided into factions, each of which seeks some separate object."

At this time Niebuhr, irritated apparently by the prominence which the Hamburghers were giving to their own affairs, and especially to their own differences, took a view of the position of Hamburgh and

the other Hanse-towns, and of their claims in the settlement of the general question then engaging German
statesmen, which caused a temporary estrangement between him and Perthes. "I need not tell you my
opinion of yourself," he wrote to Perthes; "you have
done what your friends expected of you; but we must
not expect the historian to hear the fame of an unwar-
like people like your Hamburghers, whose thoughts
are bounded by their trade and whose city has inglo-
riously fallen, made so much of without ascribing it to
a vain and partial exaggeration."

"For a long time," wrote Niebuhr subsequently,
"the isolated Hanse-towns have existed by a kind of
sufferance, without any political activity worthy of the
name. Such civic communities, in fine, have been contented with the reed's destiny, and have regarded it as
a privilege to bow before the wind. Bravery is the
attribute of cities full of free and vigorous life, and
which by virtue of their own resources are capable of
defending themselves. A full and free life is now only
possible in great states, in which all homogeneous elements are concentrated."

Many passionate and hasty words passed between
the friends in the spring of 1814, and Perthes wrote so
bitterly of Niebuhr, that Nicolovius replied.—"I like
quarrelling in such times as these as little as you do,
and I am convinced that in no circumstances are we
warranted in speaking hastily, or otherwise than as
the good spirit prompts, and that in this respect, as in
the Gospel, a mite is of more value than large gifts and
mighty deeds. You must not do injustice to Niebuhr
as you do in your last letter to me. You make erro-
neous combinations, and draw false conclusions. Con-

tinue to him your full and entire confidence, for he deserves it. He is not only one of the most profound and most original of men, but also one of the most upright. He is excitable, and may, therefore, be occasionally unjust, but he is full of humility in the presence of the good, the great, and the godlike."

It was at the price of what then seemed an irreparable breach of friendship with the man whose sympathy of heart and mind had attracted him in a period of national suffering, that Perthes learned the inevitableness of a contest between those who sought to develop the future destiny of Germany through the German people, and those who sought its development by means of Prussia. Many perplexing anxieties were, indeed, involved in the prospect of such a struggle, but that help from above which had wrought deliverance in the hour of greatest necessity, was not now to be distrusted.

Nicolovius warmly pressed this home to the heart of Perthes. "As I have an opportunity of forwarding a letter, I send you a few lines, my dear, noble, old Perthes. God above has certainly understood and willed matters better than the wise heads at Châtillon, who are seeking to reconcile themselves with the evil one : they don't know how wonderfully God helps when we are but in earnest in our pursuit of what is truly great. This great, and mighty, and all-sufficient help, must have given you also new life in heart and soul, and is the earnest of a glorious reward for all the sacrifices you have made. Whatever you may henceforth become, and I am glad that you mean to return to bookselling, no man can take the crown from your head, or the order from your breast, or the consciousness from your heart. Blessings a thousand-fold await

you in this life ; such is my belief, and I hear the amen
from above confirming it."

On the 25th of May, the old Senate declared itself
restored to place and authority, and on the following
day, the hereditary Bürgerschaft met, and chose twenty
men who were to form a commission for three months
for the reorganization of the city. The attempts to
secure the extension of the constitution and to infuse
greater energy into the executive were thus resumed.
" Henceforward," wrote Perthes, " I can have no other
bearing on public affairs than such as springs out of
my position and rights as a citizen, and my influence
with my friends ; and I thank God from my heart that
He has been pleased to give me a larger share of the
affection and confidence of my fellow-citizens than is
usually the lot of any one who steps out of the limits
of his own immediate sphere."

The day when Perthes and his family were to leave
Blankenese and return to Hamburgh, now drew nigh.
" These six weeks in Blankenese, have been the sweetest part of my life," wrote Caroline to her sister.
" Perthes with me, the children well, and the hope of
the deliverance of our city gaining strength day by day.
Suddenly the white banners waved once more at
Harburg and from St. Michael's tower : in all directions
outcasts might be seen streaming into the city. We
lived near the Elbe, and could see all those who were
hastening back from Bremen and Hanover. One day,
a carriage full of little children, whose parents had
died in the Hospital at Bremen, arrived at our door.
Troops of starving people with many children and but
little luggage, passed under our windows, and it was
touching to witness the love for home and hearth that

was manifested, though, for the most part, the poor
creatures could look forward to nothing but trouble
and wretchedness.   As they came through the country,
each silently broke a branch from the trees by the
wayside, and bore it in his hand, and old and young,
and even little children, amid tears of grief and shouts
of joy, thanked God for their deliverance from the
great and universal calamity, little thinking all the
while that each brought his own burden with him, and
that a heavy one."

On the 31st of May, General Benningsen made his
entrance with the Russians, and the Burgher-Guard ;
and on the morning of the same day, Perthes and his
family left Blankenese, and in the midst of the advancing troops returned through Altona, to the home from
which they had been driven a year before.

XX

The Return—Summer of 1814.

N the 31st of May, 1814, Perthes had returned to the home and the city which he at one time hardly expected to see again. Many an anxious thought was mingled with his feelings of gratitude. "God be praised that He has brought us thus far, that He has stood by us and helped us in this year of heavy trial," wrote Caroline to her parents on the day of her return. "I will be glad, and forget all, except my dear Bernard. We have many troubles before us, even under the most favorable circumstances: God grant that my Perthes may be spared to me with strength and spirits for the heavy daily toil now before him."

It was, indeed, no easy task to take up the links of the old life after so long an interval,—an interval filled with suffering and privation. Even to render the house habitable was a difficult undertaking. The pleasant and beautiful apartments on the ground-floor had for many months been used by French soldiers as guard-rooms. In the middle of the largest room was a huge stove; trunks of trees had been dragged in through the windows to feed it. All the woodwork that could be pulled down had been burnt; the smoke had found an outlet through the windows. The upper

part of the house had been inhabited by General
Loison, but even there the soldiers had conducted
themselves so riotously, that the whole house was little
better than a heap of filth.   All the furniture had been
taken away ; some of it, by kind friends who had concealed it where they could, and the rest by the French
prefect.   There was not a single habitable room—dirt
and rubbish, a foot high, covered the floors.   Chairs
and tables, beds and bedding, and the whole apparatus
of the kitchen, had to be replaced ; while the want of
money and the heart-breaking spectacle of numbers of
hungry and sorrow-stricken exiles flocking into the
city, made the strictest economy a duty no less than a
necessity.

It was a heavy recommencement for Caroline ; but
before winter all was once more in order, though not
without considerable labor and anxiety.   To place the
business, which had been entirely broken up, on its
former footing was an undertaking of far greater difficulty.   A numerous family had to be maintained, and
many liabilities to be met.

Along with a number of adventurers, sharpers, and
revolutionists, times of great political excitement
always call forth the most talented and energetic
members of a State, turning their attention away from
their usual avocations, and drawing them into the current of events in which unusual powers are required
to meet unusual circumstances.   When the waters
have returned to their accustomed channel, these men,
whose minds had been kept in a state of continual
activity and excitement, and who had been intimately
associated with all the great events of the period,
have to return to the quiet, uniform, and narrow circle

of their own peculiar vocations. Such a step has been difficult even to men of strong natures, and many who were deemed worthy of all praise in critical times, become, when order is restored, a species of intellectual vagabonds, who, at home in no calling, occupy themselves first with one thing, then with another, unsettled in their minds, discontented with themselves and with the world, and a source of grief to others.

Perthes felt that if he would escape this danger, the time was now come when he must devote all his talents and all his energies, to the business of his calling, and he was able both to form the resolution to do so and to carry it out. In spite of seasons of trial and difficulty, it was not without a certain pleasure that he had taken part in the weighty and complicated political events of the period ; but, fortunately, he had sense to see the limited orbit in which he was henceforward to move, and courage to keep within it. The actual state of his business was such as to render a return to its daily cares and labors doubly difficult : " I dislike this transition," he wrote to Villers, "from the poetry of my previous existence, to the prose of common life, and the more so, because I see labors and anxieties of all kinds before me."

On the day following the reöccupation by the French, in the previous year, Davoust had sealed up Perthes's warehouse, and had given notice that all debts due to the firm were to be paid to the French authorities. He then issued an order that all the serviceable books were to be seized and divided between the libraries, schools, and the officials, and the rest sold by auction. A great part of the valuable stock of maps was distributed, some to the topographical bureaux, some to the different generals, while many valuable works fell into the hands of individual officers : the auction was, however, delayed. It was impossible for Perthes to pay any attention to the concerns of the business during his exile, but Besser, though also an exile, never lost sight of it. Ever watchful, and on the alert to take advantage of any favorable turn to save what might yet be saved, he was ably seconded by the dexterity and zeal of a faithful servant named D'Haspe.

The first thing to be done was to separate the books in the large commission warehouse, which were the property of other booksellers, from the rest : it was accordingly committed to the safe keeping of the firm of Hoffmann and Campe.

D'Haspe then paid all tradesmen who had claims on Perthes, not with ready money, but with small bills to such persons who were in debt to the firm, from whom, owing to the dissolution of all order, he would himself have found it difficult at that time to obtain payment. Finally, an attempt was made, and not absolutely without success, to carry on the business through the firm of Hammerich in Altona, and that of Michelsen in Lubeck, and either personally, or by means of friends and connexions, to solicit debtors in the neighboring districts to pay what they owed into the hands of Besser, in spite of the prohibitions of the French commander-in-chief.

But it was not so easy to stop the threatened dispersion and sale of the books in Perthes' own warehouse. In the hope of accomplishing this, however, the creditors were secretly invited to come forward and state that before any division of the property could take place, they must have satisfaction for their claims. As they could take up quite a legal position, Davoust, after making careful personal inquiries, yielded, and ordered that the creditors should be paid first out of the proceeds. Thus one point was gained. But before the sale could take place, it was necessary that a catalogue should be prepared ; and this, Besser, in the expectation of a speedy deliverance from the French, proceeded with as slowly as possible. He gained his object, though Davoust more than once threatened to have the books sold by weight, if the catalogue were not forthcoming. The warehouse being required as a residence for the French officials, the 30,000 volumes which it contained were removed in wagons to another place, and thrown together without any regard to order. The catalogue was nevertheless begun, but before it was ready, the Allies had crossed the Rhine, and, under this change of circumstances Davoust carefully avoided any step that might have led to claims being made on what he considered as his private property. The books accordingly still remained unsold and in safe keeping.

Such was the state of things when the two friends, Besser and Perthes, met a Kiel towards the end of February, 1814, and subsequently at Blankenese, to deliberate as to their further proceedings. Although the whole of the customers were dispersed, both partners were of opinion, that under the circumstances, it was not only possible to resume the business without involving any culpable risk, but that it was a duty to do so, as being the only means of securing the creditors from loss. With this view, Perthes issued a circular in 1814 :—" No one could expect that I should at once fulfil all my engagements, and I am aware that many of my correspondents expect a proposal for an accom-

modation. But now that the position of our fatherland has enabled me to reëstablish myself, I trust to
God to end as I began, and to pay every man his own.
I have, indeed, no longer the youthful energy with
which I set out eighteen years ago, and I have a numerous family to support; but on the other hand, I
have experience, and am thus saved paying the appren-
tice-fee of ignorance. I have the confidence of my
fellow-citizens, and also a large circle of friends and
patrons, and an extensive connexion in foreign countries. I resume my business confidently in reliance
on the friendship of my correspondents, and with the
resolution to pay all my debts, and to let none suffer
loss through me. The how and the when of payment
I must ask you to leave to myself, but within three years
all liabilities shall be discharged." In this circular
Perthes announced that the name of Besser, who had
long been actually in partnership, would "now appear
in the firm, and would thus afford to the commercial
world a further guarantee for the security of the
house."

It was not their intention immediately to resume
their business in all its former extent, but to proceed
with prudence and caution. There was little to be expected from Hamburgh or the immediate neighborhood
under existing circumstances, and not much from Germany in general, since the present distress was likely
to tell on the literary market for many years to come.
The attention of the partners was thus turned to
England, where the results of the war of Independence had awakened a degree of sympathy with the
Continent, such as had not been known for centuries.
The time appeared especially favorable for arousing a

taste for the wider diffusion of German literature in England, and more particularly for directing the attention of the many great and wealthy collectors to German classics of all kinds, and to works on philology. The very defective state of the English book-trade also induced them to hope that the German booksellers might be constituted the medium of the English foreign literary traffic. Besser had passed some time in England, earlier in life, and had perfect command of the language, and introductions to the most influential persons were at his disposal. It was therefore determined that he should go to England and endeavor as much as possible to extend the previous connexion in country. The preparations were soon made, and on the 4th of May Besser embarked at Ritzebüttel.

In the meantime Perthes was left to make the necessary arrangements for reopening the shop as soon as possible after the retreat of the French. " Yesterday," wrote Perthes to Villers, " I was invited by the Prefect to enter the city, in consequence of the Marshal's resolution to release my premises from the embargo he had placed upon them ; and I was also informed, that 700 francs had to be paid by me for a catalogue which they had prepared. You see, that under the white flag they are still the same people. Thus, for having hung me on the gallows in effigy, for having hunted me out of house and home, for having destroyed my trade, stolen the half of my books, and burned my furniture, the scoundrels ask 700 francs !"

Perthes having at once and decidedly declared that, as it was not at his request that the authorities had given themselves the trouble of taking charge of his books, or preparing the inventory, he was not disposed to reimburse them for their pains, the warehouse was, on the 19th of May, unconditionally surrendered to Runge, as his representative.

On the 30th Perthes himself returned to the city, and thus wrote to Besser :—"I shake hands with you from our old house. I dare not express in words the emotions of my heart. It is, indeed, like a resurrection from the dead."

The labors involved in the reopening of the shop were begun and carried on with all diligence. "You will believe, but you can form no idea of the labor of finding one's way through all this confusion, and of putting everything in order ; if only there were some to help me!—but that is impossible. I thank God that I am well and in good spirits, and I am grateful both to Him and to men. The worst of all is the payments which require to be made immediately : few pay *us*, while every day bills, little and great, from Peter and Paul, from bookbinders, trades-people, and others, are coming in : the poor creatures are in the greatest distress, and petition us to pay them. This is very sad. Bills and notes, too, pour in upon us from abroad. I will fight my way through, but it will only be by the sweat of my brow."

Amid all his labors, cares, and anxieties, Perthes never for a moment lost hope or courage, and many a favorable turn helped him through difficulties when things were at the worst. "I am inexpressibly affected," he writes again to Besser, "by the confidence, the affection, and kindness which our fellow-citizens manifest towards us in so many ways. Our credit is not only maintained, it stands firmer than ever. The booksellers' answers to our circular are now come in.

With a single exception they are all satisfied with our proposals, and express the most entire confidence. I can assure you that our business will soon be once more in full operation."

Towards the end of June Perthes himself opened the shop, and within a few days he could write :—

God's blessing is upon us, and all promises well ; but I cannot get through the work alone, and it is absolutely necessary that you should return. One thing presses hard on the heels of another, while things are not yet in order. All are desirous to prove their friendship, and orders pour in from every side. I am overpowered, and long for your return."

Besser's stay in England was to have been longer, but he quickly perceived the position and relations of the book-trade there, and felt that his absence from Hamburgh was no longer necessary. He had been deeply impressed by the spectacle which London presented in the first moments of excitement, immediately after the fall of Napoleon. " Here I am," he says in his first letter, " in this great city, and in this wonderfully beautiful country, at a time which has not its parallel in history. The sovereigns are expected shortly ; but General ' Blutscher' is more thought of than all the rest. There is something absolutely overpowering in this enormous mass of animated and mechanical life ; but with the people, if you only understand their manner and their languarge, you are soon quite at home, spite of their want of amenity."

It was Besser's object to form acquaintance with men of all kinds and of all ranks, and his numerous introductions gave him access to the most distinguished circles. Germans, English gentlemen of fortune, lead-

10*

ing men in the "city," he freely mixed with. Now he
had intercourse with the keen business man; then with
the amiable and the good: at another time with
Methodists and Quakers; and again, with people who
knew nothing of life but its worst side. "It is a perilous thing," he exclaimed, in one of his letters, "for a
poor frail mortal to seek to take the measure of the
knowledge of so many other children of men; whether we will or not, we must place ourselves above
those whom we presume to judge. I am heartily tired
of this sort of life, and often, in the course of the
evening, find myself longing for my little lodging, where
at least in thought I can be with you." He turned for
rest and refreshment frequently to the great Museum,
and the private collections of London. "I am delighted to have Hans Lappenburg to enjoy all these
grand things with me," he writes. "There is something glorious about *youth ;* and with a young man we
ourselves feel young again." The interest evinced by
so many different men for German literature, seemed
to justify the most sanguine hopes, and Besser formed
his plans accordingly. "Through Schwabe, who is
a truly admirable man and highly respected, and
through some other clergyman and Count Münster, as
soon as he comes, I mean to suggest the introduction
of German into the schools. Why not as well as
French? Don't laugh, this is what I call going to the
root of the matter—and it will succeed. We should
also have a German periodical here, on the plan of
the English miscellanies; I do not mean that we should
undertake it, but we might give encouragement to such
a thing in connexion with a literary advertiser. I
have the right men in my eye, both authors and pub-

lishers. In close connexion with this periodical, it would be well to endeavor to establish a subscription library. It would bring together the lovers of German literature, and increase their numbers. At present there is scarcely a single German work to be found among the twenty great booksellers at Oxford. My proposals are warmly seconded by friends and acquaintances. Only take courage, I may assuredly say that my coming to London will have important results."

"Alas! I am candidly told," he wrote, " not only by Germans, but by Englishmen who are thoroughly acquainted with German literature, that the English as a people are incapable of apprehending it. Goethe and Herder they do not understand, and Klopstock they totally misunderstand. I myself now see more and more clearly that it is impossible that the genuine English should have any taste for our works. I do not speak of the men of ' the city,' who are certainly by no means the patrons of literature, but as Robinson calls them, mere *quill-drivers;* neither do I refer to my Methodist friends, to whom Goethe is a ' wicked fellow ;' but the insular character of the people generally, is intellectually exclusive, it cannot get out of itself, and it cannot take in anything foreign. Such men as Robinson are of rare occurrence in England. A better medium than this remarkable and most attractive man, it would be impossible for Germany to find. I unconsciously place him in my mind by the side of Villers, and then the different influence which a thorough German education has had on the Frenchman and on the Englishman, is very striking."

After an interval of a few weeks, Besser again writes to Perthes : " I have at last become thoroughly aware that to promise, to will, and to be able, are three very different things ; and while we may with certainty reckon on the two first, in the case of many men, we must not on that account venture to rely upon the third. I am distressed at the thought of having raised false hopes as to the results of my present visit, nevertheless we have gained much by it. We know with certainty what we should *not* undertake ; and if we cannot enter into any great enterprises in England, we may yet reap certain positive advantages. We must keep our eye upon works of science, especially of natural history and medicine, while, on the other hand, German editions of the Classics appear to be less used than formerly. Under these circumstances, a longer stay in London is unnecessary, and I hope to be in Hamburgh by the beginning of August."

" Your lamentations do not alarm me," answered Perthes ; " only be contented ; the blessing will not fail us, even in England. We are in good repute there, and the tranquillity which is by degrees winning its way all over Europe, will open to us fresh channels even on that side of the water."

On Besser's return from London in August, 1814, the two friends labored together in right good earnest, and friends far and near assisted them gladly in their constantly recurring pecuniary embarrassments. By Easter, 1815, Perthes and Besser were able to show that they had already discharged all their obligations long before the lapse of the stipulated time, and from that period the house took the important position which it has ever since maintained.

Perthes, however, did not allow the demands of business so entirely to engross his attention as to divert him entirely from the attempts which were being made to reëstablish the old civic constitution. By speech and writing he did as much as his position and the circumstances of the time permitted.

XXI.

Momentous Events.

HILE individuals were laboring like Perthes, each in his own place, to gather up the
links of social life in all parts of Germany,
the sovereigns and princes, the ministers
and diplomatists of Europe were assembling
in Vienna, to settle afresh the great European relations, and especially to reunite the
German states, which since the dissolution of the empire had been very much isolated.

From his home at Hamburgh, Perthes had followed
the course of events with the most lively interest. He
had friends and acquaintances both among those who
actually took part in the business of the Congress,
and among those who were well informed as to their
proceedings, and accordingly his correspondence during this period, and during the war in France, in-
cludes many particulars of interest.

Among the acquaintances of Perthes who attended
the Congress, there were some who regarded with indignation the attitude of Austria, and hotly attacked
Metternich. "Metternich," writes one of these, "can
not leave off the old tricks of his wicked policy; and
in order to secure some advantages for Austria, he favors the desire for an Imperial Commonwealth that is
manifesting itself on the Rhine and in Swabia, the

grasping ambition of the Minister of sovereignty-seeking Bavaria, and, in the smaller States, the wish of the Princes to establish a sort of patriarchal empire, while, at the same time, he has relations with Talleyrand, which might convulse not only Germany but Europe."

Amid all the fluctuating events of the years 1814–15, Perthes adhered firmly to the conviction that the nationality of the Germans was the gift of God, and was independent alike of the good-will or ill-will of those in power ; that it was great and good, and a mighty power on which we might and ought to rely, in spite of all the corrupt and selfish counter-workings of individual princes or merchants, ministers or artisans, soldiers or lawyers. He had already confidently stated his belief that Germany would never rest till it had attained the full recognition of its nationality ; and now, notwithstanding his esteem for the Prussian people, he rejected most unequivocally every proposal that pointed to a merely Prussian development of Germany or of any portion of it.

In the midst of the universal excitement, Perthes on the 8th of April set out for Leipzig to attend the Fair there, after an interval of two years. He found everywhere the greatest consternation prevailing on account of the future fate of Saxony then just determined. But the momentous aspect which European affairs now began to assume, soon diverted the general attention from this unhappy country.

Soon after the return of Perthes from Leipzig, the opposing armies met, and the decisive day drew near. Minds long since exhausted by the perplexities of politics, were now inspired with military ardor.

Two days before the battle of Belle-Alliance, Perthes wrote as follows to Fouqué, who, after a short stay at Hamburgh, had gone to visit the Counts Stolberg and Reventlow : " You have by this time become acquainted with the honored Count Stolberg and his noble consort, and with the pious, humble family at Altenhof.   How gladly would I spend a day with you there !   We would, together, take a cheerful survey of history, and see how a spirited, self-confident, and vigorous youth—brought to God and to humility by grappling and struggling with dangers and difficulties—is about to recover for Germany its ancient free constitution, developed and fortified by the experience of centuries.   I would fain never cease preaching to that perpetual youth, courage, progress, and loving hope. Time broods and ferments long before he takes a step, but then it is a giant's step, which treads many wriggling, creeping worms into the dust ; this must not disturb our faith and trust.   We must step forward, difficult as it may seem, not in proud self-confidence, but beholding with awe how God has forewarned and prepared the world for the step.   It is necessary, however, to fight manfully with those who, shutting their eyes to the truth, would fain avert the course of events, either for the purpose of ruling with despotic sway, or of reposing in selfish ease and enjoyment on the last remaining pillow of a bygone age."

Sooner than any one could have ventured to expect, the hopes of Germany were realized by the victory of Waterloo.   Caroline had been residing for a few weeks at Wandsbeck, and when the first uncertain rumors of a great and decisive battle reached her there, she wrote at once, in the greatest excitement, to Hamburgh.

"Is is true, dear Perthes? Oh, why are you not here, or I with you? Write to me immediately if it be true. I cannot believe it, and stand listening for voices in the air."

Caroline had posted her children on the path leading from Hamburgh, in order to have the first news of the approach of the expected messenger. At length a horseman was seen in the distance advancing at full gallop, and waving a white flag. It was a friend whom Perthes had despatched with the Gazette of the victory, and these words,—"Behold the wonderful works of God; give thanks and praise to Him."

"That is indeed a victory," replied Caroline: "may God help us still further, and may it be without fighting and conquering, if this is not asking too much. You write that Hanbury is shot. Alas! for the poor mother at Flottbeck. But she must bear up; she sees what he has died for."

Events now succeeded each other with wonderful rapidity. "The first great act of the European drama is ended," wrote Perthes on the 20th of June. "Napoleon is dethroned. You will read the rest in the Supplement to the Gazette; the French, if they give up their idol, set the crown on their own degradation. I expect it, and, on this account, I shall illuminate, and not because of the fall of the monster, who has long ago appeared to me as fallen." And again, a few days later,—"In France all is confusion, and this kingdom of hell is going to pieces. What a judgment from God!"

On the 26th of June, he again writes to Caroline,— "Yesterday came the report of the taking of Napoleon, but it is not yet confirmed. Believe me, the person of this monster is not now of the importance that you and half the world imagine. Look at the fate of the French! their present downfall, their terrible prospects! The dispersion of the Jews is nothing in comparison."

The events which had again convulsed Europe had, indeed, driven the citizen from the seclusion of private life, and forced him into the wide circle of political sympathies and affairs. But the individual and his purely human lot retains his significance in a period of political excitement, as well as in a season of political repose. While States are struggling with each other, and conquering or falling, cold and hunger, bodily and spiritual privation, are still inflicting their sufferings on the individual. While great battles are being fought, and great congresses are being assembled, the individual still requires our sympathy with his present and his eternal wants; for even the poor perishing man occupies a far higher place than the State: he is connected with eternity, the State has to do with affairs of earth alone. It would have been no sign of political greatness, but a symptom of moral decay, if MAN, as an individual, had been forgotten in the mighty rising of the War of Independence. In fact, the distress had become everywhere so great, during the eighteen months between the first and the second peace of Paris, and had reached such a height, especially in Hamburgh, that none but the hardest hearts could have been unmoved by it, even amidst all the excitement of political events.

For many months the numerous workmen of all kinds that, in Hamburgh, earned the daily bread of wife and children by daily labor, had, perforce, kept holiday : the whole trade and commerce of that world's emporium had given place to a stillness like that of death. From the moment that labor ceased on the quays and in the warehouses, hunger began to tell upon strong and active men. Thousands had lost home and all, when Davoust had set fire to the suburbs ; and though death had made provision for a large number of the 120,000 of grey-headed and helpless men, women, and children, whom Davoust had driven out of the city in the cold of a December night,* still thousands survived to return, bringing sickness and sorrow with them, and no property of any kind, save what they carried on their persons. To provide food and lodging, and a bed of straw for each, was the least that could be done. Artisans, too, required tools to enable them to resume their work ; while the many petty dealers who ministered to the daily wants of the great city required some capital, however small, to meet their first outlay ; in every corner wants were springing up that craved immediate attention.

The public charities were turned to the best account, and were admirably worked : 148,000 marks were expended annually in alms, clothing, and lodging ; but the distress that had been occasioned by extraordinary circumstances called for extraordinary exertions. Collections were made among the wealthy burghers, and sums, greater or smaller, came in from the different European cities. Distant Malta sent a large sum, and in London Von Hess labored with indefatigable zeal to procure fresh contributions for his unhappy countrymen. A number of the most experienced citizens

---

* In the meadow behind Ottensen 1138 of these lie buried.

distributed the supplies thus sent. Perthes, with a few others, undertook the distribution of the English contributions, and the minute accounts, still preserved, attest the care and conscientiousness with which he discharged this duty.

As the dispenser of these contributions, Perthes had come in contact with individuals who were suffering the extremity of privation, and in every instance he had found that they were suffering from other than mere bodily wants. Thus in September, 1814, he wrote, "I have gathered much valuable experience among the lower classes, and, thank God, I have often found that suffering and sorrow have been the means of rousing many from their former spiritual death, and of awakening in many hearts a sense of divine and eternal things. Hundreds of families would fain seek help and comfort in God, but they know not the way that leads to Him, and, under our former circumstances, *could not* know it. What would our handful of clergy do with this multitude of people? The Bible, too, is known only to few families ; I have found it wanting even in schools."

It was at this time that the London Bible Society, founded in 1804, began to direct its efforts towards Germany. The missionaries Steinkopf and Patterson were first deputed to request that Rambach, Perthes, and Gilbert van der Smissen would form an association in Hamburgh and Altona, for the distribution of Bibles; in the event of their doing so, a contribution of several hundred pounds was promised. Perthes and his friends were well aware, that owing to the tendency of the times, such an undertaking would expose them to the reproach of pietism or mysticism, or some such term of reprobation, and in order to avoid, as far as possible the suspicion of anything clandestine or sectarian, Pethes had recourse to the men who then held the first ecclesiastical and political offices in Hamburgh, and requested their personal coöperation.

On the 6th and 13th of October, 1814, the preliminary meetings were held at Perthes' house ; and on the 19th the Hamburgh-Altona Bible Society was founded. When its twenty-fifth anniversary was celebrated in 1839, the important services which Perthes had rendered to the Society in its infancy were gratefully commemorated.

Perthes regarded the Bible Society as but one of many means for bringing about a revival of religion, and he gladly recognized the labors of those who, in a variety of different ways, were seeking to influence the people. But to make the theatre, although frequented by great numbers of persons who were inaccessible to any other influence, a means of rousing religious feelings, seemed to him more than doubtful. " Be temperate," he wrote to Fouqué, " and don't seek to bring your religious feelings, or rather your convictions regarding our holy religion, on the stage. Life and nature, and therefore destiny, belong to the theatre, but not the consolations of religion. These man must seek in his chamber or in the church, and there God will reveal himself to him."

Popular works by which the dormant Christian consciousness might be revived, Perthes viewed on the other hand as an absolute necessity. Thus he wrote to Fouqué, " We greatly need a national-historical religious catechism for our primary schools, through which our youth may be taught that God made man,

that the human race fell by sin, of the coming of the
Redeemer, and of the means by which Christianity
was spread ; how a way was made for its introduction
by the migrations of the Germanic tribes, how we
Germans, thus born again, advanced in the new world-
career, and how the seed of better times was and is
still preserved among us. I do not understand how
to put it together, but you have it all at your fingers'
ends. It must be short, and in question and answer,
or else in simple propositions. The man who should
give us this would be an unspeakable benefactor in
the sight of God and man."

It was upon the youth of our land, and on their yet
uncorrupted susceptibility, that Perthes built his hopes
of future improvement among the people, and as a
favorable opportunity of advancing their interests now
presented itself, he did not suffer it to pass unimproved.
A committee of twelve was appointed to make an extraordinary collection for the education of the poor of
the city. " We got 30,000 marks at once," he says to
Fouqué, "for the education of poor children, and we
hope to get a great deal more. We twelve have now
gone minutely through the town, and what numbers
of fine children we have found ! The blessing of God
is indeed upon our people. We have taken seven hundred of the destitute children of the city." The Hamburgh schools for the poor, since so widely extended,
owed much to this collection.

That it was possible to form well-organized associations to minister to the temporal and spiritual wants
of our perishing people, was a thought that lay beyond
the horizon of 1814 ; but Perthes regarded with lively
hope the female associations that had been instituted

in Germany during the war, for the purpose of nursing the wounded, and taking care of the widows and orphans of the slain. "Whether two, three, or four German cities shall by these means be henceforward united, no one can tell," he wrote; "but these associations of ladies may certainly do much to unite all Germany in one blessed circle, in spite of all intestine divisions and all future struggles with foreign enemies. They may hold on their way undisturbed, if only they steer clear of all interference with the State, and carefully avoid mixing themselves up with any of the questions of right and wrong, which will have to be determined so soon as peace is reëstablished." .

XXII.

Death of Claudius.

THE anxieties and privations of the year of exile had told severely on Caroline's health. Her freshness and vivacity of mind, however, never forsook her; and on this account she felt only the more painfully the pressure of the bodily disease which had its origin in great excitability of the nervous system, and in an incipient complaint of the heart. "I have not yet recovered my strength and energy," she writes to her friend, Madame Petersen, in Sweden, "and I often find my household duties so heavy, that I almost despair."

But although occasionally depressed, Caroline was neither indifferent nor ungrateful for the many blessings she enjoyed. "The old song is every morning new," she once wrote, "that, if possible, I love Perthes still better than the day before. How inadequate seems all the gratitude I feel for having been permitted to retain him!"

Death was now to be revealed to Caroline in its most solemn form: she was called to attend her father, as he approached that awful moment when time and eternity meet together. Claudius had suffered severely in the years 1813 and 1814. At the age of sever three, he had been driven from the house and home to which he was attached by the happy memories of half a century, to seek an uncertain asylum and a precarious subsistence in Holstein, where he was often exposed to poverty. "We are pretty well off here," he wrote on one occasion to Caroline from Lubeck : "we have a little room, with a bed and a sofa which almost fill it. We cook groats and potatoes for ourselves, but fuel is extravagantly dear. You will have seen in the papers that Wandsbeck is in the hands of the Allies. Fritz is there taking care of our house, and has sold the cow : he writes me that the cellar is, like the universe before Creation, waste and void."

A few weeks later he wrote,—"We are now living in a larger, I might say a large room, but it is very cold, and we have not the means of making and of keeping it warm."

The outward difficulties were great, but it was not these which affected Claudius the most sensibly. "The still vigorous man of seventy-three, had strength to bear all his personal sufferings and the dispersion of his children," says Perthes in a letter of that period ; "but his sincere and patriotic heart was broken by the conflicting emotions and the doubts for his fatherland to which the war with Denmark had given rise. He felt that the exaltation and victory of Germany involved the defeat of his own king, whom he had good reason both to love and honor. This inward struggle, during a season of such violent outward excitement, was too much for the simple mind and the loving heart of the noble old man."

Claudius had returned to Wandsbeck in May, 1814, but never again to enjoy his old home. Wearied with

11

the burden of years, and worn by bodily infirmities, he struggled through summer and autumn. In compliance with the earnest entreaties of his daughter, he removed to Hamburgh in the beginning of December, that he might be within reach of medical advice. "Papa is weary and languid," wrote Caroline, soon after the arrival of her father and mother; " but we have reason to be thankful that he is free from pain. He is so calm and so kindly, I might even say so satisfied and contented, that I am too happy to see this, to give utterance to the grief which I really feel."

It soon became evident that recovery was not to be expected; but life was prolonged for seven weeks,— to Claudius a season of thankfulness and of almost uninterrupted calm and love : the blue sky above, the rising of the sun, the sight of his Rebecca, of his children and grandchildren, were all perpetual sources of enjoyment. One night he called Caroline to his bedside, and said, " I must take something from the night, for the day is too short to thank you, my dear child."

Caroline, writing a few days before his death, says, " He is confident, peaceful, and, except at very short intervals, even joyful. Yesterday, after half an hour of distress from difficulty of breathing, he said to Perthes, ' Well, dear Perthes, this is all just as it should be, though not pleasant.' He then spoke of the approaching struggle, of Him who is mighty to save, and said that he had placed his whole confidence in God. He is wonderfully kind towards us all, and likes our mother to sit by his bed.   He is also anxious that you absent ones should have daily tidings of him, and never fails to send you his greeting."

His mind continued active to the last, and he was

able to trace the daily progress of his own dissolution —of the great mystery of the separation of soul and body. " I have all my life reflected by anticipation on these hours," he said to Perthes, " and now they are come ; but I still understand as little as ever about the manner of the end."

During the last few days he prayed incessantly, and was pleased when he saw the bystanders praying, although he did not like prayers or exhortations to be made aloud. He never relinquished the hope that God would vouchsafe him a glimpse into the realms beyond, while still on this side of the grave ; but although sight was not vouchsafed, his faith was never shaken.

" The 21st of January was the day of his death ; about two o'clock in the afternoon he became aware that his end was approaching, and prayed, ' Lead me not into temptation, and deliver me from evil.' An hour later he said ' Good-night !' several times, and in the moment of departure he opened his eyes, and looked lovingly upon his wife and children, as though they had a right to the last outgoings of affection."

" His mind was quite unimpaired, and he retained all his originality and all his peculiarities to the very last hour," wrote Perthes on the day of his father-in-law's death. " He died without anxiety—I may say, he died rich ; for even in temporal things the fulness of hope was, as usual, at his command. The expression of the whole person is still very striking ; there is an air of weariness, as if he were satisfied and pleased to have done with the earthly ; while the brow still retains the beauty and power, and the mouth all the fulness of affection which characterized them in life. The end of this man was indeed great and noble."

" May God forgive us," writes Nicolovius, " for feeling that such a man could have been better spared in heaven than upon earth."—" Death is a hard step," wrote Caroline, " but to take the step as he did is inconceivably great."

The solemn experiences of these weeks, during the whole of which her husband had been at her side, took deep hold of Caroline's mind ; and with her lively fancy and a heart ever seeking sympathy, she felt it to be a heavy trial, that Perthes, laden with cares, business, and interests of all kinds, could devote so little time to her and the children.   " My hope becomes every day less that Perthes will be able to make any such arrangement of his time as will leave a few quiet hours for me and the children.   There is nothing that I can do but to love him, and to bear him ever in my heart, till it shall please God to bring us together to some region where we shall no longer need house or housekeeping, and where there are neither bills nor books to be paid.   Perthes feels it a heavy trial, but he keeps up his spirits, and for this I thank God."

To these and kindred feelings which she had long cherished in her heart, Caroline now gave expression in letters which she wrote to Perthes during his absence.   After eighteen years of trial and vicissitude, her affection for her husband had retained all its youthful freshness ; life and love had not become merely habitual, they remained fresh and spontaneous as in the bride.   She always gave free utterance to her feelings, in a manner at once unrestrained and characteristic, and felt deeply when Perthes, as a

husband, addressed her otherwise than he had done as
a bridegroom. Now that he was detained for some
weeks in Leipzig, this state of feeling found expression
on both sides, half in jest and half in earnest.

" You have indeed renounced all sensibility for this
year, because of your many occupations," wrote Caroline a few days after her husband's departure ; " but I,
for my part, when I write to you, cannot do so without
feeling ; for the thought of you excites all the feeling
of which my heart is capable. Not a line have I yet
received. Tell me, is it not rather hard that you
never wrote me from Brunswick? At least I thought
so, and felt very much that your companion G. should
have written to his newly-married wife, and you not
to me. It is the first time you have ever gone on a
journey without writing to me from your first resting-
place. I have been reading over your earlier letters
to find satisfaction to myself, in some measure at least,
but it has been a mixed pleasure. Last year, at
Blankenese, you promised me many happy hours of
mutual companionship. I have not yet had them ;
and yet you owe many such to me, yes, you do indeed."

Perthes answered, " You write, telling me that I
have renounced all sensibility for this year. This is
not true, my dearest heart, it is quite otherwise. I
think that after so many years of mutual interchange
of feeling and of thought, and when people understand
each other thoroughly, there is an end of all those little tendernesses of expression, which represent a rela-
tionship that is still piquant because new. Be content
with me, dear child, we understand each other. I did
not write to you from Brunswick, because we passed
through quickly. Moreover, it is not fair to compare

me with my companion, the bridegroom ; youth has its
features and so also has middle age. It would be ab-
surd, indeed, were I now to be looking by moonlight
under the trees and among the clouds for young maidens, as I did twenty years ago, or were to imagine
young ladies to be angels. Nor would it become *you*
any better if you were to be dancing a gallopade, or
clambering up trees in fits of love-enthusiasm. We
should not find fault with our having grown older :
only be satisfied, give God the praise, and exercise
patience and forbearance with me."

"I wish you were here on this your birth-day," answered Caroline on the 21st of April, "and had half an
hour to spare to celebrate it with me and the children.
The children do their best, but you are always yourself, and have ever the first place in my heart. Thank
God, my Perthes, neither time nor circumstances can
ever affect my love to you. It is, indeed, beyond the
reach of change. May God be pleased only to spare
my life and restore my health, and preserve you and
the children, and maintain your love for me unimpaired. It is all I ask ; but there is no end of wishing
and praying, and happily, none too, of granting,—if
not in our own way, at least in God's. Your last letter is, indeed, a strange one. I must again say, that
my affection knows neither youth nor age, and is
eternal. I can detect no change, except that I now
know what formerly I only hoped and believed. I
never took you for an angel, nor do I now take you for
the reverse ; neither did I ever beguile you by assuming
an angel's form or angelic manners. I never danced
the gallopade, or climbed trees, and am now exactly
what I was then, only rather older ; and you must

take me as I am, my Perthes :—in one word, love me, and tell me so sometimes, and that is all I want."

"Your answer," says Perthes, in his next letter, "was just what it ought to have been; only don't forget that my inward love for you is as eternal as yours is for me; but I have so many things to think of. How much of us belongs to earth, and to man ?—how much to heaven? for we belong to both." And so ended the correspondence upon a subject which, perhaps, is not altogether unknown to other married persons.

In the middle of May Perthes returned to Hamburgh, and soon became aware that Caroline's health required serious attention. The physician, Dr. Schröder, an old friend of the family, had told Caroline that her nervous system, although still unimpaired, was over-wrought; and that by stimulating the bodily powers to exertions beyond their strength, she was gradually preparing the way for disease. A change of scene was desirable, and Caroline, with her younger children, went to pass the summer of 1815 at Wandsbeck with her mother.

During this period, almost daily letters were exchanged between her and her husband. While those of Perthes were devoted to warnings and entreaties to take care of her health, the few lines in which Caroline was wont to reply, were full of expressions of love, and of sorrow on account of their necessary separation.

"I am seated in the garden," she writes, "and all my merry little birds around me. I let the sun shine upon me, and make me well if he can. God grant it! if it only be so far as to enable me to discharge my duties to my family; for I feel myself too unhappy as

a mere cipher." And again, " I hope, my dear Perthes,
that you will again have pleasure in me ; the waters
seem really to do me good. Come to-morrow, only
not too late. My very soul longs for you."—" You
shall be thanked for the delightful hours that I enjoyed
with you yesterday," she wrote after a short visit to
Hamburgh, " and for the sight of your dear, kind face,
as I got out of the carriage."—" I only live when you
are with me," she writes a few days later ; " send Matthias to me if it does not interfere with his lessons ; if
I cannot have the father, I must put up with the son."

"The children enjoy their freedom, and are my joy
and delight : alas! for those who have none ! " she
says after telling some childish adventures. " But you,
dear old father ! you, too, are my joy and delight.
Let me have a little letter ; I cannot help longing for
one, and will read it when I get it ten times over.
Pray don't forget the poor people in the mud-huts at
Hamm : the house is easily found, it is in the lane, opposite to something particular, but I cannot remember
exactly what."

With many fluctuations of health, Caroline had passed the time at Wandsbeck ; August had now come,
and with it was brought vividly before her mind the
many years of happiness she had spent with Perthes.

" It is eighteen years to-day," she writes, " since I
wrote you the last letter before our marriage, and sent
you my first request about the little black cross. I
have asked for many things in the eighteen years that
have passed since then, dear Perthes, and what shall I
ask to-day ? You can tell, for you know me well, and
know that I have never said an untrue word to you.
Only you cannot quite know my indescribable affection,

for it is infinite. Perthes, my heart is full of joy and
sadness—would that you were here! This day eighteen years ago I did not long for you more fervently
or more ardently than now. Thank God over and
over again for everything! I am and remain yours in
in time, and, though I know not how, in eternity
too! Be well pleased, if you come to-morrow. Affection is certainly the greatest wonder in heaven or
on earth, and the only thing that I can represent to
myself as unsatiable throughout eternity."

In the middle of August Caroline returned to Hamburgh, and although not fully restored to health, she
was yet able, with sundry interruptions, to superintend
the large household, and to continue to minister comfort and joy, support and assistance, to many persons
of different classes and ages.

We have already seen the alienation that had arisen
between Niebuhr and Perthes, when in 1814 the latter
had regarded Niebuhr as exclusively Prussian rather
than German in his political sympathies. In 1815 he
had bitterly attacked Niebuhr's answer to Schmalz, as
written from a merely Prussian point of view. These
violent political contests between the former friends
seemed to offer little probability of a renewal of friendship ; and on this account it was with no small emotion and pleasure, that Perthes received the following
lines from that great and noble man, written shortly
before his departure for Rome in the spring of 1816 :
—" Dearest Perthes, I would not willingly impoverish
myself, or part poorer than inexorable destiny may
have decreed. That destiny has beggared me in those

11*

nearest friendships in which but one short year since I felt myself so inconceivably rich.   Three days ago was the anniversary of my father's death, with which sad day the destruction of my possessions began.   My friendships I know have suffered from passion and irritability ;—let all be forgotten between us, and let every misunderstanding be removed before I leave my native land.   Will you accept this?"

XXIII.

Journey to Frankfort-on-the-Main.
1816.

PERTHES had never regarded the book-trade merely as a means of subsistence and of personal gain; he had always looked upon it as one of the institutions by means of which spiritual vitality is maintained in a nation. His business had indeed secured to him a comfortable livlihood and an independent position; but he never forgot, in the enjoyment of these advantages, that it also involved the responsibility of quickly discerning and diligently supplying the literary wants of the nation within the sphere of 'his own business operations. It is in this perpetual and practical recognition of the indissoluble union existing between his private interests and the public welfare that we detect the secret of the success that, to the end of his life, attended all his undertakings. In 1816, he believed that the time was come when the German book-trade stood in need of a fresh impulse and a partial transformation.

In furtherance of this object he resolved to undertake a journey, hoping to extend his business connexions and at the same time to effect a more cordial and fraternal union between North and South Germany, with regard to the book-trade.

On Friday the 19th of July, Perthes left Hamburgh in company with his son Matthias, then sixteen years of age, with the intention of travelling by way of Cologne, Frankfort, and Munich, to Vienna.

"Our journey has been prosperous thus far," he writes from Bremen. "The night was clear and mild, and the postilions were good. The carriage is convenient, and holds me and our boy very comfortably. I am somewhat fatigued in mind and body; the labors and efforts of the last two years, coming immediately after the terrible anxieties of the fearful time that preceded them, have shaken me. To you, my beloved Caroline, I know not what to say concerning our present separation, but that I believe I am going where God calls me. I commit you and the children to His protection."

Perthes travelled without stopping to Münster, where he meant to stay some days. "It is sad," he writes, "to see the fine Chaussée, made by the French with German money and German labor, entirely neglected by the Hanoverian government; the displaced stones are left by the wayside, and in many places between Bremen and Brinkum, for instance, it is impossible to travel by night; yet the tolls are everywhere exacted. Till you approach Osnabrück, the country is dreary and tedious; towards Böhmte it is more interesting. Here we drove to see the oak of a thousand years. Its circumference at the base is twenty paces. This giant of antiquity stands towering to the sky, but bears neither bark, branches, nor boughs; on one side only where a vein of living sap still runs, the trunk is

covered with tender green sprouts ; a touching sight
this monument of grey antiquity, standing like some
ancient watch-tower, clothed with clustering ivy.   It
is a pleasing custom they have here of giving proper
names to horses.   The horse is a noble and intelligent
animal, and quite as deserving of such a distinction as
the dog ; and when it has a name, it has made some
advance towards personality."

"Here I am once more in old Münster," he says in
another letter, "and find it as usual, devotional and
lively.   Yesterday, at noon, July 22d, we arrived, and
as we alighted I saw Count Joseph Westphalen, riding
across the Square, and I am sorry to say about to
leave the town, but we enjoyed a quarter of an hour's
cordial communion : after this I inquired for our old
friends, and paid many visits.   Bishop Droste is on a
journey, but is expected back to-morrow.   I was invited to the President von Vincke's, and found several
members of the council of Münster there, and a few
also from Minden.   The conversation was animated
and unrestrained, and the men seemed to me to be of
the right German sort, simple, intelligent, and well-
intentioned : Vincke bears the impress of a gifted
man, capable of accomplishing much by the union of
power and promptitude.   In his carriage and his ges-
tures he often reminds me of Niebuhr, while in acuteness, solidity, and genuine German character, he may
be compared with Möser."

"Early this morning, July 24," he writes to Caroline, "the dear Bishop took me to his house, which,
though comfortably, is very simply fitted up.   We were
alone for two hours, and spoke together with perfect
openness.   We understand each other, though on cer-

tain important points we are not on the same track. He is calm, stedfast, decided, and liberal in the best sense, for his liberality is the fruit of love. I went with him to visit his brother Clement, and thence to call on the other brother, Canon Francis, where we met Katerkamp and the vigorous old Vicar Konrad, who now has a living in the country ; the venerable Overberg, alas! I did not see, for he was travelling. The hours that I spent in the society of these men will always live in my memory : it did one good to look at the three brothers. Clement is matured in every quality which can call forth respect, is full of fire and energy, simple and sure : Francis is talented, acute, and lively. They are all alike distinguished by honesty of purpose and purity of heart, and in each the outer man reflects what is within. It is an advantage to the Roman Catholic Church to have men of social distinction among its priesthood, but they must be of the right sort. Clement has lately returned from Rome, and is laboring zealously for the freedom of the Church, ' in order,' as he says, ' that aspirations after divine things, and the free movement of the higher spiritual life, may not be subjected to the supervision of the State and the control of the police.' In a higher ecclesiastical position he might become too dependent on Rome to work freely."

"On the 24th of July we left Münster," says Perthes in another letter. "From Hagen, which we reached next morning, the country assumes an aspect unusual in Germany. In the valley, which is about two miles broad, with a number of lateral valleys opening into it, lie closely crowded together factories and mills and smithies, all encircled by trim gardens.

The slopes of the low hills are covered with corn, the summits with wood. For four hours we travelled through this wealthy district, till we got to Schwelm, and looked from the height into the Wupperthal, and down on a little clustering town. From the summit the view of the valley is very striking,—the hills crowned with wood, and their declivities clothed with grain, or adorned with emerald meadows, here white as snow, there with a purple hue, or glittering in various colors according to the dyes of the outspread manufactured stuffs, and far below, on the banks of the Wupper, lordly mansions, with their fine flower-gardens and luxurious and sometimes tawdry decorations ; the fruits of that incredible manufacturing activity which will be the grave of our character, our morals, and our power. The children work in the factories from eight, or even six years of age ; become cripples and beget cripples ; and the efforts of the so-called pietists to put a stop to this style of things have hitherto been as unsuccessful as the exertions of the government."

It was at Düsseldorf, and by the light of a fine sunset, that Perthes first saw the Rhine. "The glorious river makes a grand impression," he says ; " it is true that, like the Elbe at Hamburgh, it flows through a level country. I should not say flows, but *streams* impetuously, for there is a vast difference ; yet the Rhine can never form so beautiful a mirror as the Elbe occasionally does. We have now, my beloved Caroline, the Elbe, the Weser, the Ems, the Ruhr, and soon we shall have the Rhine, too, between us ; but love and devotion recognize no boundaries. Be confident. Your glances into the past, and fearful and hopeful longings, are in-

deed guarantees for the great future beyond the grave ;
yet do not forget that a vigorous grasp of the present
is our duty so long as we are upon earth. It is the
present moment that supplies the energy and decision
which fit us for life. Retrospect brings sadness, and
the dark future excites fears, so that we should be crip-
pled in our exertions were we not to lay a vigorous
grasp upon the present."

Perthes passed some days in the family of his brother-in-law, Max Jacobi, who had lately exchanged the
post of Director of the great Hospital at Salzburg, for
that of State-councillor at Düsseldorf. They had not
met since 1808, and in reminiscences of the great
events in midst of which both had lived, the hours
passed quickly away. It was with deep emotion that,
at Pempelfort, Perthes looked on the spot, where in
bygone times, before the stormy season of the first revolutionary war, Frederick Henry Jacobi had formed
the centre of a highly cultivated circle, and had received as his guests, Goethe, Herder, Lavater, Hamann, Schlosser, Heinze, the Princess Gallitzin, and so
many others : and thus in recollections of the past,
rather than in observation of the present, the time was
spent in Düsseldorf. But the general impression that
even the passing traveller almost inevitably receives,
was not favorable to the inhabitants of this town.
" There is an appearance of restlessness and incon-
stancy in the countenance, bearing, and manners of the
people ; their features are not well defined, and they
do not look like men whom one would choose as associates in a time of peril."

" Hoffmann and Keetmann accompanied us to Benrath,
a summer palace, commanding a fine prospect, where

Murat, when Grand-Duke of Berg, used to pass much of his time; thence we travelled through an exuberance of fruitfulness, by Mülheim and Deutz to Cologne."

"It is difficult to give you any idea of Cologne," he writes in a letter to Caroline, "for all is so new to us—men, manners, and customs, the city, the houses, and the institutions. We have already seen much that is grand and beautiful, and also much that is comic. Don't be alarmed at our having become somewhat Catholic: in the cathedral there was a service against the rain, and at night there were torch-light processions, the priests praying aloud. and were we travellers to keep aloof? As soon as we arrived, we wandered through the city. The streets, lanes, and alleys, very appropriately called *Spargassen*, are strangely intricate and perplexing. Houses of all periods, antiquities of all ages, are here seen side by side; in a few paces you walk through the history of the old Roman times. The Colognese dwell among the stones and the ruins of fifteen hundred years; they are distinguished by peculiarity of dialect, carriage, and manners. On the street floor most of the houses have only a counting-house or shop with a dark room at the back; above are warehouses and large rooms without windows, the frequent dwelling-place of the bat and the owl. But on passing through the ground-floor to the back of the house, you find well-built. spacious rooms, in which the family live as quietly as if they were in the country, and which frequently open into large gardens surrounded by venerable walls festooned with ivy and other climbing plants. We saw a number of small houses built against the old Roman city wall, and clustered together in mid air, like swallows' nests. How many generations with their joys and sorrows have passed away within them! But amid the ruins of the past we were pleasantly re-minded of the present by a glass case, protected by wire-work like a parrot's cage, and containing three merry and fine-looking children, which was let down upon us as we passed under a window. These floating children's rooms are hung out of the windows in the sunshine, or when there is anything to be seen.—We went to the cathedral on the day of our arrival though it was already half dark ; our cicerone unceremoni-ously tapped on the shoulder a very old priest, who was kneeling and praying diligently, and the old man rose at once from his knees, in order to do the honors of the cathedral to us, while the cicerone knelt down in his place, and carried on the prayers. To-day we went again for the third time to the cathedral. On entering the choir, every one is expected to drop his alms. What honor has been conferred upon man in making him the instrument by which the Spirit of God produces such wonderful works! It is impossible to write about it. St. Peter's has now recovered the pic-ture of the Crucifixion of Peter, painted by Rubens, and presented by him to this church in which he was baptized. It was taken to Paris by the French, but I am afraid that the barbarity which did not scruple to tear even this precious legacy from the very altar will soon be forgotten by the inhabitants. This morning, after visiting the Wallraff collection of Colognese an-tiquities, *where I might have learned much if I had known more*, we went to the house of Schauberg the bookseller, a very well-informed and highly cultivated man, and there met Professor Wallraff, State-councillor von Harthausen, Captain Birsch, and a Herr de Groot.

Several hours passed rapidly away in animated conversation; Catholicism and Protestantism being among the subjects discussed. On my mentioning the incident of the cicerone and the priest, and referring to similar indecencies of daily occurrence in Catholic churches, I was told that it was the office of this priest to show the relics, and that whether praying or not, he must needs be always ready to discharge the functions of his office; that among Catholics it was the custom to treat God with familiarity, as a father, and thus they could occasionally put Him on one side with child-like confidence, while Protestants who, on the contrary, always make an effort when they pray, must be on ceremony with Him as they would with some stranger of rank! This reminded me of the drunken Catholic peasants who, before they begin to fight, with a similar confiding spirit, put the crucifix under the table, that the Lord may not be a witness to the scandal!"

On the 31st of July, Perthes left Cologne for Godesberg. "At Godesberg," he writes, "there is a mineral bath. Everybody is dispirited by the incessant rain. I am determined to be cheerful, for the enjoyment of nature was not the object of my journey; yet the farmers have but too much cause for uneasiness. All have failed—corn, grapes, and fruit—and the prospect is dreary enough: 'Believe me,' said an intelligent man, 'the winter of 1816–17 will bring famine.'"

Perthes reached Coblentz on the 1st of August, and early on the following morning, the anniversary of his wedding, wrote to Caroline:—"You are awake I am sure, and looking towards me as I to you. We have known fulness of joy in our nineteen years of wedded life, and have also experienced much trouble and sorrow ; God be praised for both! I again hold out my hand to you, beloved one! for the years that are yet appointed to us ; let us meet them bravely. Matthias is just awake, and he, too, greets his mother. The day is breaking : the dark majestic rock of Ehrenbreitstein rises in the east and hides the sun, which, nevertheless, casts kindly rays athwart into the valley that winds between the heights, while a thick grey mist is still brooding over the rushing Rhine in the plain beneath."

"This morning," he says in a letter written on the evening of the same day, "I went to Görres.* He is a tall, well-made man, energetic and plain-spoken, but withal somewhat affected. The genial spirit and the kindling fancy appear at once. In figure he reminds me of Benzenberg. only he looks abler ; he speaks like Steffens. I found him alone ; his wife was at the bleaching-field with a great washing ; she came in afterwards—a cordial, unaffected, and very amiable woman, with a good, clear intellect. The children were with her, a very pretty girl of fifteen—a frank, lively boy of twelve, whom I would gladly have taken with me, and another little wild girl ; altogether an amiable family, and a well-ordered burgher household, simple and beautifully clean. Everything bears the impress of Görres' strong moral sense ; the same cannot be said of all gifted men. At noon we went in company with him and President Meusebach to the Procurator-General Eichhorn, and afterwards Görres

---

* J. J. Gorres was born at Coblentz in 1776. He was celebrated as a political orator, and was for some time editor of a Journal called "Das Rothe Blatt." He held an eminent place among the politicians of the time. In 1827 he was appointed to the Chair of History in Munich.

and the President accompanied us to Ehrenbreitstein, and like experienced guides, showed us, through the chinks of the demolished fortress, wonderfully fine glimpses of the vale below. Meusebach was delighted with Matthias, and chased him from rock to rock. This Görres was pleased to call a mere literary predilection for the grandson of Claudius, whom, indeed, the President does not deem sufficiently honored till his works are printed in grand folio volumes, instead of in their present octavo form, or else written on parchment! Among these antiquarian gentlemen, the value of a book is determined by the antiquity of the form, by the type, and the binding. The evening was spent in cheerful society at Görres' house."

In the house of Görres and all along the Rhine, at that time, there was no escaping political discussion. "The dinner to-day was very animated and interesting," says Perthes in his next letter from Coblentz. "Meusebach and a hard-headed old knight of the iron cross* formed the Prussian party *versus* the Rhenish-Görres, and set down all the liberal ideas and institutions developed by the Revolution as 'Napoleonism,' declaring that that was what the Rhenish people loved and would fain have back again. 'You are Lithuanians,' cried Görres from the other side of the table— 'Lithuanians with the fetters of serfdom yet hanging about your heels.' This mutual esteem between Prussian and Rhenish does not appear to me to be limited to the intercourse of the table. The Rhenish are, however, genuine Germans in spite of their twenty

---

* The iron-cross was a decoration conferred on those who had fought in the war of Independence.

years' subjection to France ; although, of the Germany
on the other side Frankfort they know nothing whatever. They regard their own concerns as all-important, their own as the only beautiful country, and
theirs as the only liberal ideas : to them barbarism
begins where Frankfort ends, and they only take occasional cognizance of what lies beyond, and then with a
kind of condescending compassion. I like the Colognese best ; with all their petty State notions there
mingles somewhat of the great City-feeling of olden
times when cities were principalities. They, and they
alone, have a history, and therefore are entitled to self-
respect. It will be hard for Prussia to win over
Düsseldorf and Coblentz ; there is an unsteadiness
about the people, and a disposition to gainsay everything, even in matters of religion. Catholicism is well
adapted to Münster and Westphalia : it is at home
there, and appears as the growth of the soil ; but on
the Rhine it is like an exotic, or something ingrafted
or assumed, and therefore a mere external ornament.
It was in the midst of this state of things that our Protestant Bible Society began its work of furnishing
Catholics with Bibles, and this often by means which,
if adopted by Catholics, we should style Jesuitical
and proselytizing. The future welfare of the country
and its position with respect to Prussia depend greatly
on the personal character of the bishops who are about
to be appointed. Kaspar, Droste, and Sailer are mentioned. What an infinite amount of labor and of influence they might take from the government if they
were inclined! This evening I have taken leave of
Görres. The force of his understanding must be evident to every one who hears him speak ; but there is

great confusion in his views. His letters and his
writings had prepared me for hasty conclusions, start-
lings paradoxes, flights of fancy and of wit, but not
for his often self-contradictory and really revolutionary arguments.   Görres does not know what he wants.
The elements of the positive are in him, but the district, the time, and the city in which he lives, have ingrafted on it a spirit of opposition which is not worthy
of him.   Beyond the limits of Frankfort and Heidelberg, he, like the rest, is absolutely unacquainted with
our fatherland."

In order to speak with Baron von Stein, Perthes
chose the route by Ems and Wiesbaden, rather than
that by Bingen and Mainz.   "On leaving Ems," he
writes, " you see on a hill that rises before you the
ruins of the castle that was the cradle of the Nassau
race, and beneath, raised upon a rocky eminence, the remains of the castle of Stein.   In the valley below, the
Lahn winds its way through charming meadow lands,
and in a narrow bend of the stream lies the little town
of Nassau, and near it Stein's present castle.   I sent
in my name, and was received by him in a very friendly
manner, and recognized as an old acquaintance, on account of our meeting here in December, 1813.   He requested me to sit down.   ' You are going to Vienna ?
What do you want there ?   What do you want with
me ?'   Assuredly, he who did *not* know precisely what
he wanted with Stein, would very quickly find himself
outside of the door.   I explained my views and intentions in few words, and he went into the whole
affair at once, heart and soul.   He then asked me
about the Hanse-towns, and whether any fresh blood
had found its way into the Hamburgh Senate,—the

perukes he had once seen there had made no pleasing impression.

Görres, he said, was a genius, a learned and upright man, but he would not listen to counsel, though the Chancellor had done his utmost to keep him within bounds ; finally, that both in and out of Prussia there were blunders and evils, and so it had ever been, and so it would be to the end of the world. 'Nevertheless, even in Frankfort,' he added, ' you will see that good also is in store for Germany, and, therefore, for Europe ; for the present conservators of freedom—the English—will hardly continue so much longer.' Stein invited me to dinner, and on my refusal, accompanied me to the door, in order to show me a stone tower in process of erection. On my saying, ' that will be a Zwing-Uri, not *against* the people, but *for* them,' he laughed heartily, and shook my hand, and thus I left a man, who, after a world-wide experience, is yet open to every new impression ; and who though so many of his schemes have foundered, and though he has been so often compelled by the will of the Prince, or by an unfavorable majority in the council, to withdraw his plans for the progress of the people, is still full of hope. We got on afterwards as far as Wiesbaden, and this morning, August the 4th, arrived in Frankfort."

XXIV.

Perthes' Letters to Caroline.

T Frankfort, Perthes found letters informing him of the sudden and serious illness of Caroline. He had resolved on a hasty return, when, in a letter from Caroline herself, he was assured that all danger was over. "How can I thank you for your letters," she wrote, "and for the lively enjoyment that they afford me? If I were not altogether yours, I would now give myself to you anew. You cannot conceive how thankful I am. To-day I have another letter, while I am still enjoying those from Cologne and Coblentz. They are living pictures of your inner life, and of all that you are seeing and doing, and are inexpressibly dear to me. Often I can scarcely persuade myself that it is only a narrative, it is so exactly as if I were present at all you describe. Ruben's picture of Peter hangs before me day and night, and yet it is too terribly beautiful to have always before my eyes. I am also thankful to God for keeping you so well, after so many years of wearing labor."

His mind set at rest by this letter, Perthes could now surrender himself without anxiety to the manifold impressions of Frankfort life. "I did not find one of my personal friends here on my arrival," he says, "and was consequently obliged to make my own way; and

12   (265)

first I sought out Frederick Schlegel, whom, notwithstanding our long correspondence, I had never seen. He is a fat, round man, with very bright eyes, which, nevertheless, look coldly out : he has shortness in his manner, which you may call straightforwardness if you will. He gave a very friendly reception, and yet I did not feel myself constrained to open my heart to him. I passed the evening at his house in company with Buchholz ; you remember this accomplished, amiable southron of 1813. Frau von Schlegel made a very favorable impression on me. She may, indeed, have passed through a hard apprenticeship ; but she seems to me to have won the victory, and appears to be an unassuming, sensible woman.

Among those who were accounted the most zealous Protestants, Perthes found almost as much to dissent from as among the Catholic circles of Frankfort. "I shall name first the Senator J. F. von Meyer," he writes, "the same who, under the signature Imo, wrote the criticisms in the Heidelberg Annual, on Jacobi, Goethe, and Claudius, which so much charmed us. I met him with feelings of respectful anticipation, but quickly found myself repulsed, and in a few minutes involved in a violent argument with him. You see at once that he is a man of talent and weight ; but he is ever ready to do battle for petty points of controversy, in support of which he has an infinite number of texts at his fingers' ends. He is undoubtedly a man of piety, and full of genuine humility towards God, but what he says, he says in the name of God, and carries it very proudly towards men. To him Rome is Antichrist, Stolberg a castaway, who does not know what the grace of God is ; every other Christian community is good only when compared with Rome, in other respects they have only the external form of Christianity."

Wilhelm von Humboldt, an old personal acquaintance, received Perthes with great cordiality, and took up the book-trade question with zeal. After an afternoon passed in his family circle, in company with the Secretary of Legation, Count Flemming, and Von Bülow, Perthes wrote, "There is a wonderful atmosphere about a really great man; nowhere do we feel so much at home; nowhere does one feel so free and happy. Through all the light play of conversation, in which he takes quite an equal share with his wife, the real, actual greatness of Wilhelm von Humboldt comes out, and I am confirmed in my old opinion, so often laughed at, that under an ice-cold exterior, and a keen-edged sarcasm, this man conceals deep and warm feelings, and a lively interest in Germany."

At the end of a week Perthes prepared to leave Frankfort. "I am," he wrote, "so thoroughly tired of eating and drinking, of speaking and hearing, and of the exuberance of talent and wit which I have here encountered, that although there are still influential men I would fain see, I have determined to depart. I have received letters of all kinds for Vienna. Schlegel, whom I met this morning at breakfast at Smidt's, after partaking of some fresh herrings that our host had just received from Bremen, asked me, on my conscience, whether I was not a Freemason, or a member of some other secret society, and when I said I was not, he commended me to the Director of the Police at Vienna, Councillor von Ohms. And now for the southern Tetrarchy—Darmstadt, Baden, Würtemberg, and Bavaria."

As he left Frankfort on the 12th of August at noon, Perthes cast a last look, from the Sachsenhaüser Tower, across the broad plain, with its innumerable towns and villages, watered by the silver stream, and stretching itself in luxuriant fertility at the foot of the Taunus range. "It is from this point," he says, "that one first learns to appreciate the splendid situation of Frankfort. How many memories of former times, and of its grand old history, are awakened as one looks upon the outspread city; and how many conflicting efforts in which the welfare of Germany and of Europe are involved, are now mutually clashing there! Immediately on leaving the Sachsenhaüser Tower, you are in the Darmstadt territory, which is like a piece of patchwork. Here—the capital with the original domains of the Landgrave—in the distance isolated Giessen, and, on the other side of the Rhine, Electoral Mainz, with a portion of the Archiepiscopal territory. The little place seems to have been bent on great things, for the gates are a mile and a half from the city. But though the greatness is yet unachieved, things seem in good order, and much has been done to promote science and literature. I went to Leske the bookseller, and asked him if he could tell me where Claudius had formerly lived? 'Here, in this room,' he replied. 'My house was the printing-office of the journal which was begun under the superintendence of Claudius, for the benefit of the invalids.' Late in the evening I saw the house again. The moon was shining brightly, and I thought of the little Caroline who had played here so many years ago. On the well-known Bergstrasse between Darmstadt and Heidelberg, we were met by large parties of emigrants, whom a characteristic restlessness

drives from this earthly paradise to the barren steppes
of Russia. On the other hand, what numbers of peasants from the Breisgau* flock hither for the harvest!
We encountered a large party of these reapers talking
a simple Hebel† language. The girls, with their pretty
faces, short petticoats, and short morals, were quite
on simple Old Testament terms with the lads who accompanied them. The Heidelberg students who find
their way into this Canaan, must have a hard time of
it."

At Heidelberg Perthes passed three days full of interest and instruction. His first visit was to Professor Thibaut, whom he had known at Kiel. Under his
guidance he saw the castle and the Königs-stuhl, and
feasted his eyes on the fine outlines and luxuriant
verdure of the mountains. He was particularly struck
with the graceful melancholy of the weeping willow,
which there attains a size and height unknown in
North Germany; while the famous Vat delighted him
as a specimen of genuine German humorous folly. At
the house of Mohr, the bookseller, he spent a pleasant evening in company with Daub and Kreutzer, with
whom he had no previous acquaintance. To his great
delight he also met Pastor Zimmer, who had formerly
served in his own warehouse, and had left him to establish a business of his own in Heidelberg. Amid
all the hindrances of a laborious business life, he had
acquired the classical languages, studied theology,
passed his examinations, and had now assumed the
priestly office in Worms. " When I see my dear Zim-

---

* A district of Baden, in which wooden clocks and toys are made.

† A writer of great naïveté and simplicity.

mer, I feel proud of human energy ; we see in him
what a man is capable of accomplishing, when he is
resolved."

Voss, also, was one of Perthes' early personal acquaintances ; and on the day after his arrival he went
to visit him, anxious to know his manner of bearing
himself in his altered circumstances. "Voss has a
healthy look," he writes, "and what was decaying in
him has passed into the tough ; but Ernestine is worse,
and does not look as if she would live long. I received a kind and friendly welcome from both, and a
cordial greeting for you. The old man took me into
his garden, and was very amiable among the flowers.
At first he spoke patriarchal *Luisisms** about God's
beautiful nature, about flowers and plants, old times
and simple-hearted men ; and then, suddenly, at the
mention of Fouqué's name, gave expression to a spirit
of hatred which I was really terrified to see in the old
man. ' Ah !' he exclaimed, ' that Fouqué, who has misled the whole crew of booby priests and aristocrats, is
seeking to make Catholics of them, as he has done of
Stolberg !' He next inveighed furiously against the
worthless spirit of the Mecklenberghers and the Hol-
steiners ; then attacked Claudius, and said, it was his
intention to publish an edition of the 'Wandsbeck
Messenger,' in which all the priestly legends should be
expunged, which he said had been the suggestion of
the dark spirit of superstition. I was silent for a
while ; but to this last sally I replied, that I, on the
contrary, was thinking of publishing a new edition of

---

* Voss had, in his youth, written a sentimental Idyl, called " Luise."
Vide p. 76.

Stolberg's ' History of Religion,' to the extent of several thousand copies, believing that I should have
cause to congratulate myself on the speculation, not
only as a matter of business, but as one that was likely to have a great and good influence throughout the
whole of Catholic Germany.   Upon this the old man
said, that he had read nothing of Stolberg's since his
apostasy.   I then endeavored to turn the conversation,
for I do not willingly speak of Catholics, or of the
Catholic Church, except with those who have themselves received the faith of Christ in all humility.
With such persons we can contemplate, from a firm
and intelligible stand-point, the various forms in which
the spirit of Christianity has expressed itself ; but
with a man who is ever revolving in the circle of
his own self-constructed religious system, it is nothing but idle or passionate disputation.   After dinner,
Voss went with me alone into the garden ; he hastily
ran over a string of names, adding to each some epi-
thet, such as ' sneaking fellow, mischief-making trai-
tor, scoundrel,' &c.   At last, I got up and ran away.   I
would not answer the worthy old man as he deserved,
and I felt that I ought not to be silent.   Believe me, in
spite of all the domestic spirit and garden joys that are
visible here, there reigns in this house a spirit of hatred
that has surprised and deeply pained me."

It was not alone in Voss's house that Perthes observed the presence of a prevailing spirit of bitterness, which, manifesting itself as it did chiefly in political questions, caused him deep anxiety for the future.
" It is as if scales had fallen from my eyes," he says ;
I was in no wise prepared for such scenes.   Here,
when, during the reign of Napoleon, circumstances

might have justified some exhibition of political hatred, it was scarcely known, and now it rages with wildest fury against their own government. For the first time, I understand much that I heard and overheard at Frankfort.

"In an hour we leave for Stuttgart. I should have remained here some days longer, for one can hardly see the game these men are playing so well elsewhere : but notwithstanding all this wonderful beauty of scenery, I am oppressed and dispirited. There are few here who recognize in their lives, fewer still in their words, the mystery of love in its uniting and saving energy, the point to which the inexhaustible goodness of God is ever leading us back. The moral nature becomes rank through license, and the spirit hardened ; and although there are many who have escaped the snares of sensuality, there are few who have been delivered from those of pride. Here, in this earthly paradise, grief and dejection have overtaken me. Tonight we put up at Heilbronn."

From Stuttgart, where he remained from the 18th to the 20th of August, Perthes continues his narative : —" I passed a night of the wildest fever-fancies at Heilbronn ; body and mind were both over-excited by personal fatigue, by speaking and hearing, and the experience gained at Heidelberg had impressed me deeply. But the fresh and glorious morning chased away the spectres of the night, and, refreshed in spirit, we drove through the valley of the Neckar, a valley so highly cultivated, that the artisan can scarcely find a spot to settle in undisturbed. I heard of nothing but the apportioning of lands, and emigration. We reached Stuttgart at noon. Cotta drove us to see the fine en-

virons, and with this remarkable man, in whom the
greatest contradictions meet, I passed the evening.
On Sunday morning I called on the Medical-councillor
Jäger—he was absent ; then on the Russian Ambassador, Von Strüve—gone to church ; to Von Wangenheim—not at home ; then to the Parade—which *was*
at home. I dined at Cotta's with a small circle of
very interesting men, among whom was Wangenheim,
whom I had known long ago at Gotha, as a wild
youth. His imposing person, all covered with decorations, offers a singular contrast to his careless manner of
presenting himself. Full of talent, he is apt to be overtaken in conversation by flights of fancy, and to hurry
his hearer with him over hill and dale up to the clouds
of speculation, and down into the depths of human nature. In his place, I should not have spoken so freely as
he did of public affairs. Yesterday afternoon and this
morning I spent in calling on many distinguished people. This country is truly in an extraordinary and
perilous situation. Its princes are possessed of a
kind of heathen greatness—wicked and powerful ; just
such as men in the olden times required as rulers, in
order to keep them quiet. As to personal affection
for the king, that is not to be thought of. A Stuttgarder said to me with evident pride, ' Our princes
have always been wicked fellows, and have deserved
to occupy even higher thrones.' The people of Würtemberg are proud of the vastness of their palaces, the
magnificence of their gardens, the beauty of their theatre, and of their model highways. They are proud
that their king should have better horses and dogs
than any other king ; that he is the best shot known,
and that, what he wills, he accomplishes in spite of any

amount of opposition from his subjects. Every Stuttgarder knows, and makes no secret of it, that the wildest beast in the whole menagerie of kings has fallen to his share. Freedom of speech is at the same time so unlimited, that I could not write the half of what was told me openly close under the palace windows. Order reigns supreme ; the ministers appear to be honorable men, and are so situated as to be kept out of the range of popular hatred, the burden of which the king takes pleasure in keeping to himself, by a series of offensive and tyrannical enactments. In vigorous and determined opposition to this powerful prince, stand the Constitutionalists, regarding the voice of the country as the voice of God, and looking neither to right nor left ; while between them, the world, with its selfishness, its corrupt principles, and its interested views, plays a cunning and wicked game."

XXV

𝕽𝖊𝖙𝖚𝖗𝖓 𝖙𝖔 𝕳𝖆𝖒𝖇𝖚𝖗𝖌𝖍.—1816.

CORRESPONDENCE CONTINUED.

N the 20th of August, Perthes left Stuttgart, and travelled by way of Esslingen, Geislingen, and Ulm, to Augsburg. In spite of the hurried journey, he found abundance of material for observation among a country and a people, which, to a North German, were foreign. He halted for a few days at Augsburg, attracted by the social life of this old, art-loving, imperial city.

"On the 21st, at noon," he writes to Caroline, "we drove to the magnificent hotel of the Three Moors, and in the course of the afternoon I visited several book and map-sellers, and have wearied myself yesterday and to-day with walking and listening. Augsburg is a large and handsome city, but it does not impress one with the idea of antiquity. There is not a single public building, and but few private houses, that date from our great architectural era. Centuries of prosperity have enabled the inhabitants to renovate their dwellings according to the fashions of the day. It is within the houses and in the mode of conducting business that we find the family manners and customs of ancient artistic Augsburg. I am much mistaken if we are not here among a spirited and determined population, hard to bend or to break : we find here 'originals' in character and even wild eccentricities. At the present time, a vast traffic is carried on, and many factories are in full operation ; while works of art in silver and other materials are still objects of desire with the burghers ; and yet there are tokens of decay. Such a life, so prodigal of labor, energy, and invention, can only be sustained in these days by men possessed of civil and political freedom. The good people of Augsburg firmly believe that, on his accession, the Crown Prince will again declare their city and Nuremburg to be free cities." "The present state of the literary traffic here," he says in another letter, "is really extraordinary, and it has been at the expense of much labor and fatigue that I have got a glimpse of it. I shall write the details to Besser."

The journey from Augsburg to Munich offered little that was attractive in natural scenery ; but the Sunday brought out the peasants in all the picturesque variety of their singular but grotesque costume, richly adorned with silver lace, buttons, and coins. "They may be at once distinguished from the Swabians," wrote Perthes. "These are stout, cheerful fellows, well-fed, and vigorous ; in Swabia, the men have a downcast, oppressed look, and are often thin, sallow, and ill-shaped."

On the 25th of August, he reached Munich, and went straight to Jacobi. "He received us as if we had been his children, and with the feelings of a child I embraced the dear old man. In appearance he is little altered, and his health is quite as good as can be expected at his age, especially for one so delicately

organized, and of so susceptible a temperament. In
conversation, when only two or three are present, there
is the same power as ever, the same clearness and
readiness of mind, but for general society he is dead ;
being somewhat deaf, he does not follow a conversation quickly. If possible, he is even more affectionate
and cordial than ever ; and he bears his altered and
now narrow circumstances with the composure of a
wise man ; it was only when he referred to the pension
that he had lately been obliged to ask of the king for
his sisters that his voice failed, and the tears came into
his eyes. He still takes the liveliest interest in public
affairs, and carefully watches the progress of events.
He listened to my account of the death of his friend
(Claudius) at Hamburgh, and seems to dwell with
interest and thoughtfulness on this last event in human
life, but yet without seeing further into Christianity
than he did ten years ago."

"I have seen few *things* in Munich, because I felt
that my time belonged to Jacobi ; but the Picture
Gallery has great attractions. For some time I was
perplexed, till from the mass of the great and beautiful,
I was able to fix on something definite : the contrasts
are too strong. With wonderful power has Rubens
penetrated into the dark side of human nature, and
with equal power has he exhibited it. His drunken
Silenus is a horrible compound of devil and sow ; the
woman just falling into hell, and still recking with lust
and passion—the torments of the damned portrayed in
her countenance—is not less horrible than the principal
figure in the same picture, a bloated glutton. Gluttony
and the dread of future hunger are both depicted in his
face, the latter somewhat diminished by the conscious-

ness of having a resource for a while in his own fat. The evil that is in man is as truly represented by Rubens as a man's heavenward aspirations and pure affections are by Guido Reni and Raphael. Man is in both : we feel, and are conscious of the contradiction that we carry within us, at other times and in other places, but here we see it in pictures—it becomes visible to itself. It was strange to see again the pictures that were in the former Düsseldorf Gallery, and which I had helped Tischbein to take, one by one, out of a chest in a barn at Glückstadt."

"Matthias shall have special thanks to-day," replies Caroline, "for his descriptions of nature, which really did me good, after you had frightened me with Rubens' dreadful picture. I hold it to be sinful and wrong to pervert such a divine gift as Rubens had received to such corrupt and monstrous uses. I rejoice over one who has passed through life without having known, seen, imagined, or been susceptible of such abominations. How dare a man, by the medium of pictures, realize to better and purer souls, who dream not of them, things which are the disgrace and brand of humanity ? In a word, I hate such pictures, in spite of all the art with which they may be painted. It is a black art. Matthias should not paint such pictures if he could ; I glory in God's work,—Nature ; she comes from Him and leads to Him, and happy is he who has it in his power to look upon these works as you have done. Dear Matthias, fill your soul with *such* pictures, and let them live there till you have learned to draw nigh to your Creator in another and higher way : bring back to me all that you can apprehend and can communicate—I long for it."

The position of Bavaria, as a state, appeared dark indeed, as Perthes contemplated it, during his visit to Munich, and he says,—" What political form Bavaria may ultimately assume, no one here seems to have any idea. As to any feeling for a common Germany, or for national union, it is wholly unknown here ; but if a German spirit were awakened, the Bavarians would be one of our bravest, most powerful, and loyal races. All is uncertainty as regards the internal policy. The king is cordially loved as a true, warm-hearted citizen, but he will not hear of representative chambers or constitutions, and has said that whoever speaks of them attacks the throne." " I have again spent some hours with Jacobi," wrote Perthes immediately before his departure from Munich ; " he took me into his room alone, and spoke of many things, and his voice was often tremulous : he was always beginning the conversation afresh, and I could see plainly that he dreaded the parting moment. He felt, as I did, that in this life we shall never meet again."

And now that Perthes was entering on the hitherto unknown world of the Alps, he forgot kingdoms, literature, and the book-trade, and surrendered himself with all the freshness and joy which were peculiar to him, to the overpowering impressions of that glorious region. He passed some days at Salzburg, and thence visited Berchtoldsgaden, the Königsee, the Eiscapelle, and the Salt-works of Hallein. In spite of these demands on his physical strength, he preserved sufficient elasticity of spirit to write to Caroline late in the evening, and to convey to her living and graphic pictures of the sublime Alpine world.

But the human element in man never, even amid such

scenery, lost its attractive and abiding interest for
Perthes,—"I have," he says, "seen many men, and
men of all kinds, in my long journey from Hamburgh
hither ; and my love for man is in nowise diminished.
I have found far more intelligence, ability, and uprightness, and far less outward immorality than I expected.
If only we meet men with confidence, and are not repelled by differences of manner, and peculiar modes of
viewing things, we everywhere feel how nearly related
the individuals of our race are to one another. I have
felt in some degree at home even in the rigidly Catholic
countries, and have seen much that is attractive there.
How touching, for instance, was it to see in one of the
churches at Augsburg, the childlike thought of a whole
row of little chapels, each devoted to special prayers,
suited to different circumstances,—first a marriage
chapel, where, under garlands and orange-flowers,
bride and bridegroom come to be united ; then a chapel
to the Virgin Mother, to entreat her blessing on the
marriage ; a third, in which maidens pray for good
husbands ; and a fourth for parents whose darlings are
sick or dying. In the Salzburg district you see a crucifix at the summit of every declivity, and a crucifix or
an image of the Virgin on every bridge ; and the
driver never passes any of these symbols without a
grateful reverence and a friendly look. After all, the
people of Cologne were not far wrong when they talked
about the Sunday-God of the Protestants and the
family-God of the Catholics, to whom they can resort
in work days, and in all the petty circumstances of
life."

To this Caroline replied,—"The little chapels for
prayer interested me, but, nevertheless, you are very

unjust to Protestantism, dear Perthes. I can tell you, as before God, that *I have many little chapels in my heart, to which I resort in time of need*, although not so fervently or so purely as I ought, and as I could wish. At present, the chapel of thank-offering takes up most of my time, and you must retract what you said of the Catholics being more familiar with God than we, and of our making a rush to Him only on Sundays."

The character of the South German, as he saw it at Salzburg, struck Perthes forcibly. " At the *tables-d'hôte*," he says, " I met chiefly officers and employés. Everywhere I found good common sense, expressing itself clearly and decidedly on all the circumstances of life, without exaggeration and without losing itself in vague generalities. Learned or book-borrowed phraseology you never hear. Cheerfulness and gayety prevail unchecked. The different dialects, with their simple hearty accents, suit all this. To many travellers this appears tiresome, unpolished, and insipid ; some, in the pride of their refinement, have thought themselves justified in animadverting on this simplicity of manners, and have, for the most part, been answered as they deserved. I have often found the people draw back suspiciously from the North German, leaving him to himself, as though all belonged to the class of commercial travellers, with whom they are most familiar, and who are indeed often very ignorant, and unblushingly immoral in their talk. For myself, I have everywhere found the South German easy of access. If you ask about the inner man, I must say that, here as elsewhere, we find self-sufficiency and arrogance ; and here as elsewhere, one is forced to admire the wisdom that planned the world, and is ever renewing it by means

of children, and the love they bring with them ; and
restoring men when their faith in their own wisdom is
at the strongest to the simplicity of childhood, and
placing marrying and giving in marriage in the middle.
Here we walked for a while in the churchyard, and
read the inscriptions.　They are, in general, very singular, and many of them provoke a smile ; but there
are no flowery, fantastic, or sentimental phrases, and
no heathen philosophy ; all is from the heart, and ex-
pressive of a firm faith in the mercy of God.　There is
much love and good-will in our people, and where the
materials are still, or I should rather say, *already* so
good, the right political form will surely not be long
wanting, if we would but try to work in existing forms,
however unfitted they may be, and—satisfied with a
gradual development—not insist on having everything
ready-made."

It was with no small regret that, on the 3d of September, Perthes took leave of the Alps.　" We travelled through a fine and pleasing district, but our hearts
and minds were closed, and, like one who sighs for his
home, we often turned to look for the splendor we had
left behind, till at length even the last of the Salzburg
hills had vanished from our eyes.　In the evening we
passed Neumark and Vöcklabruck, and at night reached
the Austrian frontier, and were harshly wakened from
our soft slumbers by the officials on duty.　The officer,
roused out of his sleep, asked sternly, ' is the business
then so urgent that people are obliged to travel by
night?"　But on my replying politely that the explanation of my business would only detain him the longer
from his bed, he looked at the passport, and muttered,
' Drive on—but at Lambach you must stop for the

night.' In some anxiety as to the reception that might await us, we drove on, and stopped at Lambach, in front of a large building. The postilion unharnessed his horses, called out, 'This is the custom-house,' and rode away. The question now was, whether we should patiently wait for day-break in our carriage, or knock up the custom-house authorities. At last I took courage and knocked, and soon an old soldier, with a lantern in his hand, came out, and said, 'Follow me.' He brought me into a large hall, where there were at least twenty desks, went into a side-room and returned immediately, bringing two large wax-candles, and followed by a man of very gentlemanly appearance, in snow-white under garments, who very politely asked to see my papers. The soldier again said, 'Follow me.' We went to the carriage, and he searched the pockets,—'Cards, maps, and schnapps, the rest only dirty linen.' For the third time the old man said, 'Follow me;' and reported at the bureau, 'The gentlemen have all in order.' Thus satisfied, the officer bowed, returned my papers, said, 'All right,' and disappeared. The old soldier procured horses, took a two-guilder token, and at the end of an hour we drove free from these mighty perils."

Without further delay they travelled through Wels, Amstetten, and Mölk, to Vienna, where they arrived on the 5th of September.

" I soon felt quite at home here," says Perthes in his first letter. " In the midst of so many people and of so much activity, a man soon finds freedom of life and action for himself. I feel uncomfortable and ill at ease only in a place where I am conscious of being observed, and where I am liable to come in contact with individuals of peculiar and different characters, who have as yet given no intimation whether they are friendly or hostile—however, this does not apply to Vienna. Here the stranger sees neither officers, orders, signs of rank, nor official costume in the streets or public walks—at the *tables-d'hôte,* or in the theatres. He sees no *individuals,* but everywhere Viennese, all seeming to be on equal terms, and none allowing himself to be disturbed in his ways and enjoyments by a third party, or even recognizing the existence of such a third party. In Vienna the stranger observes only life and pleasure, not the living and the pleasure-loving ; all is freedom and equality, as these are to be found only in great cities."

In the Austrian capital there was so much to be seen and done, so many persons to be visited, that the time till late at night was fully occupied, and apart from the fear of committing everything to paper in Vienna, it was impossible for Perthes to record the impressions received there, and to continue his journal-like letters to Caroline—a jotting down of names was, in general, all that he could find time for. Even of his audience of the Archduke John, his dinners with Gentz, his visit to Collin, where he saw the young Napoleon, and of his frequent meetings with Hammer, Baron Stahel, Stift, and other eminent men, we find mere passing notices, but the general impression made on him by Vienna life appears in all his letters. Many questions were there debated, on which Perthes was already well informed, but the religious movements of a small, yet decidedly Catholic circle in Vienna, touched and interested him deeply.

" Pilat," he writes to Caroline, " is a talented and

imaginative man ; but he is also a man of strong passions. His bearing and manner are remarkable. He
works daily with Prince Metternich, who has given
him the Austrian Observatory for his services. Diplomatic he undoubtedly is, but I believe him to be honest,
and he certainly has at heart the interests of religion,
and of what, as a Roman Catholic, he regards as appertaining to religion. Towards me he has really behaved like a friend. Our old acquaintance Klinkowström I also believe to be an honest man, in spite of
the opinion of some."

Perthes, having expressed a wish to hear a good
genuine Catholic preacher, was recommended by Pilat
and Klinkowström to Father Pascal, a Franciscan.
" To-day," he writes, " was the festival of the Saluta-
tion, a great day for a church boasting the possession
of a miraculous picture of the Virgin Mary. The high
altar was splendidly lighted, the church crowded.
Behind the pulpit is a gallery, some paces long ; in this
the father walked up and down, laid aside his sack-
cloth, &c., and made himself quite at home. His voice
and gesticulations are powerful and violent, his idiom
is that of the common Austrian dialect. We were reminded of everything from Abraham to Sancta Clara,
whether we would or not. He had taken the power
and graciousness of the Virgin as the subject of his
discourse. Two-thirds of it were directed against the
prevailing corruption of morals, one-third against
heretics, that is to say, heretics within the Church, for
with those without the father declared he was in that
place no way concerned. The comparison of the Virgin bearing the spiritual world within her, with the
ark of Noah containing all the beasts, was clever, but

far from delicate in the details. The pictures of famine and its accompaniments, disease and crime, as
similitudes of a famine-stricken, unbelieving heart,
were very good, and the concluding prayer was admirable. When at every fresh petition the father, turning himself towards the miraculous picture, devoutly
supplicated the Virgin, people could not fail to be
affected, and overlooked the comic element. On the
whole, it was an able discourse, and effective."

But the interview with Father Hoffbauer of the Re-
demptorists, to whom his attention had long been directed, had greater interest for Perthes. "To-day," he
writes on the 18th of September, " after many ineffectual attempts, I succeeded in meeting Father Hoffbauer.
I found him in a large gloomy saloon, whose very
windows were converted into small latticed chambers,
within which young ecclesiastics were sitting, some
reading, some writing. During my visit one of them
came forward, and took a slice of bread and butter
out of a safe attached to one of the pillars. Hoffbauer
seated himself by me in the centre of the room ; he is
over seventy, and small of stature, but vigorous and
smart. He has not the usual downcast look of a
Catholic priest : his eye is full of fire, and his glance
keen and steady, with great variety of expression ; yet
withal there is a repose of countenance that one can
only call heavenly. Hoffbauer began the conversation
with great politeness, by speaking of common friends ;
then, of my youth and manner of education. From
Claudius he passed to F. L. Stolberg and his joining
the Catholic Church. He soon won my heart, and I.
talked quite freely of Stolberg and his connexion with
the Princess Gallitzin, whom I spoke of as my motherly

friend, and said, that considering Stolberg's peculiar
temperament, and the state of the Protestant Church
at the time he left it, with reference both to doctrine
and practice, I regarded this step not only as natural
and intelligible, but almost as inevitable. When, however, I perceived the impression that my words had
made, and found that they were received as having immediate reference to my own position, I immediately
added, in order to set the worthy old man right, ' Had
I been born and brought up in the Catholic Church, I
should have remained in it ; or were I now to be
transplanted to some land where there is no Protestant
congregation, I should, if obliged to remain there, join
the Catholics ; and even, in the event of the present Protestant Neology getting the upper hand, and becoming
generally acknowledged in the Protestant congregations, I would, in order to secure Christian communion
for my children, follow Stolberg's example. But this,
I said, will never happen, and such a step is nowise
necessary for the salvation of my own soul, inasmuch
as consciousness of sin, the necessity and certainty of
redemption through Jesus Christ, humility, faith, and
walking with God, are entirely independent of adhe-
sion to the Catholic Church ; while the passing over
of individual believers from one church to another, except in peculiar circumstances, might be an anticipation of the Lord's purposes, and an obstacle to the
future union of all Christians as one flock. The Catholic Church has already given way in many matters
of form ; the Protestants will also have much to retract, and the course of time must and will unite them
again.' While I was speaking, Hoffbauer regarded me
steadily but calmly, then grasped my hand, and said,

' I, too, believe in an invisible church. I will pray fo
you, that you fall not into temptation. And now le
us talk on without disturbing the explanation whicl
you have just given.' We then spoke of the Reforma
tion, and Hoffbauer said, ' Since I have been enabled
as Apostolic Nuncio, to compare the religious positior
of the Catholics in Poland with that of the Protest
ants in Germany, I am convinced that the apostasy
from the Church arose from the need which the Ger
mans felt, and still feel, of genuine piety. The Refor
mation was propagated and upheld not by heretics anc
philosophers, but by men who were seeking a religior
for the heart. I have said this at Rome to the Pope
and Cardinals, but they would not believe me, and
will have it that it was enmity to all religion of what·
soever kind that brought about the Reformation.'
Hoffbauer then listened to much that I had to tell him
about the religious and ecclesiastical condition of
North Germany, and, on my departure, the gentle and
pious old man extended his hand to me with his bless·
ing."

A young Catholic priest, named Hörni, who, on the
death of Claudius, had written to Perthes a letter full
of respect and sympathy, made, indeed, a different but
not less interesting impression. " This morning," he
says to Caroline, " a young man in the dress of an
ecclesiastic entered my room, and approached me
with great respect. It was Hörni, whose letter written
on the occasion of your father's death you will remember. He entered on his family history, explained to
me his personal circumstances, and the course of his
education, in a very amiable and intelligent way. ' I
too, like most of my associates,' he said, ' was a victim

to the religious free-thinking that prevailed in Austria under Joseph the Second ; but my truant soul was led back to the way of truth and grace by the writings of Claudius. How wonderfully great he was! In the hottest of the battle waged throughout Germany, Protestant as well as Catholic, against all revealed religion, he clung but the more closely to the Lord Jesus Christ, and when all the so-called philosophers of Germany were perverted by the prevailing systems, he remained unmoved, and recognized the delusive enchantment, when at its culminating point, as what it really was—a dazzling nonentity. His wisdom was, indeed, too little like that of this world, to be acceptable to the children of this world. His contemporaries did not understand his lofty simplicity, and esteemed it lightly ; they spent their energies spinning cob-webs, and seeking out many devices, and only went the farther astray. For my own part, I shall be thankful as long as I live, that the wisdom of the single-minded Wandsbeck Messenger was revealed to me in its height and its depth.' Hörni then asked me for further particulars of your father's last hours. ' For though,' said he, ' it is possible that, in the death-agony Claudius may not have had the power of expressing what the soul experienced in prospect of approaching union with its Friend and Redeemer, I believe that after such a uniform and singularly Christian life, his death must have been beautiful and Christian, and that the consolation poured into his soul by the Redeemer must have been evident to the happy witnesses of his passage " to the land of life and truth."' On taking leave he asked me for a picture of Claudius. ' It does a wrestling man good,' he said, ' to be surrounded con-

13

stantly by tried wrestlers ; evil thoughts are put to
flight when the eye falls on the portrait of one in
whose living presence one would have blushed to own
them.' All that Hörni said bore the impress of truth
and of pious conviction. The intelligence with which
he spoke indicated great accomplishments ; his manner
of speaking is fluent and pure, such, indeed, as you seldom meet with here, even among people of rank and
learning.

Towards the end of September, Perthes had brought
to a close the arrangements preparatory to entering
into literary undertakings in Austria, and delighted
with the fruitful weeks, and the confidence that he had
enjoyed in Vienna, he took his departure from that
city on the 22d of the month.

After a hurried journey and a halt of four days in
Nuremberg, he found himself on the morning of the 2d
October in the neighborhood of Blankenburg in the
Thuringian forest, and within a few leagues of Schwarzburg, the home of his childhood. The heavy rains of
the last month had swept away the bridge over the
forest-brook between the village of Schwarza and the
little town of Blankenburg. Perthes, well acquainted
with all the footpaths, ordered the postilion to drive
round by the stone bridge while he with his son walked in the direction of the paper-mill, where he knew
that a lofty narrow foot-bridge was thrown over the
stream ; but this also had been carried away, and in
its place two trunks of trees had been laid from shore
to shore. As they were setting foot on these, a by-
stander asked if the travellers thought it safe to venture to cross on so narrow a ledge. They went forward, however, without hesitation, both having risked

far more perilous paths in Salzburg. The Schwarza swollen to a torrent rushed rapidly beneath them : they were within two paces of the opposite shore, when Matthias, who was foremost, called out, "Hold me, I am falling!" Perthes seized the falling boy by the collar, and was instantly precipitated with him into the water. He soon regained his feet, but both were again carried away by the impetuous stream. Once Perthes rose to the surface and cried, "Don't lose your presence of mind," then immediately sank. Wife and children flashed across his mind, and then he lost all consciousness. Both were being swept along towards the wheel of a saw-mill about two hundred paces distant, but when within a few yards of this, Perthes was vigorously grasped by the left arm, and slowly dragged to the shore. In the struggle for life he had kept convulsive hold of his son, by the right hand, and now, all unconsciously, dragged him to the bank.

The stranger who had warned them of the danger— Stahl, the owner of the paper-mill—when he saw them precipitated into the torrent, had hastened over the narrow bridge and along the bank to a shallow which extended far into the Schwarza. Here, up to the middle in water, he waited, seized the floating body as it passed, and, while expecting to save only one from certain death, found he had saved two. In the warm drying-room of the paper-mill the rescued father and son speedily recovered under the treatment of a surgeon from Rudolstadt, who happened fortunately to be on the spot. They then hastened to Schwarzburg, where, well heated by a rapid walk, they arrived towards evening. The hand of death had been upon them, but had left no tokens of his having been so near.

Amid the scenes of his childhood,—cherished and affectionately ministered to, as if he had been still a child, by the old Colonel, the old Master of the horse, and the old Aunt Caroline,—Perthes rested for a day or two after the excitement of the two preceding months. Then, after a short stay in Gotha, he hastened back to Hamburgh by the way of Göttingen and Hanover. He reached home on the 8th of October, and found Caroline, whose health had often been a source of anxiety to him during his absence, stronger than he had left her.

XXVI.

The Summer of 1819.

SHORTLY before the return of Perthes to Hamburgh, Besser had written to him: "You went out to see Germany, but, as it appears to me, you did not find it." This was undoubtedly true. On the Rhine, in Würtemberg, in Bavaria, and in Austria, Perthes had indeed met with truly German manners and modes of thought, and even with the wish for a great and powerful fatherland; but at the same time, he had found the South Germans unwilling to diminish the independence and integrity of Baden and Würtemberg, Bavaria and Austria, which yet would be a necessary consequence of their becoming parts of a whole. The North German adhered as tenaciously as the South German to the independence of his own particular State, but less consciously, and arose from an impression, that in any alliance with the South, the preponderance would still be his.

Perthes regarded these struggles and conflicts as the necessary result of the course that events had taken in Germany. He says in a letter to Jacobi, "Men of action are never far from men of thought; but the struggle is violent and wide-spread in proportion to the rapidity with which history is enacted. Formerly op-

posite movements of thought and effort were separated
by centuries, but our times have united wholly discor-
dant elements in the three cotemporaneous generations.
The immense contrasts of 1750, 1789, and 1815, acknowledge no transition state, and appear to men now
living not as succeeding one another, but as coëxist·
ing."

The fact of conflict was not only intelligible to Perthes, but even matter of rejoicing. "You remember
what I said to you in 1815," he writes to Fouqué,
"that the real hard fighting would only begin with the
war of minds, when the external warfare should be
over. And now, do you think I should be sorry if I
turned out to be in the right? By no means. Remember, dear Fouqué, here below, in some way or another, work is God's will for man. Man has more time
on hand than he can spend in mere love and contemplation; therefore, pray and work ; now warfare and
struggle are a sort of work. It is in vain that as friends
we give each other the hand of love; as soon as we
would come to an understanding, by word or deed, on
any subject of human interest, we find ourselves in mutual opposition, and a conflict is inevitable till the goal
be reached. You do not yourself like the stagnant
waters of indifference, the slough of compliance and
servility ; why then be disquieted by conflicts in these
times, even when they arise among friends? But let
no unfair weapon be ever made use of, and let us give
even our opponents credit for intentions good and noble as our own. It is only when experience has proved
them to be otherwise, that indignation, driving the liar
out of the sanctuary with sword and scourge, can become well-pleasing to God."

Perthes was, however, reminded by serious and thoughtful men, that conflict is not itself true life, and that it does not always, as a matter of course, end in victory.

A letter which Perthes received from Görres about the end of the year 1818, expresses the opinions of many eminent men of the period. "You, my dear Hanseatic friend," he says, "have now seen what reception my address has met with from the most dastardly and the coarsest of despotisms. The slightest stimulant applied to these people brings on delirium and convulsions, and without stimulants they sink into dulness and lethargy. The Rhenish Mercury was the very thing for them. Every other day it came out with an ointment, compounded according to circumstances, of bitter, stimulant, sedative, gently purgative, or nauseating ingredient. Thus an equilibrium was maintained, a gentle perspiration induced, the excessive irritation carried off, and the animal spirits set once more into regular circulation. After three years of silence, I thought it well to send a rocket among the parties again, in the form of an address, but I cannot say that it has revealed to me anything agreeable. It showed me princes who have been in the school of adversity without having learned anything there, not even so much as to take care of their own dignity: ministers who have good intentions but no ability, decision, or courage: a Court opposition,—bad rather from the absence of all good than from the presence of positive evil, stupid to brutishness, awkward as a Rhinoceros, cowardly, contemptible, and beneath all criticism throughout: a democratic party without unity, without standing-ground, inactive, yet running after every Jack o' Lanthorn, always hoping that over night things will shape themselves anew; without skilful leaders, without principles or comprehensive views; arrogant, frivolous, scatter-brained, and negligent; barren and inconsistent; at once cowardly and boastful; without dignity, vigor, and repose. Such are the magnificos of this crotchety time; they are worthy of a generation that has stood on the pinnacle of the temple, and yet waded through every sort of mire; which has shown aptitude only in destroying, complete impotence in building up. Like the Jews, who spent forty years in the wilderness and never saw the promised land, so these men will accomplish nothing, but only lay the foundation of something better. Another generation, however, is growing up now, from which we may reasonably expect much good."

The year 1819 is rightly regarded as a turning-point in the history of Germany.

Perthes himself distrusted the noisy orators of 1819. He thought that civil freedom could exist only when the members of a state think less of themselves than of the general good; and to the question whether this were the spirit of the liberals, he answered, "No: division and discontent characterize the popular leaders, because they are in bondage to the spirit of selfishness, which, I fear, is at present the prevailing spirit of liberalism."

The murder of Kotzebue by Sand, on the 23d of March, 1819, revealed to every one the form which the spirit of the times might assume in overheated imaginations. Perthes wrote,—"That which gives such a frightful aspect to the deed, is that it seems almost to have been necessitated by the course of events. It is

not detestation of the murder that should move us first
and most ; it is especially important that both rulers
and subjects should recognize in this crime, a last and
terrible warning, which, since all milder intimations
have proved vain, should open our eyes to the state of
things which has rendered so bloody a deed possible,
and to the terrible future that awaits us without a
thorough political regeneration. The germs of other
terrible events lie in this act, which is, only *apparently*, the crime of an individual. Fanaticism once armed with the dagger will not stop at the comic drama-
tist."

A statesman wrote to Perthes in the summer following :—'· The murder of Kotzebue is like a jet of fire
from a volcanic abyss ; the flame may be put out, but
the sea of fire still surges beneath. The judgments
passed on the horrible deed are more frightful than the
deed itself, and show that the state of feeling which
engendered it is not confined to a few excited students.
The individual criminals may, and should be punished
with the utmost rigor of the law ; but a system of ter-
rorism would only multiply the chances of a revolutionary outbreak ; for every hydra-head cut off, two new
ones would spring up. The Germans have a profound
longing for common objects of affection, reverence, and
hope ; but this craving received no satisfaction after.
the victory over France. On the contrary, the victors
see the vanquished in possession of great national
treasures ; honored and respected as a people, while
they themselves are deprived of all political co-
herence and importance. The result is, that, failing
objects of common love, the Germans have found out
objects of common hatred—and it is impossible for any

government to maintain the existing political order long in opposition to such a state of opinion."

" The whole German nation, governments, and people, are turned hypochondriac," writes another distant friend ; " you all talk so much about perils and destruction, that you will actually die of the fear of death ; get rid of this death-phobia, and you will find yourselves well, at least as well as man can be on earth. You have many imaginary evils and much real good ; but being, as I said, hypochondriac, you must needs be angry when any one says to you, ' My dear friend, you are really not so *very* ill.' Just look at France—where there is much imaginary good and much real evil ; but there everybody is cheerful, and rejoices in the delightful consciousness of belonging to ' *la grande Nation*.' If the German nation could but make the tour of Europe, it would on its return find life very bearable at home."

Perthes shared the universal dissatisfaction at the inactivity of the rulers. After giving vent to it very decidedly in one of his letters, he proceeds : " The appearance of Madame de Staël's ' Considérations sur la Révolution Français' may be useful. This talented work will be read by princes, for it is written in the language of their drawing-rooms. When they see how the murderous axe of revolution hung over the king's head they will tremble at the sound of the tempest that is approaching their own thrones, and when all other inducements have failed, fear may perhaps force them into action."

" The sovereigns of Europe," wrote Perthes, " have placed themselves in opposition to the half-slumbering, half-roused peoples, and seek, like master-tailors, to

shape governments for them.   Governed, indeed, we
must be, and kings and princes we must have, but we
need not be bondsmen for all that."

A lively representation of the public excitement occurs in a letter written to Perthes about the end of
December, 1818 : "At Weimer I rubbed shoulders
with the Emperor Alexander this time, as twelve years
ago with the Emperor Napoleon. Now, as then, I
found everybody in excitement ; even Goethe spoke of
nothing but the masquerade in which he was to declaim his own noblest pieces to their high mightinesses.
Twelve years ago Napoleon was in a great hurry, but
he came from Paris, and went I know not whither, and
had a hundred cannon in his train. Alexander was
also in a great hurry, but he came from Aix-la-Cha-
pelle, and is going to Petersburg with twelve carriages
full of lacqueys, gentle and simple—some with pointed,
others with flat noses. It thus appears that an emperor is not always the same thing : so at least I
thought, when, at Erfurt, I heard Napoleon abused in
the most outrageous manner by the officers after he
was sent to St. Helena ; which reminded me of Blumenbach's furious anger at the mischievous disposition
of scorpions, when, at the very time he was exhibiting
them to his auditors preserved in spirits !"

XXVII

The Religious Conflicts of the Period.

HE men to whom in his youth Perthes had been accustomed to look up with child-like reverence; by whose faith and convictions he had strengthened his own; and in whose strivings he had found a guide through the intricacies of his own inner life, were no longer in the arena on which the great religious conflicts of the age were to be fought out. The man, to whose words he once listened as to those of an oracle, had now become a loved and honored patriarch, who required and received the most tender consideration.

In December, 1818, Frederick Henry Jacobi, then in his seventy-seventh year, wrote to Perthes a few lines concluding thus:—"It is really wonderful how, in old age, men often gain what they had previously striven for in vain; I, for instance, can speak of an increasing cheerfulness."

Perthes answered,—"You have certainly every reason to be cheerful; it is assuredly no misfortune to have reached an advanced age, and few even of the most distinguished men retain so much clearness and activity of mind. But don't look for production any more; historical narration is the province of age. I very much wish you would let alone Part Fourth of your works, and devote yourself to gathering and arranging the experience of the last forty-five years of your life. It would cheer you, by bringing vividly before you the entire circle of ideas and course of thought belonging to an important period. If it has not been granted you to accept with child-like confidence the Divine Revelation, because you have eaten too largely of the tree of knowledge, this is indeed a great spiritual loss; but he who can ask as you do in your last letter, 'Where and what is truth?' possesses humility before God, such as few inquirers like yourself attain to; and humility is the very kernel of humanity, and the way to God."

Throughout the length and breadth of Protestant Germany, the rationalism of the 18th century, as propounded by Roehr, Bretschneider, Paulus, and others, had exercised absolute dominion, but its very existence was now endangered from two opposite quarters. The profounder scientific theology had appeared in alliance with the new philosophy, and in Schleiermacher especially, who was then at the zenith of his influence, had found a powerful champion. It withdrew from rationalism the loftiest minds, limited its influence to the less intelligent, and threatened its extinction. Scientific theology might at first escape the notice of the laity, or it might be suspected of merely defending the old errors of rationalism with more approved weapons, and of making the ascertainment of truth the first object, while sanctification in the truth was not even the second. Doubts of this kind may have been expressed by Perthes in the letter to which a theological friend sent the following answer :—" We ought not to forget that, as the majority, and among these the most eminent men of our times have been seduced from Christianity by science, it is only through science that they can be brought back. She alone can heal the wounds which herself has made. In saying this I am advancing nothing new ; none of the Fathers thought otherwise, though undoubtedly, they were as ready to sacrifice life and fortune for their convictions as any of our present zealots can be ; nevertheless they always acknowledged that the word of life revealed in Christ was reflected in the philosophy of the East and West, and that, as the Jews by the law, so the heathen might by philosophy be prepared to receive Christ." Perthes' doubts were in nowise removed by this and similar representations ; he still feared that the theologians, rejoicing in the newly discovered or newly established scientific ideas, would not resist the temptation of bringing them into the Church, which, as it neither was, nor could be a scientific institution, would find in these only a new element of disruption.

On the other hand, Perthes took the warmest interest in another movement that threatened rationalism from a different quarter. The deeper spiritual life which had been called forth, first by the heavy pressure of the French yoke, and then by the popular rising to shake it off, was actively working and penetrating into the heart of the nation. The craving for remission of sins and godliness of life, apart from all scientific theology, had manifested itself in individuals, in congregations, and here and there in whole parishes. Not finding satisfaction in the prevailing Rationalism, the subjects of this craving betook themselves to a new, or rather to a very old method ; in all parts of Germany, associations were formed of men seeking spiritual help, and finding it in the old faith of the Church.   The links which had held the whole of Germany in the grasp of Rationalism were broken, and its prestige as the universal Protestant creed disappeared.

Perthes had attentively observed the new movement; and though he was by no means insensible to its perils, its aberrations, and its caprices, he yet rejoiced in it, in so far as it was earnest and healthy.   "Harms is now pastor in Kiel," he writes to a friend, "and all Holstein goes, drives, and rides to hear him, even the professors; and if Voss should come to Holstein this summer, it will be at the risk of becoming a low German* Christian.   Harms, as I hear, has no personal advantages, and an unpleasant delivery; but his earnestness and his steadfast belief in Divine revelation, aided, perhaps, by his provincial plainness, carry all before them.   Falk tells me, that his preaching has already made other preachers somewhat more careful in disseminating their rationalistic wisdom, so that they at least refrain from pulling down what a more godly era had built up."   In mentioning another earnest and pious man, who headed another religious movement, Perthes regrets his arbitrary use of Scripture passages, whereby they can be made to say anything.

A friend in Berlin wrote to Perthes, that certain young men in that city were attracting attention by their earnestness in the matter of salvation; but that they were of a sombre mood, regarding everything secular, and even art itself, as sinful, and were very eager proselytizers.   Perthes answered, "If the zeal of the young men be sincere, you need not alarm yourself about

---

* Platt-deutch, low German, the dialect in which Harms preached.

their gloom. Sadness and cheerfulness are things of temperament, and the same earnestness and faith are variously manifested, by some in seriousness, by others in cheerfulness, according to the bodily constitution, and we may not, on account of the earthly husk, quarrel with the heavenly substance."

Another theological friend writes :—" A very peculiar view of Christianity is just now manifesting itself here and there among the Moravians. They split men into two parts—the natural, which, as such, according to Kant, has no knowledge of the infinite and the divine, but appreciates only the finite and temporal relations of things ; and the intuitive, which sees God and eternity everywhere."

Perthes answered :—" It is not the business of Christianity, by fine-spun theories, to immortalize the contest which goes on within us all, and to show that each of the combatants is justified in its own department ; rather it is *by means of saving faith, to make of twain one new man.*"

" He who has not felt the internal working of a great mystery which is ever alienating us from God," wrote Perthes, " will never attain to that humility without which the saving virtue of the atonement is inaccessible. The flesh is not the root of evil, pride,— pride is the real devil. The flesh is but the means of punishment and cure, ever reminding, even the proudest, of his misery and helplessness. Little that is positive is revealed to us, but that little is all. What form shall be given to revealed truth is an open question, for it breaks into rays of the most various colors, according to the fancy and modes of thought peculiar to individuals and epochs. But when you say that the

Christian revelation, if received as truth, at once shrouds history and philosophy in a haze, in which man is confounded, and dreams rather than thinks, I reply, that to every one who ignores the redemption through Christ, history becomes one immense tangled skein, and every philosophical system a sum in arithmetic, the correctness of which, for want of proof, can never be ascertained.   Inquiries into the nature of the Trinity, and of our Lord, into redemption and atonement, are great and noble, but the craving in which they originate is scientific, not spiritual.   We are lighted and warmed by the rays of the sun, whether we understand the laws of light and heat or not.   On your expression, ' The swinish multitude do indeed require a faith which surpasses comprehension,' I must observe, that the arrogant contempt of the people which it betrays, is very remarkable in so determined a liberal as yourself.   In conclusion, I have only further to say, that a man who, like you, has never been seduced by the allurements of sense, and never felt the swellings of pride, nor ever needed any to help him, would only be wasting his time by bestowing further attention on me.   Such a man might choose for his spiritual adviser a preacher in this neighborhood, who selected two Jews as sponsors to his own child ; and he might repeat daily, till his last hour, that men are all in the right, and all in the wrong."

An upright and gifted man, far gone in rationalism, endeavored in lengthy communications to justify to Perthes his position with reference to the Christian revelation.   " My words will not have pleased you," he says in conclusion, " but I cannot help it, and you

have too much sense and fairness to expect fresh bark
on an old withered trunk."

" You say," replied Perthes, " that with the mysteries of Christianity your religion ceases. To this I
reply, that the God of Rationalism baffles conception
far more than does any mystery of Christianity. But
for Christianity there could have been no Rationalism ; and apathy alone enables it to remain where it
is. By the idea of an Eternal Being, exalted above
time and space, the Rationalist seeks to satisfy himself and others,—but what he means by these words,
he neither says nor knows. Man cannot conceive of
a personal God without investing Him with a human
form ; every religion is an incarnation of Deity, and
so far an obscure anticipation of God's manifestation
in the flesh. It is true, indeed, that men have never
attained to an incarnation of God, but only to carica-
tures of it ; and they are right in saying that by no
effort of human thought *can* they attain to a proper
incarnation, to atonement and redemption. But how
does that effect the truth involved in the historical
fact ? In no way. The most acute thinkers could not
by thinking discover the Roman Empire ; but had it,
therefore, no existence ? You, my dear friend, will be
obliged to go either forwards or backwards, since you
cannot, like others, shut the eyes of your understanding."

" You say that Christianity is forced upon man,"
wrote Perthes to another friend, " and are displeased
that it should be so. I, at all events, cannot complain
of any such violence. Neither upon me nor upon any
of my contemporaries did any teacher or pastor, force
eternal truth, nor so much as bring it near to us, by

an injunction to attend church or read the Bible. But
as every year strengthened the conviction of my divine
origin, I felt but the more deeply the degradation of
my shameful bondage through the flesh and the mind.
My trouble on account of selfishness and impurity
drove me to seek reconciliation with the God before
whom I trembled, and thus led me to recognize and
lay hold on revelation. Christianity was not forced
upon me, but I upon Christianity ; I was thrown by
an inward necessity into the arms of the Saviour, and
so, I believe, are many others."

" Our existence is that of fallen spirits," he says in
another letter ; " but we have retained a yearning
after the purity of our divine origin, and this elevates
everything. We all are conscious of an effort to soar,
to climb, or to creep upwards ; many get the length of
struggling with evil, but none gain a victory over it ;
the most elevated, as well as the most grovelling natures, need a Helper and Mediator in order to rise ;
and he who is unconscious of this necessity, wearies
himself out in ineffectual endeavors. For him who,
in the anguish of his heart, cries out, ' I am a miserable sinner,' and stretches forth his arms to the
Saviour,—for him, I say, Christ died. How closely,
then, is faith in the Redeemer allied with the realization of one's own sinfulness ! Many, who no more
recognized Christ than did the disciples at Emmaus,
may yet have prayed to Him, and in their perplexity
made an idol their mediator. Such men Christ will,
in His own time, bring to that truth, which is rest and
light ; and many will sit down on the right hand of
God, who in this life never uttered the name of
Christ."

"The Divine light," says Count F. L. Stolberg in one of his letters, "has so thoroughly penetrated the modern mind, that our civilization could not be preserved if that light were extinguished. The heathen philosophy found an element of preservation in that yearning after light in which it originated; but the false philosophy of our times originates in insensibility, audacity, and vanity, without any yearning after light or truth. The Divine light, indeed, will never be extinguished, but the candlestick, on which it is placed, may be removed from a land that has rejected it, to another; and of this, history furnishes alarming examples."

The certainty to which Perthes had attained in matters of faith, did not extend to ecclesiastical questions; but he did not consider his own salvation or that of others endangered by uncertainty with reference to these. He, nevertheless, considered the external Church to be of inestimable value as a depositary of the faith. "God has, in the Holy Scriptures," he writes to a friend, "taught us the way in which He delivers men from their self-imposed slavery. Man, however, is so obstinately self-willed, that he cannot apprehend the directions of Scripture; he overlooks them, perverts them, or stares at them stupidly in the letter, so that, in fact, he requires a second helper, in order to avail himself of the help which they contain. But who is to open up to him the depths of their meaning? Who is to keep, disseminate, and expound the Scriptures? This is the grand and the hard question. Scripture needs protection against the perversity of man; man needs an interpreter of Scripture, and the visible Church is the institution charged with both these functions."

XXVIII.

The Marriage of the Eldest Daughter.

LTHOUGH neither the political commotions nor the manifold religious and ecclesiastical controversies of the time ever became uninteresting to Caroline, or failed to draw forth her sympathies, they never again engrossed her whole soul as in 1813. Her heart was in her home, and there she ever found fresh cause of joy and gratitude.

Her eldest daughter, Agnes, had been betrothed, since the summer of 1813, to William Perthes, who had formerly taken part in the business at Hamburgh, afterwards campaigned as a volunteer, and now managed the business which he had inherited from his father in Gotha, and which, under his auspices, had become very flourishing.

"God has again showered down joy and gladness upon us," wrote Caroline about this time; "how can I thank Him enough for so manifestly protecting us and our children! It is certainly a great happiness to be able to commit so pure and innocent a child to the man whom we have so long esteemed, knowing that he will cleave to her with his whole heart, loving and cherishing her as long as he lives."

On the 12th of May, 1818, the marriage took place.

and on the 16th the young couple departed for their new home.

The following is the first letter of a correspondence which supplied the lack of personal intercourse :— "My beloved Agnes, you have hardly been gone from me three hours, and I am already writing to you, because I cannot help it. When you left, I watched you till you had passed the bridge, and then gave you up in the sure confidence that you are, and ever will remain, in God's hands. You, dear Agnes, know that I love you, and can imagine the rest. How well I remember the moment when you were first laid beside me on the bed, when I looked at you for the first time, and gave you the first kiss. Since then, I have rejoiced in you every day, I might say every hour, through twenty years. Should I not thank God, and if He has willed it, consent to part with you? He will forgive me if I cannot do it without tears. And you, too, my dear Agnes, must and ought to weep ; and your beloved William will understand you, and forgive you if you weep too long. Never conceal from him anything that relates to yourself, even if you think that it may displease him ; you will soon find that even with the fondest love, there is room for mutual forbearance. I rejoice beforehand in your future, for we, too, shall be sharers in it : remember that you are never to be weary of communicating your joys and sorrows, that so we may still live a common life."

Joy and gratitude for the happiness of her daughter, and for her own, was the groundwork of all Caroline's letters. " Perthes has just brought me your letter," she writes in answer to the first news from Gotha : " I have read it again and again, and rejoice and thank God, and

also your dear William, for making you so happy.
You know how confident I was of this beforehand, and
it will be permanent where God has given His blessing. Conjugal happiness lives in the depths of the
heart even amid the sorrows and trials of life ; indeed
it is by these only the more deeply rooted, as I know
from my own experience, thank God. I rejoice with
you, and on your account, dear children, and school
myself to bear your absence cheerfully ; so does your
father ; it is a real pleasure to look at his face when
he comes to the door with one of your letters."

"We cannot think of anything but William's birth-
day," she writes somewhat later ; "we would gladly
have lived in the same place with you if God had so
ordered it. Ah! what a pity that the world is so
wide! how delightful it would be if we, and all whom
we love, could live together, and we could have kept
this birth-day with you. But I will not complain, I
will rather rejoice and be glad even in your removal.
May God preserve your happiness to you and us, and
with it a thankful and watchful heart. I cannot tell
you often enough that you are always with me and
at my side ; and none knows so well as myself how
gladly I would hear you answer when in thought I
speak with you. At the same time, I do not grudge
you to your dear William, and it is my constant desire
that you may become dearer and dearer to each other.
That you are in the right path I am fully pursuaded ;
yours is indeed a happy lot, my beloved Agnes, and if
every day finds you walking more humbly before God,
and more lovingly, you will have a heaven within you.
Your dear father is well and cheerful. Would that he
could only secure a quiet hour for me occasionally !

this is my only want, and it troubles me more and oftener than it ought."

In July, 1818, Caroline went with Perthes for a few days to Lübeck to visit her family, returning by Rheinfeld, the birth-place of her father.

" We have actually been to Lübeck, and have enjoyed it very much," she wrote to Agnes. " Your father was young again, and very merry, and so was I. We stayed two days with my brother, and were truly happy. I am really well, and hardly know which is best, to awake or to go to sleep in health ; but I think the latter. Oh, Agnes, pray that I may remain so !—St. Mary's Church is large, and I believe that many earnest prayers and cries ascend to heaven from it. The long row of tombs, with their great stone coffins, and the obscurity of the place, impressed me deeply ; one can hardly realize the destruction of these heavy coffins, and this is to me an unpleasant thought, seeing that the body, on account of which they are erected, is so soon dissolved. The Cathedral Church is very fine, and I would gladly pass an occasional hour there. On Tuesday evening we left for Rheinfeld ; the quietness of this place passes all description ; it is situated on the shore of a large lake, richly wooded on one side. It was a still, peaceful evening : we had escaped from the world, were alone, and inconceivably happy. Would to God we had more such hours ! When our busy life in Hamburgh occurred to me, I felt rather discouraged, and yet I am convinced that my work there is, on the whole, better for me than this calm blessedness. God has led me by a very different way from that which I had laid out for myself, but it has been the right way—this I not only believe but know ;

He has given me in labor and tumult what I would gladly have sought and found in quiet and solitude. We also went to the church of your dear grandfather, and to his grave, and into the confessional where there was an old arm-chair in which he had often sat, and a few books in which he had often read. The next morning we again went out for a walk, and rested ourselves in a beautiful spot. How did I rejoice in the happiness of Perthes, he was so delighted with me and everything! But to return to you and your letter : what you write of N.'s children is true, and distresses me greatly, for I am convinced that heartfelt love, which lets itself be seen, and in a manner felt in everything, is the dew and the rain indispensable to the growth and bloom of children. I believe that the more children are loved, and the more conscious they are of being loved, the better ; of course there is also a time for seriousness and discipline. But I know many people who think it right carefully to conceal their affection from their children. They should study 1 Cor. xiii, and they would see that there is nothing to fear in that direction. You know that with reference neither to children, nor to anything else, am I fond of words ; but to give occasional expression to the feelings of the heart, I consider not only not wrong, but right ; the mouth naturally overflows with whatever fills the heart,—and how can it overflow but in words ?"

Caroline was anxious to instruct her daughter in housekeeping, and often desired her to write all sorts of details. In return she sent many an approved receipt, and many a useful hint, and also gave news of her daughter's friends. Thus :—" You ask after

14

Z. ; she was here lately, and was so ingenuous and confiding, that, to my horror, she did not shrink from saying that she believed all unmarried women had missed
their vocation, and had but a melancholy prospect. I
pray God to defend every girl from so miserable a
notion. No ; God has provided love and happiness
for all who will accept them, whatever their rank or
sex. No one need want objects of affection, dear Agnes ; you cannot for a moment doubt that I, like you,
regard a good husband as a great and precious gift
from God ; but God can send His blessing directly into the heart, without attaching it to any intermediate
object, and make us happy without husbands. For,
dear Agnes, your mutual love can be a means of happiness and blessing only as it increases your love to
God ; and can you not imagine, that to turn directly
to God, and love Him without the intervention of any
human medium, must be far, far better ? And even
with a human medium I can imagine unmarried to be
quite as happy as married life, else poor maidens must
indeed despair, and we with them, and for them. If
we but propose to ourselves some serious object, pursuing it with our whole heart, and laboring for it in
dependence on God, His blessing and happiness can
never fail us. This is my honest opinion, and I believe
that every young woman acts wisely when she turns
her affections to God, instead of looking about her
with yearning and anxiety for an earthly object ; this
is a melancholy condition which withers and dries up
the heart, and annihilates all happiness. I know nothing so sad as a poor girl in this condition, especially
if she be pure and good. If, however, a woman finds
such a dear Perthes as you and I have found, or rather

as God has given us, let her close with him at once, and be thankful."

But Caroline's anxiety about the spiritual influences that her daughter might find in her new home, took precedence of every other. "I thank you for your letter," she wrote, "but not at all that you have not yet looked out for a real friend of your own sex. I earnestly wish one for you, so that you may have something to fall back upon, when William cannot be with you. If you are sketching a model of perfection in your friend, I can quite understand how it is that you have not found one ; but you must make allowances, and go forth with a generous confidence, not suffering yourself to be ruffled, as you too often do. It is often easier to tolerate weaknesses and failings, than manners and modes of speech to which we are unaccustomed. Only bear perpetually in mind that there is no difference at heart between the people of Gotha and Hamburgh ; there, as here, there is much shortcoming and much good, and many little things that you would rather do without, yet which you must take along with every acquisition. It is very natural that the good qualities of your friends here should appear to you in the liveliest colors ; their weaknesses and failings, on the other hand, in the faintest ; and yet, there were not many of them with whom you could speak of the deepest and holiest things, and to whom you could pour out your whole heart. Nevertheless you loved them, and took pleasure in their society. Only make the attempt in Gotha, let your heart speak in truth and confidence, and you will find that what comes from the heart, goes to the heart ; you will be met more than half way, for the necessity and the pleasure of loving and being loved is common to us all, and the young ladies there have no William as you have."

Perthes also wrote to warn his daughter against seclusion from others :—" Make the most of your own happiness, but remember that you are not alone in the world ; and do not shut up your house from your friends ! it is perilous, and leads to family egotism, and brings its own punishment. I am glad that you have young men living with your dear William ; continue this custom even to old age ; it will preserve you alike from the gossip and the tedium of company. Communicate freely with others, and show that domestic happiness does not estrange you from them. The earth is God's house, and we may not live only to ourselves. I know, dear Agnes, that you will not let any needy person whom you can help go empty away ; but neighbors and acquaintances wish to talk of their affairs, their joys and sorrows, and those of their friends, and nothing is so offensive as cold reserve, as though we were beings of a superior nature, able to live, and suffer, and rejoice alone."

" That you do not find in the pulpit what you seek," wrote Caroline, " distresses me greatly, but does not surprise me, since the clergy for the most part preach only morality, which is but meagre fare. But do not be cast down on this account, my dear Agnes ; take refuge in your inner church : God can serve up a better table than any preacher, and will assuredly feed you, if only you are hungry. The old hymns and chorals have ever been my best stimulants, and are so still, whenever the inner life grows languid ; in particular, those beautiful hymns of longing after. God, in

Freylinghausen's book, have often revived me, and will, I trust, support me even in death. But if the preaching be not satisfactory, do not on this account absent yourself from church; there are seasons in which you are more likely to be aroused and quickened in the church than in the house, where I at least seldom have a quiet hour."

"I am indeed sorry," she says in a letter of later date, "that you are obliged to live without music; still, my advice is, not to form any intimacies only for the sake of music; you might pay too dearly for it, and not perhaps find it easy to draw back. My piano is also dumb, I cannot sing one of *our* songs to it; when I sound the first note, I feel that you are no longer by my side; tears then come and choke the rest. Yes, dear Agnes, I feel that it is a hard duty to part with a gift in which God has so long allowed us to rejoice."

In this, and in many other letters, we see the struggle in Caroline's heart, between her joy at the happiness of her child, and the sorrow of separation. "I know that you are happy, and that is the chief thing; but, my dear Agnes, a mother's heart is not at all times to be quieted by reason, and has its own rights too. Only it must not be intractable; that it should not be so is, in quiet hours, my daily study. As long as you were with me, I was wholly yours—heart and soul, mind and body, hands and feet; if you have no longer need of my hands and feet, you may yet find my affection useful, for in this consists the glory and excellency of love, that if we are only pure, it can never hurt us; of its giving and receiving there is no end here, and it endures throughout eternity."

" That you still think of us with warm affection and attachment, and would gladly be with us, I find quite natural," she writes in another letter ; " you could not love your William so well if you could forget us. I am fully persuaded that I love you as truly and fondly as William does, and have done so for twenty years ; and thus it is but just that you should continue to love me for at least twenty years, and what will be yet better, my dear, long-loved Agnes,—forever. Preserve then your affection for us in all its fervor, it is quite consistent with that to your dear William. The soul is so constituted, that, while we are here below, wishing and yearning are not only compatible with our happiness, but our best and proper happiness is only realized when this wishing and yearning are directed towards the best things."

" To-morrow is our wedding-day," writes Caroline, in a letter on the 1st of August ; " it is the first on which I have had to look back on gifts resigned. Do you enjoy the onward road, it also has its cares and troubles ; but, as I find by experience, the retrospect is harder and more painful. Youth has its dangers, but those of age are, I fear, greater and more trying, though, thank Heaven, I observe this rather in others than in myself, and in God's name I also am going forward. Dear Agnes, love me still, and keep as close to me as you can. My dear bridegroom is quite well and cheerful, and as dear to me now as he was twenty years ago. I never believed it possible that affection could continue so uninterruptedly for twenty-one years —and how much longer it will continue is not for me to say."

Again, on the following day,—" The children had

adorned our breakfast-table with flowers and wedding
garlands ; we sat in a bower of leafy green, and exam-
ined the little presents that your sisters had prepared
for us. It appears very strange to me that you should
be wandering about the world without me on this
day, and that I should not know whether you are at
Schwarzburg or Rudolfstadt, or where you are."

But it was not only the joyful anniversaries that
Caroline loved to devote to correspondence with her
absent daughter ; those consecrated by sad remembrance were also spent in the same way. " It is six
years to-day since my angel Bernard was born," she
writes on the 27th September, " and his earthly body
is already so decayed, that I can now see only his dear,
bright eye, which, when I was in trouble, used to revive
and strengthen me, and renew my confidence and joy
in the Lord. You also recollect how he rejoiced and
comforted us all at Aschau, and how kindly, and pleasantly, and lovingly he looked on us all. Would that,
though unseen by me, he still looked upon me, and
raised my soul to God ! The angel-child must be able,
and he is certainly willing, to do even more for us
now. How gladly I would know more about the
nature of the happiness of my beloved, departed children ! God does indeed allow us to apprehend it in
the depths of our hearts, as something transcending
thought ; but whenever I would realize this presenti-
ment of the heart in my understanding, it dissolves and
vanishes altogether ; and yet, I cannot help thinking,
though I know that it is in vain, and that on this, as
on all other great questions, we can do nothing more
in this world than keep alive in ourselves the yearning
and longing after truth, not allowing it to be dis-

turbed and destroyed by external influences of any kind."

A new source of happiness was opened to Caroline in the prospect of becoming a grandmother. "I have just received your letter, dear children, and am beyond measure delighted, affected, and thankful. You can have no idea of the happiness that, if it please God, is awaiting you, neither can I explain it to you, although for twenty years my heart has been filled with it. Rejoice, and again I say rejoice, and pray to God for His blessing. If I could but tell you something of your coming joys,—but they are inconceivable and unspeakable, and come directly from God Himself; may He impart them in richest measure!"

The succeeding letters express the tenderest maternal sympathy with the hopes and fears of her daughter; but in all, the call to gratitude and joy is paramount. Thus towards the end of 1818 she wrote—"Every one has, doubtless, reason both for hope and fear, in regard to the New-Year, but God helps us all through. Farewell, dear Agnes, and don't forget your grandfather's prescription for the eve of New-Year's Day, viz.: to sit down upon a stone and pray:—you have much to remember and to hope for; but you must spare us, too, a thought from the depths of your heart."

"A happy, happy Christmas may God give you, dear children," so wrote Caroline, on dispatching a small Christmas box;—"if you have but a tenth part of the delight in unpacking which the children have had in packing it, you will be content. The three little ones have been especially busy, and the pleasure of giving and sending has often ended in tears because there was nothing more to give. Remember that your gratification is to equal theirs, or we shall not be satisfied. The box will reach you at six o'clock, and then, assuredly, you will think of us; and I, too, shall think of you, dear Agnes: you seem still a part of myself; and though I weep, I cannot tell whether they are tears of joy or of sorrow. The Christmas prayer which I put up from my inmost heart for you, last year, is more than fulfilled; let us then, now again, thank God, and place ourselves, and those who are near and dear to us, with confidence and faith in His arms, and rejoice. You must also help us to thank Him; let us with united voice sing, 'Oh, for a thousand tongues,' &c. That sweet hymn always recurs to me when I know not what to say in reviewing the past one-and-twenty years."

"Perthes is a true child at Christmas time," says Caroline, a few days later, in her account of Christmas eve; "my heart is stirred afresh by him every year at that season. It is three-and-twenty years since I first felt this, and my conviction, that one who could take such child-like delight in the Christmas tree must have a pure and simple heart, has not been falsified. This was the impression that my heart received on that evening, when I, properly speaking, first saw him; that, indeed, was the day of my real betrothal. I can never thank God enough for his affection. When, yesterday evening, at six o'clock, we sat down to table, Perthes was so wearied and depressed, that it made us sad to see him, but when the tree was lighted, he became as lively and as frolicsome as the youngest child."

At Easter Caroline writes, "God give you a joyous festival—and why should He not? since He has made every day a festival by the deep and abiding

14*

love that He has put into your heart. That He can
give us nothing better even in eternity is certain ; only
we cannot yet understand the greatness of our blessedness, because we know so little at present of pure love
to God, although we have some foretaste of it in the
delight we feel in the outgoings of our feeble love towards our fellow-creatures. The children are all gone
out, and I meant to read a sermon of Taulerus, but
you and William, your happiness and your hopes, have
stirred my heart so deeply, that I have been unable.
Dear William ! I feel real joy and happiness in having
so nursed, and cherished, and brought up Agnes for
you ; may God grant you the same pleasure in your
children that he has hitherto given us in ours. More
I cannot wish you, for I know no more. I have, to my
great delight, just opened the balcony door for the
first time this year, and am quite transported with all
that the sweet spring breathes, and with all that it reveals to eye and ear. The little birds know not how
to leave off singing and rejoicing, and I would sing
and rejoice with them."

Ever since the autumn of 1818, Caroline had cher-
rished the hope of visiting her daughter in Gotha in
the course of the following spring. Accordingly, on
the 23d of April, Perthes and Caroline, with four children, set out from Hamburgh, committing their second
son to the charge of his grandmother in Wandsbeck,
and leaving the eldest in charge of the house.

"We arrived safe, and well, and happy," wrote
Caroline from Gotha ; " the journey was bitterly cold,
but our inward joy kept us so warm, that the external
cold could not touch us. The postilions were all good
and steady except one, who had a drop in his head ;

but just as we were beginning to be uneasy, we met another posting carriage, and by changing horses got quit of him. Both the little ones behaved very well, and by their merriment and their lively observation of all that they saw and heard, and their surprise at the sight of mountains, trees, and rocks, greatly increased our pleasure, although the charge of such young travellers was not without inconvenience : I was obliged to hold one in each arm during the whole night, to keep them from the cold, and soften the jolting of the carriage. When we came near Gotha, I could scarcely restrain my feelings, and on Tuesday the 27th of April, we arrived."

After Caroline's return to Hamburgh with her husband and children, in the beginning of June, the weeks she had spent with her daughter were a source of grateful remembrance. "Since I have seen you in your own house," she writes, "I have lost the feeling of entire separation, and really live with you again ; and if your heart yearn after me, you will often find me. The happy remembrance of the days that I have spent with you so lately prevails even over the pain of separation."

A year of trouble and disquietude of all sorts awaited Caroline on her return from Gotha ; she had found her second son Clement seriously ill in Hamburgh, and it was many months before her anxiety on his account was in any degree abated. To her eldest son Matthias, who was passing the holidays at Gotha, she wrote at this time,—" Gaze, not to satiety, but till you are hungry, on the beauties of nature ; salute the rocks at Schwarzburg, and go before noon to the Trippstein, when the sun shines aslant through the firs, and reflect that your father and I have also been there, have thanked God and rejoiced. In all my present sorrow, the remembrance of that sweet spot can cheer and solace me ; in such a place one can rise higher, at least more easily, than in one's own room. As for the hours of sore and burning trial, who knows and who can reckon the benefit we derive from them! They are not appointed in vain."

On the 14th of August, in the midst of her anxiety for her sick son, the news of the birth of her first grandchild reached her, and Caroline wrote,—" Oh that I had a thousand tongues, and a thousand voices that might strive together in praising God for what He has done for you! May God Himself help me to thank Him, that He has heard my prayer : I have always the feeling that we can pray fervently much longer than we can praise ; so that our thanksgivings are all too short compared with our supplications. If I could escape from the anxiety and sorrow which surround me, I should be still nearer to you ; but my heart is divided between joy and sadness, and a divided heart brings labor and unrest. You will be astonished to find in how many new and pleasurable aspects the child will appear to you, if God grant His blessing,— and this He certainly never denies to those who honestly seek it. Pray then, that God may send His angel to guide your little one through the joys and sorrows of life, and to be very near him in the time of trial and the hour of death."

XXIX

The Marriage of the Second Daughter.

SCARCELY was Caroline's anxiety for her invalid son removed, when her repose was again interrupted by a proposal for the hand of her second daughter, Louisa, who had remained at Gotha to nurse her sister. The young suitor, Agricola, was scarcely known to her, and the decision was difficult.

"How could we commit so great a charge," wrote Caroline, "to one whom we know not?—it is always a trial to give up a beloved child to any one, and we are now called on to do it to a stranger. I know not where to find counsel or help; it seems to me the greatest trial of my life."

The confidence manifested by the daughter induced the parents to leave the decision to her alone: and when Agricola became known to them through his letters, all anxiety vanished.

In the middle of November, 1819, Louisa returned to Hamburgh for the winter. "We are anticipating," wrote Caroline, "a right pleasant winter with our dear happy bride."

The anticipation was realized. The invalid son meanwhile had made such progress, that he was able to be removed to Wandsbeck for some months for change of air. Caroline's letters at this time are filled again with joy and thankfulness ; but the present was sometimes overcast by the prospect of parting, not only with the daughter, but also with the eldest son, who was to enter the University at Easter.

"It often distresses me greatly," wrote Caroline, "that my young Louisa is so early called upon to play an independent part, and to do without me; still I have a firm confidence in her happiness. Young people who are so sincerely attached, and who express their affection so simply and naturally as these two, are doubtless sound at heart."

"The welcome New Year," she wrote in the end of December, 1819, "lies heavy on my heart, since it is to separate me from two of my beloved children. I know that I ought not to be so, yet I am quite troubled and oppressed. Rejoice in your sweet infant ; the joy will indeed be of a nobler kind when the fondling is over, but never wish a day away ; enjoy that blessed season of maternity during which you have your child in your arms, and it cannot do without you, but stretches out its little arms, and lovingly embraces you."

"To-day," she writes again soon afterwards, "Louisa's trousseau is packed up. God loveth a cheerful giver : He certainly loves Perthes, then ; for he gives almost too freely, and too cheerfully, what it has cost him so much to gather. Life is very serious to me now ; the past and the future stir my soul, but my constant comfort is in the lively and steadfast feeling that God guides and leads us for our good ; only we should not invade His office and cater for ourselves : but this I have never consciously done, at least never desired to do."

At the beginning of April, 1820, both children left the paternal roof, the son for the university, and a week later, the young couple, who had been married on the 12th of April, for Gotha, accompanied by Perthes, and his son Clement.

"I could not write yesterday," says Caroline, "the tumult in my soul was so great that I could not command my feelings sufficiently. Dear Agnes, what a powerful thing is a mother's heart; yes, I believe that the love of parents is stronger than the love of children; what wishes, hopes, fears, and anxieties, stir within me! A steadfast feeling of the presence of God supported me at the parting, and lightened that sad hour; and while my heart is sorrowful, I know and feel that all is right, and that we have much cause for thankfulness; what good would the outward presence of my children do me if their hearts were not with me? If here below we must part and give up, it is only that we may learn to submit our wills, and set forward on the road to our proper home."

Perthes had passed some weeks in Leipzig, and on his return to Hamburgh had quite unexpectedly brought his eldest daughter and his little grandchild from Gotha with him. "As soon as I heard the post-horn," wrote Caroline, "I flew to the door, and when it was opened Perthes put the little prattling healthy child into my arms; my Agnes was also there, and it was a joyful hour indeed. For a long while I could not compose myself, and forgot that Perthes was there too, which afterwards vexed me much."

"You may imagine," she writes a few days later, "how happy I am with my child and grandchild! I have not yet settled down into quiet enjoyment, my

delight is so tumultuous. God be praised for awarding
me so much!" After a stay of five weeks Agnes
returned home with her husband.

Caroline had now three absent children, each of
whom expected letters from her regularly, and they
were seldom disappointed ; she kept up a constant
correspondence with her second daughter during the
honey-moon, and the transition period between it and
the settled repose of matrimonial life. " That you are
so happy and contented with your Agricola is only
what I expected, and I hope better and greater things
still for you, for these are only gilded weeks which,
however, I do not grudge you ; but it requires many a
serious hour, and many an earnest wish with and for
each other, before real happiness and confidence are
established.   Genuine affection is the way to this end ;
perfect openness towards each other, at all times, and in
all things, is also a great help.   Strive to have common
objects of pursuit, and to support each other, when
either seems ready to faint, and let your first aim be,
to draw nearer to God, and to assist each other in
becoming more like Him.   Do not be disturbed by
occasional differences of opinion with regard to the
highest things, only be true to each other, and seek
only the truth ; you will thus, though by devious paths,
be sure to meet again.   I know that I have always
been in earnest, and that I often have been in difficulties, but I also know, that, at last, I have always
reached the same goal with my beloved Perthes—the
how and when do not concern others, and no one has
any right to inquire."

" You can well believe," wrote Caroline soon afterwards, " that I enjoy nothing more truly than what

you tell me of your happy affection. But the human heart is a strange thing; when you wrote lately that you could not understand how you could have hitherto been happy without your Agricola, I felt as if you had done me an injury. I am, at every moment, conscious of loving you with my whole soul, of hoping and wishing for you, and of doing you all the good I can ; more than this I cannot do, neither can your husband ; why, then, should you not have been happy with me ? Can you tell me ? Agricola has loved you for only one year, while I have loved you for eighteen, and with all my heart. Is not this, then, very wrong of you, and can you say that it is not wrong ? I know not what to reply except that it was just so with me when I was married to Perthes, and that I thank God that you now cause me the same grief which I then caused my parents."

Hours of home-sickness were not wanting to the absent daughter. "You cannot wish yourself by my side," wrote Caroline, "so much as I wish myself by yours. But remember one thing, would I not often be in the way when Agricola comes home? Can you deny this? I see you blushing ; but do not blush, and do not vex yourself about it, my dear Louisa ; I am contented, and can thank God that I am now only secondary with you, while I love you as well as if I had the first place in your heart."

"That you find it hard to bear the loneliness, and the distance from us, especially when Agricola is not with you, I can very well understand," she wrote. "I myself, when the children are gone out for a half holiday, am as stupid and dull as an owl by daylight, but one must not yield to this, which happens, more or

less, to all young wives. The best relief is work,
engaged in with interest and diligence ; work, then,
constantly and diligently, at something or other, for
idleness is the devil's snare for small and great, says
your grandfather, and he says true. I do not mean
that there is anything wrong in your longing after us
when Agricola is absent, my own dear child, only you
must strive to retain your composure ; and yet, if you
should be overcome by filial yearning, Agricola will
not be angry with you. You are quite right to tell
him everything that you think and feel at all times ;
where truth and affection abide, joy and happiness are
not long absent."

And again : " Is it not true that the life of a house-
keeper is more stirring than that of a young girl at
home ? It is quite right that you should take pleasure
in your little household affairs, and enjoy your clean
pretty house ; and I can see you, in the afternoons,
looking and listening for your husband, when you
expect him from the courts. How gladly would I
sometimes be behind the door when he comes in !
Fancy me on Saturdays looking through your rooms,
your presses, and your shelves, and praising you when
all is neat and in order."

And in another letter :—" I delight to find that you
take pleasure in all the little matters of your housekeeping ; great events do not often come under our
management, but if we are observant and watchful,
we find our appointed work, and we have more need
to pray for a heart to enjoy our blessings, than for a
larger share of them."—" You are quite right, my dear
Louisa, to visit your neighbors occasionally, but it is
still better that you prefer staying at home. God

grant that you may ever find the same pleasure in your pretty room."

In order to sympathize fully with her daughter's interests, Caroline desired to receive more detailed accounts of her daily life than Louisa was accustomed to give. "You have not yet got into the proper way of writing, you tell me only of things in general, and great events, but, my dear child, I want to know the most minute particulars; you always tell me how dearly you love Agricola, but I should also like to know why you love him. We understand a man's character best from his conduct in little circumstances and in daily life. Don't always seek for something of importance to write; you are writing for my motherly heart, to which everything is important that brings you more vividly before me. Write, then, without too much consideration, about trifles and anything whatever; great events constitute the life, but trifles, the interest of a correspondence. You know that Agnes fills her letters with cabbages and turnips, and so gives me unspeakable pleasure. Man, here below, consists of two parts, and thus, petty things, not paltry. recollect, are part of our existence."

Again :—" I am sorry that you tore up your letter because it was not written in a happy mood; next time send it me just as it is. I know as well as you do, that the heart is not always in the same frame; we should, indeed, endeavor to be at all times master of ourselves, but it takes a good many trials before we attain to this; and I remember how many uneasy moods and moments I myself had to pass through."

When, in the course of time, the daughter made that discovery which every young wife has to make

for herself, viz., that even in her new position, the
earnestness of life is not wanting, Caroline wrote,—
" Yes, dear child, God's gift of true love grows and
improves under all circumstances, and although we
would gladly escape the sweat of the brow, we soon
see that it is necessary, and a part of our earthly discipline ; all men have felt, that as life brings us greater happiness, it also becomes more earnest. Thank
your Agricola with all your heart for sharing his
cares with you, rather than concealing them in order
to spare you. If a wife cannot actually remove, she
can often lighten care, and sweet and bitter should be
shared by man and wife. I might indeed desire nothing but joy and happiness for you, but I do not at all
despair about you.

" Men's characters differ greatly, and with them
God's means of promoting their welfare. Your father
and I had many struggles, which were often very
painful ; but when I look back, I see clearly that all
served to unite us, and make us better acquainted with
each other, and that is a result which can never be
bought too dear."

" You are quite right, dear Louisa, to be on your
guard against all sources of irritation. It is great and
noble to attain to a state of mind which does not
allow affection to be saddened or interrupted by
the trifles of daily life. A strong determination
against this must be rooted in the heart ; but I have
learnt from good old François de Sales, and from experience, that there are many things which, though
they are not to be lightly regarded, must be lightly
handled. We must not oppose an irritable tendency
by force, otherwise the irritation may only change its

form.   To oppose one's own irritability with greater
irritability, is disturbing to others, and may embitter
our own hearts, but I am not at all anxious about you ;
you never had a fretful disposition, and a loving heart
is proof against it ; but you cannot have recourse to
any one who will understand you so well as I do, for
I have felt it all myself."

In November, 1820, her daughter was severely tried
by the illness of her husband, who was in great danger for many weeks from nervous fever, and had a
very slow recovery.

" Your father and I think of you day and night,"
wrote Caroline, when the crisis was over : " we feel
but too deeply how painful it is to have a child whom
we cannot soothe and make happy.   These have been
very sad days for us ; it was quite a new thought to
me that I might have my own dear child in my house
and in my arms, and yet that all my affection could
neither satisfy nor comfort her."

Soon afterwards she wrote,—" Let us first thank
God for having preserved your Agricola, and having
given you trust and confidence in time of need, and
then pray for his further recovery.   We need neither
be ashamed nor vexed that we are always ready to
ask ; God knows better than we do that we can do
nothing without Him."

When the invalid was beginning to recover his
strength, she wrote,—" We no longer feel the burden,
we only remember it, and now rejoice with you in the
coming spring, and the warm sunbeams ; although the
spring-time of youth has passed for us, not so, thank
God, the eternal spring, which still grows fresher as
we grow older.   Let your heart beat in sympathy with

the renewed spring-time of nature, which makes us young, and fresh, and gladsome, like the little variegated tom-tits in the oak tree behind my window. Ever rejoice in the spring and in life, dear Agricola, and be thankful that you are preserved to my Louisa and to us all."

XXX

Departure of the Eldest Son for the University.

HILE the correspondence with the married daughters devolved mainly on the mother, Perthes adding now and then a kind word on special occasions, that with the eldest son, Matthias, who had been studying theology at the University of Tübingen since Easter, 1820, was kept up alike by both parents. The doubts and difficulties suggested to the son by the study of theology, were submitted to the father. Perthes always sympathized with his son's inexperience, and endeavored to allay his misgivings.

"I have been reading over many of your letters a second time," he once wrote, "and am more and more convinced that it would not be well to answer your earnest communications in detail by a discussion of your views. In the case of a striving, energetic youth like yourself, months are more fruitful than years are to an older man ; the scales are moving up and down, and so it should be. One thing rectifies another in the course of the student's own hearty efforts, which God always blesses. This is better for you than listening to an old man's experience, which must always be some-

what strange, even though it be your own father's."—
"I cannot and dare not enter into the subjects which
you mention. It would ill become the man whose
mind is matured by age, and whose intellectual training has been so different, to set bounds which might
impede the young theologian in his career; when your
advancing age brings you nearer to my own, we shall
readily understand one another. You say, 'The God
of the many does not satisfy my yearnings, I want one
to whom I can put up my petitions in the hope that He
will be moved by my humility to grant me health and
strength.' These are your own words; keep to them,
my dear son."

In another letter, Perthes explained his views of the
difference between youth and age more fully :—" Between youth and age there is a wall of partition, which
a man does not observe till he has passed it. The
transition is generally made in middle life, but passes
unnoticed amid the necessary cares and labors of one's
calling. All at once man finds himself upon an eminence, and sees much that is varied and cheerful behind
and beneath him. This is a decisive moment for the
soul, for now arises the question, whether he shall give
himself entirely to God. and turn away from the world,
not with contempt,—for it has been his training school,
but with a glad contentedness; or, whether he shall
again mingle with the many things that should be left
behind, and thus become not only a transgressor, but
a laughing-stock in the eyes of superior intelligences.
Generally, when a man has passed through the season
of wayward minority, and stands erect in manhood, he
asks himself, What means all this? his reply must be,
All below is vain and fleeting; true joy and peace are

only to be found in spiritual life. I have done many things and perhaps well, but where is the fruit of the blossoms which looked so promising? '*The ideals have disappeared*,' but not the faculty of labor ; and therefore, clothed with humility, 'forwards,' I say, to suffer and to do. This is to become a master in the business of life ; but it is vain to expect that this can be attained without passing through an apprenticeship and the *Wanderjahre*. Here it is that so many well-disposed youths of the present day make shipwreck. They affect a simplicity, plainness, and stoutness of heart, which almost look like the repose and dignity of age ; they harden their bodies, adopt severity of manners, and are modern Stoics. But this is an unnatural condition for youth, and it will not be generally found a safe one : this contempt of the world and of the true riches of human life soon passes into repulsive egotism or sonorous emptiness ; or if the character be of sterner mould, into inhuman tyranny and wickedness.

"But there are others among our would-be men who, from misconception of the religious sentiment, would fain jump to their majority, by avoiding all conflict with the world, both within and without ; they think that they can, even in youth, pluck the precocious buds and blossoms which themselves have nurtured : but this is vanity : let us give ourselves to the LORD in humility. God's special messengers generally pass through a discipline in youth ; many persons, on the other hand, have to endure the conflict with their own hearts and with the world, in later years, and that with aggravated difficulty and peril ; others wither away in empty formalism ; and many end in the vilest hypocrisy. Both these forms of premature manhood belong

to modern times; and both have often borrowed from
Christianity forms of speech which they take for their
own proper expression. I would not have you, dear
Matthias, fasten these words of mine on any individuals; what I have said applies only to classes. We
should always take for granted that it is all right with
the individual, and that he has merely received his
coloring from the age. A wonderful admixture of
youth and age now prevails, and to the detriment of
both, each trespassing on the other; for to keep clearly in sight the real line of demarcation between the
two, is alike essential to both teacher and learner; for
the power of the Spirit and the love of Jesus Christ
have a special applicability to the several circumstances
of life. This is exactly what we find in the Acts of the
Apostles, when Paul adapts himself specially to every
variety of character and place. What countless errors
and deviations from the path of duty do we find to have
arisen in the present day, from well-intentioned preachers having laid down *general* rules of conduct from instructions designed only for *limited* application!"

Although Perthes always avoided giving an opinion
on the theological questions and religious doubts which
exercised the mind of his son, he did not object to point
out frequently, and with decision, the course of conduct which a student, earnest in his search after truth,
should adopt. Thus, on one occasion, he writes, "You
ask, if I object to your joining the Bürschenschaft.
Since the Authorities of the university are not absolutely opposed to it, and I am unacquainted with the
state of affairs at Tübingen, on which the whole question hinges, it might be better to leave the decision to
your own judgment; but it is well to consider the ex-

penditure of time, which time belongs not only to yourself but to your vocation ; and then you must not be
too sanguine in your expectation of improving others,
whom, in your youthful enthusiasm, you hope to influence.   We influence others only when the ruling spirit
of our own minds is the stronger ; such a man, for instance, as Plehwe, whom may God help, exercises great
influence, but God forbid that you should be like him.
You are much too thoughtful, inquiring, and contemplative to command the minds of young people, who
are, for the most part, under the influence of physical
temperament.   They will be led only by one who has
shown his superiority to them on their own ground.
Moreover, in carrying out that which you recognize to
be right and true, you are apt to be decided and harsh,
and to grow impatient, and would thus increase your
difficulties.   Nevertheless, I am not, as you know, one
to keep back anybody, even a child of my own, from a
path which may lead to good, merely because it is be-
set with dangers : one thing, however, appears decisive
to me,—as soon as you join this association there will
arise in your own breast a discord that will not be
easily quieted ; for duty towards God is not separable
by a clear straight line from the claims of conventional
honor.   He who will dance upon the ice must reckon
upon falls.   I cannot, therefore, but oppose your joining the Bürschenschaft."

But the correspondence of Perthes bore more generally on the broad principles connected with the vocation to which his son had devoted himself than on
details of this kind.   Thus he once wrote :—" The distinction which you make between a man of learning,
and one who only uses learning as a means to an end,

appears to me to be too subtle. In the present day
there are but few who value learning for its own sake;
even the teacher uses science as a means of forming
and influencing other minds. Still it is certain that he
who has chosen any path of practical usefulness can
never have acquired too much scientific learning; and
in your own case, if the path you have chosen be followed out, you can be kept from deviation into by-
paths, and advanced in the right way only by the most
thorough learning. But do not misunderstand me; in
the present range of scientific knowledge it is necessary that a man circumscribe himself, and rigidly keep
within certain limits, otherwise he will get lost in its
immensity, and prove superficial in all. It appears to
me that the first requisite for a theologian is a thorough
acquaintance with Greek and Hebrew, Latin being, of
course, presupposed. If a young man be well-grounded
in the original language of the text, he has won a
standing-ground for all future inquiry and investigation. Stand to your daily work, my beloved son;
study methodically and faithfully, and collect materials;
then you will have learnt what admits of investigation,
and what not."

Again he writes :—" You are not satisfied with the
conviction of the deceitfulness of all human thought
and inquiry, and you refuse to take the leap that sep-
arates reason from faith in revelation—you would fain
prove by scientific research that revelation is a reality.
Be it so. Only recollect that, for some centuries past,
inquirers and divines have trodden the same path, and
soon found themselves at the end of it. All that men
could discover in the Scriptures concerning the Life of
Christ, is certainly laid down in the early Fathers.

Have they and all their followers not been able to present a connected system that might satisfy the minds of
young inquirers like you, till you are far enough advanced in science to frame one for yourselves? Do you
recognize no authority in your teachers when they say
to you, 'This is found in Scripture, this our predeces-
sors have found, and this you will also find when you
are sufficiently advanced in the study of languages and
of history?' It would be sad indeed, if learning, which
has made such progress since the Reformation, had not
even so much weight as this with beginners."

When, in the further pursuit of his studies, the son
felt himself more and more attracted by philosophy,
Perthes wrote to him:—"Since, as I see, you have
betaken yourself to philosophy, I should wish you to
put yourself under the guidance of some able thinker,
a good man, and a theologian, even though of a different religious persuasion from my own. Would not
Professor Steudel give you an hour now and then? It
seems to me that you should at present pursue the
study of theology dogmatically and historically only, ·
disregarding for a while its philosophical basis. But
at the same time I would thoroughly study some one
philosophical system without reference to Revelation,
and run through the history of philosophical systems;
when you have done this, throw aside the one you have
mastered, take up another, and so on, until you have
found one that is tenable; only beware of bringing to
any system thoughts which it has not itself originated,
and reject with contempt that legerdemain which rep-
resents, as proper to a system, thoughts which owe
their origin to Revelation alone. Then I am convinced
that you will soon enough discover that all mere phi-

losophizing is vain, and will gladly avail yourself of
Revelation, if, indeed, any true religious feeling be
awakened within you. My dear son, read frequently
your mother's letters.—be attracted within the atmosphere of her piety,—keep your heart pure, that it may
never be a stranger to prayer : then may you investigate freely ; for prayer and earnest study will help you
to overcome in the conflict with doubt."

Caroline considered her son's determination to pursue the study of theology as a matter of primary importance. " Matthias," she wrote, " has handled a hot
iron ; but, if he grasp it rightly, he has achieved a
great matter, and God is with him." But when he left
for the university, her sense of the earnestness of his
vocation was for a while supplanted by her regret at
separation from him. " How painful it was to me,"
she wrote immediately afterwards, to part with Matthias, and to send him into the world, without being
able to commit him to the guidance of any human
heart or eye. I have had hard work with myself, but
now I have laid down my arms, and am at peace."

At the same time she wrote to her son,—" My
thoughts of you are disturbed by a painful feeling of
your solitude and distance. I know and am persuaded that in great and important matters you
cleave to God, and can do without us ; still there are
many seasons in which parental love and sympathy are
a source of great happiness and comfort. This I myself feel."

" Your letter is just come," she writes a few days
later ; " I am filled with joy and thankfulness to God,
who has so wondrously heard and blessed our wishes
and desires in placing you amongst the truly good.

But you know not, dear Matthias, how wholly I have committed you to God, praying that He may guide, and teach, and care for you in great and in little things. I am persuaded that you are in His hands, and am happier and more reconciled than I could have thought possible, although there are moments when the yearnings of the mother's heart prevail over these better feelings. We have also letters from Gotha with the best tidings. I do not know how to make enough of the happiness which God has given us on all sides, and must take refuge in the hymn-book."

Again, she wrote, "When I am sitting alone on the sofa in the parlor, before the children come down in the morning, and your father has just gone to business, I thank God, and pray for you with all my heart, and look at your portrait which you gave me last Christmas. It brings you vividly before me, and often it seems as if you saw my thoughts, and responded to them."

"Your grandmother, at Wandsbeck, will rejoice to see that people love your grandfather, and you for his sake," wrote Caroline shortly afterwards. "Indeed, dear Matthias, how many advantages you enjoy that others have not! God will expect more from you, and you must expect more from your own self, on this very account."

In several other letters Caroline urges her son to realize the responsibilities involved in his choice of a calling. "It is quite clear to my own mind," she writes, "that there are many more inquirers for counsel and encouragement than there were ten or fifteen years ago, and it is a great privilege to guide such ; but it is no easy task. We get over many difficulties in our own minds, because the solution does not require to be put into words, which must, however, be used when we would help another."

In another letter Caroline writes,—" I was well aware, whilst you were still with us, that the time would come when you would see many things, both within and without, in a different light from us ; but I did not *say* this because I hoped and believed that you were earnest and truth-loving, and because I trusted that God would give you right views and opinions at the right time. Moreover, I know that man can impart but little to his fellow-man ; each must seek and find for himself. I can say with truth that I have been for many years in trouble and perplexity, from which I am not even now free. I have found that it is better not to think of one's self so much, but rather to think more of God, and to long earnestly after Him ; and if we have fallen, to rise at once and go on, trusting in God : thus we are continually advancing, by God's grace, towards a peaceful and blessed end. The Princess Gallitzin once said to me, from her inmost soul, and with a deep sense of her insufficiency, ' But I will still *will.*' This word often recurs to me, and cheers me when I am cast down. We often become more free and happy when we look at ourselves as a whole, rather than in detail. If we keep all the good thoughts that have occurred to our minds continually present, we shall easily be led to think more highly of ourselves than we ought, and so shall in reality retrograde."

" I am not distressed to hear," wrote Caroline at another time, " that you find yourself unable to pray with as much faith and confidence as you desire, for we are at best but as reeds moved to and fro by the wind ; if we only yearn for living faith, God will not fail to help us on, and all doubts and discouragements will eventually cease ; but it is almost too much to expect that you should be as yet near to this happy consummation. Socrates thought that inward peace was not to be attained until a man had reached his fortieth year, and Confucius has placed the goal still farther forward ; but I do wrong in referring to Socrates and Confucius when we have Christ ; consider it then as unsaid. I always take comfort from that man in the Gospel to whom our Lord Christ said, that he must *believe* before he could be helped ; and who replied to him, ' Lord, I believe, help thou mine unbelief.' This is all that we can do, and where we can do nothing, God is ever ready to aid ; besides, there may be much unrest and unbelief in the head whilst the heart holds firmly by its anchor—' God is love, and he that dwelleth in love dwelleth in God.' I know of nothing more certain, imperfect as our love must needs be here below."

Great as was the importance which Caroline attached to this anchor of the heart, she was far from wishing to make it an excuse for indolent security. " Dear Matthias," she once wrote, " accustom yourself to laborious study. It is not mere ignorance, but the want of the power of application, which is found to have such evil and bitter consequences. Tell me, then, whether you are bravely diligent : I wish and hope it may be so ; and I should like to know how you arrange your studies. I do not believe that it is possible for a young man, however earnest and well-intentioned, always to see the why and wherefore of

15*

his studies. You would relieve me from a great anxiety if you would commit yours to the direction of some sensible, learned, and older man, who might take your father's place, and direct your scientific career. Without pretending to understand more, I know that experience makes the best guide. Perhaps, dear Matthias, you will laugh at this counsel ; you are quite welcome; only consider it, and tell me what you think of it. I would so gladly know that you are on the straightest road even to human learning."

" You may imagine," wrote Caroline, in transmitting some controversial pamphlets, " the *pros* and *contras* that these have occasioned ; it is very sad and grievous that the holiest and brightest truths of religion should be treated as mere topics of conversation and amusement—and yet it has this good, that it leads men to ask themselves on which side they are. I believe with you that, in order to deal honestly with your future congregation, and with your own understanding, you must diligently investigate, in order that you may come to the steadfast knowledge, and the clear consciousness, that ' in Christ Jesus are hidden all the treasures of wisdom ;' but I also trust in God that, if you wrestle and strive earnestly, He will give you a yearning, and a steadfast faith by which He will carry on the work of grace in your heart, even when your understanding labors under perplexity."

" In answer to a letter in which her son had told her of the many valuable friends whom he had found at the University, Caroline replied,—" I was rejoiced to receive your last letter, and although I make allowance for youthful enthusiasm, and am well aware that your best moments are not lasting, yet I see that all your hopes and efforts are in the right direction, and we are thankful that you have joined such a circle of friends. Tell me how you generally spend the Sunday, and whether you have found a preacher who proclaims the truth without any human additions, and with the inward confidence that he has the same interest as his hearers have in what he says. I hope that you are pursuing the study of logic right earnestly ; many feel the want of it. Last Sunday I heard a sermon of much ability, and containing much that was good in the details, but the whole so confused that it was almost impossible to follow it ; thought and learning are, in general, necessary before we can teach others. I thank God that you are committed to teachers who unite in themselves learning and respect for the faith."

But it was not only in the studies and perplexities of her son that Caroline was interested, she also sympathized warmly with him in the pleasures which the University offered. "Your external life is somewhat monotonous, but you must vary it a little, and I think you should do so as far as is consistent with order and regularity." "You have given us great pleasure by the narrative of your journey," she wrote, when the young student had sought recreation for a time in Switzerland ; "open your eyes wide, look at everything, so that the impressions, which are to be the materials of thought when you are set fast in the yoke, may be permanent. If you keep your eye and your heart steadfastly fixed on the goal, the yoke will be softer and lighter : this your father finds, for God does not send him empty away : he also has his circle of influence where God blesses his efforts ; of this I am certain,"

"Your letter from Zurich is just come, and tells us that you are well, and in dear Switzerland, where my heart has so long yearned to be. I have got the map out, and have followed you from place to place, and have calculated distances, and have seen everything with you as far as possible. No one can sympathize with you more than I do, in the enjoyment of the works of God ; only, they must lead you into the depths of your own heart and to prayer."

The mother's care extended to the minutest details of the student-life, and warned him against bad habits, so easily acquired when removed from the paternal roof. "It is long since you have written about yourself," she says in one of her letters, "and of your daily life at home and abroad, so that I can see exactly what you are about. If such a letter is not already on the way, sit down at once, and tell me, circumstantially, whether you are in good spirits, what you are at work upon, and whether you are making progress ; also about your friends, your amusements, your chairs and tables, your coats and shoes, in short, about all that appertains to the nourishment and necessities of this mortal life ; I am longing for such tidings."

Shortly after this she writes :—"Make a point of keeping your room clean and neat, and of opening the windows every day : and then, dear Matthias, I entreat you, out of love to me, dress yourself on first rising, and don't sit for hours half dressed, and with shoes down at the heels : I dislike it very much ; dress yourself for the day, and you will feel fresh and cheerful, and ready for anything that may come."

But while Caroline thus fully entered into the life of her eldest son, she kept up his interest in home by communicating all those trifling events which make up domestic life : all anniversaries were especially noticed ; thus, on the 2d August, 1820, the anniversary of her wedding-day, Caroline wrote,—" We were sitting at the breakfast-table, almost buried in garlands, as you have seen us,—joy and pleasure in all hearts and eyes—when your letter and congratulatory verses were brought to us ; we read it, rejoiced, and thanked God. I was especially affected by your wedding-garland, for if you had not been my own very child, you would not have sent it. I have wept my fill, but rather from joy than from sorrow. My whole heart thanks you for your affection, and I pray to God that He may strengthen and uphold your purpose, and enable you to act upon it. We have need to will, and will afresh every minute, for thus we generally bring something to good effect, often unconsciously indeed ; but what is unconscious is often best. At least there is nothing that I fear so much as self-satisfaction ; for the feeling of need, and of insufficiency, and the reaching after God's mercy, are our best safeguards here below, because this is our real and natural condition. That God may help you, and all of us, my dear Matthias, is my constant prayer."

" The 18th October," she writes on another occasion, " the anniversary of the battle of Leipzig, was right festively commemorated. Early in the morning all the bells were ringing, all the churches were full, and crowds waited without ; at noon the whole town-guard turned out ; the streets were so full of holiday folks walking, driving, and riding, that I could not hear myself speak ; in the evening there were fire-works in every direction. I sat at home and thought ; the rec-

ollection of that great epoch is engraven in my heart ;
I have lived those iron months over again with all their
joys, and sorrows, and anxieties ; you will believe that
my eyes overflowed, and I thanked God as well as I
could, though not so fervently as I wished, for all His
goodness. If I could but once keep this day in the
Aschau cellar, gratitude would rise spontaneously, and
overpower all other thoughts : that cellar I shall remember as long as I live ; how perplexed I often was
when I left you all for a quarter of an hour, to be
alone, and to give free course to my tears. I am really
angry with all who on such a day can allow themselves to be dissatisfied with things as they are ; on
other days people may be angry, and demand reforms,
but on the 18th of October we ought only to rejoice
and be glad in the deliverance which God wrought for
us. And when I think of ourselves in particular, what
overflowing pleasure do I see ; only my darling, blessed
Bernard's place is empty ! we miss him, and shall miss
him till we go to him."

In another letter she says,—"All my anniversaries,
now that we are so dispersed, are spoilt, and no longer
yield the same enjoyment, for it takes much thought to
bring you all before me now ; still, so long as nothing
disturbing comes between you and my longing after
you, I shall rejoice."

"The empty places at the Christmas table," she
writes, " did indeed mar my joy, but not my gratitude
to God, for you, my dear absent children, and for the
persuasion that you have set out on the good and right
way. Though I cannot see you, my heart is glad in
its affection, and especially on dear Christmas eve ;

still it was a quiet festival, and less happy than usual on account of our anxiety for Agricola."

The 16th January was Matthias' birth-day, and his mother wrote, "How I long to see you face to face, and to hold you in my arms, tall as you may be, for maternal love is not appalled by height, and the child is a child still though he be a man. You, my dear old Matthias, I would so gladly have with us; keep well, and enter on your one-and-twentieth year with joy and energy : may God be with you, and preserve you, and grant all my wishes for you, and bless you forevermore, as I believe He will. I send you the birth-day wish and prayer, with which I this morning awoke, that you may make it your own. 'O thou Eternal Light and strong Rock, let the light of thy life-giving word shine upon him, and teach him to know thee aright, and to call thee Father with his whole heart ; teach him that Christ is our Lord and Master, and that there is none besides, that he may seek thee only, and trust in thee with all his strength.' My beloved child, may God grant it !"

XXXI

The Last Days of Caroline.

THE bodily sufferings to which Caroline had been subject, ever since the trying scenes of 1813, had been greatly aggravated by the cares and anxieties of the last summer. The irritability of the nervous system, and the heart disease had now reached an alarming height; but her serenity of mind was undisturbed; her Christian faith and hope waxed even brighter and stronger as the body approached its last resting-place. "I have lately had feelings, thoughts, and views, formerly quite unknown to me with reference to our earthly life and our appointed work therein, and in connexion with these, a greater serenity." This she wrote in the spring of 1820.

And again, about the same time, "How differently I regard my position, now that I am consciously going down the hill, and find myself so much nearer the end than the beginning of life. If I am not self-deceived, when I examine myself as in the sight of God, I find an increase of peace and assurance, and there are seasons when I am even confident. God grant that the peace and confidence may be abiding, and not a mere play of fancy! God will surely help me. The desire of my heart is for peace and submission to His will, but I cannot always master the desire to live here on earth. I have still much enjoyment and happiness in life, and I have my Perthes."—"It refreshes my spirit, dear Agnes, to hear that, like me, you are seeking and finding God in many things that appear insignificant, but that do really gently stir and rejoice our hearts all the day long. I cannot say much about them, but I can thank God, and long for more. Let us only be faithful and earnest in little things, and perhaps, in heaven, great things may be committed to us."

An anxious, doubting state of mind was unknown to her, and she was not inclined to regard it favorably in others. "N.," she writes, "has left us; he has failed to discern much that is good here, and also much that is not good in the circle of his own friends, I fancy, because here as elsewhere, externals cast a veil over the inner-man. He is certainly a pious man, but his misfortune is that, for the most part, he has an eye only for what he dislikes in the lives of Christians."

In another letter she says :—" we are anxiously looking for a man of truth and earnestness to prepare Matilda for confirmation, and, as yet, without success. Pl—'s sister has gone from Riga to Kiel for a year and a half, that her daughter may enjoy the benefit of Harms' instruction : gladly as I would avail myself of his teaching for Matilda, I could never have taken such a step, because it seems to me to involve a distrust of the Divine power and influence ; and besides, how could one look other children in the face, whose parents were unable to do so much for them ?"

That it was possible for a Christian to be, for a longer or shorter period, depressed by anxiety concerning his spiritual state, Caroline was well aware, for she had herself experienced it. "Come to my arms," she wrote in the spring of 1821, to a deeply dejected friend, "and pour out your heart with all its hopes and fears, its anxieties and sadness. I understand you, and have not forgotten my own griefs, but I believe that God will look upon us for good, if even one groan escape from our breasts. Only we must be willing at every moment to take up our burden, and to bear what God sends; and that He often sends heaviness no one will deny. I cannot say that I have never murmured, but I have often asked God with tears why He has weighed me down; and then I have been strengthened by the thought that it is all His doing, and cannot be without reason; that He knows our anxiety and cannot be offended by it."

Although well acquainted with the cares and sorrows of the inner-life, a feeling of joy and thankfulness was nevertheless habitual to Caroline, even when her bodily sufferings were severe; the source of this joy she indicates in a letter to her eldest daughter :—"That you are a happy woman I know, and I desire with all my heart that you may continue so : nor do I doubt it; perplexed you may be, but not unhappy ; for one who strives from the heart to be resigned to the will of God, under all circumstances, can never be unhappy."

Caroline possessed, in a remarkable degree, the power of tracing the sources of happiness, and of not allowing them to pass by unnoticed and unenjoyed. On the day preceding the last anniversary of her betrothal, which she survived, she wrote :—" To-morrow will be my day of days, the first of May, and gladly would I wander with my beloved bridegroom amid the hills and woods, where I might see and hear none but himself, and might thank God, that, after four-and-twenty years, I can keep the day with feelings of the most thorough joy and satisfaction. A few sighs may escape, for my breath is but short; but joy shall be continually renewed: yes, certainly, the woods, the green woods, would be my chosen home; though, when I look through the fresh green leaves at the blue waters and the unclouded sky, all is so beautiful, that it is only with shame and self-reproach that I can really wish for more. Such a fullness of spring splendor and beauty, I think I have never before seen; the loveliness of the trees and foliage, grass, and flowers, is inexpressible. And this great change from death to life has come to pass in a few days, I might say, in a few hours. When we stand in the sweet spring-tide, looking through the tall, bright-green trees to the pure blue sky, one can scarcely realize all the trouble and sorrow that may be within us and around us: yes, spring is the time of joy; and that joy carries my heart upwards to that bright and happy land, where there shall be no more pain or sorrow."

When nature was dark and wintry, Caroline had many other sources of happiness. Her affection for her husband and children was, above all other earthly things, an inexhaustible fountain of joy and gratitude: "I must tell you, my dear Matthias," she wrote in 1821, "that, notwithstanding my difficulty of breathing, I am not cast down: and, indeed, I have no reason for being so; for God overpowers us with blessings and joys, by making our children happy and prosperous. We hear nothing but good from Gotha, and we hope that you also are in the good way, and that God is with you. Matilda is a sensible though merry child, and has made herself useful, beyond what one could expect from her age, in the season of severe sickness ; she delights to go about with me and to take care of me as far as she is able. Perthes is specially fond of his little daughter. Eleanora is a nice girl, and her heart grows full of kindliness and love : and my Andrew is my delight from morning till evening, when he does not happen to be passionate and naughty. My dearest Perthes grows daily in earnestness and grace, as regards his own soul ; towards myself he could not be better. Can I then do otherwise than thank God and rejoice ?"

In a letter to her eldest daughter she says again, " I must tell you more about your father—how he continues to gain peace, quietness, and stability, in spite of the disturbance and confusion by which he is surrounded. I would that you knew this as surely as I do—it is so comforting and encouraging to see God's blessing so manifestly resting upon him. It may be difficult for those who look only at separate features of his character to realize this ; but I, who am so thoroughly acquainted with him, know, that year by year he draws nearer to God, and is working out his own salvation with earnestness. I call upon you to thank God with me for having given you such a father, he is almost too dear and good. If I could only have him a little more, or rather talk with him a little more ; for I certainly have him wholly—of that I am persuaded. Nothing in heaven or earth can sur-pass genuine affection ; it will certainly make the happiness of heaven, only there it will be greater, and purer, and uninterrupted ; and, according to my present feelings, I should desire even there to keep my Perthes and to love him."

In the autumn she wrote, "What a constant and profound sense have I of God's mercy, in the bright hopes He has given me, and to so great an extent already realized, in and through you all! You cannot imagine what bright and blessed hours your father and I enjoy when we sit down together, to think over this. It is a gift of God's grace, unspeakably precious, to see our children walking in the way to heaven, however great may be our fears and anxieties respecting them ; for God who has begun the good work will perform it in us all, and will perfect that which concerneth us."

In a letter written on the last day of December, Caroline says, " One could not have believed it possible to have sailed along the world's sea of sorrow and suffering, throughout three hundred and sixty-five days, and to find our fragile bark so little injured. Again, I feel that I cannot be thankful enough ; and yet how many wishes and petitions are ready for the opening year."

From the commencement of her married life, Caroline had longed for more of outward calm and quiet, that her enjoyment of Perthes' society might have been more undisturbed ; but the course of time convinced her that the bustling life to which she had been called was a needful and salutary discipline.

" I rejoice with you," she once wrote to her daughter, " that you have returned to your wonted quiet and peaceful life, and that I still long with all my heart for quietness and peace ; for this longing proves to me that my unrest has not injured me. Who can say that it has not done me good ? I should certainly never choose to live in a whirl, but God makes all things work together for our good."

Her anxiety, however, lest the health of Perthes should suffer from the pressure of business could not be allayed. "Perthes," she once wrote, "works more than is good for him. Ah! if I could but get him safe out of this tumult! I can only live with him in thought, for the worry of incessant toil does not leave me a single quiet moment with him. But I must not, and will not complain, for he is in good spirits, and would rejoice if we could be more together."

Ever since Caroline's eldest daughter had been settled in Gotha, she had cherished the hope that, at no very distant period, Perthes would commit his large business and its unceasing cares to others, and at a distance from the tumult of the great city retire to Gotha, where he might live more to himself and for his family. In many letters she joyfully alludes to this cheering prospect. "If God will, we shall come nearer to you and enjoy a common happiness. Yes, in the depths of my heart, I anticipate that you, dear children, will be the joy of my old age, as you were of my youth."

Somewhat later she wrote,—"I notice that Perthes is constantly endeavoring to bring matters to a point, in order that we may join you; but when I would express the delight that this gives me, he grows restive, and says, that I ought not even to rejoice in my heart, while all is still so uncertain."

Perthes, in the meanwhile, was no less earnestly occupied with the hope of deliverance from the wear and tear of such a business. Thus, in the spring of 1821, he writes to his eldest daughter and her husband,— " You are indeed privileged in being able to enjoy your youthful years so free from care; mine has been a tumultuous life, and it is but seldom that a quiet hour, unburdened with anxiety, has fallen to my lot. I would thank God with all humility for His guidance hitherto, and commit my way to Him for the future. My desire is for quiet and repose. I would not be unemployed ; but I long to feel at liberty to follow my inclination, and gradually to obliterate from my heart and mind the world's unrest, that I may be ready for that time when all reckonings here below must be forever cancelled."

Caroline's hope to spend the latter years of her life in quiet union with Perthes and her married daughter, was not to be fulfilled. The disease that had attacked her heart and nerves, increased to a painful degree in the spring of 1821.

" I am restless, and my nerves are weak and weary," she wrote in April, "and my breathing is become very difficult. This is not a healthy condition, and Dr. Schroeder does his best, but he has not yet found the right medicine." Some weeks later she writes, " I am now drinking the Geilnauer waters, and am in the garden from six to eight o'clock ; and happy to receive any visitors there. I take all sorts of journeys in imagination, and hold long conversations with you, my beloved children, when I am wandering about alone."

Early in June she was brought to the gates of death by nervous fever, consequent on a severe attack of internal cramp ; and she now became fully aware of her danger. " I am weary and done," she wrote when the danger had passed for a season ; " and if you should see me, you would feel that my days are numbered. I give myself up to be nursed and cared for by Matilda, as the representative of you all. She ministers to me

with child-like love, and with great judgment and caution.   I have often had you by me, dear Matthias, and
have wished you good-morning and good-night.   I
thank God that I can think of you with joy.   Once,
in my delirium, I thought you were become a Catholic ;
I took it sadly to heart, and now I rejoice the more that
it is not so."

Serious thoughts of death had been familiar to Caroline throughout her whole life.   She had always regarded it with solemn awe, but it had, perhaps, never
excited in her mind that terror with which it is frequently associated even in the minds of pious men, and
of which the majority of people are insensible, only
because wholly given over to frivolity.   The letters in
which Caroline refers to the death of those near and
dear to her, are the expression of distress, but never
of alarm—she is peaceful and resigned.   Thus, in one
of them she says—"This is another anniversary of
death : ten years ago, my beloved John departed from
us.   In this long interval I have always, thank God,
been able to love him, but not, alas! to see and hear
him, and who can tell whether he is still capable of
loving me ?   I believe that the relation of mother and
child ceases in heaven ; but God will assuredly so
order all things that we shall still love each other."

Again she says, "It is hard for the survivor, with a
heart full of love and yearning, no longer to hear and
see the dear departed one.   How deeply and vividly
I feel this when, with my motherly heart, I think of my
beloved children in heaven.   I cannot help asking
why our Heavenly Father has appointed these painful
partings ; and though I receive no answer, I am reas-
sured and comforted by the knowledge that it is His

will, and that He wills nothing but good, even when it does not seem so to us."

In another letter she writes :—"Old Mrs. N. gently fell asleep yesterday. I rejoice to think that she was ready : she could no longer enjoy anything here below ; and her weakness and confusion of mind were, as far as we could judge, a hindrance to the enjoyment of the presence and consolations of God Himself. Now her dormant love is rekindled never to be dimmed by the thousand trifles that clouded and dogged it here."

Again : "I have passed some very serious hours at S.'s death-bed. He died with wonderful peace and resignation, retaining his consciousness to the last. I rejoiced to look upon the corpse as it lay in the still repose of death, no longer constrained to cough, and tortured for want of air. It is remarkable, and I have often observed, how high and clear death makes the forehead : even S.'s was very fine after death, though certainly it was not so in life."

On receiving the news of the decease of Count F. L. Stolberg, in December, 1819, Caroline had written to her eldest daughter,—"The dear, pure spirit will now see God face to face, of that I am persuaded ; but we have one dear friend less on earth. The last month of his life was spent in writing a little book on Love : this was a good preparation for the enjoyment of the Eternal Love. May God enable us all to grow and stand fast in His love ; then we shall be prepared for all that may happen ! I would so gladly have ministered to Stolberg in his illness and at his death : there is no greater comfort on earth than to see a man die in full consciousness, committing himself peacefully and joyfully to the mercy of God in faith. Dear Agnes,

16

we have once seen this together in my dear father. Do
you still remember the wonderful beauty of his eyes in
those last hours, even to the last minute?"

But while Caroline did not shrink from the thought
of death, she thoroughly enjoyed life. "When at our
outset in life we have surmounted one hill, we are apt
to think that we have left all hills behind, and have
nothing but smooth walking to the end of our days,"
she says to her daughter Louisa; "at least I have often
felt this; and then I came to little hills and great
mountains which I must needs cross, and so it will be
till we have climbed the last, and laid down our burden. Still, notwithstanding the hills, life is pleasant
and valuable to me, and were it God's will, I could
gladly live among you yet awhile with my beloved
Perthes, especially if he could find a place of rest
where I might be more with him. In that case, I
should indeed wish that my breathing were somewhat
more free, so that I might go about and enjoy life with
you." And soon after,—"It ought not to be so, but
the thought of keeping time in our grasp often occurs.
Assuredly God cannot have less good in store for us in
heaven, but that which we have here we see with our
eyes, and thus it has a stronger hold on our hearts
than the anticipation of even the better things awaiting us above. But even here below there are moments
of great and inconceivable assurance and blessedness,
if we could only keep them; but my special sorrow is,
that I am not at all times master of my own heart, and
my greatest comfort is, that God knows me perfectly;
and certainly, I desire far more than I can accomplish."

In the middle of July, Caroline was taken to Wandsbeck, in order to be away from the bustle of home, and that she might take the air without going up and down stairs ; she now suffered much from difficulty of breathing and cramp in the chest. "When I sit still, I am pretty well, and enjoy the beautiful weather quite forgetting my pain, but the slightest movement reminds me of it at once."

"It is now three months," she writes another time, "since I have been able to do anything in the house, the kitchen, or the cellar, and this distresses me greatly. I long indescribably to return to my duties, and to spare my dear Perthes any further anxiety about my health. I cannot do any kind of work, not even knit, neither can I read ; but I feel no tediousness, and am in very good spirits. I must not write any more, my dear child. It it not my heart, but my head that is weary."

These were almost the last lines that she was able to write to her distant children, but her affection continued undiminished, and she rejoiced with them, as warmly as ever, on the occasion of the birth of her second grandson in July. "God help those poor creatures," she wrote, "who have no love in their hearts ; you dear, happy children, how glad I am to be your mother, and how I rejoice in all your happiness!"

In the last letter to her son at Tübingen, on the 2d August, she says,—"We passed our wedding-day very happily at Wandsbeck ; I went round the beautiful large meadow many times with my dear bridegroom, sitting down occasionally, and cannot be thankful enough for this delightful walk. We were alone, and it was many years since I had such a walk with my dear Perthes ; our conversation was very comprehensive and hopeful ; since it is not only the past but the present which is ours, we thought of you all."

But Caroline's health was not improved by her stay at Wandsbeck :—" How gladly would I tell you that I am strong and hearty," wrote Caroline to Perthes on the 8th August, " but I cannot ; I do not feel strong. Pleased I am, but not cheerful, though I might be so, could I sit on my bench in the open air ; the pleasure of being out carries me beyond myself, but within doors I do not easily forget myself, and my short breath : perhaps to-morrow God will send the doctor the right thought. My general health is still good, and the one weakness may yet be found out. My feelings tell me that I may be perfectly restored, though my understanding speaks rather differently."

A few days after this Caroline returned to Hamburgh, in order to be near her physician, but the hope of recovery diminished day by day. Although Caroline was not at this time living in the immediate expectation of death, she enjoyed a closer communion with God. The old hymn,* " Lord, I would venture on thy word," was her delight. When, through the severity of her sufferings, and the restlessness of fever, she could with difficulty keep before her the contents of the hymn, she would take up her pen, and write a few verses, in order to impress these breathings of prayer on her mind.

Perthes had long been aware of her danger. Thus in a letter written somewhat later than this, he writes :—" I have long suffered on her account, and for many months have been weighed down with grief.

---

* " Herr auf dein Wort soll's sein gewagt."—German.

My lonely walks have been spent in endeavoring to realize the heavy trial that is before me, and, with God's help, to prepare for it. Ever and anon hope revived, but only to be dashed again. No one, who knew as I did, the weight of the fetters that a weary body imposed upon so active and intense a spirit as hers, could believe that she could long endure it. She has suffered much for a long time, and it is a hard struggle for one so excitable and energetic, to feel herself constantly bound. It was only her genuine Christianity, and the consideration of the sufferings of our Lord, that supported her and kept her patient, yea cheerful, and preserved her sympathies to the last. I alone knew how weak she was, and how much she suffered; her friends and acquaintance saw only her kindness and her mental energy."

On Friday, 24th August, frequent and violent attacks of inward cramp placed her life in immediate danger, and from this time she alternated between wild delirium and exhaustion, struggles for breath, and profound sleep; but there were occasional hours of freedom from pain, and of perfect consciousness, and then the peace of faith, the assurance of hope, and the joy of love, were victorious over suffering and death. During these last days, Perthes enjoyed the most perfect resignation and peace.

"Your mother is very ill," he says in a letter to his sons-in-law, written on the 28th August: "we are in God's hand, and may hope, although we have more cause for fear: I find my comfort and support in submission; Thy will be done, O Lord. If God has ordained the death of your pious mother, His will be done: I could not count much on my own strength,—

the rending of such ties is terrible ; it is terrible to be
left without the only creature who entirely knows me,—
sad, desolate loneliness, long or short, is all that remains, no more comfort of mutual coöperation, no
helper in all joys and sorrows.   I cannot and dare not
hope ; it is only when I realize the worst that I find
comfort and support."

On the evening of the day on which this letter was
written, on 28th August, 1821, shortly after nine
o'clock, a stroke of paralysis put an end to Caroline's
life so suddenly, that no pressure of the hand, no word
or look of love, gave token of farewell to those
around her.

> " Welcome the tomb!
> Immortality's lamp burneth bright 'mid the gloom ;
> The pillow is there on which Christ bowed His head ;
> How sweetly I'll slumber on that holy bed!
> But sweeter the morn that shall follow that night,
> When the sunrise of glory shall beam on my sight,
> While the full matin song, as the sleepers arise
> To hail the glad morning, shall peal through the skies."

XXXII

Perthes and his Motherless Children.

ITHOUT making any unnatural efforts, without constrained resignation, Perthes gave himself up to the sorrow so natural on such a loss, but which yet is found only in connexion with Christianity, because it presupposes the necessity of submission and hope.

"Here I am with my poor children," wrote Perthes on the following morning to his son-in-law, "and life looks empty and desolate ; we seek for the overflowing affection that has been so richly granted to us ; and yet, since we could have it only by bringing back my Caroline and your mother, could we wish that her free and pious spirit should be again imprisoned in the body ? My poor little children,—you older ones have had the benefit of your mother's mind,— but the younger ones must for ever miss her love and her watchful spirit : God help them and me. It breaks my heart to see the little ones seeking up and down for their mother everywhere, and to hear their sobs when they do not find her. The corpse is inexpressibly beautiful, from the height of the forehead and the sweet loving smile that plays about the mouth."

In a letter written on the same day to his son Matthias, Perthes says,—"Her love can no longer bless us

here below ; she is at rest with God, while we mourn
her loss : weep as much as you can, then compose and
command yourself, and come to us."

" My sorrow does not make me idle," wrote Perthes,
a few days afterwards, to his daughter, "it rather
rouses my affections, and excites me to be helpful to
all around me, as far as I can ; I have abundant cause
of thankfulness, that for four-and-twenty years God
permitted me to enjoy this treasure of affection, energy, and intelligence, and I would render thanks to
Him for this. Now she knows how and wherein I
sinned, as she could not know here below, but now she
also realizes the full measure of my affection. How
many are the hindrances, and limitations, and circumstances, great and small, that oppose our recognition
of the love that is in other men's hearts! That she
now knows me thoroughly, and helps me to cleave to
God and to walk before Him, I am fully persuaded,
though I am aware that Revelation gives no express
countenance to this belief."

In a subsequent letter Perthes says,—" All that I
have done and planned, that was not immediately connected with business, has for four-and-twenty years
been solely in reference to your mother ; she never
knew, at least in full, how dependent I was on her ;
she only thought, through the depth of her love for me,
what sacrifices I had made. But now all this is over,
I am no longer bound, I can do what I will, and next
to the yearning after her, I am most oppressed in my
solitude by the consciousness of freedom. I know by
long experience the instability of man when he is left
alone, and if humility can bring down help from above,
I may venture to hope that it will not be denied. If

it were not for you, children, my wish would be to depart, but my course is not yet ended, and I must continue to struggle and to act."

In a letter to his son at Tübingen, he says,—" In my
heart all is dark and desolate ; I long for communication with some loving soul, as if communion with the Invisible were not enough, and to this disquiet is added
the anxious fear, lest when time shall have cooled
down my burning sorrow, my affection for your mother should also suffer some diminution."

Again, after a few weeks, he wrote,—" I am now
more reconciled to the transition from that yearning
which arises from bereavement, and neither can nor
should be permanent, to a continued life with the beloved one in the immediate presence of God and our
Saviour : I trust I have found that peace of God,
which is the only rest of the soul."

In a letter to Helena, the sister of F. H. Jacobi,
who had been a motherly friend to Caroline from her
girlhood, Perthes gave a lively picture of the great
blessing which he had possessed in Caroline. " You,
indeed, early appreciated the worth of my Caroline,
but, removed as you were from her in these last years,
you could not see the development of her mind ; her
piety and loveliness, and the simplicity of her character, were untouched by years, and her affection, while
it retained all its strength and depth, expanded in every direction, and showered blessings and benefits on
all within her reach. She had counsel, comfort, and
help for all who approached her, and won love, and an
esteem bordering on reverence from persons of the
most opposite character and circumstances. Caroline's
imagination was of unparalleled vivacity, and origi-

16*

nated the deepest sympathy with all that was passing in the world. She had much experience of human nature, but her judgment was always loving and pitiful, her faith was free from the narrowness of the letter, and great as was her affection for me, she was perfectly independent in mind. For four-and-twenty years we have lived together through cares and anxieties, sometimes through sorrow and trouble, but in all she was happy, for every moment was filled with love and lively sympathy ; always resigned to the inevitable, she preserved her heroic spirit in great events. That poverty of spirit, so extolled by Taulerus and Thomas-à-Kempis, was hers ; she had acquired it in struggling with a vigorous nature, to which passion, impetuosity, and ambition were not unknown. From her earliest youth she had lived in continual intercourse with God, and she was sincere as I have known few besides. And now this great and rare blessing is lost to me in the grave,—in vain I stretch out my arms ; humanly speaking, I am alone, and yet I have a foretaste of a previously unknown blessedness, since our souls may now meet unfettered ; but this may not be put into words, since once uttered it becomes untrue."

After Caroline's death, Perthes felt the constant bustle of business more painfully than ever, while for the motherless children a quieter life and a simpler style of living seemed indispensable. He had long planned the transfer of the Hamburgh business to Besser, and the removal of his own residence to Gotha. There, in the centre of Germany, he proposed to establish a publishing business, and henceforward exclusively to devote himself to this quieter and less wearing vocation. After Caroline's death, he resolved on carrying out the long-cherished purpose with as little delay as possible. "Next Easter we shall come to you, and, if it please God, stay with you; this resolution is not forced on me by excited feelings, but has been carefully considered, and is wise and necessary."

"The housekeeping can be carried on as usual," he says in a subsequent letter; "Matilda is active and sensible, and has conducted it with discretion and judgment beyond her years, during her mother's illness. She still continues to take care of the younger children; but apart from all other considerations, I should be doing injustice to Matilda, if by remaining here I were to oppress her youthful spirit of seventeen, by leaving so much under her charge."

The winter of 1821-22 was occupied with preparations for the transfer of the business and the removal to a new home. Mauke, who had long borne the burden and care of the vast business with Perthes, was now taken in as a partner, and things were put into such a train, that, if the Gotha plan succeeded, the final arrangements would not be difficult.

But the separation from the friends of his youth, and from all the associations of his past life, was far more painful to Perthes than the dissolution of his business relations; with the former he had experienced the full joy and the full sorrow of life; amid these he had learned and suffered, wrestled and enjoyed. Thus he wrote in January:—"I will not tell you how I passed Christmas and the New Year; they were heavy, heavy days, and heavy days are still before me. Every step, every stroke of the pen vibrates in my heart, and seems to say, At last! Thirty years of my life have been passed in this neighborhood; here I have won all that was

dear to me, a calling, influence, and consideration ; here
I met with Caroline, and here I found God. It is no
light matter to leave a house and city, men and associations, with which my own life has grown up, and I
feel it deeply ; but it is needful for me to keep up my
spirits, since I have not only to preserve my own composure, but also to keep my heart for others, well-re-
solved indeed, but not cold or insensible. I do my utmost to bridle the outer man, and may God help me to
overcome the weakness that is within."

At the close of February, Perthes wrote :—"An hour
ago, your Wandsbeck grandmother left our house for
the last time. How many days of joy and trouble, of
sorrow and anxiety, she has passed here! Here two
of her grandchildren died; from this house she saw us
driven out into the world as wanderers ; in this room
she witnessed the departure of her husband and daughter—and now, in a few weeks, our place will no longer
be found. When such depths of feeling, usually fast
sealed up, are opened, and a heart that retains in
advanced age all the energy of youth, gives way
to the profoundest grief, it is hard to preserve one's
calmness. It was one of the hardest and most painful
trials of my life."

Just before he left Hamburgh, Perthes wrote a few
farewell lines to the Countess Louisa Stolberg :—"The
time is come when I must take leave of the home and
place where I have enjoyed so large a measure of happiness in affectionate and intelligent communion ; my
heart is oppressed with sorrow, but I humbly trust that
strength will be given me ; to you, my dear maternal
friend, for the sake of our old associations and acquaintance, I send a parting greeting. How often has

my beloved Caroline taken up the pen to bid you farewell—but she could not : deeply did she feel and return your love ; of this you are well aware : let us
cleave to each other in faith, till we too are gathered
to the abodes of peace and light."

On Wednesday, the 22d of March, 1822, Perthes, with
his four children, left Hamburgh, and on the following
Monday reached Gotha, where, as he had anticipated,
a calm and peaceful, but not inactive, life awaited him.

XXXIII.

Gotha.

ERTHES had lived exactly half a century, when called upon to begin, as it were, a new life, under new circumstances. He had exchanged the bustle of a great seaport for a quiet retreat containing about 12.000 inhabitants, an independent commercial republic for a small German capital. Gotha cannot fail favorably to impress all who visit it. It forms a crescent at the foot of the Schlossberg, from whose summit the palace of Friedenstein looks down on a green and fertile plain, and southwards to the glorious extent of the forest of Thuringia. Park-like grounds, rich in old trees, grassy slopes, and flourishing plantations, front the town on the opposite side, sheltering the remarkably fine orangery of the ducal palace together with many a pleasant pavilion, and giving to Gotha the appearance of standing in the middle of a spacious park. On the other hand, the narrow stream of the Leine, diverted with great skill from the hills. rather displays than supplies the want of water in the district, and the wide extent of treeless, level ground, between the forest and the town, intersected, at the period of which we speak, by no good roads, removes the mountain range to a considerable distance.

Together with the rest of Germany, Gotha was dragged into the whirlpool consequent upon the first French Revolution ; but however strongly the period, dating from Luneville to the second peace of Paris, had convulsed the whole country, it had not been able to overcome the tenacity inherent in German character and outward circumstance. In many a small state the good old times had passed over unchanged into a new epoch, and in the Duchy of Gotha when Perthes first settled there in 1822, both town and country afforded a picture of manners, customs, and regulations, which carried one back to the years immediately preceding the Revolution.

Every evening the streets of one-storied houses were filled with cattle returning from pasture, and by night the only sound heard in them was the loud horn of the watchman and his pious caution,—" Put out fire, and put out light, that no evil chance to-night, and praise we God the Lord." The streets were lively only on the weekly market-days, when the robust form of Thuringian peasants, with their gaily dressed, healthy-looking wives and daughters, selling corn and wood, butter, flax, fruit, and other country and forest produce, filled the square in front of the old town-hall, on whose roof a greedy-looking wooden head opened its mouth at the striking of the hour, as if uncertain whether to speak or bite.

There were a multitude of strange relics of a past time, which met the stranger at every step, though the inhabitants of the place hardly remarked them. Day by day a little man, in a blue coat with shining buttons, mounted on a pony smaller still, might be seen wending his way midst the confusion of heavily laden wagons,

which were wont to rest a night in Gotha, on their
way from Frankfurt to Leipzig. This functionary was
the Weimar escort, the terror of the wagoners, looking
out for any defaulters among them who had not paid
the tax formerly levied in return for an armed escort,
which served as protection against the assaults of
knightly highwaymen. Long as this custom had become obsolete, the fee was still rigidly exacted, as well
as the town-toll, from wagons which were not permitted to go through, but only around it.

Not less notable to the youth of the place were the
giant forms of the guard, with their wide white cloaks
down to their heels, their great swords at their side,
their heavy boots and clattering spurs, though horses
they had none. Peaceful, friendly, obliging people
they were, carpenters, locksmiths, joiners, who, while
following their respective trades, were accustomed to
figure as warriors, so many times a month, for a moderate compensation. There were only about six or
eight uniforms for the whole body, which were passed
on from one to the other.

Any one crossing the town at mid-day, was sure to
meet an elder scholar, followed by ten or twelve
smaller boys, running in breathless haste through the
streets, singing a chorus the while, in hopes of thus
collecting a few pence. On Wednesdays and Saturdays the choristers of the Gymnasium stationed themselves, in their black cloaks and three-cornered hats,
before the doors of the wealthy, thus, by means of their
persevering quartettes, extracting enough to support
them during their school career.

As for family life and social intercourse, nothing
could be more simple. The men assembled in the

evenings in groups, composed of those of the same trade and condition, and enjoyed their long pipe over a glass of beer; and even the womankind of the more cultivated families made afternoon visits to each others' spinning-rooms.

The theatre consisted of a large room in a mill, where all classes, indifferently, might, for a zwanziger, gain admission to benches from whence to contemplate the strolling players. Any expensive outlay in eating and drinking was reserved for extraordinary occasions; the rooms were, according to the old fashion, small and low, the furniture generally of deal, was at the very utmost of the cherry-wood of the district; and, in short, unostentatious comfort and scrupulous cleanliness everywhere prevailed. In trade and business, too, the old customs still endured. The different guilds were assiduous in preventing those who were not members of them from procuring employment; the saddler might not make a portmanteau, the locksmith was forbidden to interfere with his brother of the anvil, and the tailors were sure to institute a crusade against any needlewoman who might venture to overstep the limits of their peculiar calling. The right of brewing was confined to certain firms, which, according to rule and precedent, supplied the citizens with a beverage, thin and sour enough. All intercourse with the small villages around was carried on by means of a walking post, who indulged in a perpetual warfare with the post-office authorities of Thurn and Taxis. The Thuringian forest was only traversed by the Tambach and Schmalkalde roads; and though the great highway through Gotha from Leipzig to Frankfurt was kept alive all the year by countless wagons, it did not yet boast a mail; and when in the September of 1825, the first Diligence entered Gotha, the whole town assembled to gaze upon the phenomenon, and for months nothing was spoken of but the energy of the Postmaster-General, Nagler, who had actually brought seeming impossibilities to pass. In other directions the roads were impassable after rain, and journeys, whether of business or pleasure, had to be postponed till dry weather.

Nor could any one have guessed from the political condition of the Dukedom that it had belonged for long years to the Rhenish Confederacy, and that Duke Augustus had been one of the most fervent adherents of Napoleon. The law of the land was still, and had been for ages, a heterogeneous medley, which no one could understand, and yet which all needed to understand in self-defence. The higher departments of office were almost exclusively filled by the numerous nobles of the small territory. Without an army in which to take refuge, without state-diplomacy in which to entangle themselves, and without extensive landed possessions to fill up their minds, the nobility assumed, not indeed, a political but an exclusive social position, partly because they themselves desired it, but still more because the untitled classes pressed it upon them. The State College was at once the chief tribunal and the highest administrative power. Now, because in the solution of legal difficulties it was obliged to decline all interference from the Duke and his ministers, it grew impatient of their control in affairs of civil government also, and assuming an attitude of almost complete independence, became inactive through very arbitrariness. The reigning Duke since 1804,

Augustus Emilius, had, in the days of Napoleon, averted many a misfortune from his country, but later, his out-of-the-way love-affairs, strange sallies, and wayward fancies, had injured his reputation, and the ministers, among whom was Herr von Lindenau, did not exercise an elevating influence over the affairs of the community. This state of things corresponds closely with the position of the nobles and towns which, in the year 1809, united to form the Rhenish Confederacy. In short, the epoch of the French Revolution had passed away, scarcely leaving a trace behind, and in the year following the union of Coburg with Gotha, and the personal peculiarities of Duke Ernest effected a far greater transformation than the French Revolution, the Rhenish Confederacy, and the war of Independence together.

Although the political, ecclesiastical, and social forms of Gotha belonged to bygone days, yet there was, not indeed in them, but coexistent with them, an amount of life, and intellectual excitement, not often to be met with in towns of the same size. The Gymnasium numbered amongst its teachers such men as Döring and Schulze, Ukert and Kries; Rost and Wüstemann; the library had attracted to Gotha, Friedrich Jacobi, the Observatory Von Lindenau and Encke; Bretschneider was general superintendent; the natural sciences were worthily represented by Von Hoff and Von Schlotheim; Stieler had already begun his geographical labors, and Andreas Romberg had, until 1818, led the services of the ducal chapel.

All these men were cordial friends, and every one was welcome to their periodical meetings who possessed any scientific tendencies whatsoever. Tradesmen and mechanics were, generally speaking, active and enterprising. They had planned and established, at their own expense, excellent schools for their own order, and many other useful institutions besides ; the educational efforts of former centuries were continued and developed ; free schools were carefully supported, and societies formed for the benefit of orphans and prisoners. The living influence of the town extended beyond its own confines. The Fire Insurance Office established in 1821, and the preparations for the Life Insurance Company which followed, in 1829, the getting up of the universally circulated geneological pocket-books, as well as the great geographical undertaking of Justus Perthes, called out a spirit of enterprise on all sides. Mental influence of various kinds was diffused by the many born or educated in Gotha, and thence transplanted to German universities, while the parents of the numerous pupils who flocked to the Gymnasium from all parts of Germany, as well as from Denmark, Poland, and Russia, brought with them foreign interests into the town-circle.

With this fresh and vigorous intellectual life, the confusion and deadness prevailing both in politics and religion, was singularly contrasted. Here, as in the rest of Germany, the creed of political rationalism, handed down by the last century, was combined with the national efforts, as also with the fantastic characteristics resulting from the war of independence and its concomitants.

In almost every respect, Perthes' new home afforded a fair epitome of the state of Germany. Death and life, disease and health, reason and unreason, old and new, were in close juxtaposition, as indeed they are everywhere, but here, perhaps, still more singularly blended than elsewhere.

Perthes had keenly felt his departure from Hamburgh, and the shadow of the last sad months there spent followed him into his new home. Writing to Count Adam Moltke, he says,—"It is a heavy year that lies behind me. My childhood was spent in poverty; as a youth I was thrown about from place to place, till, as a compensation for all besides, Wandsbeck was given me as a home. Home died with Caroline. The gradual removal from my desolate house of objects endeared by memory, the last look into the now empty rooms, which for eighteen years had been consecrated by the closest ties, all this cut me to the heart. We must be unspeakably guilty in God's sight, otherwise when through the darkness in which we walk, light shines through love, death would not be permitted to take it away. My nature could never endure to give itself up to a great and deep sorrow, and on this occasion it was only the labors and the efforts, essential, in order conscientiously to part from my home, my business, and my social and civic relations, that enabled me to bear the rending of so many ties by which my very life seemed bound. Our journey was a prosperous one, and a slight accident was the means of enriching us with a pleasant impression. At a village near Netra, our axle-tree broke. I shall never forget this little village of Rittmannshausen. The four-and-twenty families living there made but one; they were all related by love and friendship, and mutually behaved with the most refined politeness. The women were handsome—the lads well grown, the men Hessians, who had seen service, with their medals on their breasts, all of them alike intelligent and helpful. For twelve hours they helped Wagner and the smith, and I had difficulty in getting them to take anything in return. In short, I met with an idyl in real life, which rejoiced my heart. On the 20th of March, at mid-day, we reached Gotha. Our meeting was a mournful one without 'the mother.'"

During the first few weeks after his arrival, Perthes was occupied with the various small matters connected with the arrangement of his new way of life. In April he wrote as follows :—"I have not yet begun my regular habits, the many things to be done just at first, and the presence of my son Matthias, who is come from Tübingen to see us, having filled up the time. Our provisional dwelling stands in a free and open situation, surrounded just now by a very sea of flowers, and commanding an extensive view. We see the Seeberg and the Inselsberg, and even the Brocken in clear weather. My daughter Matilda governs the new household judiciously and firmly ; Clement I have sent to the Gymnasium ; the education of the two youngest is provided for, and the most necessary visits made. We are a good deal with my married daughters and their husbands, and I already foresee that my new mode of life will suit me."

Towards the end of April, Perthes, having completed his necessary family arrangements, was obliged to go to Leipzig. But the impulse given to the book-trade by the confluence, from all parts of Germany, of men of every kind, no longer excited him as of yore.

In a letter to Besser he says :—" It is not the labor, nor the turmoil, but the emptiness of the pursuit which weighs upon me now. Everything seems to me null and void, and I can no longer get up an interest in things as I used to do. Many objects which a short time ago were bright and varied, have become grey and monotonous in their hue, and the life of life is over for me."

In the middle of May Perthes returned to Gotha in melancholy mood. He again wrote to Besser :—" My spirit is deeply troubled. This returning home without Caroline, without finding the love, the fulness of soul from which I drew my life, is horrible. I can impart nothing, receive nothing, all is barren and dead. My arrival yesterday was most painful—no welcome, no life in our communications ; the poor children cannot supply that want."

The Countess Augustus Bernstorf *née* Stolberg wrote to him :—" The wilderness within, the blank, the loss, —ah ! who knows these as I do,—the love, the longing, the home-sickness, and yet the consolation and the hope ! Most heartily do I stretch out my hands towards you ; we are one in faith, and strive towards the same goal—may eternal love and mercy help us to reach it !"

However sad Perthes may have been during the first few weeks of his residence in Gotha, this did not prevent his excitable nature from receiving new impressions. He wrote to Count Moltke :—" Very notable to me is life and action in this little ducal town, and the contrast between it and the commercial republic in which I have grown grey. Here there are no State and social restrictions for me, scarcely, indeed, for those who hold office here. There is no place where one lives more unconcerned as to prince or governments, and that is not well ; for what import-

ance can these small duchies retain unless they preserve
more intimate relations between prince and subject
than is possible in great towns?" In a letter to
Besser we find him saying :—" As I write, the village
bell is sounding in my ears. Last night, the 16th of
May, Duke Augustus died. All medical skill was in
vain, for this half crazy prince could not deny himself
the stimulus of the hottest spices."

" Perthes writes to Rist :—" The funeral was a melancholy spectacle, no sympathy shown by high or low,
town or country. The domestic servants were the only
mourners, and the Duke's favorite cock, who was almost
always with him night and day, alone looked solemn
and tragical. And yet this prince had injured and
oppressed no one ; he was both clever and feeling, but
he was early ruined by an education founded on the
principles of the French Encyclopedists ; he took dis-
torted views of everything, and his conduct bordered
on insanity. On the morrow, when the country heard
of the death of the old Duke, there was another ready,
and the Saxon Dukes, who would gladly have succeeded, had to practise patience, and not only to con-
dole upon the occasion of the death, but to congratulate
on that of the accession. If, in the other smaller States,
prince and people are not more closely united than
they are here, we shall have some ugly experiences to
go through.

" The theologians and philologists are much the same
here as elsewhere. Poetry and Art have no representa-
tives, but we have no lack of originals. A gentler, more
cheerful, and child-loving head of a school than Döring,
the director of the Gymnasium, you could nowhere
find. Though not far from his seventieth year, he

wears a grass-green coat and a sulphur-colored waistcoat; though decidedly humpbacked, he is a great
rider, and a thorough Nimrod; he keeps and feeds
singing-birds, reads Horace, and is good-humored and
jovial in his manner to his pupils. In short, society,
in despite of the narrow limits of the town, is so exciting and many-sided, that one need never be obliged,
like Richard Parish, to take frequent journeys, in order
to rub off the cryptogamic growths with which a long
stay in one and the same place is apt to incrust the
human soul."

At another time we find him writing :—" No one is
indispensable, no dead man is long missed ; the waves
close over him, and the place that knew him knows
him no more. The ambition of a youth of talent cannot refrain from striving and working on a great scale,
but this will be the case with an older man, only if he
be vain ; if not, he will see more and more clearly that
he is surely influencing the whole when quietly occupied with the particular, that the thing nearest at hand
is the right thing to do, and that if there be a will,
there is everywhere and always a way. It is without
a pang that I find myself withdrawn forever from all
public activity, such as that of my Hamburgh life, and
I am thankful that my outward circumstances do not
compel me to summon up and strain all my energies,
in order to fill my future position with credit. My
present occupations and endeavors do not hinder, they
rather further my soul's meditation and the growth of
my spiritual life. Certainly, I have often trembled
when I thought of the step I was about to take. It
was no small matter to me to give up a long-established,
certainly unquiet, but perfectly secure situation for a

17

new and certainly quiet, but by no means an assured future. However, if one ever wishes to make a decided change in life, it must be while one has still strength not only to break off from the old, but to found the new, otherwise there results a wretched half-and-half existence, full of divided regrets and weak yearnings after the past, and a depressed disposition, which unfits for business, and never can prosper. Ten years later I should not have been able to carry out my resolve ; now God will help me onward."

XXXIV.

Perthes' Views of Men and Things.

ERTHES, as we are already aware, had made
over his prosperous Hamburgh business to his
brother-in-law, Besser, and chosen Gotha for
a residence, with the view of establishing a
publishing business there. He writes,—"I
am too old to take part in the disputes of the
different writers. As a publisher, I have to
remember that when Peter was hungry and would eat,
he saw a sheet filled with creatures of every kind let
down before him. Now, a publisher is not exactly in
the same plight as to killing and eating, but he has to
collect historians of all sorts, whether wild beasts or
fowls of the air, and so to get the History of Europe
written."

While Perthes was thus collecting all his energies
to lay the foundation of his new business, he had at the
same time to dissolve his Hamburgh connections, and
to settle matters with his old partner Besser. Accordingly he wrote, to him :—" We must settle our affairs
as soon as possible, for if one of us were to die before
this were done, inevitable confusion and mischief would
ensue, for then law would settle what we arrange as
brothers: therefore I urge you to make all possible
speed. After all, when this is over, I shall not be

estranged even from your affairs; (from yourself I never could be so :) but I shall watch them with delight and sympathy, and in many things we shall be able to help each other as long as we live." The only difficulty attending the dissolution of partnership between these two brothers in mind and heart, arose from each thinking himself too much benefited by the propositions made by the other. However, matters were soon arranged, and upon the occasion of his retirement from the Hamburgh establishment, Perthes wrote to Besser : —" We have now, dear brother, worked together for a quarter of a century, carrying on one and the same concern in troublous times. Not once have we taken different views as to ' meum and tuum ;' not for one moment during all those years have we ever felt it possible to waver in our mutual confidence. Let us thank God that at the hour of parting that confidence is as firm and pure as it has been during our long-associated life. Such happiness in such degree is vouchsafed to few."

Despite the great amount of labor which his calling and his temperament alike imposed upon him, Perthes, during the first year of his life in Gotha, found time to make more or less distant excursions into the surrounding country. In the beginning of August he visited the Rudolstädt and Altenburg district; and later in August he went for a few weeks to Franconia and Bavaria. In a letter to a friend he says :— " When, on the 13th of September last, I left Gotha at mid-day, a magnificent thunder-storm accompanied me over the heights of the Thuringian Forest. I travelled in the diligence, a nine-seated monster, on the top of which a seat is built for two people. If, from this perch, where one knows nothing of the heavy vehicle behind, one watches the six horses toiling up the hill, the mind naturally reverts to our humanity, which often forgets the heavy body there is no shaking off, and then childishly wonders at the trouble it gives us to rise. A diligence like this (I mean the actual Thurn and Taxis conveyance) is convenient and rapid in comparison with those of earlier days ; but yet it requires that the passengers should be good-humored, not over-sensitive, and not in a hurry. As for conductors, they are always wet or dusty. Mine made pious reflections during the thunder-storm, and did not lose a moment in taking up five blind passengers, whom I could not see, as they got in during the night, and out before daybreak. But I, the only seeing passenger, had to take the conductor's place, not only at the customary halting-places, but at every intervening public-house, where he was minded to play a game at cards with the postilion. In Schwallungen I heard an enlightened watchman cry, ' The hammer has struck one,' instead of ' the bell has struck one.' In Hildburghausen I ate at the same table with two of the prince's retainers, the one a valet, just out of bed, the other a sweep, just out of the chimney. The barefooted blackamoor was a fine-looking fellow, and discussed great European events better than many a professor. However, at Coburg, which I reached on the evening of the 14th, I grew tired of the whole concern, took a carriage, and drove to Baireuth." He then passed through the valley of the Maine to Baireuth, where he remained some days.

In a letter to a friend, Perthes writes :—"As you were once rather an idolater of Jean Paul, you shall

hear something about the impression his personality
made upon me. It is better, however, I am well aware,
to speak than to write about things and persons, that
in the course of one's travels one may have become
more or less acquainted with. How many opinions
and judgments are only rightly understood by means
of the commentary of voice and manner! A good-
natured smile softens the spoken word, and if the listener should take a matter too seriously, an additional
word removes the misapprehension. But what is
written remains hard, cold, rigid, and unalterable, and
often the reader views as black what the writer at
most meant only to paint as grey. In letters written
on a journey, and conveying the impressions of the
moment, one cannot be conscientious enough in one's
opinions about people. Meanwhile, since I cannot
speak, I needs must write. I went at eight in the
morning to Jean Paul. A tall, strong, bony figure,
like that of a farmer or a forester, entered the room,
dressed in a hunting-coat, with a badger's skin over
his shoulder, and leading a white poodle by a string.
As we had long been correspondents, we were soon in
full talk. I spent two evenings with him, the first in
his own house, the second at that of Madame von
Kettenburg's. Not only was a court lady of the name
of Stein present on both occasions, but the newly married Count and Countess Henckel-Donnersmarck.
The wish to appear in the best light, excited Jean
Paul, and, accustomed as he is only to be listend to,
my sudden interpolations interrupted him, and the consequence was, that while he proved himself a worthy
truth-loving man, and although the conversation
turned on the leading men and leading events in

Church and State, life and literature, I did not hear him utter one significant word, one deep view, one result of great inner experience : his conversation was throughout wearisome and obscure. He gave us the narrative of his daily life, as follows : 'In the summer at six, in the winter at eight, I walk about half a mile to Frau Schabenzel's (an old countrywoman ;) the poodle goes with me ; I carry my papers and a bottle in my badger's skin ; there I work and drink my wine till one o'clock ; then I do not drink again, but from five to seven I drink my beer as long as there is any in the jug. For half an hour Jean Paul put us to sleep with receipts for sleeping. None of the lightning flashes and scintillations of fancy, the striking similes, or the glowing pictures with which his works abound, appeared in his conversation ! I left him convinced that the man who, as an author, belongs to the tenderest and richest minds of Germany, is not, therefore, necessarily tender and soft-hearted. After Jean Paul, I felt most interest about a certain Councillor Kraus. In order to get at him, I applied to Jean Paul, having heard that they had been friends for years. 'We are old friends, it is true,' said he, 'but now we no longer meet. But go to him, and say, that though I never will have anything to do with him myself, I have sent you to him.' Accordingly, I went. I had to go up a steep stair, at the top of which was a closed lattice, and outside hung a long wooden hammer, with an inscription above to this effect : 'He who will enter must knock hard ; if the hammer is inside I am not to be seen.' So I knocked hard, and the door was opened. As I entered a large library, which swarmed with cats of every age and color, a friendly

old man, a bachelor with silver hair, and in a long
dressing-gown, advanced to meet me. After I had
playfully delivered Jean Paul's message, we fell into
conversation. 'Jean Paul,' said he, 'is a thoroughly
upright, feeling, good man, rich in heart and mind, but
the blossoms of his nature will never ripen into fruit,
because he has not strength thoroughly and scientifically to mature any subject; he knows much, but all
he knows is in disorder and confusion, and now that
his own mind can create nothing further, he has fallen
into all sorts of follies.' Kraus and I parted excellent
friends. 'Farewell, my dear good foe,' said he, as I
rattled down the steps. I have found out since then,
that Kraus, together with Lang, wrote the well-known
journey to Hammelburg."

From Baireuth, Perthes went for a few days with
the son of the bookseller, Grau, to the Fichtelgebirge,
and wandered on foot to Kemnath. "This is the true
home of the German kobolds, dwarfs, and little mountain spirits, this barren, gloomy mountain range, whose
far-stretching dark ridges, mighty detached granite
blocks, and long winding valleys, make a deep, if not
a pleasing impression on the traveller. Everything
here is grey and mysterious. The rock is hardly
covered with earth; stunted fir-trees, with ragged
foliage, heath, and blackberry bushes, give the district
all it has of color, and dark moss shrouds trees and
stones, hills and valleys alike. Colossal rock-masses
are heaped together in hundreds on the east side of
the Luchsberg; some of them rounded, some table-
shaped, but all perfectly detached, and most of them
in the boldest positions, a world in fragments, a true
picture of the ruins of the old German empire. Here

we were overtaken by a heavy thunder-storm. 'That's a loud noise,' said our guide, 'but there was a louder one when these stones were rolled together here." Another time he pointed a rock out to us, 'called the Prince's Head, but if closely looked at,' he said, 'you will see that it is an inverted heart.' He was a rough man, this guide of ours, but full of sense and wit, and his talk was one series of bold, lively pictures. What he had heard from others he told in good German, but he gave his own thoughts in the rude yet melodious *patois* of the mountains."

Perthes' life flowed on in uniform and undisturbed occupations from the autumn of 1822 till that of 1825. We find him writing,—" The day, which, according to Rist, was to consist of forty-eight hours in Gotha, is still, as in Hamburgh, too short for me, and yet there is time enough if reckoned by hours, not days, for every one's work." In another letter he says:—" My home-circle and those of my sons-in-law, who are both intimate friends of mine, fill up my idle hours. William Perthes is the same stable, firm, determined char- acter he ever was; combining a healthy intellect and a warm heart as few others do. Among the younger men, I most frequently see Fritz Becker, Encke, and Ewald; Jacobi and Ukert among the elder."

The uniformity of Perthes' life was broken in upon also by visits from such men as Heeren, Rehberg, Harms, Savigny, and many of his Hamburgh friends. Perthes, who up to the last year of his life delighted in long walks, began during this period to explore the Thuringian forest in all directions, sometimes visiting familiar spots, such as Schwarzburg, Liebenstein, &c., and sometimes, accompanied by his boys or his son-in-

17*

law, William Perthes, making his way through remote
valleys, and exploring solitary crags, thoroughly enjoying the discovery of new wood-paths, ravines, and
views, as well as the little difficulties and inconven-
iences attendant upon such rambles.

In the beginning of September, Perthes, accompanied
by his two unmarried daughters, went to Hamburgh to
settle his affairs there. "If this journey were not
necessary," wrote he, "it would not be taken, for a stay
in Hamburgh will be to me a look into the grave, and
yet it is well for man's frivolous nature to have sometimes the pain of ending before his own end comes."

The weeks he spent there were restless ones indeed;
hard work, melancholy reminiscences, his relatives, as
well as his countless friends and acquaintances, civic
interests, great dinner-parties daily, an excursion to
Lübeck, and a visit to Count Moltke, divided his time.
He entered with much animation into all these various
interests. Haller tells him in a subsequent letter:—
"I found you younger in mind and older in mildness
of temper."—"Your stay here," Rist playfully wrote,
"has been a perfect ovation."

Meanwhile his third daughter had betrothed herself
to Frederick Becker in Gotha, who, as soon as he had
received her consent, hurried off to Hamburgh, and
there remained till Perthes left. Perthes had written
a year before to Besser:—"Of all the friends of my
sons-in law, Becker suits me best; he is a noble-hearted
good man, thoroughly intelligent, and well-informed;
indulgent to others, and, perhaps, only too severe
towards himself. One may learn from him the nature
and influence of truly conscientious order."—To another friend he writes:—"You have heard from me of

my warm attachment to Becker, and will, therefore, readily believe that I am rejoiced to give my child to him."

Towards the end of October, Perthes, accompanied by Becker, returned through Bremen to Gotha.

Soon after, the following letter was written to Rist : "I look back with gratitude to my stay in Hamburgh, where I met with so much love and confidence. Some degree of self-complacency will mingle with the recollection of how poor, destitute, and dependent upon my own exertions I was, when I first entered it thirty years ago. Our journey home was prosperous, and fraught with small incidents. On the way between Hamburgh and Harburg, the steamboat had to lie to several times in a thick fog ; the Duke of Oldenburg was on board ; the passage lasted seven whole hours, and the honor of his presence, of course, for the same time. We talked over every conceivable subject by way of diversion. Amongst other things the question was put whether one would like to live one's life over again, and whether it were not to be wished that the duration of man's full powers extended from twenty to fifty years, or even longer. I negatived both these propositions, the first, because, amidst all the pleasures of this life, men have still a yearning after their departure from it ; the second, because a prolonged grant of life's full powers did not improve men themselves, and would, by confirming them in pride, make them a terror to others. But the old gentleman seemed to know nothing of the yearning I spoke of, and the continuance of bodily powers seemed to him inexpressibly desirable. He stated that in his youth he had been very hasty and passionate, so much so that, when he first joined the

army, his Colonel had said to him,—' Prince, you will
be lost in four weeks unless you learn to control yourself.' ' But,' continued the Duke, ' I did control myself,
and I am no longer passionate, impatient, or hard,
though no occupation affords more temptation to be so
than mine.' At which his adjutant sighed deeply, and
stroked his moustache, and his chamberlain made desperate attempts to look as he ought. Then the Captain asked whether he might fire a salute in the Duke's
honor ; ' Yes,' was the reply, ' if the ladies permit it.'
The ladies did permit it, but the bottles of the Restaur-
ateur were terrified to pieces to his comic distress. The
Duke made it up to him, and then the whole crew drank
to the Duke's health out of the broken bottles, and, in
short, there was nothing for it, *nolens volens*, but getting
into the best possible humor. As the Duke took leave
of me he said ' that Providence had compensated for
the length of the journey by my good fellowship.' To
make up for lost time we travelled by night to Bremen, where I found our friend Smidt cheerful and active
as of old, and had great pleasure in the friendly and
intellectual society of the place. I have visited Hamburgh, Lübeck, and Bremen in succession, and it was
striking enough to see the contrasts between these independent powers, and to walk through their states,
that is, their streets! After the excitement of all this
travelling, quiet and occupation will do both soul and
body good."

During the winter of 1823, Perthes had not only his
betrothed daughter, but his eldest son Matthias at home.

As the spring of 1824 approached, Perthes resolved
to go, for a few weeks, to Bonn and Frankfurt, and his
letters to his children and to Hamburgh friends give an

account of his way of life there.   Here is one of them :
" When I left you on Monday evening, I had to scram-
ble over legs, carpet-bags, and cloaks, and, with much
difficulty, to take my place as number six, in the middle
of the back seat—five people being in already—but it
was too dark to see their faces.   A light that we passed
threw a momentary ray over an odd-looking figure who
went on with a discussion which my entrance had interrupted, about Walter Scott's account of the Battle
of Waterloo.   The speaker was a Scotchman, and after
a week spent on the field, having been a good deal dis-
gusted with pretended mementos of the battle, he had
begun to dig himself, and had had the good luck at
length to find a hero's skull, which he carried away,
confident that he should easily find out to what nation
it belonged, as a friend of his had once upon a time
attended Blumenbach's lectures.   'Devil take the fellow, leave skulls alone, and the dead to rest in their
graves,' muttered a deep voice in the corner next to me.
'What do you mean, sir?' answered the Scotchman,
hastily.   In short the quarrel had begun, hot words
passed—the Scotchman got the worst of it ; we had
universal commotion in a dark box, and no one knew
what would come of it.   'Messieurs,' said a young
good-humored voice, 'shall I show the Scotch gentleman, for his collection, the letter of the Chinese that I
met in Halle?'   The Scot pricked his ears, forgot the
rebuke he had received, and thought only of the genuine
Chinese document.   Peace was restored, and at Eisen-
ach, on went the whole party, skull and all, to Frankfurt, I diverging to Cassel, which I reached after a
journey of seventy-seven hours.   We seldom see princely
splendor, handsome palaces, and the independent tur-

moil of trade, brought in such close juxtaposition as in Cassel. I spent the evening with the brothers Grimm; they are the same as they were ten years ago, and yet different too. Then they were almost feminine in their bloom, filled with the tender dreams and hopes of youth, now they are almost exclusively devoted to severe study."

Perthes spent a few weeks at Bonn, in the house of his brother-in-law Max Jacobi. He writes, " The being with my dear old brother, Max, and with my Caroline's sister, who, in sprightliness and mental gifts, is all she was five-and-twenty years ago, reminded me vividly of a time now long past, when I too was rich. No one knows what a poor human heart feels, when such echoes of a vanished world pierce his soul. The joy of meeting was mingled with grief; the joy I shared with others, and kept the grief to myself."

With the theologians, Sack, Nitsch, and Lücke, with Welcker, Brandis, Arndt, and many others, Perthes was very intimate, and much enjoyed their companionship. But he was, above all, impressed by his first meeting again with Niebuhr. A warm political quarrel had, in 1814, separated the two old friends, and though it had been long ago made up by letter, yet they had not since met. From Bonn Perthes wrote to Besser :—" I was prepared for a painful meeting, and should not have wondered at a distant manner, or formal bearing on Niebuhr's part, but the very moment I saw him, I found the old heart and the old friend, and there was not a shadow of reserve between us. His wife had just given birth to her second son, and the three elder children were running about their father's room, with all their playthings; and during our conversation, I was engaged first with one and then with the other of them. For five days I daily spent several hours with him. Our conversation was almost entirely political. Niebuhr's disposition is very melancholy ; the purer his heart, the deeper his sensibilities, the more he feels the want of some firm support for his soul ; he fights with uncertainty, and quarrels with life. He said to me, ' I am weary of life, only the children bind me to it.' He repeatedly expressed the bitterest contempt for mankind ; and, in short, the spiritual condition of this remarkable man cuts me to the heart, and his outpourings alternately elevated and horrified me. To see such a heart and mind in the midst of the convulsions of our time gives a deep insight into the machinery of our poor human life. Niebuhr needs a friend who would be a match for him ; he has not one such in the world. The wealth of his intellect and the extent of his knowledge are absolutely appalling, but his knowledge of the present is only the result of historical inquiry and political calculations—he does not understand individual or national life. ' I do know and understand the people,' replied he, when I made the above remark to him ; ' I read, and inquire, and hear ; and my residence abroad has afforded me an impartial point of view.' And yet I maintain, he has no knowledge of human nature. One thing I am more and more sure of : men of giant intellect and high imagination are little fitted to govern ; the practical man, if he will avail himself of the intellect of others, makes the best minister."

A few days after Perthes had left Bonn, Niebuhr wrote to him as follows : " The unlooked-for pleasure of seeing you again still remains in the form of memory ; your visit has awakened the illusion that old times have not quite vanished. And yet they have ; and could I become a sceptic, I should begin by denying a man's identity at different epochs of life."

Perthes wrote in reply, " You yourself would afford me a proof of identity if I needed one. Only look within you, how love has endured, how much you are still the same! Thirty years ago I have seen that very same love shine forth from your whole being, which still has power to melt all the frost, and rub away all the rust of the world."

In 1818, E. M. Arndt had been appointed Professor of History in the Bonn University ; in 1820, he was forbidden to teach ; in 1821, he was subjected to an inquiry instituted on the plea of demagogical stratagems ; but do what he would, he could not obtain a decision one way or another. Perthes had never seen him before, but they had corresponded long, and had many mutual friends.

He writes from Bonn,—" Arndt is just what I had pictured him,—sound-hearted, stable, lively and clever in conversation, never wearisome with his etymological and historical derivatives, odd as they often sound. Everywhere the poet peeps out, and it always does one good to hear his just and discriminating views of men, even of those who have done him wrong. His hard fate has left no trace of bitterness in him ; and his good heart peeps out through whatever hasty expression he may, on the spur of the moment, utter. The many points of contact afforded us by our past lives soon made us feel intimate. He has been very unjustly treated, and that is Niebuhr's opinion as well as mine. He is an imaginative man, and exciting and stimulating to the young, but that was well known before his appointment, for his whole character, as well as his writings, is perfectly transparent. And now there he is, in a beautifully-situated house, a quarter of a mile from the town, but without any scope for the exercise of his rare talents."

Perthes spent several mornings with A. W. Schlegel, and writes about him thus : " We had not seen each other for years. At first Schlegel gave me a stately reception ; but old recollections of former meetings soon made him open, tender, and natural in his cordiality. It was in 1793, just after his marriage, that I first saw Schlegel ; then we met in 1803 and 1805 in Leipzig and Dresden ; in the summer of 1813, I spent some weeks with him ; and again, in the December of the same year we had a very pleasant day in Saalsund in Hanover, with Rehberg, Smidt, Sieveking, and Benjamin Constant. These old pictures having first flitted past us, the political and religious opinions of past days gave way to the present. Schlegel expressed himself very strikingly about the men and the occurrences of our own time. I called his attention to the importance, historically speaking, of a new collection and edition of his works. He owes it to the history of our literature, to show the origin and the aim of his detached essays, so as to prevent further misunderstanding and confusion, for however different the decisions of different parties respecting him may be, still his views, his criticisms, his praise and blame, will have considerable influence over our literature for all time. Schlegel agreed with me, and remarked that he must needs be much misunderstood, for that his labors

in the early part of his life had almost entirely consisted in reactionary efforts against particular errors
and perversions, and that his views had met with such
a one-sided apprehension, and been carried to such ex-
tremes by his adherents, that he had subsequently been
obliged, for truth's sake, to appear as their opponent.
But he added, that his position, in regard to his brother Frederick, prevented an edition of his collective
works. They had formerly accomplished the greater
part of these together, but their opinions were now
diametrically opposed on the most important subjects.
He could not give up his own convictions, and his
feelings forbade him publicly to oppose his brother. I
then requested him to prepare a posthumous collection
of his works, saying, that when our race is run, natural
ties cease to fetter, and that the open confession of
what each held to be truth would do honor to both.
Schlegel spoke very openly of his relations with Niebuhr. The latter is so offended with his criticisms on his
Roman History, that he will not see him. 'Niebuhr,'
says Schlegel, 'has no ground for this ; no one made
such efforts as I to follow him in his investigations in
all directions, and this is the highest proof of appreciation and respect. Niebuhr might have forgiven me
a few witticisms and jests, which he knew to be a part
of my nature ; but so it is, no one in Germany understands criticism, and so I keep to myself my opinion
of Voss' performances, though I could express it in
three words. I begged him to tell them me, and he
replied, ' Voss has enriched our literature with a stony
Homer, a wooden Shakspeare, and a leathern Aris-
tophanes.' Schlegel took me to see his Indian printing office, and I could not but admire the simplicity

and practical wisdom of his arrangements ; indeed, on this occasion I saw nothing but the good side of his character. His faults are better known than those of most of us, and every one speaks of his incredible vanity, but it lies so on the surface, that one can hardly suppose it sinks deep. He has always been distinguished for strict conscientiousness in all affairs of business, and now he is firmly attached to Bonn, and a regular and active life may still further improve him. Good-natured he certainly is, if not exasperated or tempted by a sally of wit."

On the 9th of April Perthes arrived at Frankfurt. In a letter to Besser, he says, " I have done and seen much here in a few days. The first morning I spent with Friedrich Schlosser, and there met his brother Christian again, who had just come from Paris. With his smothered ardor, his cold liveliness, and his curt cutting sentences, he is really a remarkable man, and a striking contrast to his gentle and lovable brother."

" Yesterday," wrote Perthes a few days later, " I had to dine twice : at two o'clock with Schlosser, and at four with Gries, who had invited several of his colleagues. A circle of great or small diplomatists is always a little world apart ; and the scenery is an essential in its performances. During dinner, persons and things were discussed with much point and spirit."

On the morning of the 14th of April, Perthes left Frankfurt by the diligence. In one of his letters he says, " At Schlüchtern, a man got in whom the conductor called Mr. Post-Secretary, an impudent fellow, who was bent upon drawing out a sulky old Englishman ; but the latter pulled his cap over his ears. By this time it was night. So the talkative man turned

to me. 'Is the gentleman asleep a travelling tradesman?' 'I do not know.'—'You, however, are a minister?' 'No.'—'A professor?' 'No.'—'A merchant?'
'No.'—'A government official?' 'No.'—'Then you
must be a private gentleman, the happiest race of all,
who live on their income?' 'Yes,' said I, 'if they have
capital.' A little later my friend asked suddenly, 'How
morals stood out of Hesse?' I replied by asking what
morals meant. Upon which he thought me a fool, and
held his peace. He got down at the last Hessian station, and then, for the first time, it occurred to me that
he was very probably one of the Cassel police, a so-
called Erfurt spy. This honored company does not
seem to employ very clever agents. I could not get
the conductor to speak out; but he said, 'The man
is one of those who try to find out why frogs lose their
tails when they grow up.'" After an uninterrupted
journey of thirty-eight hours, Perthes found himself
once more at Gotha. A fortnight later he had to go
to Leipzig. "I do not like going," wrote he; "many
things combine to make me supine and sad, and anxious
for repose. If the wear and tear of strong feelings could
kill, I should be no more; but the human heart is a
hard nut, and destiny, sharp-toothed as it is, cracks away
at it, till it is tired, without breaking it."

XXXV

Perthes' Inner Life.—1822-25.

THE new circumstances of a new abode, and the varied exertions consequent upon his new calling, as well as his numerous journeys and the changes they involved, had an exciting influence upon Perthes' susceptible nature, deprived as it now was of the gentle restraint exercised by Caroline's affection for nearly twenty-five years. For hours and days he would feel restless and excited, and for this very reason dissatisfied with himself.

"It is no easy matter for me," he writes, "to conquer myself; the effects of fifty years of unrest have to be subdued by a naturally restless man. My life hitherto has passed away in care and toil; now I have the opportunity of quiet and undisturbed occupation, and perhaps external repose might bring me the peace of God if I were only at rest within."

In a letter written at this time to Friedrich Jacobi, he says:—"The battle of youth is over and gone, and evening is at hand. Much during all these years might have been done otherwise and better, and discipline is still necessary. The passage from man's prime of life and strength to age is a difficult one, and the gate is wide that leads to the company of old sinners. Passion blazes up anew, love of pleasure still lurks near, and I sometimes suspect that youth is not the only season of temptation."

In another letter we find him saying : "Sometimes my heart can rise above the region of disquiet, and my mind grow calm when I walk alone in a neighboring wood, and look at all the life and love around ; but still, after much profound experience, the heart is not to be roused by nature alone, it needs a previous education to fit it for her influence, and, perhaps, in our later years, she works upon us less through what she is herself, than through what we ourselves are. But God can help, and I pray and implore Him to help me in overcoming the unrest I suffer from."

The consciousness of the influence of the outer world upon his inner life was specially roused in Perthes, by the thought of the difference made in his whole being by the mature age he had now reached. In one of his letters he says :—" Half a century now lies behind me, and old age is not far distant. So much in me is changed, that when I consider myself with the eyes of the natural man, I could almost doubt my indentity with the self of five-and-twenty years ago. This subjection to the outer world were horrible, if liveliness of feeling, play of thought, and energy of action constituted the essence of our being ; but thank God these are in relation to our real personality but as the waves to the sea, which have their origin in the wind and not in the sea itself. The sea is the sea still when unstirred by the wind, and I am still I, when the special stimulus, be it of youth, passion, or society, is over. It is not I that am grown old, but the means of stimulating me. Time may blunt the nerves and stiffen the limbs, but it has no power over love which is the life of men, the core of their personality. Despite my half century I feel no diminution of love, nay, I am certain that viewed as a faculty of my nature and apart from its particular objects, it grows both in scope and depth. Love is the sum-total of life, and it is only according to our measure of it that we are accessible to truth. But I feel more and more how mysteriously love, although belonging to eternity, is bound like ourselves to nature and the world. I find it manifested in my own heart under a threefold character—divine, human, and animal, or, in other words, the love of the soul, the heart, and the senses. On the confines of these separate regions lies the wide domain of fancy, which blends the human with the divine, the animal with the human, and often enough leads us to mistake the one for the other. We aspire after the divine and are captured by the earthly. The love of the senses soon passes away, and because that of the heart—human love—is also of the earth earthy, time can soften even the most agonizing loss of the object of that love. Man has part in the eternal only in so far as he cherishes in himself the divine spirit-love. The history of a human being resolves itself into the history of his affections, and at the close of his life his only question should be, How sincerely and strongly have I loved God, my neighbor and myself, with that spirit-love which is divine?"

In order to revive within his own heart the history of the past, Perthes had begged his friends, far and near, to send him back all the letters his wife had ever written to them. To these he added those addressed to himself and to the elder children, and thus repeated

as it were in uninterrupted succession the years spent
with Caroline.

"A past life of five-and-twenty years lies before
me," wrote he to his sister-in-law Anna Jacobi ; "this
little bundle of paper contains an infinity of love and
thought, truth and conflict, and evokes from their
graves many a forgotten fact and feeling.   Yes, life is
a dream, but a very serious one, and our dreams are
solemn truths veiled in airy fictions."

In the midst of all his excitements and disturbances
Perthes deeply yearned for repose, but this yearning
made him feel himself very lonely in Gotha.

" I find no one here," he writes, " with whom to share
my inner life: in this respect it is even more dead than at
Hamburgh.   People are taken up with the visible, and
have only a few trite commonplaces to bestow upon
the invisible.   If I were to speak of what most deeply
moves me, no one would understand me.   The more at
rest and at home I become in my new position, the
more painfully, in spite of all the amusing and attractive conversation, do I feel this want of sympathy."

Another time he writes :—" I would not willingly
be unjust, but I cannot be blind.   I know in how many
respects I ought myself to be different, and may say
before God and my friends, that my heart is humbled ;
but here I find that I must either be silent, or else let
myself down,—I cannot express my meaning otherwise—although I would so gladly be improved and instructed by men who stand above me.   The elder
among them have lived in an exclusively literary or
scientific circle belonging to the past.   The experience
of the younger is too limited, not reaching to the War
of Independence, which gave a new direction to the

whole of our social life. They are ignorant, and choose to remain so, of a number of important facts, believing in their youthful self-confidence that they stand independently of the intellectual life of our past days. As the elders live but in the past, so do these but in the present, and the majority of the educated give themselves up to indolence and commonplace enjoyment. This dead state of things is in great part accounted for by the insignificance of their political condition."

In another letter we find Perthes saying:—"To throw one's self in one's later years amidst strange scenes and people as I have done, makes one fully alive to this world's transitoriness. This year has brought me nothing unexpected ; I knew from the first how it would be, but still many a tie of youth and early manhood has been snapped asunder, which would not have been weakened had I remained in Hamburgh. Here no one knows the circumstances of my former life, and hence no one can understand the point of view to which experience has brought me : and I need an apprenticeship to learn to bear this."

Perthes' firm Christian convictions had become universally known by his public controversy with Voss,[*] and he was not the man to seek to hold back what he believed true. His religious opinions and himself were accordingly looked upon as a phenomenon, and many were at a loss how to reconcile his strong impetuous character, his constant activity, and wide circle of interests, with the quiet *pietism* expected from every

---

[*] Perthes had, sometime before leaving Hamburgh, sued Voss for libelling the memory of his father-in-law, Claudius, by his criticisms on the opinions of the latter.

Christian.　The curiosity excited by this seeming contradiction led to much conversation and much controversy.　Perthes' life had been less pervaded by doctrinal speculation than by practical certainty, and this certainty he had acquired from his own wants, his own experience, from the testimony of good and great men, and, above all, from the Bible.　In his youth he had never had any systematic religious instruction, and the business of after years had prevented his supplying the want.　But in Gotha he was confronted by men of all kinds, who often pressed him hard by their historical knowledge, their philosophical aphorisms, their scientifically and logically trained intellects.　He could not appeal to a sense of need or to the inward experience, for these men had never known them, and if he quoted Claudius and Hamann, Spener, Franke, Tauler, Thomas-à-Kempis, &c., he found that no one knew anything about them, or else he was called an enthusiast, and met with sayings of Kant and Fichte, Krug, Fries.　Scripture proofs availed him nothing, for either they were not recognized, or they were explained in the sense of Paulus or Bretschneider.　Perthes, sure of the truth of his cause, but not always able to refute the attacks made upon it, was often irritated and impatient, and his impetuous character led him to make use of many bitter and unguarded expressions against his opponents, whence arose many an unpleasant consequence.　Perthes himself felt that this was doing no good to others nor to himself either.

"I am not so skilful a controversialist as others," he once wrote; "I cannot always find the happy medium between the too little and the too much, and my opponents are very skilful in avoiding the main points of the argument, and directing their attacks against the weak sides of non-essentials. On both parts springs up a hard feeling, which should least of all find place in holy things. Theological strife brings, if not gall, at least wormwood, into religious life."

One of his friends writes to him in reply :—" My case is the same as yours ; the older and the more experienced I grow, and the deeper through God's grace my insight into Christianity becomes, the more convinced I am that demonstration and disputation do no good. So long as a man does not feel that he is a poor sinner, and deficient in all that God requires of him, he will not be reconciled to Him ; and in order that we may convince him, it is in our own selves, our personal character and conduct, that we have to build up a temple of the Lord, so that the enemy may see what he will not else believe in."

Perthes often resolved to avoid religious discussion altogether. " My knowledge," writes he, " is more imperfect than should be possessed by one who speaks on such subjects, my speech is but stammering, and that every one is welcome to see and know, but I will not be the means of injuring the cause. There are good estimable men to whom, owing to the circumstances of their lives, their parents, their education, their age, the study of Christian evidence has been a sealed book. Now, if such hear me, they only perceive my weakness in argument, and my impetuosity, and the holy cause bears the blame that should attach to the unholy man. I will not be guilty of this any longer, I will hold my peace."

This was a wise resolve, but to carry it out was very difficult to Perthes. It was only in his last years that

he had attained such self-control as to be silent when
speaking was useless, or to speak with mildness and
moderation.

But these theological conflicts awoke in him a desire
for a knowledge of systematic Christianity, and led to
his diligent study of the dogmatical and historical
works of Protestant and Catholic theologians. He
wrote essays by way of defining his own views, and
sought through a correspondence with his friends in
North Germany, with Poel, Neander, Nicolovius, and
even with the Catholics, Friedrich Schlegel, and the
Countess Sophie Stolberg, to attain to a deeper understanding of special questions. For many years he had
been well acquainted with the Scriptures, but princi-
pally with particular passages and chapters. While
in Hamburgh he had never had time for the systematic
study of them, to which he now applied himself, and
which he continued up to the day of his death. He,
too, had his difficulties and hindrances of various kinds,
as all have had before and will after him, though to
each probably these will be of a different nature.

In one of his letters he says, " I find that the benefit
I receive from Scripture, in great measure depends upon
myself. How often on turning to it to clear up some
historical sequence, or some obscure doctrine, to find
material for imagination or ground for hypothesis, I
only get at the shell instead of the kernel : or, again,
if in high-wrought times a clearer insight be afforded,
how prone we are to seek to improve and define it by
our own strength, and so to bring human fictions instead of Divine truth to light. The mysteries of Holy
Scripture are only revealed to us when we are seeking
for nothing else but for the way of reconciliation with

God, and for help in our battle with selfishness and sin."

Perthes having written very fully to a friend about St. Paul's Epistles, received the following reply :— " You know that to me Judaism and Christianity, Old and New Testament, do not appear as they do to you, to constitute one great whole. What I most admire in Paul's Epistles is, the triumph of Christianity over Judaism, and therein I acknowledge rather the expression of Divine inspiration than the result of human perception." " Your opinions approach very nearly," replied Perthes, " to the now almost universally prevalent notions respecting Scripture. The earlier theologians have, perhaps, too little remembered that God has not spoken immediately, but through John, Peter, and Paul, in the Bible. At the present time, however, we are certainly in danger of overlooking the unity of the Scripture, while dwelling on the individual writings of Paul, John, or Peter. In short, the trees prevent our seeing the forest, and we forget that it is not with a collection of separate writings that we have to do, but with the Bible as a whole, as being the word which, during the course of the world's history, God wrote down for man's salvation, and which contains nothing more indeed, but still nothing less than is necessary to reveal the ' mystery of godliness.' It is not so much from the individuality of the writers of the Epistles and Gospels, that we are to understand their writings, as from the relation of these to the whole."

It was not only with inward but with outward difficulties that Perthes had to struggle. His ignorance of the original was a hindrance to him, and the whole generation to which he belonged had been deficient in religious instruction and early familiarity with the Scriptures. Perthes writes to a friend :—"The Bible is certainly one and the same for all ; but the best method of studying it varies with the individual, and without a guide, few are able to discover it. The peasant, the mechanic, feels no want, because unable to understand many a historical and circumstantial detail ; without stumbling at this, he quietly passes them over ; but behind his plow, or at his daily toil, he has much unbroken time for meditation and introspection, and it is with reference to this point of view that he must be directed to the Bible. The man of business has different requirements ; his hours are broken up into fragments, and he must devote his few free moments to the great essentials the Scripture reveals, without having them perplexed by what is comparatively immaterial. As for many of the educated in Germany, who have plenty of leisure, and who, without being learned theologians, yet feel a spirit of inquiry within them, they ought not to be perplexed by external difficulties, which only learned theologians can remove, but should have the result of profound science and learning afforded them in a concise form, so that, supported and enlightened by it, they might progress in spiritual understanding. If the numerous ministers who spend, and often spend in vain, their energies in producing well-conceived and well-expressed sermons, would strive to give to seekers after truth the special guidance their different positions and wants require, there would be a great improvement amongst us."

A friend wrote :—"However lofty Tauler's views may be, they are not practical ; his system does not seek to build up, but to destroy, and must therefore be faulty."

Perthes replied as follows : " We are not so much opposed as your letter would imply. The truth of the saying, 'All is vanity,' does indeed come home to the man of ripe years, when he reflects upon all that in life's vicissitudes has charmed and enchained his heart and mind ; but he who, because all things are vain, should cease to take a part in them, would merely vegetate, and no longer live. An entirely contemplative life is an impossibility, the instinct of activity is innate ; at all events hard work is to me a habit with which I cannot dispense.

" He who should attempt nothing on earth but to meditate on God, and feel His presence, would soon cease to do either. The Christian is set in the midst of the world, and, let him stand where he may, will always be called on to fulfil various external duties : in these he is to act as skilfully, expeditiously, and energetically as his faculties will allow, and he may not extinguish his earthly nature or his senses, for he needs them all in order to be God's faithful servant and steward.

" If therefore I have gladly and actively used my physical energies, that is no contradiction to my Christianity ; but if I have failed to sanctify and employ them as in God's sight, then I have been untrue to my convictions. No one knows better than I how little progress one makes. When I remember, that, six-and-twenty years ago, I expressed to Caroline my earnest desire to approach God, and purify my life, and then consider what I am at this day ; alas, how little improvement I find ! The conflict is different, now less

violent indeed, but not easier; and I often feel as
though my whole past, from earliest childhood, came
crowding into the present.

"Brought up by worthy, well-intentioned relatives,
I yet heard hardly anything about Christianity. I did,
indeed, learn Luther's Catechism by heart, but its meaning was never explained to me; and as to my confirmation, it might well be called blasphemous. I owe
some facts and good impressions to Hübner's Biblical
History; Lavater's Diary, too, fell into my hands, and
left some religious impressions behind.

"When I was fifteen years old, I went to Leipzig and
was there taught a rude lesson. While licentious books
inflamed my imagination, I started in the track of
Garne, Reinhard, and Kisewetter, and was only saved
from ruin by my deep and sincere love for a modest
girl.

"When I was twenty years old, and full of internal
struggles, I went to Hamburgh, where I was surrounded
by a new world, filled with all kinds of interests. The
writings of Schiller and Jacobi attracted me; I became
acquainted with Besser, Runge, Hülsenbeck, and Speckter, and my education, properly speaking, then began.

"I became acquainted, too, with Caroline, and through
her, with the blessing of my life. The first six years
of our married life were full of internal and external
difficulties, and then the great public events of the time
intruded into our domestic circle. The spiritual struggle went on. Pride and arrogance never belonged to
my character, and good sense saved me from petty
vanity; but I was always ambitious. As for the impetuosity of my nature, it has often helped me forward,
and the excess of it is punished and restrained by the

conditions of life. My besetting sin has always been sensuality. I have fought a hard battle with it, and only triumphed, or rather found the way to triumph, by becoming a Christian ; and it was not Caroline, nor Claudius, nor any one else that made me a Christian, but the deep yearning for help which I felt to be necessary in battling with my sensual nature.

" Until manhood, the moral law performed for me the functions of the Old Testament, by convincing me of sin, and of my powerlessness to conquer it, and so breaking my presumptuous spirit. As soon as I had relinquished my self-reliance, the gospel renewed the humbled man, comforted him for the sins of the past, and promised and afforded him help in his future struggle. I am not conscious of ever having experienced any special act of grace, though I have yearned after such for years, and I know very well where and what the hindrance in myself is, which stands between this desire and its accomplishment. That many others possess what I still only long for, I firmly believe, though they may perhaps have begun to work in the vineyard some hours after me ; but that God has worked in me, and is still working in many ways, I feel. I have found the sure, the only way to spiritual peace, but the end of that way cannot be reached on earth ; I am neither dead to the world, nor made sinless ; and, indeed, I believe that the effect of regeneration is not to transfigure a man while here below, but to make him childlike and humble. As regards Tauler, it is true that he aims at a wholly interior life, a withdrawal from the world, which is possible only for those who have no earthly calling or earthly ties ; but you must not forget, that Tauler is here addressing himself

18*

especially to unmarried ecclesiastics; for who else could have understood or even read his works at that time? His sermons to the people, on the contrary, are full of practical wisdom, and contain many cautions against the danger of undervaluing one's lawful calling in favor of the inner Christian life; but even in these respects, the infinite difference comes out clearly between human writings, be they even as profound and lofty as Tauler's *Medulla Animæ*, and the divine sublimity, simplicity, and moderation of Holy Scripture."

About this time Perthes spoke out with equal distinctness to his son Matthias. "Neither Tauler, nor Thomas-à-Kempis," wrote he, "desires such a separation from the world as would interfere with the performance of even one of our duties towards our neighbor. I do not know what Terstegen may advocate, for I am but little acquainted with his writings. To withdraw one's self entirely from contact with the world is impossible under the conditions of time and space; and if a man does come into contact with it, though at only one point, that contact gives the devil a hold over him. However, if the attempt to lead an exclusively inner life be hopeless, we have the comfort of knowing that such a life is not ordained of God, but devised by man's own deluded will. We may, indeed, with the loftiest sentiments, and the sublimest ideas, imagine it, but we are deceived by Satan. Behind the lofty sentiment lurks sloth, which hopes for the crown without the conflict; and behind the sublime idea lurks pride, which, in its independence of the world, would fain assume divinity. We are to suffer and strive, but to suffer and strive in love; if this love has degenerated towards our neighbor into coldness, towards ourselves into sensuality, or towards God into presumption, we ought to feel that we need atonement through Jesus Christ. We can do nothing but fight to the end. If we have conquered the grosser and ruder forms of temptation, we have hourly to guard against more subtle and gentle attacks. This world is not made for the rest after victory : fight on, love, and trust God's grace!"

In another letter Perthes says :—" You say that to live with God can only mean to have intercourse with Him, and that he who has such intercourse must needs be conscious of it. Now, the latter proposition is true, but not the former, for intercourse supposes strangers who seek to become better acquainted : intercourse is, indeed, but a repetition of attempts to abolish an existing separation, but it does not abolish the communion of those whose hearts are already one. Friends and acquaintance have intercourse with one another, but who would use that word to express the relation between mother and child? He who has not only intercourse with God, but who, according to Tauler, allows the *ego* within him to be dumb, or, according to Thomas-à-Kempis, 'abandons himself, and is filled with the presence of God,' or again with Tauler, exclaims—' God within, God without, God round about me ;'—he, I say, will neither be troubled by the past with all its sins, nor by the future with all its punishments ; for him, indeed, there is no past or future,—all is present : or rather he lives beyond the conditions of time altogether, for he already has eternal life ; and Consciousness in eternity means something very different from what we call consciousness here on earth."

" As for your being without consciousness," replies a friend to Perthes, " I would, first of all, inquire the exact sense of the phrase, for I can attach no meaning to the words." Perthes says in answer :—" I cannot, indeed, fully and clearly express my meaning, but I can refute the charge of having none. I can recollect, more than thirty years ago, lamenting to Runge, with tears in my eyes, that I could not guard against the consciousness of my best feelings ; does not the experience of others in this matter respond to mine? When an able man accomplishes a noble enterprise with self-sacrifice, that is his Being : but when he is conscious of the goodness and nobility of what he has done, and self-complacent because of it, this Consciousness destroys the excellence of his Being, and ' verily they have their reward.' The Being was noble, the Consciousness ignoble. The Bible says, ' When thou givest alms, let not thy left hand know what thy right doeth.' Does it not in these words imply Being without Consciousness ?"

Perthes writes thus to Rist :—" My youth, with all its passions, my efforts to get on in the world, my labors and cares, the quarter of a century spent with my blessed Caroline, consist of months, days, hours, each filled by its own life and love ; but now all these infinite complexities resolve themselves for me only into their results, and are all fused into the present moment : the past has left in me, as a precipitate, my consciousness of it. I am still able to call forth all these moments, and to make them pass before me like the pictures of a magic lantern, otherwise they are like dead things buried within me : my consciousness of the past perishes with me, but, nevertheless, that past has been, and will continue as Being, though it find no place in any man's Consciousness."

However warmly Perthes longed for internal rest and peace, he yet well knew that there were many obstacles in the way of his attaining them. Having written on the subject to Rist, he received this answer:—"If I had ever misjudged you, the sketch of your life, which you have now given me, would have served to rectify my impression. But it is just as I always supposed. From youth up strong passions have been your special enemies—your better nature strove against them—you cherished indeed higher aspirations and resolves, but you also felt your own powerlessness to carry them out. As the enemy pressed you harder and harder, you sought to strengthen the bulwarks of your religious creed; and you would, no doubt, have become a member of that Church which, on system, comes to terms with the world of sense; had it not been that too free a spirit dwelt within you, and that you were too sincerely converted to God to be perverted by man."

Perthes writes in reply:—" You call me a naturally sensual man, and you are right; I always was so, and still am; my self-reliance, worldly wisdom, and passionate temperament, will play me many a trick yet; the multitude of things that run in my head are constantly leading me astray; the weakness of the *ego*, the love of the world, and the light-heartedness essential to the fulfilment of an earthly calling, are ever making me to forget that I am not my own master; but, let sorrow come, and internal or external conflict, and I become at once aware that the hearty desire to give myself up to God does bear good fruits, and that love is more and more chasing away hatred and coldness out of my heart."

In another letter he says :—" Do not laugh if I tell you that my dog has given me many a hint upon human nature. I never before had a dog constantly with me, and I now ask myself daily whether the poodle be not a man, and men poodles. I am not led to this thought by the animal propensities which we have in common, such as eating, drinking, &c., but by those of a more refined character. He, too, is cheerful and dejected, excited and supine, playful and morose, gentle and bold, caressing and snappish, patient and refractory ; just like us men in all things, even in his dreams! This likeness is not to me at all discouraging : on the contrary, it suggests a pleasing hope, that this flesh and blood which plagues and fetters us, is not the real man, but merely the earthly clothing which will be cast off when he no longer belongs to earth, provided he has not sinfully chosen to identify himself with the merely material. The devil's chief seat is not in matter, but in the mind, where he fosters pride, selfishness, and hatred, and by their means destroys not what is transitory, but what is eternal in man."

In another letter he says :—" If, indeed, as you affirm, ' the *summa summarum* is, that we are all sinners, and that God must best know why He gave us these material bodies which are not sinless, and cannot be so,'—then, truly, we don't stand in need of mercy, for God alone would bear the blame, and the door is shut in the face of all inquirers. But were this so, we might well wonder at the sorrow which sin always awakens in us, and by which we are prevented from charging it upon the Almighty. When I look upon what I have become, what I have conquered, and what I have gained, I may sometimes feel confidence in my own powers; but then again, I know, as certainly as anything can be known, that, if the senses had been stimulated by keener delights, ambition lured on by greater prizes, if heavier trials and stronger temptations had encountered me, I should not have been what I am! Who is there that must not bow his head at the question, 'Does thy life belong to God or to the world?' that would not be saddened by the thought of all his deeds awaking with him in that future life? that would take his defilements with him into paradise? that would not be willing to blot out his past life, or at least the consciousness of it, even in this world, and how much more in the next? that would not like to drink of Lethe's stream? But the gospel hints at no such possibility; on the contrary, it states that we shall stand, and be made manifest before the judgment-seat of Christ. Again and again the all-important question recurs :—' Can and will God forgive sin?' He who does not understand the full force of this question does not know himself, and happy is he whose own individual experience affords him the answer to it. Human philosophy can prompt the question, but never solve it. Philosophers misapprehend reason as the Jews did the law : so I read lately in Hamann's letters; for they know not that reason is given us only to make us acquainted with our ignorance, just as the law was given to make us acquainted with our sins. Truth and grace alike cannot be excogitated or inherited, they must be historically revealed."

XXXVI.

Changes in Life.

LTHOUGH Perthes had rejoiced with all the energy of paternal affection at his daughter's happy betrothal, yet her departure from his home cost him a severe struggle. "From this day forth," he writes, "my child is mine no more. I shall have to see her removed further away day by day, and her love, not indeed estranged from me, but yet devoted to another. So it must ever be; the child is to leave father and mother, but the pain of it is great, the heart bleeds at the necessity, and we gain deeper insight into its depths, and into the pure intensity of a father's love."

On the day after the wedding, which took place on the 1st of June, 1824, Perthes had all his children assembled round him; but, as one by one departed, leaving him alone with the three youngest only, he was almost overwhelmed with sadness. We find him writing :—"They were indeed heavy hours when all forsook me. First Matthias went away to begin a new and independent life, then both my married daughters returned to their long established homes, at last Matilda left with her husband. The farewell of this dear daughter, who clung to me with boundless tenderness, pierced my heart, and I found myself alone—alone as

(424)

for thirty years I had never been. Henceforth I have no family circle ; the house that Caroline and I founded is fast going to pieces, and the picture of myself as the last remaining one haunts me like a spectre. One after another the children depart, in three or four years even the three little ones will have left me, then I shall be free as the bird of the air, and a long avenue of solitary years may yet lie before me. The horrors of a forsaken solitude come upon me and force many tears from my eyes."

Perthes was particularly desirous that his three younger children should not, after their sister's marriage, be deprived of the advantages of family life. " It grieves me," said he, " to inflict myself and the three children upon the young pair, but it cannot be helped. My elder daughters remind me, it is true, that the limited accommodation, and the necessity of conforming to the habits of others, will be new and disagreeable to me. But, since so much inward sorrow has been overcome, external changes can surely be so too."

Accordingly, a few days after the wedding, Perthes removed to the house of his son-in-law, Becker. " I am now sitting," he writes to a friend, " in my daughter's home ; the small house suits me, and I enjoy the extensive view on every side. Nothing can be happier than my relations with my son-in-law, and my daughter's attention is boundless. The three younger children feel at home, and for myself I have but few requirements, having never been an uneasy seeker after comforts, and can easily conform to the ways of others ; yet I will confess that it is not altogether pleasant to be no longer lord and master in one's own household.

I have had from my very childhood an almost morbid fear of becoming a burden to others, and disturbing their way of life. And now here I am with three children in this young couple's house! No one, indeed, will allow us to be called an incumbrance, but are we the less so for that? This thought vexes and grieves me already, do what I may to battle with it. What, then, will it be in future? I shudder at the prospect of old age, with mind and body getting more and more enfeebled, and requiring help and care day and night. I have never seen an old and feeble man who did not, if alone in the world, feel his position awkward and painful. Many of them I have seen fall into acts of great folly; who then may feel secure? I declare that the best provision for such a time of life is a French valet of the old stamp, such as we used to see in the days of emigration; a man who could alike cook for his old master, and feed, wash, dress, and comb him."

The truth of the matter, however, was, that though Perthes was right in saying that he had few requirements, he yet had requirements which the best of French valets could never have met. He had been for many years accustomed not only to Caroline's society, but to her perfect comprehension at a glance or a word, of all that concerned him, whether outward or inward; in joy and sorrow, in small and great things alike, he had always found in her the most perfect sympathy. This mutual life was lost to him now, and after Caroline's death, in his more serious hours, he was never for a moment without a sense of loneliness."

"I am alone," he wrote to his friend Nicolovius, "and full of yearning and longing; I deeply crave for sympathy to cheer the desert within me ; but no one understands me now, as I was once understood. If I speak out of my heart, the answer I receive teaches me that my meaning is not apprehended." In another letter he says,—" It is wretched enough to lead an unmarried life, but still worse to have known perfect sympathy of soul, and then to lose it. I possess, in no common degree, my children's love, but this cannot replace the love of which I have been bereft. The affections of youth have different objects from those of riper years, being fixed either upon present good, or the glancing forms of the future. Parents belong to the past, and the past is pale and dim for the young. Before them all is bright sunlight ; behind them cold moonshine. So it ever has been and will be, and we who also looked forward once, must needs look backward now."

In another letter he says,—" There is no comfort for the sadness I feel—night is in my soul. The outward man, indeed, makes a show of enjoyment, laughs, and seems cheerful, but there is a waste and bitter void within. Yet whither am I drifting ? When one sees in a new wedlock a new human love arising, which ignores time and decay, and then feels the phantom-world in one's own heart, truly the bones rattle, and the blood runs cold."

It was with this feeling of loneliness, that Perthes, at the age of fifty-one, became a member of his third daughter's household. In the very next house to him lived his son-in-law's sister, Charlotte Becker. She had been married to Heinrich Hornbostel, a distinguished merchant of Vienna, and had, after his death, returned with four children to her mother's house. Of

these children, the two eldest were hopeless invalids ;
but, though they had been often at the point of death,
it was impossible to foresee whether their sufferings
would extend over a few weeks, or a few years.   Perthes had, soon after his arrival in Gotha, become acquainted with this much-tried mother, who was an intimate friend of his married daughters ; he had heard
of her sorrows with sympathy, and admired the energy and cheerfulness with which she bore them.   Perthes wrote some time after this : " I was only slightly
acquainted with Charlotte, it is true, but I was always
struck with her clear intellect and quick wit, the animation of her whole nature ; the precision and skill,
shown in all she did, attracted me, and her discrimination of character, and her sensible estimate of things
in general, perfectly astonished me.   However, we had
not drawn nearer, and life's deeper chords had not
been touched."

Charlotte was thirty years old when Perthes joined
his daughter, and thus came into daily contact with
Charlotte and her children.   In a later letter he says,—
" Her real worth could not be concealed from me,—I
saw the steadfast fidelity and enduring love she displayed in nursing her sick children, and her good
sense in educating the healthy ones.   I saw how, in
spite of her liveliness and social gifts, she gave up any
pleasure as soon as the children wanted her.   Sorrow,
anxiety, and loss of rest by their bedsides had left
traces on her features, but her clear, intellectual glance
was undisturbed by them all.   I could, indeed, gather
from a few strong expressions, how heavy her trials
were, but generally speaking, I found her composed,
resigned, and cheerful.   I resolved to be as useful a

friend as I could, both to the mother and children : she kindly responded to my cordiality, and I soon possessed her confidence, though the thought of standing in a nearer relation to her never occurred to me."

Towards the end of July, 1824, Rebecca Claudius, Perthes' mother-in-law, came with her daughter Augusta, to pay a month's visit to Gotha. She was much concerned about Perthes' situation, and one day, while they were walking in the orangery, expressed herself openly to him. She told him that he was no more a master in his own house, that soon his younger children would be leaving him, and that his strong health gave promise of a long life yet to come—that for him solitude was not good, that he could not bear it, and consequently, that he ought not to put off choosing a companion for the remainder of his life. At these words the thought of Charlotte shot like lightning through his soul : he made no reply, but he had a hard battle to fight with himself from that time forth.

In September he communicated to his mother-in-law the *pros* and *cons* which agitated him so much, but without giving her to understand that it was no longer the subject of marriage in general, but of one marriage in particular, which now disquieted him. After stating the outward and inward circumstances which made a second marriage advisable in his case, he goes on to say, " I am quite certain that Caroline foresaw, from her knowledge of my character and temperament, a second marriage for me, and I am equally certain that no new union could ever disturb my spirit's abiding union with her. My inner life is filled with her memory, and will be so till my latest day, but I must own that this is possible only while I incorporate in thought her happy soul, and think of her as a human being, still sharing my earthly existence, still taking interest in all I do ; and I cannot disguise from myself, while viewing her under this aspect, that my dear Caroline would prefer my living on alone, satisfied with her memory. Again, there can be no doubt that Holy Scripture, although permitting a second marriage, does so on account of the hardness of our hearts. The civil law contains no prohibition either, and yet there has always existed a social prejudice against such a marriage, and youth, whose ideal is always fresh and fair, and women who are always young in soul, look with secret disgust upon it. I know, too, that my remaining alone would be, not only with reference to others but in itself, the worthier course ; but, on the other hand, I know it would be so in reality only if this worthiness were not assumed for the purpose of appearing in a false light to myself, to other men, and perhaps even before God, or for the purpose of cloaking selfishness under the guise of fidelity to the departed. To us, in our life here below, the love of the creature is given to educate us for the love of God. Can I dispense with this earthly help, and yet maintain love alive in my heart? Can I, without family ties to constrain me, go on caring for others? Can I escape the danger of isolating myself, and living in selfishness, gross or refined? I recall many a fearful instance of this in others! Is it, in short, weakness to say to myself, 'Thou canst not dispense with the earthly helps to a loving spirit,' or is it arrogance to believe that I no longer need such? I do not know how to answer this question."

It was not, however, by answering this question, nor

by reflecting upon the lawfulness of second marriages in general, that Perthes' irresolution was subdued, but by an increasing attachment to the lady with whom he wished to contract such a marriage.

"My own experiences amaze me," he writes a few weeks later to Rist ; "the varying moods familiar to the innocent heart of the boy in his first love, the enthusiastic tenderness that found vent in happy melancholy and universal good-will to all creation, these lay far, far behind me like a lovely dream, and no wish had power to call them back. But now I feel again as I did then. How is this possible in a man of my age? how can I, whose heart has been so tempest-tossed by time and by the world ; how can I, who have known so much, sinned so often, return thus to the innocent fondness which nestles in the newly-awakened heart of a boy ; for I can call it nothing else ? I feel like a child, I cry to myself 'Awake, and pray ;' but there is no discord, no warning voice within ; I can pray and hold the most fervent communion with my dear Caroline still."

Perthes was thoroughly aware of the strength of the influence he was under. A few days later he again wrote to Rist :—"I know that, when an attachment has once taken possession of the human heart, the balance is lost, and self-deception is almost unavoidable. There then remains but one way, prosaic yet sure, of discerning right from wrong ; and that is to prove one's heart's desire by a reference to the claims of others. Do I, in following my own heart's impulses, interfere with any man's right, disturb any man's peace? am I hindered in the activity which my calling requires, and can I fulfil my duty to her (Charlotte's) children, without failing in duty towards my own? I feel that increasing sorrow, on account of these poor little invalids, would await me, and that in regard to them I should have no easy task; but without a participation in this trial, I should not feel justified in uniting their mother's destiny to mine."

Perthes' decision was taken in the middle of September, but he did not declare himself till a month later. The answer he received was favorable, but not decisive, and time was asked for calm consideration. Perthes had believed that such a delay would have suited him exactly, but he was mistaken. In these days of suspense he wrote confidentially to Rist, saying, "I need just now the heart of a friend, and desire that you should know all." Perthes' correspondence at this period mirrors with wonderful accuracy the state of his inner man.

One letter runs thus:—" I am horrified at myself:— am I a fool and self-deceived, or am I really to bear the joys and sorrows of youth and to battle with this unspeakably excitable heart to the end of my days? I wrote to her that she was to say No, if she was unable to say Yes with all her heart, and that her refusal would find and leave me tranquil. I wrote that with perfect sincerity, and now her refusal would shatter me, and her consent give me new life."

And yet these letters of his, overflowing as they do with intense feeling, are written under the fullest consciousness of his own inward condition, and show that he was able to analyze and estimate it coolly and impartially.

In one letter, he says, "I feel as if every one who saw me must think to himself, 'Ought passion to hold such sway over a man of his age?'" In another, "I have had of late new experience and new insight into the deep places of the human heart, and this season of conflict will have a permanent influence on me for time and for eternity."

In short, in Perthes we find united the passionate youth and the middle-aged man, and the latter watches and even laughs at the former.

He tells Rist: "It is a pity that Kotzebue is no more—he would be charmed with the whole story."

To another friend he says:—"All human affairs have their comic side ; if Charlotte becomes my wife, being as she is my son-in-law's sister, I shall be my daughter's brother-in-law, and Becker will be his sister's son!" But the seriousness and stable good sense of the man finally won the mastery. He says to Rist : "It were indeed sad, if all the labor and discipline of my past life were to be in vain. I have a firm will, and with faith and prayer shall get over this ere long."

However, such a state of excitement could not long continue without obtaining a decision one way or another. The 25th October was the day of betrothal. Perthes wrote to Rist :—" Charlotte had always felt towards me esteem and confidence ; now the fervor of my love has conquered her, and she is mine. The storm is laid, and I am again at rest; but I do not believe that my peace was ever more deeply disturbed."

Somewhat later he writes,—" We have had some weeks of quiet intercourse, and easily understand each other's inner life, though this understanding is of quite another kind from that which existed between my Caroline and myself. Indeed, the characters of the two are so dissimilar, that it is impossible to bring them

19

into one and the same picture. I cannot compare them —each of them stands apart in my thoughts. Our relation to the outer world is rendered singular by the circumstance of Charlotte's having first known me in Gotha, where, a stranger among strangers, I am cut off from all connexion with the friends and transactions of my earlier life. Thus all the letters that I receive must needs appear to her fragments of an unfamiliar and antiquated world. It is impossible to me to give a connected account of myself, that is, of the external facts of my early life ; I must trust to Charlotte's gradually finding them out."

Towards the end of December, Perthes writes :— " Behind me lies a year filled with anxieties, occupations, conflicts, and experiences ; before me a period which will not be less rich in all these, and will bring me more work than ever. Free as I was a little time ago, I was able to embark at once in important measures connected with my new calling, without any painful anxiety as to my means. But now, greater foresight and increased effort are necessary, and hard continuous labor is the path my nature points out for me. So I need not fear that Charlotte should be obliged to take time from her children to devote it to me ; indeed, it is a blessing to me that she should have her special duties to fulfil, for a woman who depended upon me for the filling up of her time, would make me wretched. Our common task is to labor, watch, and pray, and God will add His blessing and support."

In February, 1825, Perthes went to Berlin, where he remained till the middle of March. " I thank God, I thank Him with all my heart," he says in his first letter to his betrothed, " that He has led me to thee, thou dear, pious, noble soul. Thy letter lies before me ; between ourselves, I have kissed it just as a youth might do ; and why should I not ? If feeling be true, it is always young, though time and the world may have aged the features. Thy letter makes me very happy. My Charlotte, all that thou sayest springs from so simple and upright a mind, that it promises a firm and perfect understanding between us. Thou wishest to be strengthened, elevated in spirit by me, as I was by my Caroline. Dear Charlotte, I know, indeed, that I can lead thee to a knowledge that affords security for thy whole being, yet a security only for what thou already hast ; for God has been with thee in thy trials, and He is with thee still. God has been, and is with me also, and I have the knowledge of eternal truth ; but thou art purer, better, more stable than I. I have an excitable fervent heart of love, but formerly, my beloved Charlotte, it was Caroline that sustained me, and thou, too, wilt have enough to do. Hold me fast to thy heart. My restless spirit needs to be restrained by the arm of love, and by the eye of love that looks to Heaven."

A few days later, he says, " My heart is true and loving, but much that is unstable, wild, transient, impulsive, and uncontrolled, still lives and stirs in me, and the repose of age is as far off as ever. But take me as I am,—have patience with me,—love me ! Thou must support me, and I, too, shall support thee,—that I know well."

In the middle of March, Perthes returned to Gotha, but he was soon obliged to leave it again for Leipzig. On the 15th of May he was married. On the day following he wrote to Besser :—" I parted from you in Leipzig with deep emotion. Standing at the gate of a

new life, it seemed as though I was bidding an eternal
farewell to you, the companion of my earlier days.
The coach that carried me off seemed transformed into
a ship, that bore away the sailor from his familiar
scenes into an unknown waste. My past lay behind
me like the receding shore, becoming more and more
indistinct each moment, and my future stretched out
before me like the wide untried ocean, in which no
anchor that I cast would hold. The evening before
last, I returned with bleeding heart and mind to Gotha,
and Charlotte alone restored me to peace and security.
Yesterday morning, at seven o'clock, we were married,
and we spent the day in such quiet as we could. To-
day the newly united family have sat down to our first
dinner, and I feel marvellously composed and peaceful.'
A week later, Perthes writes :—" I have never in all
my life felt such thorough satisfaction and security
respecting any step I have taken. I feel as though the
peace of God had settled upon me, and accordingly I
say, ' God be praised.' "

Although the rest after which Perthes yearned
throughout life was certainly not conferred upon him
by his new connexion, yet this second marriage proved
a source of blessing and happiness greater even than
he had anticipated ; though, on the other hand, it made
many claims upon him. He had not only to provide
for the education of his three youngest children, but he
was now responsible for four step-children beside. At
the age of fifty-three he had to begin a new and complicated domestic career, and to fulfil many duties commonly reserved for the high spirits of earlier life.
In addition to all this, four children were born to him :
Rudolph in 1827, Caroline in 1828, Augustus in 1830,

and Eliza in 1832. The illnesses of the children, the care of their education, and the noise of a large household, certainly affected his excitable nature more than they do that of most men ; but not for a single moment did he feel them a burden : on the contrary, the feeling of gratitude for the happiness conferred upon him, remained with him till his death. He wrote as follows to Niebuhr :—" I have won a great treasure : I am loved with woman's utmost tenderness, and my Charlotte's noble mind discovers nothing in me which lessens her esteem."

Perhaps *any* second marriage would have proved a blessing to Perthes, at all events *this* second marriage was so to such an extent, that they who knew him intimately could not imagine what would have become of him had it not been brought about. He himself says, " I feel in deep humility how great are the claims that God may justly make upon me. Even in my later years he has done great things to preserve love alive in me ; and though I spake with the tongues of men and angels, and had not love, what were I but sounding brass and a tinkling cymbal ?"

XXXVII.

Correspondence on the Relations of Life.

T was about this time that Besser's health began to fail ; and, in consequence of this, he had fits of deep melancholy, which often found vent in his letters to his old friend, who tried to comfort him, now in one way, now in another. "It is your body which again inflicts upon you the well-known 'grey season,' and no one is perfect master over bodily moods, but sometimes you are needlessly uneasy about your ability to get through the work that lies before you. You might very often scare away the 'grey' mood, by calmly considering how trivial are the causes of your anxiety, and with what ease you have overcome such before. But, indeed, I know only too well how it is with man ; the head may be weary, and the heart full of love and devotion, or, on the contrary, the head clear, and the heart barren and cold ; but sorrow weighs down head and heart alike, just as joy brightens both."

In another letter, he says : "I know that you are often conscious of great bodily depression ; you call it sickness, but this has been your case ever since I have known you, and it is necessary to be as intimate with you as I am to appreciate fully the wealth and clearness of your mind. So you see you announce nothing new to me, and I can only reply, ' Take courage, till life's phantasmagoria are over.' I, too, have been ailing these last few days, and then I felt as though I had been presumptuous in beginning life anew, and uniting another's existence to my own ; but, however, I let my Charlotte comfort me, and she does so effectually."

Again we find Perthes writing, " You say that life becomes a burden ; so it must to us all as we grow old : but we should try to accustom ourselves to a new race of men, or rather to the same men differently dressed, on whom the divine Father still looks down with a smile, as in the Berlin painting. While we live we must put up with novelty, but I shall be glad to die ; one gets tired of evermore picking off one husk after another from the kernel of truth."

The sufferer wrote in reply, during the summer of 1826, " You have found out, though I was unwilling to trouble you about it, that, for some months past, my spirits have been much depressed. I am always expecting better days, and they will come, I know, but this physical and mental exhaustion gives me many dark hours. Dejection and faint-heartedness do not improve the health, and body and mind react unfavorably on each other. I deserve reproaches for not being happy in my happy circumstances, and I expect them from you, but sympathy as well. Ask for me strength and courage from Him who. alone can give them."

Perthes replied as follows : " Ignorant as I am of your present circumstances, it is difficult for me to write to you, my dearly loved brother. I see that your spirits are depressed, and knew it indeed before you stated it plainly, but I know not whence this depression comes. Deeply grieved indeed I am, but how reach out a helping, comforting hand? You speak of your 'happy circumstances,' and you are right. The companion of your life, the mother of your children, stands at your side in the prime of life; your children grow up satisfactorily, you can look at them all with glad hope, and you have given your daughter to the worthy, true-hearted Mauke, who is at the same time a support to you. You have friends who cordially love you, you enjoy great social consideration, your means are liberal and independent, and, if it pleased God to take you away, not one in a thousand could feel equally at ease as to the temporal well-being of those left behind. God has greatly blessed you, and you yourself own it when you say,—'I deserve reproaches for not being happy.' Now, as to happiness, commonly so called, only the innocent child, or the day-dreaming youth can really experience it. The earnest-minded man cannot thus be happy, it is only the shallow and self-sufficient who can trifle on gaily through life. For here nothing endures; what most we love is torn away; all is brittle and perishable, and we ourselves are but broken reeds. Our heart overflows with love to some dear object, and yet how imperfect the union, how weak the sympathy! And even he who knows that love to God is the only enduring love, and that it is the only anchor of the soul, how deeply he feels that he can but seldom draw near to his Father with perfect resignation and sincerity. Who, then, can be happy in such a state as this? We are not to be so, nay, we are to feel that we lie in chains, that we live in an element uncongenial to our nature, and, fighting humbly and manfully, we are to follow the light that leads us out of our darkness. Now all this, dear brother, you not only know but feel. So long as I have known you, you have been loving and lovable to all around you, you have never given way to pride or vanity ; you have endured hardness and weariness in full reliance upon God, and the way of reconciliation through his Son has long been open to you. Therefore the core of your being must be sound, the burden is only a material one, it is your body that oppresses you, and physical causes reach deep down, not only appearing in actual disease, but exercising an invisible influence over the spirit itself. Your bodily frame is not in unison with your loving nature, your lively fancy and elastic activity ; therefore you have always felt hampered and have become a humorist, who has good and bad hours and days, and many a sudden alternation of sun and shower to undergo. Even in your youth you had dark seasons when you shrank within yourself for fear of grieving others : and now that your blood is no longer young, you need not be surprised if the old enemy return, and cast a dark pall over everything. You have been weaving again a dark web of feeling and thought, which holds you fast as though it were of iron strength, while in reality it is but a spider's web. Tear yourself away from it all, for three or four weeks, I beseech you. I demand this as your friend and brother ; I demand it for the sake of your family and that of the business. Tear yourself away and come to us ; make up your mind and set off without delay."

Besser did not come, but he recovered somewhat.

19*

However, the improvement was not lasting. On the 6th of December, tidings reached Gotha of Besser's having been fatally attacked by nervous fever. In a few hours Perthes was on his way, travelling day and night, and reached Harburg on the evening of the 8th, too late however to cross the Elbe. A newspaper lying in the inn apprised him of Besser's death five days before.

He wrote home :—" I arrived too late, they had already buried my beloved Besser. In him I have lost the friend of my youth, the only one who knew what I am, and how I became what I am. Many have experienced his affection and benevolence, but I alone fully knew the capacities of his mind. We had been friends in joy and sorrow for more than thirty years."

Besser's death brought about another change in Perthes' outward circumstances. " You see, my dear friend," says he in a letter to Niebuhr, " that I am in my old place once more, and must go out again into the great market, where I did not wish to end my days. It is almost impossible that Mauke, able and worthy as he is, should carry on so large a business alone."

However, it did not prove necessary, as Perthes had feared, that he should return to Hamburgh ; but henceforth all manner of hard work was added to the joyful and sorrowful events with which his life was filled. Children and grand-children were born to him, and manifold were the sicknesses and deaths, pleasures and anxieties, which agitated the large family circle.

In 1827, Perthes lost his eldest step-son, and he writes thus concerning him :—" We could not but wish to see him freed from his sufferings, but even I miss the boy's sweet, sad look, and his affectionate ways more than I could have supposed. Our little Rudolph is a real godsend to his mother, and even in her grief she cannot resist his liveliness and loveliness."

Perthes had, in 1827, taken his second son, Clement, to Hamburgh, to attend the academical gymnasium there, before entering the University. But the father's anxiety was not decreased by this removal of his son from his immediate care. A great number of distinguished men, too, paid him longer or shorter visits during this period, amongst whom were Ranke, Oken, Bunsen, Tholuck, Haller, Parish, &c., &c. Perthes in his correspondence touches with pleasure upon these visits.

In one of his letters he says : " Haller of Hamburgh was with me a few weeks ago ; his judgment and penetration surprised me anew, and I truly esteem him for having in spite of them, preserved such a benevolent heart, and such childlike ingenuousness."

While in Bonn, Perthes again spent most of his time with Niebuhr. He writes of him thus :—" On seeing Niebuhr, after a long interval, I always experience a painful degree of shyness ; because in spite of his intellectual greatness, his universal knowledge, and his keen discrimination, I am conscious that I take a truer view of many subjects than he does, and, consequently, often feel myself obliged to oppose him in spite of his superiority. Added to this, the strange, almost unpleasant peculiarities of his manner ; for example, his restless walking up and down the room all the time he is talking. But this shyness soon gives way, his natural candor and good-heartedness triumphing over all. I am more than ever struck with the singularities of his character, and yet I never found him so cordial or so

gentle. His emotion at parting overcame me much.
He came to me twice after I had taken leave, and said,
with tears in his eyes, ' I have hardly one other old
friend like you.' Niebuhr is happy in his present situation, and with his present employment, and yet were
a political post offered him, he would hardly refuse it.
His political opinions are not irrevocably fixed : once
he remarked that time corrected many of his judgments ; that he now justified much that he once condemned, and condemned much that he once justified ;
and that thus he had become more cautious in his decisions. This time, too, he avoided, evidently on purpose, all conversation about religion. When he dis-
puted Schiller's influence being beneficial to youth, I
asked him whether he himself remembered any interval
between the personal experience of the boy and the
learned man. He grew melancholy and was silent.
But it is very certain that Niebuhr never had a season of
youth, yet he now exercises an extraordinary influence
over youth. Young Dr. Classen of Hamburgh, with
his industry, acquirements, and sincere attachment, was,
he told me, a daily delight to him. One of Niebuhr's
strange peculiarities is his stammering, not over words,
but sentences ; he will repeat the same sentence six or
seven times in the most different ways. The reason
is, that owing to his wide range of imagination and
immense amount of information, language cannot keep
pace with his thoughts. In Niebuhr there is a strange
mixture of the statesman and the *savant*, of refinement
and awkwardness, yet he is truly a great and noble
man. He keeps himself quite independent, and says
openly whatever he thinks. Before I saw him, a man
high in office said to me with a dash of envy : ' Niebuhr

can say and do what would be allowed in no other person ; he is a crony of Schleiermacher's, is often with Cousin, and enjoys the unlimited confidence of the Crown-Prince, who is ever asking what Niebuhr says of this and that.' I found Schleiermacher wonderfully changed. Formerly I had known him for a keen, sarcastic, violent humorist, but now, whether lively or quiet, he is uniformly serene and indulgent ; his sharp features have acquired an expression of peace ; repose and gentleness are now his, and love, which struggled so long with intellect, will conquer yet. God has vouchsafed him an excellent wife, who will assist him to gain the final victory. The impression he made upon me answered exactly to his own words some time ago, viz.,' I wish neither to offend nor to injure any one by my theological writings : I strive in all things with all my might to "speak the truth in love," and hope, by God's help, never to be moved again from this position.' "

Of the numberless letters written and received by Perthes, the majority related to business, many to politics, and many to ecclesiastical affairs : but he also received communications from men of the most varied character, who asked his advice, his aid, or his sympathy, in circumstances the most miscellaneous, sometimes the most singular.

One man, whom he had never seen, consulted him on the choice of a wife. For six years this person had daily resolved upon matrimony ; but the fear of embittering his whole future life, by a mistaken choice, ever restrained him : he was now thirty years of age, and felt certain that, left to himself, he would remain undecided to the end of his days. " Choose for me a bride," he wrote to Perthes, " and, at a word from you,

I shall set out, marry her, and, as long as I live, revere you as the author of my happiness."

To this "strange but honest fellow," as Perthes called him in a letter to Besser, the following answer was made : "Marry you must ; for yours is a case in which science and business would not be adequate safeguards against onesidedness. I am not one of those who liken the choice of a wife to a man fumbling in a basket of snakes for the single eel which is among them : I am rather inclined to think that marriages are made in heaven, not, however, without the coöperation of men. A frank boldness is required. Youthful fancy is often most successful, catching at once the right object, or being caught ; but whoever, like you, racks his brains, and scrutinizes every possibility, finds of course on all sides dangerous rocks. You should remember that the absence of positive badness is itself a great point in creatures such as we are, and that too much positive goodness is not to be expected. Look out, then, among the daughters of your own land ; and, if that avail nothing, make a tour in the wide world. A man, thirty years of age, should do nothing by halves, and if he go to work with sound sense and an earnest purpose, God will be his helper."

To another young man : "Beware of disclosing too freely your religious convictions to the lady you name. Except in marriage, a thorough understanding cannot exist between a man and a woman : out of it they are enigmas to each other."

Again : "Instruction and training have comparatively little influence on the position of women. A naturally intelligent woman shines everywhere, even with little acquired knowledge and refinement : on the

other hand, if she be nothing in herself, then, spite of
all instruction and polish, she appears awkward and
common. A man, however, counts for something, if
he have but the superficial acquirements and polish
obtained by intercourse with the world, or if, though
stupid and awkward, he have learning."

To a young man, whose age may be guessed at from
twenty to thirty : "In early youth every girl is charming, and the object of desire ; in the later years of
manhood, again, one sees in both girl and woman, above
all things, our common humanity ; we rejoice over the
good, and put up with the bad ; but at your time of
life, a man is neither quite blind nor yet perfectly open-
eyed, and consequently his judgments are at fault."

After congratulating Henry Ritter on his marriage,
Perthes continues : "Marriage is God's chief gift.
The bachelor may, indeed, accomplish great things in
the outer world, but he cannot penetrate into the inner
life of men and things. The community of earthly
joys and sorrows in marriage discloses to us the heav-
en of our origin and destiny. In the course of a long
married life, I have had much suffering and sorrow,
much care and anxiety : but, unmarried, I had not been
able to live."

On another occasion : "As, since the introduction of
Christianity, woman, from being a mere instrument in
the propagation of the species, and a beast of burden
to man, has acquired an independent position, and a
distinct recognized value of her own, so likewise man
has made a step in advance. He has begun to form
ideals. First of all he idealized woman, and his relation to her ; but this resulted in a disposition to
idealize everything—a disposition of which the Greeks

and Romans, and the whole ancient world knew nothing, but which has exercised an incalculable influence on modern history. Christianity makes large and heavy claims in regard to the relation between man and woman, such, indeed, as were never dreamt of before : every man has now a secret history of his own in regard to these claims ; and that history varies according as, in his struggle to satisfy them, he has simply persevered, actually conquered, or fairly succumbed. No third party can be a witness of this struggle ; yet on its issue, the man's whole life, as noble or base, useful or baneful, essentially depends."

Having congratulated Rist, whose children were as yet all young, and at home, on his domestic happiness, Perthes continues : " This, too, is but for a time, and it will be far otherwise when your children begin to entertain thoughts, wishes, hopes, and views of their own,—when, one after another, they leave the nursery and the house on their several ways. The tenderest strings of your parental heart will then be broken. I have experienced it myself, and I may freely say so, as my own children have given me cause only for joy ; still they go their own way and must do so."

To a dear friend who sought consolation for himself and his wife from Perthes, on occasion of their son's death : " To lose a child ! What that means no man can know but by experience. From earliest childhood we indeed see that the ties of affection are broken asunder : but what comfort does that bring to the sorrowing father and mother ! Cling to one another in your grief ; let neither conceal it from the other ; do not try to calm one another down, but rather let your sorrow flow out into a common stream ; it will then be changed into a quiet happiness, and will unite you more intimately than mere prosperity ever could have done. Cling to one another, I say ; community of love changes the profoundest grief into a blessing from God." On receiving a letter of thanks, in which the same party acknowledges Perthes to have proved the best comforter among all his friends, and adds, that henceforth the period of unbroken domestic happiness lies behind him, like an ancient world. Perthes writes again : "It is even so. From the moment of a child's death, the parent's eye is dulled, and the beauty of life gone. Every little accident, a cough, a change in the tone of voice, excites cruel anxiety. All know, that a family seldom remains unbroken, but no one applies the observation to himself, till a loved one is taken away, and then he believes it indeed ; for deep down in his breast sorrow gnaws on. The parent submits to the stroke, but cannot get above it. Gone! gone! yes, that is it! To be no longer able humanly to love this particular child, no more to receive from it a caress; that is the eternal pang! Then, to be obliged to leave a child's corpse—which is always heavenly—for the world outside, is horrible! Everything appears so little and trifling, compared with the great experience just made. You were right not to keep away your other children from the death-bed and the coffin. To talk children into sadness is vain ; but we may not too anxiously keep them from the view of realities : they should early learn to look the lot of man in the face, and they can bear it. A mother, by the sick-bed of her child, teaches us the full power which lies in human nature : the husband is appalled at his own comparative backwardness. Time, also, has less power over woman's grief than over man's. Faithfulness is the noblest thing in human nature ; and it is the peculiar property of woman."

To an aged man who had lost a son twenty-two years of age : "The younger the child, the closer the bond, as its very flesh and blood seem still to be ours : the older, the more does it differ from us ; it becomes even, in a sense, estranged by the possession of a will and of feelings independent of ours. The loss of a son in the bloom of youth brings with it both a peculiar sorrow and a peculiar consolation ; for the purity of youth is nearly allied to the ideal. The youth's expectation of accomplishing great things is sure to be disappointed in after years ; but your son has carried with him all his hopes with their bloom untouched. Twenty-two years, as you write, is a fine age to die at, better than forty-two or fifty-two ; yet for me at least the battle of life was necessary ; and I am still attached to life chiefly by the hope of gaining a complete victory within."

A friend, residing at a great distance, wrote to Perthes complaining that, in ripe age, he was humiliated by onsets of passion, such as he had never experienced before, and could not resist. Perthes thus endeavored to allay the storm :—"He who is assailed by passion, as you are, is not old, no matter how many years he can count. It *is* exceedingly humiliating to find one's self overcome by the animal powers ; but, when these fail, it is not the man who has left sin, but sin which has left the man ; and he will find it not easier, but more difficult, to rise up to God. In this world war is life, peace, death ; and we must battle on to the end to gain the crown."

Often as Perthes bestowed a glance on the inward
and outward condition of others, his own development
was still ever with him the chief subject of examination, nay, of wonder, and even anxiety ; and he frequently unbosomed himself to his friends. Thus to
Rist :—" Few men have enjoyed all along such opportunities of intercourse with children as myself ; and,
through observation of them, many things in my own
development are only now becoming clear to me. The
child, as soon as it can use its senses, feels itself to be
only a fragment of nature ; it sees and hears things
which are new, but, because the child is itself, as yet,
merely a bit of nature, it wonders at nothing. For a
few years it lives only with what is close at hand.
The clear-running stream is dearer to it than the heav-
ing ocean ; the flower more charming than the forest ;
the hillock on which it tumbles about is more to it
than the mountain ; the child finds everything in harmony with itself. When, however, thought awakes,
when the child comes into contradiction with its own
will, and enters on a struggle, of which the object and
the issue are alike unknown, then does the boy begin to
feel himself severed from nature, and the youth to
long for something which shall correspond to him, to
his heart and mind. Alternately deceived and un-
deceived, the man must then work through the years
of life-apprenticeship. Throughout the whole season
of youth, man communicates, by fancy and love, through
nature and the creature, with God. Youth is poesy,
but advanced life has quite a different character. To
love mankind in old age, and to remain steadfast in
love even to death, is exceedingly difficult. Things
are in the end reversed : youth rises through man to

God—age descends through God to man. A youthful warmth of feeling can be preserved in old age only by faith and humility ; and, whereas there is hardly anything more repulsive than old age without warmth, love, on the other hand, or even kindliness, gives peace and assurance to the conscience, notwithstanding the profoundest conviction of sin." •

Genial old age was illustrated by Perthes himself in an eminent degree. He greatly enjoyed the renewal of old acquaintanceships, even when these had been of the most casual description ; and his method of procedure appears in the following letter :—" One cannot be long with a stranger, in a diligence for example, without noticing his peculiarities, his strong and weak points, his taste for this or that beauty in nature, his perception of this or the other relation among men. One proceeds accordingly ; and, if the stranger be equally complaisant, there arises an agreeable relation. capable of producing all manner of fruit. I have frequently contracted such travelling marriages, as I may call them, and during the last few hours of our common journey, I have always been saddened by the thought that a kindly relation of man to man was about to be broken up. I have ever afterwards heartily welcomed a fellow-traveller of the sort, even when his face looked quite different in the house from what it did in the carriage. Men differ in understanding, but love brings them together." In another letter :—" I have shown much kindness to some men, for which I have received no thanks ; and that pains me : but I have received much more kindness from others, and I often search in vain for lively gratitude in my heart, which pains me still more."

Perthes' native kindliness did not prevent the decided expression of his views.   He was not easily, and never long, irritated by the opposition of others, provided he thought it sincere ; but against insolence, falsehood, indifference, and baseness, he blazed up instantly and violently, even in cases where he was under no obligation to speak.   His views were these :—
"I would have nothing to do with the man who cannot be moved with indignation.   There are more good people than bad in the world, and the bad get the upper hand merely because they are bolder.   We cannot help being pleased with a man who uses his powers with decision ; and we often take his side for no other reason than because he does so use them.   No doubt, I have often repented speaking ; but not less often I have repented keeping silence."

In administering reproof, Perthes generally hit the nail on the head.   To an inflated personage he once wrote : "You may see by Jacobi that, if scholars have often an insufferable temper, a petty character, and selfish dispositions, scholarship, at least, is not to blame."   Again : "You insist on respect for learned men ; I say, Amen.   But, at the same time, don't forget that largeness of mind, depth of thought, appreciation of the lofty experience of the world, delicacy of manner, tact and energy in action, love of truth, honesty, and amiability—that all these may be wanting in a man who may yet be very learned."

To a young man : "You know only too well what you *can* do ; but, till you have learned what you *cannot* do, you will neither accomplish anything of moment, nor know inward peace."

To a man who, in order to escape the annoyances of

public life, confined all his intercourse to his wife and
children, and boasted of his seclusion, Perthes wrote :
" Beware ! The fear of unpleasant collisions outside
the house, and not the joys of the domestic circle
itself, may account for your boasted seclusion. The
domestic life does not mean seclusion from others, but
discipline of one's self ; it is not negative, but positive,
and he only can enjoy domestic life who has borne, and
still bears, the burden of public life."

Not only in letters of reproof, but in many others
also, does that bold freshness come out which characterized Perthes' youth. A friend had written him that
whoever lives to eighty years of age may be sure of
outliving his reputation, alleging that all the octoge-
narians, from Blücher to Wieland and Goethe, had
done so. Perthes answered : " Certainly, the age beyond fifty brings with it peculiar dangers, among
which, however, I do not reckon this, that of late
years I have had a son and two daughters baptized.
No doubt, I can look back on much sorrow, care, and
trial ; but I am still of opinion that a sterling man is not
complete till old age. In my own case, I cannot complain of too much age, but rather of too much youth,
which torments me with unrest, and with whatever
else you please. In presence of so many old young
people, I often fear lest there be in me something of
the wandering Jew !"

Perthes' later years exhibited the same struggle between energetic activity and a longing for repose, which
pervaded his earlier life. Once he wrote,—" I still
take an interest in a thousand things, yet only by fits
and starts ; for, after all, in order to be cheerful and
content, I require, besides my family relationships

only a quiet room with a few books, a mountain and a wood, a couple of intelligent men, solitude when I want it, and freedom from bores. This is little, and yet much." Again : " I cannot learn to be at rest ; and I often fear lest, by way of a refining-fire, blindness or lameness be reserved for my latter days ; which the good God in His mercy forbid !"

Later still : " Besser's death has increased the number of those who attract me to the other world. Manifold indeed is the attraction : my Caroline and Besser stand beside each other : then the old Schwarzburg lieutenant-colonel, who was the father-like guide of my youth, and my first love, Frederika ; then Claudius and Jacobi ; then my children who died young ; and, which is strange, the attraction to my father, whom I never saw. Whether the inborn impulse towards energetic activity, or the no less profound capacity for repose in love and contemplation, or whether both shall fill up our eternity, who can tell?" About the same time : " Life seems to me monstrously long ; what a terrible sameness in the midst of variety. To-day, as fifty years ago, I see sparrows and dogs, sheep and goats ; they are always different, yet to me they seem always the same. Viewed from a distance, it does not seem difficult to die : yet they only who have experienced death can tell what it is ; and they who have experienced it are silent to us."

XXXVIII.

Christian Enterprise.

ERTHES had watched with intense interest the progress and the increase of evangelical religion in Germany. He wrote to Rist, in reply to one of his enthusiastic letters, as follows:—" The eye of youth is ever attracted by some lofty aim, and its heart blessed by ingenuous faith in success. But when youth passed, and the grown man wished to realize his former dreams, the whole was found to be a gross deception. What did many of those become who, in the Kantian period, thought themselves the *élite* of mankind ? Mere red-tapists, lost in paltriness. What did many of those become, who, in the era of mighty genius, or in the period of Gleim, Georg, and Jacobi, seemed to overflow with spirit and fancy ? Mere organ-grinders, a weariness to themselves and others."

Perthes considered that a great improvement had taken place in Germany during his own lifetime. In 1826 he wrote to the Countess S. Stolberg : " The contemporaries of your youth were also mine ; my recollections of the middle and lower classes run parallel with yours of the higher, and are equally sad. But since the French Revolution, the rod of divine chastisement has not been wielded in vain on our lacerated country. The sensual, godless frivolity of last century wanders about now only as a dusky obsolete ghost; good seed has been sown; and it will bring forth by and by the genuine fruits of Christianity."

In many parts of Germany, endeavors were made to satisfy the profound wants of the human soul; but the Christian life can neither become nor remain sound, unless Christian thought and feeling go out into action.

In carrying on Christian enterprises by joint effort, Protestant Germany remained far behind England. Isolated attempts were indeed made, but they were exclusively the work of individuals, and ever bore the stamp of their individual origin. With some such Perthes coöperated in Hamburgh; but the most remarkable of them all was commenced at Weimar, by John Falk, councillor of the embassy.

In the vicinity of the battle-fields of Jena, Lützen, and Leipzig, there were to be found a multitude of boys, partly belonging to the district, partly brought from all parts of Germany, by the armies that had fought there; they had run wild, and Falk, selecting the most destitute, determined to make honest men of them. A native of West Prussia, Falk had been in Weimar since 1796, had appeared on various occasions as a lyric poet and satirist, and was frequently pointed to as a type of the national literature in decay. It seemed incredible to many that such a man should have a genuine vocation for such an enterprise. Because, notwithstanding all Falk's labor and care, many of his *protégés* turned out ill, some concluded that none of them were reformed; and others pretended that the outlay of zeal, effort, and money, was in ridiculous contrast with the paucity of results.

20

A friend wrote to Perthes : " Falk is so impressible and fanciful, that the dreadful destitution of the youths, and their subsequent improvement may very well both be creatures of his imagination. Then he is importunate in seeking subscriptions, and aid of every kind : he is, in fact, a bore. He has a few enthusiastic followers ; but, in general, he is not liked here : people avoid him, and laugh at him behind his back."

Yet this same man, the butt of ridicule, was the author of that movement for the reformation of children, abandoned in every sense of the term, which continues to this day. In 1820 he had 300 children in his own house ; and had stirred up Jena and Erfurt to similar efforts.

Although Perthes entertained some scruples about Falk himself, he yet recognized at once the real importance of his undertaking, awakened an interest in its behalf in Hamburgh and Holstein, and procured for it considerable pecuniary aid.

In 1821, Falk wrote to Perthes :—"Amid the children I find consolation and support, when I am tempted to despair ; for this is indeed an evil time : insurrection lurks behind the constitutions, and Sand's dagger lies concealed behind the Gospel of St. John. Men pass like wind-bags : they eat and drink, work and sleep, as if there were no such thing as an immortal soul ; they do not, indeed, in so many words deny God, but their whole life is practical atheism : nor will matters be mended so long as men regard preaching and the hearing of sermons as a Christian act, whereas Christian action is itself the true sermon. The death upon the cross is the sermon of sermons, and the pattern for all others : acted sermons, not sermons preached, is the want of our age. God has deigned to make me his instrument; truly in the fire of affliction He has moulded me, in the valley of tears prepared me. I have put my hand to the work in reliance on the mighty God; and you also, my dear friend, has God chosen to be a powerful coadjutor. Work along with me then, while it is day, that what has been begun in God's honor may be joyfully finished in His name. The idea which has possessed me, will spread throughout Germany and all Christian Europe; already, indeed, it has risen up in might, and, with hands and feet, may be seen walking and working at Dorpat and in Paris alike: already the doors of the children's prisons are being thrown open, both in Germany and France. Hitherto we Protestants have been like the hermit-crab, which takes possession of a shell not its own, for we robbed the Catholics of their cloisters, in order to provide a refuge for our children: that is convenient, but not noble; and it is amazing what resources are in the people themselves, if we but knew how to call them forth. What we want, however, must be obtained from God by prayer and love, not as hitherto by violence and craft. The military knights have played out their part; not even against the Turks is the sword now drawn: the arts of diplomacy are worn out; not even a fratricidal war can all the congresses prevent. O ye kings and fathers of the people! One thing is needful; let the fear of the Lord be established in your hearts, and in those of your subjects; otherwise you and they are destroyed together."

Again :—" Could you see us, you would rejoice and bless God. The children of robbers and murderers sing psalms and pray : boys are making locks out of the insulting iron, which was destined for their hands and feet, and are building houses, which they formerly delighted to break open. Yes, it is indeed true that, where chains and stocks, the lash and the prison were powerless, love comes off victorious."

Later still :—" I and my 300 children must leave our old habitation, because the proprietor has sold it ; and no one is willing to receive us, because, as may easily be fancied, no one is willing to give up his house to 300 such children as mine. We shall build then, and with the hands of our own children too, so that every tile in the roof, every nail in the walls, every lock on the doors, every chair and every table in the rooms, shall be a witness to their industry."

Of course Falk concluded with pressing solicitations for pecuniary aid. Perthes did what he could, and, in the spring of 1822, paid him a visit in Weimar.

Perthes thus reports in a letter to Benecke : "About fifty journeymen and apprentices, all of them former inmates of the Ragged Hospital, were working at the new building as masons and carpenters ; they were served by boys still in the institution ; horrid, cannibal-like faces had they all, with the wolf of the desert unmistakably imprinted on their foreheads. In the expression of many, however, there were traces of a new life ; and Falk says it is a real pleasure to see how the claws and the shaggy tufts gradually fall off.

Falk's own room is a perfect gem, with this intention, perhaps, that the children may recognize in him their true father ; but it seemed to me that he had also an eye here to the gratification of his own fancy. Altogether **Falk** appears to me an exceedingly remarkable man : his command of happy and striking images in conversation is wonderful ; the rapidity of his fancy hurries along first himself and then his hearers, so that fact and fancy dance at once through the minds of both. He is at the same time shrewd, yea, cunning, and knows right well what key-note to strike, according to persons and circumstances. I am, however, quite convinced of his thorough earnestness, now that I have seen him and the institution ; and it is not his fault, if he be a poet into the bargain. He himself, and still more his undertaking, deserve our support ; many have much good to say of him, and even his bitterest enemies know no ill."

To Falk himself Perthes wrote : " Your success in impressing the hearts of these neglected children, and in winning over new supporters to your cause, arises from this, that you yourself are entirely occupied with one idea : what has no relation to it is nothing to you, and what has only a slight relation you consider only as auxiliary to its realization ; small successes appear to you great ; obstacles and failures do not appear at all. He who is thus filled, thus prepossessed I may say, by one impulse, when he listens to his inmost soul, may hear only profound truth ; but when he speaks to others, *they* may hear, according to Goethe's happy expression, ' Wahrheit und Dichtung.' He who cannot recognize the deep truth of inspiration, will not understand you, may even misunderstand you ; and therein lies a danger both for you and your cause."

Baron Kottwitz, whose antecedents were in striking contrast with Falk's, had even before him carried on a similar work in Berlin. In the spring of 1825, Perthes visited repeatedly that truly pious man's institution, and he thus reported of it to some of his friends : " I have known Baron Kottwitz for five-and-twenty years. For a long time I considered the dullness of his eye, and the gentleness of his whole nature as signs of feebleness, and consequently, though respecting his piety, I was little attracted to him, for I have never been a friend to pale, sharp-featured ascetics. In Kottwitz, however, I have been mistaken. To know him, one must see him in the midst of those wretched creatures whom he has gathered about him. I have left him with a feeling of reverence ; and, though seventy-six years of age, one cannot too much admire his decision, perseverance, and that all-piercing knowledge of mankind, whereby he detects not only the sins, but even the petty tricks of the human heart."

Again : " After having made valuable observations, among the mountains of Silesia, on the misery of the poor, and the best means of alleviating it, and sacrificing a considerable portion of his property, Kottwitz went to Berlin. ' There,' said he to me, ' is a population of the most abandoned character, brought together by the establishment of factories in that city, at the instance of Frederick the Great : there are 20,000 of them, and it shall be the business of my life to diminish their number.' All this misery—profligate women, stunted children, disbanded soldiers of the old Prussian type, famished factory work-people who lived on brandy,—he collected in an ancient royal edifice, ceded to him for the purpose : twenty long years he spent in the midst of this wretched and disgusting filth. He forced no one to come, or to work, or to receive Christian consolation or instruction ; but to all he offered, with mild earnestness and love, the comfort and aid of our Saviour, and an opportunity of work. That the offer was not made in vain I could myself see from the confidence and freedom with which these poor wretches, cast off by all the world besides, approached him. His object is, so soon as they get accustomed to regular work, to distribute them among the small towns in the neighborhood, where hands are scarce. Then, at his request, the magistrate assigns them a cottage and a patch of potato-land at a small rent, and the Berlin manufacturers send them work to be done at home. He says that a considerable number of men, who have passed through his hands, are now leading a moral life, and enjoying that health which is insured by cleanliness, fresh air, and easily accessible field-work ; he thinks, too, that the mass of the debased population in Berlin has been diminished, though no doubt this is chiefly owing to the clearance which time makes in such a population, and to the gradual extinction of the military rabble."

Perthes was connected with undertakings of the same description on the lower Rhine. Count Adelbert von der Recke, laying to heart the misery begotten by the wars, and the subsequent dearth, opened a house of refuge, in 1819, for orphan and criminal children at Overdyk, and in 1822 a larger one at Düsselthal. In 1827 the chaplain wrote to Perthes the following notice of these institutions : " We have 240 boys and girls under our care, and thirty Jewish proselytes who, besides receiving instruction, learn a handicraft. Instead of trading on their conversion, as such persons often do, and so bringing disgrace on the Christian name, they will be able to earn their own living honestly, by having been employed with us, as locksmiths, weavers, joiners, or brewers."

Perthes hoped that Protestantism, now in course of revival, would not only sustain and carry out these attempts, but in due time convert them into ecclesiastical establishments.

The following proof of the far-seeing wisdom of Perthes is remarkable :

" Napoleon's conversations at St. Helena are like his whole former life, filled with contradictions. He holds legitimacy to be a necessity, and yet seizes at the crown by force ; he seeks to do away with class differences, and yet bows low before the aristocracy ; he intensely despises the French, and yet considers it the highest earthly honor to be born a Frenchman ; he abhors England, but believes France and England united could sway the world ; he has completely done with life, and yet his fancy is ceaselessly occupied in devising means of regaining freedom ; he is filled with the loftiest pride, and yet tortured by the lowest vanity. But this does not involve falsehood, each of these contradictory moods being for the time earnest and true. Napoleon was not like Frederick the Great, the same at all times, a distinct personality asserting itself equally under all varieties of external circumstance. Napoleon was rather whatever some inward impulse or some outward impression might for the moment make him. Like Goethe, he was constrained to give form and shape to whatever he was feeling at the time ; his changing mood expressing itself not in poetry but in bulletins and notes ; his passionate feelings not in romances and dramas, but in diplomatic negotiations."

A friend in North Germany wrote to Perthes : "A few days ago I went into a print-seller's shop, and saw a multitude of copper-plates in honor of Napoleon and his family, which have newly appeared, and are forbidden in France. 'Who buys them?' I asked.— 'Who!' said the man ; 'they are the very things which sell best at present. Confectioners, hucksters, and mechanics, all are cursing England now, and buy greedily the like.'" Perthes answered : "*Napoleon will yet become the idol of the age; many are already longing for another such despot to appear; and it is quite possible that their desire may be gratified, for, out of fermentations like the present, dragons may well arise.*

There are thousands who would destroy everything, that no one might possess more than themselves, and other thousands would be quite pleased to lie in chains, provided all who either have more, or are greater than themselves, were reduced to like degradation." To an invitation from a friend that Perthes would join him in some social festivities on Napoleon's commemoration-day, Perthes answered : " Certainly I consider Napoleon to be one of the greatest and most remarkable phenomena in the history of mankind ; but I set too high a value on freedom and the free development of our race to accept your invitation. Napoleon was a mighty instrument in the hands of Providence, and when he had done his work, and was no longer needed, he was thrown, like other worn-out tools, into a corner ; for not in himself, but only as an instrument, had he any importance."

20*

XXXIX

Death of Niebuhr.

OWARDS the close of his life, Perthes himself came to see that theology was aiming at a position in the Christian life which no science could possibly hold. In a letter to Dorner, dated June, 1842, after expressing his conviction that Strauss and Co. were hastening to their downfall, he continues: ' But would the condition of the Protestant Church be thereby improved? · Even if to-day we argue the devil down into the abyss, who knows but his grandmother may rise from it to-morrow with more subtle analysis, and a glibber tongue? Truly, dialectics are a fine art! For myself, it was through the consciousness of sin in the forms of sensuality and pride, that I came to recognize my need of redemption, and the truth of God's revelation in Christ. Whoever disdains this way, will wander through speculation and mystic symbolism, to pantheism, if he be intellectual; or, if he be superficial, will take the convenient road of progress to perfection, Jesus of Nazareth being the trainer-in-chief. You say, that many can hardly attain faith till certain difficulties are solved for them scientifically, and that, for that reason, the Church has need of science. I doubt if any one was ever led through science to faith, till his very bones and mar-

row quivered under this question : ' Oh, wretched
man that thou art! who shall deliver thee from the
body of this death ?"

Again : " Now-a-days science is at once the starting-
point and the goal of Protestanism. Even with the
best among the theologians, Christianity is but a stage
on the way to science ; and, whilst they are anxiously
ferreting out scientific results with which to prop up
their faith, the age is demanding not Christian theology
but the Christian Church, not notions but deeds, not
the ideal of Christ but His very person."

It is not often that a man who carries on his calling,
be it what it may, with great energy and an unflinching
sense of duty, has the good fortune to be popular. But
Perthes had always inspired esteem, liking, and confidence in all with whom his profession brought him into
contact. Authors, old and young, sought his acquaintance, and works of every sort were offered him in pro-
fusion. About two thousand such offers were found
amongst his papers, and they afford many a significant
insight into the all-pervading tendency of our nature to
rush into print. We find the well-known author side
by side with the village school-master, the gentleman
of rank, the man of office, and the man of wealth, and
endless is the variety of forms in which they all give
out that they are occupied upon a work of rare importance, while, at the same time, all betray their uncertainty as to the reception the public will give it. Here
an earnest man firmly believes that he is making over
with his manuscript the best part of his life ; there a
bold, *brusque* fellow plainly declares that gain is the
only motive for his activity.

Perthes was on confidential and friendly terms with

almost all the authors with whom he had any permanent connexion. The countless letters which he wrote in his professional career are of a singularly mixed character, revealing the experienced man of business conscious of his own capacity.

To a man who had occupied an important position under Napoleon, as a tool, and who applied to Perthes in November to assist him in publishing a periodical of revolutionary tendency, Perthes replied :—" I am astonished that you should dare, at this time, to appear again among us Germans ; and indignant that you should suppose me capable of helping you. A man who, not twenty years ago, betrayed his prince, and for filthy lucre's sake accepted a situation which obliged him to perpetrate the most horrid cruelties, should keep silence, and thank the invisible powers that he is forgotten. You are a wretch and stand on the brink of the grave ; therefore I shall hold my peace ; but if you speak out publicly, then so shall I, undismayed by the fate of two men, whose blood is already at your door."

On the 17th December, 1830, Niebuhr sent to Perthes the following letter, the last but one he ever wrote :—" My afflicted heart would find relief in writing some such address to the Germans as you indicated in your last ; but prudence dissuades me, and indeed it could not produce any great effect. If I write, and it please me, I shall send it to you. Never has Germany been so untrue to herself as now ; and, since the revolution in Poland, not only is salvation by her own strength hopeless, but there is no room, which yet there should always be, even for a miracle to reëstablish order in human affairs. I understand that my Preface has given great dissatisfaction to the wise men of the age. Posterity will judge otherwise. You, dear Perthes, are at one with me, of course."

Perthes answered :—" When you say that Germany has never been so untrue to herself as now, 1 allow it in respect to the half-educated of the nation, who, by manifold writing and reasoning, form and direct public opinion ; but the recent tumults have not betrayed a thorough corruption in Germany. Either they have been mere outbreaks of popular joy, such as happen now and then in all countries, or there have been causes for them such as are always followed by the like consequences."

Niebuhr was dead before the above answer reached Bonn. In a letter to his son, Perthes thus refers to his deceased friend :—"At our last parting, which I little thought would be our last, Niebuhr shed tears. Great is the loss to our youth, to science, to our country ; for rarely have so much talent and learning, views at once so profound and so extensive, been united with so loving a heart. He has been taken away from the evil to come ; for whatever turn things may take, much must happen that would have exasperated him, and he would not have been able to stand it long. His death will enable you, who are young, to measure how great or how little a single man is in this world."

A few weeks later :—" I shall feel the loss of Niebuhr as long as I live. Hardly a day passed but I saw, heard, observed, or thought something which I treasured up for the purpose of consulting him about it."

On the same subject Rist wrote to Perthes :—" One more is taken away of those who worked their way through this mighty period ! And what a cotemporary ! The terror of all bad and base men, the stay of all the sterling and honest, the friend and helper of youth. You knew his foibles as well as his strong points, and, unlike many others, you never came into collision with him. I know not whether I should have been able to maintain daily intercourse undisturbed with one who was no less passionate than intellectual, so susceptible in fact as to be somewhat peevish ; but I do know that no friend, from whom I had been separated for years, ever gave me so agreeable a surprise as he did eighteen months ago, when he greeted me after a long absence with all the cheerfulness, sincerity, and elasticity of youth. Two-and-thirty years ago, when we were both in the flower of youth, I recognized his immense superiority ; but it appeared to me still greater at our last interview, when I saw how he had preserved the purity and ingenuousness of his mind, and that power which, instead of bending to externals, breaks through them. In spite of his favor for the English aristocracy, he was ever, in thought and act, a true people's man, and on this account I feel myself intimately allied to Niebuhr ; but I still hold up my head, whilst he, misled by a sort of piety, despaired, and went down to the grave with a broken heart."

From Count Adam Moltke to Perthes on the same subject :—"Three weeks before his death, I received from Niebuhr a letter : it was a single night-thought. The quiet of resignation, founded on the providence of God, and a lively hope which rejoices in itself, were not his. He was more a citizen of the ancient world than of the modern. He saw through the ancient world by virtue of that inspiration which love only can impart ; he knew the modern world intimately, but he did not understand it, because he did not love it."

Perthes' Domestic and Social Life.
1830–37.

"ERTHES," writes his intimate friend Frommann, " was not only honored in his large circle of acquaintances on account of his uprightness, candor, justice, and liberality, but also on account of his mental energy : his distinguished reputation continued to spread every year more widely. That it was well deserved is proved by the multitude of his friends amongst Germany's noblest and best. Friendship, indeed, was a necessity not only of his heart but his mind, and this necessity was satisfied by his relations alike to his superiors in years, position, intellect, and attainment, and to those who were his inferiors in these respects. The weaknesses of his friends did not escape his quick eye, but he loved them none the less, and was always prone to exaggerate those points in which they excelled himself. To his younger friends he was especially indulgent. Differences of opinion in religion and politics neither blinded him to the faults of partisans nor the merits of opponents, and he was always ready to help and advise both. He was by no means despotic, but quite as little given to be servile ; perhaps he was rendered over indifferent to external political forms, because conscious of maintaining his liberty and independence under them all. His frankness of speech was remarkable, and he gave many a striking proof of it. He understood the art of speaking with the utmost calmness and *naïveté*, truths which people were not accustomed to hear, and which they hardly knew how to take; and this peculiarity he would display not only in presence of his equals but of those in a higher rank, as well as to those far below him. Impetuous he certainly was, yea, very impetuous, but he never nursed his anger nor allowed his ultimate judgment to be biassed by it."

Perthes' life in Gotha had, as we have already seen, become rich and full beyond his expectations, and he continued to retain all his old friends and acquaintance. "When I reflect," said he, "on the extent of my acquaintance, Goethe's words occur to me, 'The stream rolls wider and its waves increase,' and I would call out to all to 'hold together with all their strength alike in the sunshine and the storm.' To me at least it is almost impossible to let any go from me who once stood near, and of all the inward gifts God has given me, I am most thankful for the consciousness of constancy. It has always been exquisitely painful to me to see any one who once was closely united to me by head or heart now pass me coldly by."

Another time we find him writing: "What you young people call friendship will certainly not last forever, least of all now-a-days; its warmth and intensity belong not to the immortal element in man, but to the fresh feelings of youth. A few years hence, and feelings, opinions, convictions, will have got developed which even the most intimate friends will fail to understand. Amongst older men friendship, except as it belongs to memory, consists in confidence in each other's earnest striving after truth, and this confidence can outlast all changes." To all that Perthes had so long possessed, much of every kind was added during his residence in Gotha. The number of distinguished men who came from all parts of Germany to visit him went on annually increasing, and his continually extending correspondence with historians, theologians, and politicians, introduced him to all the interests of the period, while his constant study of the biography, correspondence, and private annals of the previous century, led him to look upon the events of the day not as detached, but as links in the great chain of the world's history in general, and of our own important epoch in particular. It was an unfailing source of recreation to him to express his views of the present and the past to a certain distinguished friend of his who had a very strong hold upon his heart.

George Rist, member of the Danish Legation, born in 1775, was descended in direct line from the old lyrical poet; he had studied at Jena in the days of Fichte and Schelling, and had then been appointed Secretary to the Danish Minister of Finance in Copenhagen. In 1801, he went with the Legation to Petersburg, in 1803 to Madrid, and in the eventful year 1807, his diplomatic duties led him to London. From 1808 to 1813 he had lived in Hamburgh, in 1814 he was sent to Paris, from 1817 to 1832 he spent his time between Hamburgh and Altona, and then went as member of the newly established Schleswig-Holstein Government to Schleswig, where he died in 1847. Rist was a noble man in the fullest sense of the word, sincere and stable, and equally distinguished by the qualities of head and heart. Even in his later years he continued devoted to the ancients, especially the Greeks; he had been attached to philosophy from the time he had listened to Fichte and Schelling; was perfectly at home in English and French literature, and well acquainted with the Spanish. Perthes and he differed no less in their views and opinions than in their outer life. Rist was intimately acquainted with the history of the former century, yet notwithstanding he gave the preference to the men belonging to it over those of the present day, and sure of not being misunderstood, he used to tease Perthes by making this preference conspicuous. "Our youth was far more enjoyable than that of the present day," he once wrote : "how pleasant the sentimentality-period was, and Fichte, and Goethe, and the Revolution on the top of all. Those were days indeed ! Now all is cold and old."

In religion Rist was a pious Christian, but he always declined entering into dogmatical questions. "I read no theological works," he once said ; "they have the unvarying effect of raising in me doubts which Scripture itself never raises."

Aristocratic in appearance, manners, and habits of life, his politics were extremely liberal. "It is wonderful to me," Perthes once wrote to him, "that you who have had such a distinguished career, should so often take pains to present yourself as a plebeian to me, the tradesman."

"That should not surprise you," replied Rist, "I have had to fight with patricians half my life, even against such as loved me and were loved by me." Ever since his first settlement in Gotha, Perthes had carried on an unbroken correspondence with this friend of many years, in which both freely exchanged political, literary, and ecclesiastical opinions, and understood and opposed each other. The very difference of their points of view gave to this correspondence a peculiar charm. As Rist once said in a letter to Perthes: "One writes so easily and comfortably to you ; what with unity in great things, difference in small, even a. conscious exaggeration of our own views on both sides, and, above all, an unchangeable conviction that though sharp words may be used, there is always kind feeling at bottom. Spite of all our protestations, our practical life paths run parallel ; we are both good citizens, good parents, good neighbors, good men of business, we give rather than receive, strike out if people come too near our heels, bring up our children in the fear of God, and live in hope of a joyful resurrection. Now, this I call the practical part of life, and in this we agree intimately."

Another time he writes : " Our children will learn much from our letters as to the time in which we lived, and will see that there were two independent men in Germany who wrestled bravely with each other and with the world, and who, if early placed under different circumstances, would have developed other aspects of character which must now remain undeveloped to the end."

The variety of interests and impressions which Perthes owed to his calling and his correspondence were sometimes a little oppressive to him in his latter years : " From early youth," we find him writing, " I have been subject to a habit of fancy-painting, to a sort of internal novel-writing, which often followed and disturbed me in business, which did not entirely absorb

me. Hence arose faults and mistakes, and the vexations and loss that followed these taught me to conquer the tendency. But in another form I have still
to battle with the play of fancy. However persever-
ingly I have striven to acquire a habit of concentrated
feeling and thinking, I still have to struggle with
desultoriness, with sudden inroads of the most uncon-
nected ideas ; and my calling is a great snare to a
man of this temperament, showing me, as it daily does,
the world in its most varied confusion, and men in the
craziest fool's caps and bells. Both when reading and
writing, my attention is most easily disturbed. I know,
indeed, that a quick imagination is the salt of earthly
life, without which nature is but a skeleton ; but the
higher the gift, the greater the responsibility." Pray
and work, is " the great maxim here, too, for young men
and for old." Another time he writes : " Nitzsch's sermon upon the sanctification of the imaginative faculty
has deeply impressed me ; but I wish the language had
been plainer. Perhaps few have had such bitter contests as I to subdue wandering thoughts, and gain the
power of continued meditation on things above. This
susceptibility of temperament and over-activity of imagination, are idiosyncrasies over which flesh and
blood cannot prevail. And, besides, from my early
years, my calling required me to retain in my memory
an innumerable quantity of things and circumstances ;
but now I cannot recollect anything in which I am not
interested ; all these things moved me more deeply of
yore. Thus it is that a million different things now
lie garnered up in my semi-spiritual, semi-material or-
ganism, rising up, God knows how, seeming to possess
an independent existence, beyond my control, and dis-

turbing my inward composure and my strivings God-
ward.   In the conflict with these foes, the best method, according to my experience, is an unvarying habit
of devoting daily a certain portion of time to the contemplation of, if not to communion with God.   Moments of glowing aspiration and occasional attempts
to command religious emotions will not do.   Thy
grandfather spoke a deep and important truth when
he said, ' *Ponamus*, that thou wert on a mountain
height, at break of day, looking at the sea below, from
out of which rose the sun, and that thy heart being
touched, thine impulse was to fall down on thy face ;
why fall, with or without tears, and do not feel ashamed of it, for the sun is a glorious work of the Most High,
and an image of Him before whom thou canst never
bow low enough.   But if thou be not moved, and must
squeeze hard to squeeze out a tear, why let it alone,
and let the sun rise without one.'   However, one must
not decide hastily for others./ Nature, art, and the
temperament of different men are infinitely varied, and,
consequently, the means by which we help ourselves
onward must needs vary too."/

While Perthes thus expr   himself to one friend,
respecting the struggle for   nal composure and recollection, he endeavored to excite a differently organized nature to courageous endurance of the changes of
mood brought about by external life. · To a young
man, who seemed inclined to take trifles as well as sorrows too much to heart, he wrote as follows : " Go
forward with hope and confidence ; this is the advice
given thee by an old man who has had a full share of
the burden and heat of life's day.   We must ever
stand upright, happen what may, and for this end we

must cheerfully resign ourselves to the varied influences
of this many-colored life. You may call this levity,
and you are partly right; for flowers and colors are
but trifles light as air, but such levity is a constituent
portion of our human nature, without which it would
sink under the weight of time. While on earth, we
must still play with earth, and with that which blooms
and fades upon its breast. The consciousness of this
mortal life being but the way to a higher goal, by no
means, precludes our playing with it cheerfully ; and,
indeed, we must do so, otherwise our energy in action
will entirely fail."

However varied Perthes' domestic life might be by
visits and correspondence, he did not the less take
great pleasure in seeing and judging for himself of new
places and new circumstances. In 1831 and 1834, he
spent some time in Berlin ; in 1835, on the Rhine ; in
1836, in Hamburgh ; in 1840, in Vienna, in all these
places seeing and hearing much that he never could
have clearly understood from the accounts of others.
Even in his latter years, he constantly wandered with
a son or son-in-law through the hills and valleys of
the Thuringian forest, giving himself up, as soon as he
had left the town behind him, to the delight of a boy
who sees the world for the first time, feeling strengthened and improved by the now lovely, now grand
views that this mountain range abounds in, and certain
to meet with some singular character, or some strange
adventure to interest him.

That Perthes was able, without injury to his character, to respond to such a number of external claims
upon his attention and interest, may be attributed to
his life being so firmly rooted in his home and family

circle. It is true, this family spread out yearly more
and more. His eldest son Matthias had been a pastor
in Moorburg since 1830 ; his second son, Clement, became in 1834 a public tutor in Bonn ; his son Andrew,
after a preparatory residence in Hamburgh, Prague,
Switzerland, and France, had become a partner in his
father's business. All these sons were married. His
step-son Henry, for whom he had a true father's affection, left the Gymnasium in 1838, to study first in
Bonn, and then in Berlin.

Perthes had always encouraged a great amount of
independence of manner and feeling in his sons, respecting their personality even in their childhood. When
they became men, he entered into such free and friendly relations with them, that on each side the very
depths of the heart were unreservedly revealed.
Public and private events, religious and political
opinions, formed the staple of the unbroken correspondence carried on between father and sons. Nor
was his intercourse with his children settled in Gotha
at all less intimate. Three of his daughters had long
been established there ; in 1831, his fourth daughter
married Moritz Madelung, and his step-daughter
Bertha, Carl von Zeche. None of these daughters
would allow many days to pass without seeing their
father in their own houses, were it but for a quarter
of an hour, and few weeks went by in which the whole
family, daughters and sons-in-law alike, did not spend
one evening at least with their parents. The circumstances of these different families were indeed widely
varied, but in spite of all manner of obstacles, they
contrived to keep up the animation of these meetings.
Even after a hard day's work, Perthes would enter into

a spirited conversation with youthful ardor, and would unconsciously excite each to exert to the utmost the faculties he possessed ; indeed, it was almost impossible for any one to remain supine or feel weary in his society.

Perthes had four children by his second marriage, and the number of his grandchildren yearly increased. In so large a circle there was, of course, no lack of anxious weeks and months, of sicknesses and deaths. The sad year 1831, in which the cholera first appeared in Germany, was well calculated to excite alarm, but it did not disturb Perthes' composure, though two of his sons were living where it raged most fiercely. "I am convinced," wrote he in the June of that year, "that if natural causes do not stay the pestilence, it will overspread Europe, and that all attempts to fly from it will be vain. It is not my nature to feel any great dread of falling into God's hands, but I am horrified at the prospect of the evils that selfish precaution may inflict upon our social relations. Self-love in the garb of fear is something terrific, and will corrode both public and private life. The state of Europe during earlier pestilences cannot be compared with what is now before us, when all are so intimately and closely connected and narrowly confined. But God will help us!"

No member of his large family, however, was struck down by the epidemic, but sorrows crowded upon them in after years, especially in 1833. In the month of June Perthes wrote as follows : "Six months lie behind me, all filled with fears and hopes. Our distresses began about Christmas time. I have often remarked, that in cases of sudden trouble, families gain much in courage, endurance, and composure. Each is sustained by a

consciousness of duty, and each has his special post.
But nature fails under long-continued pressure. Sor-
saw loses its exciting, energizing influence ; it exhausts,
and the danger is lest a certain passiveness should result from it, which is not strength but weakness, not
resignation but stupefaction. Prayer, and nothing but
prayer, is the one and only remedy. We still hold
out bravely, and I am still able to bear our daily trials
patiently and submissively, but anxiety about my wife,
whose burdens are almost too great for mind and body,
perturbs and distresses me. God will help us on."

Towards the end of July low fever broke out in the
house, attacking not only five children, but Perthes
himself. "These trying weeks," he wrote, "have been
to me a season of new and important experiences. I
have been quite unequal to the business of life, but the
union of my soul with God has remained undisturbed
by the pressure of sickness, my mind is quite clear, and
I can express my thoughts more clearly than when in
health. Nitzsch's sermons have been a support and comfort to me. I have got over the difficulties of the language,
and I find at each reading new treasures in the mind
of this man, who is certainly the deepest of our living
theologians. For the last week my second son has
been with us, and he will not leave till matters take
one turn or another. I daily spend hours with him
alone, and I have endeavored to convey my views sys-
tematically to him. Our conversation has chiefly turned upon the origin of things in general, evil included ;
the wide circle within which man is free, and therefore
responsible ; the direction of the world's history by
God ; Jesus Christ the centre of all history ; material-
ism and pantheism, political and ecclesiastical order."

21

Towards the end of August, it became apparent to Perthes that the illness of his only son by his second marriage was of a fatal character. He had been more closely knit to this lovely and gifted boy than to any of the others at the same age. When his elder sons were boys, he was immersed in Hamburgh business, and could but seldom occupy himself with them. But he had watched this child's life through joy and sorrow alike ; even when at his occupations he used to have him playing by him, and in his walks he made him his companion. " It is a rare bliss," he once wrote, " to be, in one's latter years, the father of such a child. A parent of my age contemplates such a young existence with different eyes from those of a young man who is himself but entering into life. It is delightful to watch the germ of love and sensibility, and very striking to see that the nursery is a little world, whose daily incidents require and cultivate self-control and reflection, awaken penetration, and even the sense of the ludicrous."

Accordingly, when this beloved child's life-powers were struggling with death, Perthes felt as keen and deep an anguish as any he had ever before known. " I prayed with my whole heart's fervor," said he, " that my Rudolph might be spared to me, and I saw that I prayed in vain. Faith and despair struggled within my breast, and I have gained a deeper understanding of the prayer, ' Lead us not into temptation,' than I ever had before."

On the evening of the 31st August, just as the setting sun reddened the sick-room, the child died. " God has taken away the delight of my age" wrote Perthes, " but he has given me tears such as I had not hoped to weep again. You wish me to tell you much about my

Rudolph, but I cannot do so. To a third person all children of that age are so much alike, and the loss of a child is such a common occurrence, that no details could give a clearer insight into the individual case. Each father and mother's heart knows its own bitterness, and no third person can enter into it."

Later he wrote to Nicolovius : " Since the death of my Rudolph, I begin to feel the evening of life closing in, not because of any diminution of bodily or mental powers, but because of a certain indifference to human pursuits and interests. But God will uphold me with His love and truth, so that I may not grow supine and incapable cheerfully to do and bear according to His good pleasure." Incapable or gloomy Perthes indeed never became, but the yearning for his lost child haunted him as long as he lived, often forcing from him, as he paced the room alone, even after years were past and gone, the cry, " My Rudolph, my Rudolph, where and what art thou now !"

Many an hour, too, of inward conflict besides, had Perthes during these years. We find him writing : " How far beneath our wishes and our will are the works and ways even of the old amongst us ! Love without work, and work without love. How cold and weak our sorrow for sin seems, and yet, perhaps, God sees more in it than we do, and knows how deep and strong and abiding a sinner's repentance really is."

Another letter runs thus : " ' Be ye holy even as I am holy. These words often pierce me through marrow and bone. I have known many who have experienced in themselves the immediate working of the Spirit, and who believed that they had been made holy by it. That there may be such saints even in our days, I will not dispute, but I do not belong to their number. I have striven and wrestled, but the world and the flesh have hindered me. Only for moments have I, in and through prayer, tasted of the peace of God. Not to shut our eyes through indolence or despondency to the sin remaining in us, not to mistake death for life, sorrow for repentance, and imagination for love, not to grow weary in our upward course, or to substitute wishing for willing ; this is our ceaseless task here below, a task impossible without faith, but without which faith is impossible too."

Whenever his heart was heavy, Perthes would turn by preference to the Epistles of St. Paul. He once wrote, " Look for comfort in the Epistle to the Romans ; in it is the whole truth of God in as far as we need to know it here on earth. Fight the good fight to the end, this is Paul's teaching to you, as well as mine."

In another he says : " I have often, very often, read the Epistle to the Romans ; it is the portion of Scripture which has most impressed me, has given me most light, and most stablished my faith. Should another prefer some other portion, that need be no matter of dispute : it is a proof of the divinity of the Bible, that different books affect different Christians most, according to their difference of temperament and education, while yet all books lead to the same end."

Not only was Perthes inclined by natural character firmly and fervently to express his convictions, but he believed it his duty so to do. " We should give honor to the truth," said he ; " we should not suffer others to seem to despise it ; we should not practise a false toleration, but shun all intimacy with those who do not acknowledge it."

It is true, that even in these his latter years he was often wont to be more vehement and sharp in his tone of controversy than his conscience approved, and he was well aware that he had thus offended and temporarily estranged many.

" I feel," said he, on one occasion, " that I must be very careful as to what I speak or write about Church or State, lest I be misunderstood, and injure both myself and my cause. It must be in some measure my own fault that you should believe that I wear a pair of eye-blinders, so as not to be disturbed in my convictions by what lies on the right and left of my path. Not so ; I have sharp eyes for what is not good and true in matters that I deem essential. I see things plainly, and like to see them so, even when they do not fit in to my views, but I do not allow my positive tendencies to be disturbed by them. He who knows what he wants, and determines to accomplish it, be it in small or great matters, cannot afford to weigh everything so closely as to darken it by his criticism, and bring into prominence every weak point ; this would but lead to a habit of scepticism, and where that exists there is an end to all action. I know, indeed, that in this great world-drama, the doubters and deniers have their part to play, and do not *all* belong to the great club-footed denier, but to the children of God, though not to the active workers among these. However, my province is to affirm and establish. I will wrestle with evil when it comes in my way, but neither in great things nor small, politics nor religion, doing, thinking, nor feeling, will I consent to the overthrow of God's

Church, because the devil has built or may build a side-chapel of his own against it."

However earnestly Perthes may have held and asserted that without ecclesiastical and dogmatic authority neither theology nor Christian feeling could hold their ground, still his own individual life was very independent of both. " My Christianity," he once wrote, " becomes each year more simple. That not to love God is sin, and that to love Him again constitutes deliverance from sin ; this as infinite truth, this as the solution of every problem, has been transmitted from the Bible to my spiritual life. Christianity is thoroughly practical in its nature. Scientific inquiries and absorption of the soul in religious emotion, are of themselves little worth. I learn more and more to discern the Divine wisdom, which has set limits to revelation ; all that we need for our happiness is given us, and were the curtain lifted further from holy mysteries, man's utter bewilderment would be hopeless."

XLI

Last Years.—1837-43.

FTER a severe attack of influenza in 1837, Perthes took a small house at Friedrichroda, about nine miles from Gotha, in order, with his wife and children, to spend the summer in the woods. "You see, my dear friend," wrote he in July, "that I have fled to the mountains to drive away the consequences of influenza. My hearing is still much affected, and I have difficulty in making out human babble, but I hope to be able to hear the vulture scream and the trout splash. If anything can restore my health, it will be life in the woods. You know Friedrichroda, so I need not speak of its charms. Everything is in our favor,—the sky blue, the woods dark, the meadows green."

It was indeed a lovely spot that Perthes had chosen. On the north side of the Thuringian forest, a long valley runs down into the plain, at the entrance of which lies Schnepfenthal. Half a league further up the valley you encounter numerous mountain tarns, along which there is just room for the road to wind beneath the shadow of the fine old firs. Higher up, the valley widens out till you come to meadows of the brightest green, in the midst of which stood in earlier days the old Benedictine cloister of Reinhardsbrunnen, now replaced by the castle of the Dukes of Coburg-Gotha. Other wildly beautiful valleys run down from the hills into that of Reinhardsbrunnen, while rocky ridges, clothed with noble beech and fir, and bold mountain peaks, offer an abundance of fine views. Divided from this valley by a low ridge stands, in a wooded basin, the little village of Friedrichroda, and at about a hundred yards from it, the house Perthes had chosen. Being built in a hollow, the front rooms looked out upon a new blank wall, and he had to bear many a joke about the situation he had chosen ; from the back and from the little garden, however, there was really a glorious view, and the Black Forest, with its shade, its solitude, and countless footpaths, was within a few steps of the house. A few years after Perthes' death, Friedrichroda became a much frequented place, but at the time we speak of, the country retained its lonely character, and you might have wandered half a day in the wood-paths, and met only a herd of timid deer. a forester, children in search of strawberries, or women in search of firewood, while nothing was to be heard but the woodman's axe or the herdsman's horn. In the evening, numbers of wild deer were in the habit of gathering in the meadows.

From 1837 it became Perthes' custom to spend every summer at Friedrichroda, and each year he loved it better. In the morning, after his hard work, he used to take a short solitary walk, and in the evenings, two, three, nay, sometimes four hours' rambles with his wife and his three little girls. It was his constant delight to find out new points of view, and when found, to show them to others ; and he had abundant opportunity of doing this. On Saturdays and Sundays the house was all alive, grandchildren, daughters, sons-in-law came, till the rooms were too small to contain them, and kitchen and cellars were put to strange shifts; and often Perthes was the youngest of the party in spirits and enjoyment. His sons, too, generally came from a distance to spend some weeks with him; and even of historians and theologians there was no lack.

Tholuck, Lücke, Marheineke, de Wette and Olshausen were his guests; and of all those who visited Perthes in Friedrichroda, however different their character or callings might be, there was not one who did not carry away with him the recollection of some pleasant and interesting hours. It is true, that he who was without a sense of natural beauty had but a poor reception; for Perthes looked upon him with wonder and pity, much as if he had been born deaf and dumb, or without arms and legs. Any under-rating of the special beauties of Friedrichroda he took almost as a personal offence, and treated it accordingly. But, on the other hand, the visitor who had an eye for wood and hill was comfortably housed, and Perthes led him here and there, to show him the beauty of the district in the best light.

It was a perfect marvel to the country people, why an old gentleman, who had neither to burn charcoal nor to prepare tar, persisted in threading the long and toilsome paths their day's work led them to traverse; but they all liked him, and knew that he had a heart for their joys and sorrows.

The oftener he returned to Friedrichroda the fonder they grew of him; and to prove this, they, in 1841, gave him the freedom of their little town, with which he

21*

reported himself more pleased than with any honor ever before conferred upon him. Many such tokens of respect had attended Perthes in his later years. In 1834, the inhabitants of Leipzig had made him free of their city, and in the summer of 1835, the Prince Regent of Saxony had given him the cross of the civil order of merit.

"I would gladly possess civil merit as far as Germany is concerned," wrote Perthes, "and I like to be done honor to by such a prince as this. In former years I once sat next to him at dinner, and he spoke very intelligently about literature and the book-trade, the Hamburgh government, the July revolution, &c. ; but what most surprised and pleased me was, his spontaneous, benevolent sympathy and respect for the social condition of all grades alike, combined, as his sentiments were, with a full consciousness of rank. It is only he who honors men for their humanity, who thus reverences every position and calling. Such a state of mind as this implies genuine cultivation, which I would distinguish from what is merely learned and fashionable ; for all ranks alike may possess it, and it does not come more easily to high than to low. Wit, information, penetration, birth, station, all oppress and alienate those who are deficient in these respects, but this cultivation makes all who come in contact with it free, and excites esteem and confidence. What a change has taken place in this respect during the last fifty years ! God grant that our nature, having learned to esteem every human condition, may not now run into the extreme of despising the difference between one condition and another."

In 1840 the university of Kiel conferred upon Perthes the order of Doctor of Philosophy. "I could not," wrote he, "have marvelled more at this honor done me if I had been Vladica of Montenegro. The learned company has not, for a long time, seen such a bungler as I in their midst; my Latin is as rusty as that of my Orfort colleague Dr. Blucher, and that is saying much."

A friend, however, remarks in a letter to Perthes : "The faculty has done well ; he who has practised wisdom throughout a long career may well be styled Doctor of Philosophy even though his Latin be rusty."

Another honor enjoyed by Perthes, during his latter years, was the kindness shown him by the ducal house of Coburg. In 1826, on the Duke of Coburg's accession to Gotha, Perthes had written as follows : "My monarchical principles have gained many new adherents ; for all fall suddenly down before the new prince : certainly he, like Saul, is head and shoulders taller than the rest of the people, full of princely dignity, very judicious, and consequently very popular. He knows and is interested in every subject ; in short, the whole world is bewitched with him, and men of all parties have suddenly become ducalized."

The great wisdom and experience of the Duke, as we have seen, interested Perthes, and his benevolence won him entirely. On his side, the Duke was very partial to Perthes, and always saw him when at Gotha or Reinhardsbrunnen. The forest and its inhabitants, recollections reaching back as far as 1806, as well as the political events of the day, formed the subject of their conversations. But Perthes' peculiar delight was in the young princes. It was in 1836, when the Coburg Princes came to Gotha, in order to conclude the marriage of the Prince Ferdinand Augustus with the Queen of Portugal, that he saw them first. In the January of that year he writes : " A few days ago I was dining with the old Duchess ; both the princes were there—fine, tall, handsome youths, fresh, healthy and full of spirits, to which they gave free scope as soon as they were out of their grandmother's sight. Prince Ferdinand, the future King of Portugal, has a noble profile, but he is still a thorough child : the poor slender fir-tree has to be transplanted to a hot soil ; perhaps his very childishness is in his favor."

In 1839 Perthes writes : " Late in the summer, the ducal household came to Reinhardsbrunnen, and with them the Crown Prince from Dresden, and Prince Albert from Italy. Their father has good reason to be proud of them both. The ardor, frankness, and healthy judgment of the Crown Prince delighted me uncommonly ; Prince Albert is, without doubt, a highly gifted and thoroughly cultivated young man ; handsome and elegant, courteous and benevolent. His thoughtful, cautious temperament will lessen the difficulties of his position. We have the Duke of Meiningen. too, and the King of Saxony ; and sometimes no fewer than fourteen princes go out hunting together. These meetings between the house of Saxony and the neighboring princes should oftener take place. Taken together, they are not without significance in German relations, and these wise, restless Coburgs will tell upon Europe too : they do not, indeed, form any very comprehensive plans, but they know, as few men and princes do, how to seize the passing opportunity, and use the present moment. They have already secured the thrones of England, Belgium, and

Portugal for their own house, and they have an eye on those of Spain and France as well."

In 1840 we find Perthes writing : "The winter months of this year have been made interesting and exciting by the chapter of history which has been enacted here ; for, at the approach of the English wedding, the Ducal Papa bound the garter round his boy's knee amidst the roar of a hundred and one cannon. The earnestness and gravity with which the Prince has obeyed this early call to take a European position give him dignity and standing in spite of his youth, and increase the charm of his whole aspect. Queen Victoria will find him the right sort of man ; and unless some unlucky fatality interpose, he is sure to become the idol of the English nation, silently to influence the English aristoracy, and deeply to affect the destinies of Europe. Perhaps I may live to see the beginning of this career." " As for your Prince Albert," writes a friend to Perthes in the Autumn of 1840, " I have every reason to suppose that you rightly appreciate him and his position in England. Still he can attain to a knowledge of things around him, and his relation to them, only after a long residence. The public seem well affected towards him, and in the higher circles he has already some influence ; but in order to influence politics, he must be older and more free to act." Another friend writes : " I have not seen the Prince during my stay in London, but I have heard much of him ; he seems to be universally beloved, and I have been often most courteously thanked by Englishmen for the noble return which Germany has made to England for the Duke of Cumberland."

Once only in these latter years did Perthes determine upon a prolonged absence from home. In July, 1834, he with his wife and his three little girls went through Coburg and Nuremburg to Ratisbon, thence by the Danube to Vienna, where he spent a month with his friend Hornbostel. "Here I have been for some weeks," wrote he, "and I have seen and heard much very different to what I heard and saw four-and-twenty years ago. All my old acquaintances are dead. Hammer was absent. Pilat was the only one left, and I spent some hours with him. With this exception, I met only mercantile men, but many of them were influential and very well informed. My high opinion of Austria's internal strength is by no means diminished by the peculiar view this visit has afforded me. The life, the intelligence, the varied information, and, above all, the faculty of enjoying life that I have here found, have amazed me. It is true that intellect and knowledge are almost exclusively directed to machinery and looms, to trade and manufacture; both the Church and the priesthood have become mechanical, and Protestantism is cold and dead. There is, indeed, a danger in this one-sided industrial tendency which the government so unqualifiedly favors, but the decomposing process going on in the spiritual life of the rest of Germany does not obtain at all in Austria, or only amongst the higher aristocracy. If great events occur—and indeed they cannot be long postponed—and men be thrown out of their present material direction, the fresh energies and natural ability of the German Austrians will soon develop themselves. The presumptuous fools in North Germany, who speak of the Austrian barbarians and the decayed empire, have no idea in their plains of the strength which exists behind the mountains—do not dream that the literary exhaustion of North Germany will probably be obliged, in the next generation, to draw life from the South."

"If people determine to call Austria a despotism," wrote Perthes again, "it must be admitted that it is one of a singular kind, the pressure being all upwards, not downwards. Perhaps in no other state in the world is the internal government so moulded and guided by ancient customs and institutions which have their origin in popular life. Restrictions and limitations of all sorts to which the Austrians have been long accustomed, and which they have therefore learnt to bear, they easily endure; but it is almost impossible for government to introduce any innovations, because an unexpressed but universal opposition of rich and poor, high and low, is at once raised against it. A number of jocular stories are circulated, in which the fruitless attempts of the government are ridiculed. A short time ago a peremptory edict against pigeons flying about in Vienna was issued. 'Are the imperial pigeons to be caged as well?' asked their keeper. 'For a day or two,' was the reply; 'if every one else lets their pigeons loose, we shall do the same.'"

"I have made the acquaintance," says Perthes in another letter, "of a very remarkable man, the Cathedral preacher Veith. He was formerly Director of the Veterinary College in Vienna, then he became a priest, and now he is a preacher in the Cathedral. I heard him twice in a crowded church. His sermons were full of geniality and practical experience, mixed up with natural science and historical narrative, and highly exciting. A friend brought me to him in the vestry, and he proved himself perfectly acquainted with our Protestant theology in general, and with Schleiermacher, Rudelbach, Julius Müller, and Tholuck in particular, expressing himself with perfect unreserve about the Catholic Church and its condition in Austria. I have read his Woman of Samaria, and gained from it many new views, and in so far as it does not treat of specially ecclesiastical subjects, there is hardly anything in it that Protestants need object to. In short, this man is a most striking character, and a matter of wonder to such as are not Catholics."

From Vienna Perthes, accompanied by his family, travelled through Ischl, Salzburg, Berchtesgarden, and Ratisbon, back to Gotha, which they reached after a two months' absence. "We have not had an ailment," wrote he, "not an accident, not a moment's anxiety nor a single day's bad weather. Yesterday, when I got out of the carriage in perfect health, and found all the members of my large family the same, I most heartily thanked God. The prospect of the journey had rather weighed upon me, for though I still feel strong, I have lost the feeling of security in taking a long journey, which I once possessed. On his return to Gotha, Perthes not only found his son come from Bonn with his wife and family, but a mass of business which had accumulated during his absence; while the meeting of philologists in September brought with it all manner of further excitement."

In one letter he says, "Two very dear friends are in my house, Ritter from Göttingen, and Nitzsch from Kiel; Lachmann is with me at my son-in-law's, and we have many an animated, and, indeed, comic hour when the whole learned body meets for business or play. It was an amusing spectacle to witness twelve postilions blowing away on their horns, and riding in advance of the three hundred school-masters, while we followed in a long procession of hired carriages to Reinhardsbrunnen, there to dine at the Ducal table."

A few weeks later he wrote: " This has been a memorable year, the birth of four grandchildren, hard work in Leipzig, the marriage of my son Andrew, the visit of my dear brother Jacobi from Siegburg, with his wife and children, the two months' journey to Vienna, the very hard work after my return, and then the philologists-- my old bones creak again."

After his return from Vienna, Perthes would never again hear of a long absence from home. "I shall take no journey till the last of all," said he, in 1841, in answer to a pressing invitation from his son. "Strength and inclination for it I still have, but change and excitement do harm to one of the advanced age you can now no longer dispute my claim to ; external quiet, that is, an unbroken routine being the right thing for body and mind. Other old men might be able to travel more comfortably, but owing to my temperament, every journey excites me, and a thousand things in succession would distract my mind. Only think of the number of men I should have to see, and how much I should have to hear and say! Why, one week's stay with you would involve at least six months' hard work."

In proportion as the pleasure that Perthes took in travelling diminished, his love for his neighboring mountain-retreat increased. But still he refused to buy a house in Friedrichroda. "I have never," said he, " had any other landed property than my travelling carriage and my corner in the churchyard; and just before the order to march comes, I do not want to bind myself down to any earthly spot."

However, he increased his accommodation and his comforts, and in the summer of 1841, we find him writing, "I have by my addition gained a most glorious view in several directions, and it was just made in time, for the elements are raging this year. The storm roars in the wood, and the trees creak and groan; the mornings are very cold, and the mountain-mists reach our windows. We make as much use as we can of the fine hours of the day, but I do not climb so high nor ramble so far as of yore. preferring the familiar paths, where I can live my inner life undisturbed, as becomes a man of seventy, who will not much longer see and feel the beauty of this earth."

However, Friedrichroda did not lack excitement in the summer of 1841, for a brilliant circle again assembled at Reinhardsbrunnen. "The quiet woods," wrote Perthes, "have become unquiet; we have the Duchess of Kent here, Prince William of Prussia, with his family, and many others. Adjutants, jockeys, negroes, lords, dogs, horses, pass our little house day and night; hills and dales, woods and rocks, are scoured in the chase, and my poor deer have a sad time of it. I once saw the Duchess of Kent alone with her brother, the Duke, who called me to him, and I sincerely rejoiced at their happy meeting."

Soon after Perthes wrote: "How strange it seems to me, in the midst of all this tumult, to look back upon my past life! Half a century ago I was an orphan, cast in extreme poverty into the world's whirlpool, without information, without help, without support, a forsaken apprentice in a cold garret, having to limp about for weeks on frozen feet, because no one attended to me but my poor and still dear Frederika. All this lies like a dream behind me, now that I am at my journey's end; my life has not been an easy, nay, often a painful one. To God be the praise that it ends well!"

Active and cheerful as he still was, Perthes now began to feel in different ways the approach of old age. He was often himself surprised at the length of days he had left behind him, when any circumstance reminded him that he had known this or that aged man as a child or a youth. He once wrote to Ullmann: "There are four men in Southern Germany whom I used to know in olden times; of late, however, I have never seen them: Rau, of whom I still retain an agreeable though indistinct impression; Schubert and Schwab, whom I last saw between thirty and five-and-thirty years ago; and Schelling, whom I met forty-two years ago, and with whom I have since maintained a friendly correspondence." Perthes was, however, destined to meet the last-mentioned of these men once again. In the autumn of 1841, he writes: "Schelling has been here. We had not seen each other since 1798. The slender, black-haired Swabian youth stood before me as a robust old man, with snow-white head, but just as cordially frank and plain-spoken as of yore. We talked over all our old experiences and our present feelings, and did not know how to part."

But there were other things besides his friend's white hair, which served to remind Perthes of the evening of life. Many a star of the first magnitude, to whose light he had been accustomed from his youth, went out one after another. Niebuhr died in 1831 ; Goethe in 1832 ; Schleiermacher in 1834. Many dear friends and relations, too, were called away, whom Perthes missed and mourned. In 1839 he wrote : " I have again lost one I loved and honored, my faithful old Nicolovius : would that I could have pressed his hand once more here below."

In a letter to Umbreit, dated 1840, he says : " If at the age of seventy I needed a warning, the departure of so many old friends might afford me one. Thibaut is now gone, a man I cordially loved and respected, and who was much attached to me. However, one can think of him with joy as well as sorrow ; no doubt, like the rest of us, he had his own struggles, but still he was a happy man, his being was a harmonious one, and despite his vigorous participation in the progress of science, his spiritual life flowed on in tranquillity." Poel had died in the autumn of 1837. To him Perthes had long been indebted for much intellectual stimulus and much information, though they differed materially both in religion and politics. Poel had spent his youth in Bordeaux and Geneva, and then studied in Göttingen. For some time he was engaged in Russian diplomacy, and was in Paris during one of the most remarkable periods of the first Revolution. Though admirably fitted for political activity, he early retired from it, and lived privately in Altona. His merits were universally admitted, and all who knew him well, loved him for his benevolence and fine moral sense. In October, 1837, Perthes wrote : " The departure of our dear Poel has deeply moved me ; there were few I so much loved and honored. He was not only a distinguished, but a very singular man,—singular, because his name and his person remained unknown, while his influence was widely felt. Many leading men have taken their literary and political bias from him."

Perthes had had his kind and earliest guardians— the riding-master Heubel, and the old Aunt Caroline —spared to him for an unusual length of time, and as long as they lived he kept up a friendly correspondence with them, and paid them an annual visit. After one of these visits he wrote : " It is singular to see how the old times and the present are peacefully blended in the dear old man. He has the liberal views of our day, and yet he considers it his highest honor to do his duty to his Prince after the feudal fashion, and the whole princely family treat him as a venerable relic of antiquity. When the Prince's arrival is announced, the old man throws on his faded uniform, and holds the stirrup while his master descends. Then the Prince takes him up to his room, and empties with him a bottle of wine of the last century." " Rare, very rare, is it," wrote Perthes on one occasion to his aunt of eighty-three, " that such strength and clearness of mind as God has given you should endure to your age. You are highly favored indeed,—you can think of the past with pleasure, you enjoy the peace of the present, and look forward with confidence to the future. I desire to say with you, God has done all things well." " Thank you, dear Fred, for all your love," writes his old uncle to Perthes, after receiving a visit from him through snow and storm ; " you love me now just as you did sixty years ago, when you used to ride upon my knee ; this consciousness is ever with me in my solitude, and I thank you for it." In 1835 the old uncle died at the age of eighty-three, and in

1838 the old aunt followed, aged eighty-seven. Perthes wrote to Rist as follows : " I heard yesterday of
the death of my dear uncle in Schwarzburg. He was
life-weary, but still in possession of all his mental
faculties : he had lived very happily, and so, God be
praised. Schwarzburg is now to me desolate ; the
playground of my childhood is no more ; there is not
a Heubel left in the house where they had lived for a
hundred and ten years. The family is now dispersed.
So goes the world ! Who can suppose that this is our
home !"

Another thing that reminded Perthes of the approach of his own death was the different impression
now made upon him by the death of others. We find
him saying : " Births and deaths, deaths and births
amongst children and children's children have com-
passed me round during the last few months, and I
have had to look upon many a sick and dying-bed.
My affection for my descendants individually is not
diminished by their number ; but the wind and weather of a long life has hardened my physical frame
against sorrow, and my soul has learnt resignation to
the loss of its dear ones. Now that I know I must
soon follow, the death of others makes quite a different
impression upon me to what it did in youth, when,
though one indeed acknowledged, one did not feel
one's self mortal. It is only the pain of suffering children that now as formerly pierces me to the heart,
and doubting questions will arise in connexion with
it. In grown-up persons one knows the why and
wherefore, and the sufferers do so themselves, or at
least they may do so." The thought of his own age
and his own death was never painful to Perthes ; on

the contrary, he used continually to refer to it. Towards the end of 1842 he writes : " When I die, the centre of a widely extended family will be taken away, and yet it is scarcely desirable that such a centre should continue very long after one's children have acquired a position of their own. They will each form their own new and special circles in the time to come. But while an old man, with remains of his former strength, sits on and on in the centre, a thousand concessions are made to him by all the other families, and horns are drawn in, which are intended to thrust with vigorously, or to be rubbed off as the case may be. The old must give place to the new! And as to the greybeard himself; when time has tugged at us long, we cease to do more than vegetate, we become a burden to ourselves and to others, and what is worst of all, we get a horrible longing for a still longer life. When I look at many old men around me, I am reminded of Frederick the Great's expostulation with his grenadiers, who demurred at going to certain death, ' What, you dogs! would you go on living forever ?' "

Again, in 1841, Perthes, after a severe illness, writes to Lücke as follows : " Recovery, indeed, one may still speak of, but the recovery of old age is not that of youth." About the same time he wrote to Ullmann : " The spring is glorious, and I often feel overcome with melancholy at the thought of seeing this earthly splendor but a few times more, and I am conscious of the same sensation in contemplating long familiar inanimate objects, but not so with reference to my living loved ones who will soon follow where others have gone before." " I yearn for the repose of Friedrich-

roda," wrote he in the spring of 1842 to Ullmann;
"perhaps it is there that the last repose of all will be
granted me--gladly would I rest in that churchyard
with its fir-trees. It is not my physical condition that
occasions this yearning, but I discover in myself an increasing indifference towards all temporal matters; I
feel incapable of effort for anything on this side; I
want nothing more here below."

This gradual loss of interest in all appertaining to
earth showed itself in the diminished importance attached by Perthes to his own external history. Formerly he had often thought of sketching out his career,
but the pressure of business had prevented his doing
so. Latterly he lacked the inclination. When his old
friend Runge lost all his papers in the Hamburgh fire,
Perthes wrote to him as follows : " I, too, lost most of
the documents relating to my youth at the time of the
French invasion. True, that in the thirty years since
then, papers enough have accumulated, and the contents of these are full of incident; but in these rail-
road times of ours, would they have an interest for the
next generation? I do not think so. My papers,
dating since 1813, will perish as did the earlier ones.
No one will hunt out the valuable from amongst
the mass, and, indeed, why should they? God looks
upon and cares for us all individually, but in the sight
of men what are we in history, but as one faded leaf
in autumn! When we return from a delightful journey, we believe that we shall never forget its incidents. Yet when a few years are over, what remains
of all the pleasures and interests, which written down
would have filled volumes? So it is with the events
of our life, and even had we written them all down

while fresh in our minds, who would read them? Perhaps a friend immediately after our death—later, one or two lovers of old stories—no more, unless indeed the autobiography were a work of art, like Goethe's 'Wahrheit und Dichtung,' owing its permanent interest to its form rather than to its contents. Those who come after us have their own life to occupy them : out of the collective existence of former generations, only the results abide, the summary of which, we call history. It is only in God's sight that the individual counts, as Job and David prophetically told us, and as our Lord revealed." Perthes had gone in the May of 1842 to his beloved Friedrichroda, and enjoyed its repose. He wrote to one of his sons : "May this morning be as fine with you as with us! the old sailor grown grey in storm and calm is refreshed by the cheerful stillness of such a day."

In the middle of September, when the cold autumnal mists began to gather over the hills, he returned to Gotha, where he spent the first winter months in his wonted health and vigor. At the end of the year he wrote to his sister-in-law, Augusta Claudius : "I am now past seventy ; I can still walk for hours over hill and dale, and I can work from eight to ten hours without tiring my eyes. God be praised for it ! I can understand everything said to myself, but general conversation escapes me. I comfort myself with the thought that I have heard enough, but I am sorry to lose the prattle of my three little girls amongst themselves. A certain inward feeling tells me that my life will not last more than two or three years. I have long fought the battle of life ; I scarcely dare hope for the crown of life ; but I know that the prayer,

22

' God be merciful to me, a sinner,' will be accepted of God." A few days later he wrote to Bunsen : " I believe that my end is not very far distant ; I have no longer any appetite, not even any spiritual appetite for what is on this side the grave. My soul yearns for more certain nourishment."

XLII.

Sickness and Death,—1843.

CCORDING to custom, all Perthes' children and grandchildren came from a distance to gather round him on Christmas day. On this occasion, none were kept away by sickness, and Perthes enjoyed himself with youthful glee in the midst of forty-nine of his descendants.

Towards the end of the year he wrote: "On that holy evening, I forgot the discomforts of my present state, but I was reminded of them on the following festival. For some weeks past, I have had premonitory symptoms of a serious illness; my sleep is broken, my appetite gone, and my afternoon hours very painful. I have been really ill, and still am so."

Perthes felt so convinced of the approach of a fatal illness, that, on the first of January, he made the following short entry in his journal: "My state of health renders it unlikely that I shall ever write 1844."

His illness soon proved to be liver-complaint, and assumed the form of jaundice, towards the end of January. For some months he varied much—occasionally his strength would sink suddenly as though a rapid termination were at hand, and then he would unexpectedly rally.

Towards the close of February he wrote : " A few weeks ago I thought the end of the journey was come ; now good days alternate with bad, but certainly the progress made is very slow, as slow as the pace of the Austrian militia. My strong constitution struggles hard to throw off the disease, but I do not believe it will succeed."

" Weary, weary," wrote he a few weeks later, "yet still the improvement goes on, and it seems as if I might really have a further grant of life."

Soon after, however, came a change for the worse, and towards the end of March, all his strength appeared exhausted. In one of the letters written at this time, we find it said, " I have seen Perthes ; his appearance really shocked me ; all his energy is gone, his voice is weak, and every movement languid in the extreme. There he is, feebly reclining in his arm chair, and emaciated to the last degree. This change is the more distressing in a nature so elastic and energetic as his was a few months ago."

Yet while he had any remains of strength left, his worn-out frame was still the obedient instrument of his active mind. It was not in Perthes' nature to lead the passive, supine life of an invalid. The health that he had throughout life enjoyed had been too good not to lead him to struggle to the utmost against the encroachments of weakness. As long as it was possible, he spent each day, or, at least, a few hours of each day in his study, and when unable to leave the sick-room, he still sat up dressed, on a chair before his desk. Even when confined to his bed, he still had letters, books, and papers spread around him, determined that his life in bed should make as few concessions to sickness as possible. As long as he could help himself, he did not like to call in the help of others. He once remarked, that his wife showed herself the very perfection of a nurse, because she never proffered help when he did not need it. As it had always been his wont before taking any journey, to settle his affairs as completely as though he did not expect to return, and to have everything ready days before he departed, so was it now, in the prospect of the last great journey. He most punctually discharged every obligation, gave directions to his son Andrew, who was to carry on his father's business, made his will, and was then able undisturbed to await the hour of departure.

Notwithstanding all these claims upon him, he still found time to write numerous letters both to his sons and to his friends and acquaintance ; in many of these he entered warmly into the different questions of the day. Even so late as March, he took undiminished interest in the newly published volume of Hagenbach's History of the Reformation, and in Ranke's German History.

In the beginning of April, his son from Bonn paid him a visit. He entered as freshly and fervently as of yore, into every subject of conversation, and he could still make many a playful speech about a letter which came from the Minister von Thiele, earnestly requesting him to attend a council at Berlin. Indeed, the friends and acquaintance who came to see him, as soon as they had got somewhat accustomed to his aspect, found it most difficult to believe him so near death.

"Perthes," wrote a friend, "belongs to that class of men with whose every idea mental and bodily health

are so intimately connected, that one forgets that they
too, are subject to the universal law of decay." In one
letter, written about the end of March, we read, "I
found him quite unaltered in mind and heart ; he is as
bright, friendly, and interesting in conversation as
formerly." In another letter : "Such a spirit as this
is mighty indeed. True, it has lost the absolute
mastery over the physical nature, but still it can assert
itself and force that nature to obey, though reluctantly,
and but for a season. I was often surprised to see
that when, towards evening, Perthes lay back, weary
and worn, a little mental stimulus availed to restore
life and strength even to the body."

Now, this in Perthes was not the result of effort. On
the contrary, activity was now, as of old, the law of
his mind, and work and cheerful conversation were as
compatible as ever with the interests of his spiritual
life. During the years preceding this illness, Perthes
had already attained to a greater mastery over the
impetuosity of his temperament. Faith and love had
become more and more pervading principles, leading
to increased humility toward God, and gentleness toward man ; nay, even in proportion as his own
convictions became stronger, his toleration enlarged.
No one, indeed, knew better than he, that he was not
yet a conqueror.

"If Paul," wrote he, "had to complain of inward
conflict and discord, no other need despair because he
has to do the same. All that man, Christ helping him,
can attain to on earth, is to prevent pride and sensuality ruling in him absolutely, constantly to fight against
them, and to bewail their remaining power. From the
first days of the Church, external methods have been

tried, in order to obtain a complete victory, and each Christian has his own special means towards the attainment of this end, but no one has ever attained it, nor ever will. Pain and sorrow have done more for me than joy and happiness ever did : the prayer for help leads to resignation, and resignation purifies the soul ; but still the fight goes on till the present day. Let us fight to the last, my dear son !"

Indeed, Perthes had to fight to the end, but months of sickness blunted many sharp weapons of the enemy, and matured the inward and spiritual life. The weakness and suffering he had to endure, were no light trials to a man who had never before given his body a thought ; but no one ever heard him murmur, no one ever saw him out of temper, his patience strengthened from week to week, he was always kind and friendly, and his thankfulness for the mercies with which his life had been filled, never forsook him. That the end was drawing near, he perfectly knew and openly declared, and he looked forward to it with wonderful composure.

To Dörner he wrote : " The consciousness of life being quite over, is to me a very peculiar and by no means depressing feeling, rather, on the contrary, exhilarating. I am full of thankfulness to God."

Indeed, as far as man could judge, Perthes had not for one moment during the whole of his illness, to struggle with the fear of death. " God is, for His Son's sake, very gracious to me a poor sinner," was his constant exclamation in hours of pain.

To Neander he wrote : "In hope and faith I am joyfully passing over into the land where truth will be made clear, and love pure."

In a letter written early in April, we find it said : " Perthes is perfectly reconciled to die, he is calm and confident. Whether this present confidence and calm will abide with him during the last struggle, he does not know, for nature, he says, often asserts her sway most strongly when just about to lose her power for ever ; and that, therefore, there may possibly be before him a fearful conflict, a seeming despair, a cry, ' My God, my God, wherefore hast thou forsaken me !' but, he hopes for a peaceful, placid falling asleep, and makes it a subject of prayer.

"A few hours after he had said this to me, I entered his little cabinet, and found him reclining in his arm- chair, his hands folded, his eyes closed, peace and joy spread over his countenance. I hoped that God had heard his prayer, but it was not so ; he was only asleep, and woke up cheerfully.

Whenever Perthes needed strength and comfort, he sought them exclusively in the Scriptures. Not one of the religious works to which he had owed much during life, satisfied his present need. Formerly he had preferred the Epistles of St. Paul to all other portions of the Bible : nor did he lose his love for them, but his love for St. John's writings increased. As of old he always turned to the Epistle to the Romans, so now, however he might be engaged, the Gospel of St. John was always open before him.

Sometimes, though not often, his thoughts would wander to the life beyond death. " In a week or fort- night I shall be on the other side, and yet I am still without any previsions as to the nature of the existence immediately succeeding my death. Shall I be in a state of painful conflict, sorrow, and struggle, through which sin will be finally destroyed, or in a state of profound repose, in which I may collect myself, and in silent resignation be healed from the wounds inflicted by the tumult of earthly life? Shall I be a fellow-worker in works of wisdom and love? Will a knowledge of the mysteries of nature, a comprehension of the course of events, or companionship with those I have loved on earth, be granted me? All these questions assume just before our death a very different degree of importance to what they ever had before, and yet we should not indulge them, since no answer has been vouchsafed."

On another occasion he said : " The season of faith will soon be over for me, that of sight is near, and yet how mysterious the word, and how veiled its meaning —Sight! I shall see with faculties that I have never possessed here! As I have only with my bodily eyes beheld the visible, with my ears heard the audible, so understanding, feeling, reasoning have only afforded me the perception of this or that aspect of truth, not the truth itself. Knowing, in fact, is not seeing. If I am to see I must have a new spiritual faculty conferred by perfect love, in order to make the reception of perfect truth possible. Fain would we question how this will be brought about, but be it unto thy servant according to thy word."

In the second week of April, there was another sudden decrease of Perthes' strength, while, on the other hand, the symptoms grew worse. " Very weak," " very wretched sensations ;" these are frequent entries in his journal about this period. On the 15th of April, he wrote to Bunsen : " The disease does not yield, and the weakness increases ; you must not be sur-

22*

prised if the tidings sent ere long be—' He died of old age.'"

On the 16th of April, on Easter Sunday, his wife and daughter were sitting with him after church; he made them give an account of the sermon they had just heard. "Do not," said he to them, "speculate or inquire into our condition after death ; it does no good, and diverts the mind from the main point. Hold simply and firmly to that which our Lord has told us, and do not wish to know more ; read again and again the fourteenth, fifteenth, sixteenth, and seventeenth chapters of St. John's Gospel : he who has these has all he needs alike for life and death."

During the two last months of his life, he lived on these four chapters, and the nearer he approached to death, the oftener did he read the seventeenth.

After Easter it had become evident to him that he had but a few weeks at furthest to live ; indeed he generally thought his last hour nearer than it was.

On the morning of the 21st of April, his birth-day, he had his children and grand-children assembled around him. All were sad and sorrowful, but he lay in his room, which had been filled with spring flowers, in such perfect peace and joy, that it was impossible for them to give utterance to their grief. "Should it be God's will," said he, "that I should still spend a · little more time with you, I shall do so gladly, and I should return with pleasure to my dear Friedrichroda ; but this may not be. A rich life lies behind me ; I have indeed had my trying days and hours, but God has ever been gracious to me. Do not mourn for me when I am dead ; I know that you will often long for me, and I am glad of it. I need not say to you ' Love one another,' but, so bring up your children that they also may do so. I die willingly and calmly, and I am prepared to die, having committed myself to my God and Father. Here there is no abiding city, we needs must part ; death cannot harm me, it must be gain."

A week later, on the 29th of April, he believed that his last hour was come. He had no pain, but he was weak in body, and somewhat depressed in spirits. During these days he lived much in the thought of his beloved Caroline, he had the account of Claudius' last days repeated to him, and liked to have his wife and daughters constantly near. He spoke lovingly to every member of his family, and when night came, as no one else was able to do so, he himself read out with a loud voice the fourteenth chapter of the Gospel of St. John from beginning to end. The next day, Sunday, he felt stronger. His eldest son Matthias having arrived from Moorburg, Perthes' wife sought gradually to prepare him for this. He laughed out in his own old way and said, " You think that because I am ill I must needs be nervous too,—let him come in at once. " Nothing in this world," said he repeatedly, " could have given me more pleasure than the arrival of Matthias." He was often able clearly and connectedly to converse with this son for hours together, although, in addition to his extreme weakness, new and painful symptoms had just set in, one of which was erysipelas in the head, of a very malignant character. But nothing interfered with his activity. He daily transacted business matters in the clearest and most systematic manner with his son Andrew, and took a cheerful part in conversations of all kinds with his friends Ukert, Ewald, and Archdeacon Hey, who had been for many years his spiritual adviser.

To numbers Perthes had been a counsellor, to numbers a benefactor, and he had friends and acquaintance in every part of Germany, from whom he now rejoiced to receive letters of sympathy and affectionate leave-taking.

Schelling wrote saying : "It was so comforting to know of one in the world from whom, in every case of need, one was sure of sincere sympathy, loving good-will, and judicious counsel."

Perthes' son Matthias had written from his father's dictation a farewell letter to Rist, which, unfortunately, cannot now be found. Rist answered it as follows, "I have, indeed, had much to bear in life. I have had great trials and great blessings appointed me, but it remained to me to have such a letter to receive as yours of the 5th of May, and to answer as I now do. My hand may indeed shake, but my heart is undismayed ; I do not dread to look upon death, with which I have been so long familiar. I draw near to your sick-bed, to thank you for your remembrance of me at such a time as this. I stretch out my hand to say farewell, if, indeed, it must be so, to edify myself by your courage, faith, and joyful trust in the new birth in Christ ; I desire to repeat your confession, and to make it mine. I hold your wife and children happy in that they stand round you, and I greet them all. My wife has still tears for her dear old friend, to whom she bids a most loving farewell. You have been much to us, your memory will remain with us all as a blessed one. Dare I express a hope that the physicans may be deceived, and that your own feelings may

deceive you!—And now farewell, here is my hand,—
we shall meet again, dear Perthes!"

Perthes had many a personal leave-taking to get
over. His old foster-father's son, Carl Heubel, to
whom he had been himself a father, had come over from
Leipzig to see him once more. Perthes received him
with heart-felt pleasure, and sent him away strengthen-.
ed and supported.

On the 6th of May he bade farewell to his son-in-law
William Perthes, who was obliged to leave Gotha for
some weeks. He keenly felt the loss of this man, who
had been for five-and-thirty years very dear to him,
and a few days after his departure expressed a wish to
see him again ; but as soon as he heard a proposal to
send for him, he said, "No, no ! one must not allow
one's self everything that is possible, he is not to come,
and I desire you to obey me, and by no means to summon him."

On the 7th of May, to his very great joy, came
Perthes' sister, Charlotte Besser. He made her tell
him much about earlier as well as present times, and
with her he reviewed once more his whole past life.

On Monday the 8th of May, his son Matthias went
through that painful parting that can only come once,
the parting from a dying father. Perthes gave him
his hand with a look of deep, earnest love, and said in
a tone of cheerful confidence, " We shall meet again."
" I used to think," he had said a few days previously,
" that in the certainty of an existence in God above,
all desire of seeing and possessing again those we have
loved, would disappear, and I never attached much
importance to the personal relations between man and
man in heaven ; but I have changed my views : I now

hope to meet and enjoy again all I have loved on earth,
and I believe, too, that I shall do so."

On Thursday the 9th of May, Perthes closed his
journal with the short entry, "Suffering much ;" and
from that time forth he could not raise himself without
assistance.   Impressed with the certainty of death
being close at hand, and with the desire to meet it in
full possession of his consciousness, he lay languid and
weary, but continually praying in the words of some
of his favorite hymns.   In a letter written at this time
we find ; "He is still indescribably patient, he never
complains, and is always kind and cheerful.   To-day,
he said, ' I am weak, very weak, would to God it were
the last weakness—my pains increase, but still death
tarries.' "

With tenderest affection, and with the composure
and energy which only experience can give, his wife
nursed him night and day : but he did not the less
appreciate the devotion shown him by others.   " Do
not," said he to his daughters, " sit up with me at night
—you only weary yourselves, and things will get worse
still ; and yet," he added, a few minutes afterwards, " I
should like one of you to sit on my bed at night, so
that I might see you whenever I awoke."

He almost always lay with folded hands, often
exclaiming, "Gracious God, help me." " Come, Lord
Jesus ;" or, "Lead me not into temptation ;" or, " God
be merciful to me a sinner, for thy dear Son's sake."

Whenever he opened his eyes, he looked lovingly at
whoever was sitting by him ; nodded, or stretched out
his hand.   Even during these last days, he looked out a
ring for his grand-daughter, Fanny Becker, on the
occasion of her confirmation, and another for his

daughter Agnes, which he gave her in a basketful of flowers on her silver wedding-day.

The 10th of May, was the eighteenth anniversary of his own second marriage. Much and long did he and his wife speak together of their mutual life, and then he added, " Death is here, and I am conscious of a most strange feeling, as though all earthly ties were dissolving ; but there is no expressing this in words."

His intimate friend, Dr. Madelung, having long promised not to conceal from him what any of his symptoms might indicate, he now asked him whether the last hours were come, and on receiving for answer, " Not yet," he said in a melancholy tone, " I had so confidently hoped to die to-day, and must I go on living ?" Alas, he had still five weary days and nights before him.

On Sunday the 12th he was lifted into his arm-chair, the erysipelas had struck inward, and his agonies every hour increased. Ice was laid on his head, and opium given. He struggled desperately against its influence, and though sometimes rendered delirious, he yet often by an effort collected his faculties, said what he wished to say, and then relapsed into a dreamy condition. He spent a day and night of fearful suffering, the opium had lessened his power of resistance, and agonizing cries of pain escaped him. " You must excuse it," he once said, " I cannot help it, and I have not any teeth to grind." " Oh that I could but weep !" said he, on another occasion. " What a long Sunday—it is a hard, hard battle ! Help me, my God, and send me death."

But there were words of resignation and trustfulness that alternated with these cries of anguish. While those around him supposed him asleep, he began in a

low touching voice, to repeat the words of a favorite
hymn.   Another time, waking from a kind of dream,
he exclaimed, "Herder, on his dying bed, sought only
an Idea : 'Light, light,' exclaimed Goethe ; it would
have been better had they cried out for love and
humility."   Early on Monday morning he became free,
not, indeed, from pain, but from the influence of the
opium ; and trying to collect his thoughts, he asked
his daughter what had been the matter? whether they
were angry with him? whether he had broken anything?   His children told him that he had taken opium,
and been delirious.   At first he repeated their words,
as though he could not quite guess their meaning, but
when, at length, it broke upon him, indescribable love,
peace and joy overspread his whole aspect, he drew
his weeping daughters towards him, laid his hands on
their heads, blessed them, and prayed long and
fervently.

Even after this distressing night, Perthes had still
some hours of unconsciousness ; sometimes, too, he
would mistake the time, and find some difficulty in
recognizing the person who chanced to come in ; but
he was never again delirious, and when he did speak
he spoke clearly, and with a kindness which was heart-
touching.

He had done now with earthly things ; he had
neither eaten nor drunk anything for weeks, a tea-
spoonful of coffee was all that he was still able
occasionally to enjoy ; his own body appeared to be
something detached from himself, whose sufferings he
contemplated with compassion.   He loved his wife,
his children, and all who approached him, more and
more, and often asked them to place themselves so that

he might see them all at once, but they felt that he did not grieve at leaving them : he had entirely done with this life, and waited in perfect composure for the last great moment. He did indeed long inexpressibly to be with God, but however weary this mortal life now seemed, he never lost the certainty of its blissful close. Those around him heard him exclaim, " Thanks be to God my faith is firm, and holds in death as in life ; for His dear Son's sake, God is merciful to me a sinner !"

On Thursday, the 18th of May, the doctor was able to tell him that all would soon be over. He had no longer any actual pain, and on being asked whether his dreams were distressing, he answered, " No, no, not now ; once distressing, now delightful." Sometimes he would pray aloud and repeat hymns in a firm voice. But for the most part he lay there peaceful and joyful, and the peace and joy that God had granted him, prevaded all that were near. " When he folded his cold hands," wrote one of his daughters, " and prayed from his inmost soul, we too were constrained to fold our hands and pray, it was all so sublime, so blessed, we felt as though our Lord Jesus Christ were with us in the room."

" The last conflict is severe," we find it said in another letter, " but we see with our own eyes that he can overcome it in love, and without pain or fear. The last enemy loses all his terrors for us, and the resurrection seems nearer us than the death."

About six o'clock in the evening, an intimate friend, the court-preacher Jacobi, came in. Perthes opened his languid eyes, and stretched out his hands to him, saying, " For the last time ; it will soon be over, but it is a hard struggle." About seven, Jacobi and the

Doctor left him ; at eight his breathing became slower and deeper, but without occasioning any distress. His whole family stood round him. Perthes had folded his hands, and for a short time prayed aloud, but his speech had now become inarticulate : only the oft-repeated words, " My Redeemer—Lord—forgiveness," could be distinguished. It had now grown dark. When lights were brought in, a great change was visible in his features, every trace of pain was gone, his eyes shone, his whole aspect was, as it were, transfigured, so that those around him could only think of his bliss, not of their own sorrow. The last sounds of this world that reached the dying ear were, " Yea, the Lord hath prepared blessedness and joy for thee, where Christ is the Sun, the Life, and the All in All."

He drew one long last breath ; like a lightning flash, an expression of agony passed over his face, and then his triumph was complete. It was within a few minutes of half-past ten. Immediately after death a look of peace and joy settled on his face.

Early on the morning of the 22d of May, he was buried in the churchyard of Gotha, and his favorite hymn was sung around his grave :

What can molest or injure me who have in Christ a part ?
Fill'd with the peace and grace of God, most gladly I depart.